Hall Johnson

His Life, His Spirit, and His Music

Eugene Thamon Simpson

THE SCARECROW PRESS, INC.
Lanham, Maryland • Toronto • Plymouth, UK
2008

SCARECROW PRESS, INC.

Published in the United States of America
by Scarecrow Press, Inc.
A wholly owned subsidiary of
The Rowman & Littlefield Publishing Group, Inc.
4501 Forbes Boulevard, Suite 200, Lanham, Maryland 20706
www.scarecrowpress.com

Estover Road
Plymouth PL6 7PY
United Kingdom

British Library Cataloguing in Publication Information Available

Library of Congress Cataloging-in-Publication Data

Simpson, Eugene Thamon 1932–
  Hall Johnson : his life, his spirit, and his music / Eugene Thamon Simpson.
    p. cm.
  Includes bibliographical references (p.   ), discography (p.   ), and index.
  ISBN-13: 978-0-8108-6038-4 (hardcover : alk. paper)
  ISBN-10: 0-8108-6038-4 (hardcover : alk. paper)
  1. Johnson, Hall, 1888–1970. 2. African-American composers—Biography.
  3. African American choral conductors—Biography. I. Title.

ML410.J655S56 2008
780.92—dc22
[B]   2007034589

∞™ The paper used in this publication meets the minimum requirements of
American National Standard for Information Sciences—Permanence of Paper
for Printed Library Materials, ANSI/NISO Z39.48-1992.
Manufactured in the United States of America.

To all the black artists who through their sweat, their tears, and their genius have witnessed their heritage and enriched our culture, but only rarely enriched themselves.

~

Contents

~

Preface

As a young black musician and avid reader some fifty years ago, I was painfully aware of the dearth of books about classically trained black performing artists. At a time that predated the aging Marian Anderson's smashing of the color barrier at the Metropolitan Opera and the passing of the historic civil rights legislation guaranteeing voting rights and access to public accommodations, blacks seemed to have no cultural history in America, save as minstrels, comics, tap dancers, and jazz musicians. Certainly, it was not until 1971, with the publication of Eileen Southern's illuminating book *The Music of Black Americans*, that the academic world discovered the identities and cultural footprints of the scores of black performers and composers who had contributed so much to make the unique American musical milieu what it is today. Only then did I learn of the signal achievements, despite segregation, of great black artists like soprano Sissieretta Jones (Black Patti); concert pianist Hazel Harrison; violinists Joseph Douglass and Will Marion Cook (a student of Joachim); and of the black composers like Cook, whose black musical *Clorindy, or the Origin of the Cakewalk* created a sensation on Broadway in 1898. Here, it is necessary to note that the greatest music schools and conservatories in the country played a significant role in accepting and training these musicians, ignoring the racial climate of the country at the time. Both Cook's mother and father graduated from Oberlin Conservatory around 1865, and he followed in 1885. Black Patti and Joseph Douglass both studied at New England Conservatory, as Warner Lawson and I did at Yale University.

But the revelations of Southern's book, for me, were just enough to whet my appetite. The few short pages that Southern devoted to Johnson's extensive career—which extended sixty years from his University of Pennsylvania graduation to his death in 1970—seemed almost as much of an injustice, because of their brevity, as not to mention him at all. It was my introduction to Johnson in the summer of 1959, and the eleven years of professional association and friendship that followed, that ultimately led to the remedy for that injustice: the writing of this book.

I recall the evening that Reginald Parker, an old friend and associate from Howard University, took me to Johnson's St. Nicholas Avenue apartment on a high floor in a rather ordinary high-rise building. As we alighted from the elevator and entered the foyer, the first thing that caught my attention was an alcove on the right that was piled high with old copies of the *New York Times* and other newspapers. Viewing the living room, there was no escaping the impression that the place was a shambles. It seemed reminiscent of the historical account of Beethoven's apartment in Vienna. Against the right wall just inside the door stood an upright piano. The other three walls were completely covered with books and record albums. It was the largest personal library I had ever seen. Beside the piano was the entrance to the kitchen, and beyond that, a single bedroom.

After the introduction, we sat and talked and listened to music. His library seemed to have any recording that I wanted to hear. Hall introduced me to the singing of the magnificent contralto, Kathleen Ferrier, whose performance of the Brahms *Vier Ernste Gesange* was, and still is, a singular one. After much musical communion, we left the apartment long after midnight, having initiated a friendship that was instantaneous and was to deepen and endure until his death. During the next eight years, after a day of teaching in the New York City high schools, I made the pilgrimage to his apartment countless times simply to visit with him, or to have him coach my performances of his works, or to accompany some of the great singers whom he coached regularly until midnight.

When I met Hall Johnson, he was seventy-two years old, vibrant, energetic, active, and still a major force in the musical life of New York. But the great massed choir he had developed during the depression and the concert choir that had toured America and performed in Berlin, Hamburg, Nürnberg, and Vienna were no more. He had been reduced to a madrigal-size group of uneven talent who met weekly to rehearse, more out of habit than for any specific performance goal. In the group were a few holdovers from the "golden age" of the Hall Johnson Negro Choir. Others were young singers with wonderful voices who were there to experience the choral magic long associated with his name. Without adequate numbers, the choral glory of the past could no longer be achieved.

At the first rehearsal I attended, I was introduced to the strange and magical sounds of the "Tongola Scene," from his musical theater masterpiece *Run, Little Chillun*. Without warning, he handed me the score and asked me to sight-read the opening bass solo, "Mo-ta-me-ko-la." Even with a small and unbalanced group, the majesty of the score was apparent. Impressed that I could both read and sing, he became a strong supporter as I made the transition from concert pianist to concert singer in the midsixties.

His rehearsal style was very different from that of the "modern conductor," that is, the post-1950 generation. The modern conductor gears his approach to working with AGMA (American Guild of Musical Artists) or AFTRA (American Federation of Television and Radio Artists) singers who have to be paid for every minute. Hall Johnson's approach, fashioned during the depression of the 1930s with singers who frequently received WPA (Works Progress Administration) compensation and who could be available all day, involved endless discussion of the music with the resulting minimization of singing time. For those of us who read music fluently and worked regularly in the recording business, although we loved and respected Hall, the rehearsals were deadly. Yet, they were valuable to me because they introduced me to the variety and scope of Johnson's works. This, his final choir, made occasional appearances at Harlem churches, singing short groups under his direction. Between 1959 and 1962, the group never sang a full concert. After his stroke in June 1961, the group disbanded. It was in that year that the Voices of Friendship, under my direction, performed the first full concert of Hall Johnson's works by a group other than Hall's own choir or one guest conducted by him.

Johnson made a quick recovery from his stroke and suffered minor impairment. His intellect was unaffected, but his speech was more deliberate and his handwriting had a new tremulous quality.

What made Johnson such a stimulating personality and mentor at age seventy-five? What made me treasure every minute of the time spent with him between 1959 and 1968, when I left New York to accept a professorship at Virginia State University? He was an extraordinary intellect, competent in both French and German, and had a broad appreciation and knowledge of all the arts, especially music, music theater, and literature. He had mastered the viola, composition, choral arranging, orchestration, play writing, and criticism. As a coach of his own works and of the classical vocal repertoire, he was meticulous beyond words, comparable in my experience only to Paul Hindemith. In the interpretation of his works, he insisted that every phrase marking, breath, and accent be observed. He was broadly interested in others, especially young musicians, and encouraged them by his attendance at their concerts and with his warm but candid comments. He was incredibly helpful to me, and to others, in learning his works and in supporting my career aspirations.

As I coached some of his spirituals with him, attended some of his rehearsals, accompanied singers as he coached, and later coached—on his compositions—students whom he referred to me, I early became aware of his greatness, of the uniqueness of his contributions, and set out to learn more and to share his achievements with others. This resulted in three New York performances of All–Hall Johnson choral concerts in 1962; the addition of a Hall Johnson group of concert spirituals on every vocal recital of mine; the recording and limited release of *The Hall Johnson Song Book*, with the Virginia State College Choir in 1969; and ultimately, the production of the three-day Hall Johnson Centennial Festival in 1988, and the release of the four-CD *Best of the Hall Johnson Centennial Festival* album in 2003.

That I should write *Hall Johnson: His Life, His Spirit, and His Music* is surely the work of fate. When I left New York to teach at Virginia State College in 1968, Johnson was a man of eighty, and I felt sure that this was the end of our close association. That conclusion soon proved to be in error when he appeared on April 9, 1970, at the age of eighty-two, at the New York concert of my touring choir. When he died, only three weeks later, I felt that I had done all I could to share his greatness with the public, and as my final tribute, I penned an article for the *Choral Journal*, "The Hall Johnson Legacy," which introduced many of his choral works to the large membership of the American Choral Director's Association. Once again, the moving hand had written, and I was unaware of what it said until I was contacted by Johnson's surviving sisters in 1982 with a request to assist them in regaining control of his estate and in representing the heirs in all musical matters. Thus, all 104 moving cartons of music, books, recordings, and newspapers (all with reviews of his performances) came into my possession, and with the help of two able gentlemen from the Glassboro State College of New Jersey maintenance staff, were moved from a New York warehouse to three rooms in the Wilson Music Building at Glassboro State. As a full professor with a touring chamber choir, the unpacking, classification, organization, storing, and cataloging of all memorabilia could only be done in my spare time, such as it was, sometimes with a single student assistant. This process took approximately eighteen years, the final two after my retirement in 2000. Of all the tasks involved, the handling, organization, and evaluation of the letters and newspaper reviews was, by far, the most demanding. Many newspapers, sixty-five or seventy years old, simply crumbled when we tried to open them. Others were so brown with age as to be unreadable. The miracle is that the people who packed these papers, which had been stacked almost ceiling high in his unused apartment dining room, had the presence of mind to realize their value. No place else on earth will a researcher find all the reviews of the Hall Johnson Choir's performances in the United States and abroad. Virtually all the letters were handwritten, some beyond deciphering, even with a magnifying glass.

By the year 2000, after several months rest from a fort-five-year teaching career, it became obvious to me—after picking up every letter, extracting every clipping, looking at every photograph—that there was no one as well equipped by dint of familiarity with the source material, and my personal relationship with the subject, to write this book. And indeed, it would be the only true validation of the twenty-year investment as curator. It also seemed clear that this was, indeed, the fulfillment of the design that fate had fashioned. So here we are!

I have carefully documented Hall Johnson's work as a violinist, violist, composer, choral conductor, vocal and choral arranger, playwright, poet, essayist, teacher, coach, organizer, and conceptual thinker. There is one creative area of his life that I have not explored because of limitations of space: visual expression. It was noted that his earliest choice of a career was to become a painter. There is preserved in the Hall Johnson Collection a single photograph of an unsigned oil painting on canvas, a still life. As this is the only photo of a painting among more than a thousand photographs in the collection, it is my considered opinion that it is all that remains of Hall Johnson's paintings. But the love for visual expression did not disappear after he became a professional musician. Rather, it morphed into a love for photography, and he was rarely seen without his Rolliflex (preserved in the Hall Johnson Collection). This photographic legacy may find publication as a separate book.

There are so many persons who have made invaluable contributions to the success of this project. Nothing would have been possible without the wisdom of Hall Johnson's sisters, Alice Foster and Susan Jordan (both in their nineties) who sought me out and then generously gave all of their brother's memorabilia to Rowan University (then Glassboro State College) on permanent loan, allowing for the establishment of the Hall Johnson Collection and for the ready availability of all the source material. The generosity extended also to Hall Johnson's sister-in-law, Bessie Johnson, who at her death, bequeathed to the collection an endowment of $44,000, which arrived in the mail without fanfare, and forms the core of a permanent endowment. I must also acknowledge the assistance of Dr. Philip Tumminia, vice president for university advancement, who had the vision to recognize the value of the collection, and to provide the in-kind support needed in transporting and housing it. Similarly, Peggy Veacock, the administrator of the Rowan Foundation, has been most helpful with all aspects of budget and personnel. Two of my assistants with the collection are most worthy of mention as they did much of the physical work of unpacking the materials and documents: Gregory Hammell and Arleen Pastin. I must also thank three of my friends—George Williams, Brian Eskenazi of Riverside Books, and Dr. Luisa Lehrer—for their invaluable assistance in proofing the manuscript, and Peter Schwender for translating a number of reviews from newspapers in Berlin, Hamburg, Nürnberg, and Vienna.

Perhaps I am alone in this opinion, but I find the new copyright laws—covering all material, copyrighted or not, for ninety-five years, whether the person or publication is dead or defunct—to be a great deterrent to scholarship, as no academic publisher can possibly afford to pay a major newspaper $250 for the reprint of a seventy-five-year-old review when the whole paper sold for 10¢ when published, and when there is no longer any demand for that particular article. Therefore, I am especially grateful to those esteemed publications that graciously consented to the reprint of their reviews without charge, and I shall name them here: the *Spokesman-Review, Boston Herald, Christian Science Monitor, Boston Traveler, Pasadena Journal*, and *Commonweal*. All other reviews, and there are many, except for headlines and short quotes, have been summarized and digested in my own words, as the main premise of the book is that it should document not only what the subject has done creatively, but also how the authoritative critics and public evaluated, and responded to it.

As I studied the history of the great European classical composers, I often thought how wonderful it would have been to speak with persons who had known Bach, Handel, Chopin, Schumann, or Liszt personally. Thus, in chapter 5, "Personal Recollections," the reader will be able to actually share in firsthand opinions of people who knew Hall Johnson personally, in varying capacities. I must thank all of those persons, some deceased since 2001, for sharing with me some of their experiences with Hall Johnson. It was a wonderful experience for me to talk with them personally. All of them, save for Elijah Hodges and George Royston, both eighty-five at the time of the interviews, wrote their own recollections. Thomas Carey wrote his recollections from his death bed, as he had recently returned home from the hospital to lose his battle with cancer. William Warfield, John Patton, and Helen Duesberg were only months from their deaths. I am tremendously grateful to all who contributed, and shall acknowledge their help by listing them here (in the order in which their recollections appear in chapter 5): John Morrison, Helen Duesberg, Arthur Bryant, Louvenia Pointer, John Motley, Thomas Carey, William Warfield, Elijah Hodges, Madeline Preston, Carroll Buchanan, George Royston, Shirley Verrett, and John Patton.

Finally, I must acknowledge the assistance of the archivist at the Spingarn Center for Research at Howard University, archivist at the University of Texas at Austin, the U.S. Department of State, Mrs. Lela Brown (aunt of Hall Johnson's son), Ruth Bernhard (photographer of the "Hands of Hall Johnson"), Gabriel Pinsky (heir of photographer Fred Fehl), Mrs. Constance Foster (administratrix of the Bessie Johnson Estate), and Celeste Robinson (the primary heir to the Hall Johnson Estate).

I trust that the confidence, patience, and attention of my gracious editors, Renée Camus and Erin McGarvey, will be fully justified by the book. My sincerest thanks go to them for making its publication possible.

~

A Historical Account

Roots

A genius of the magnitude of Hall Johnson does not, like Athena, "spring full grown from the head of Zeus,"[1] but is always a happy confluence of nature and nurture. Hall sprang from an aristocratic lineage, clearly upper-middle class, university educated, and refined—all characteristics uncommon for blacks in the antebellum days of the mid-1800s. Hall's father, William Decker Johnson, born a free man on March 19, 1842, in Calvert County, Maryland, was educated in both public and private schools, and entered Lincoln University in 1862 and graduated with the ABA degree in 1868.[2] Subsequently, he was awarded the MA degree in 1871, and a DD degree in 1880, by the same university. Ordained a minister in the African Methodist Episcopal Church in 1863, William Decker held pastoral appointments in Washington, DC; in Tallahassee and Apalachicola, Florida; and six posts in Georgia, which included Atlanta, Savannah, Columbus, and Athens, where he finally settled. He rose rapidly in the hierarchy of the church due to his skill as an orator and administrator, and served for twelve years as commissioner of education for the entire conference, and as presiding elder of the Marietta and Griffin Districts of Georgia. In 1904, he became president of Allen University in Columbia, South Carolina, a position he held until a year before his death on April 10, 1909.

Alice Virginia Sansom, born in 1857, was a slave until age eight, but was sufficiently brilliant to enter Atlanta University at the age of fourteen. After her marriage to William Decker Johnson, she remained a homemaker in

Athens and devoted herself to the education and acculturation of her children, thereby freeing her husband to devote the time required by his various responsibilities.

The fourth of six children, Francis Hall Johnson was born in Athens, Georgia, on March 12, 1888. He had two brothers, George Decker Johnson and Walter Johnson (died at age two), and three sisters, Mary Elizabeth Johnson-Glenn, Alice Irene Johnson-Foster (1890–1983), and Susan Ellen Johnson-Jordan. None of the other children chose music as a career. George settled in New York and was a clerk for the U.S. Post Office. Alice settled in Philadelphia and was a dress maker. Susan also settled in Philadelphia and was employed as a beautician. Mary became a school teacher and settled in Chicago.

Hall's musical talent manifested itself at an early age. His first piano teacher was his older sister, Mary. After learning the rudiments, he continued piano studies with James Davis, a teacher at the Baxter School (the elementary school for Negroes). Simultaneously, he studied solfège with his father and, at the age of fifteen, began to teach himself how to play the violin, using a 10¢ self-instruction manual.

There were several other significant influences on his musical persona. As the son of a minister, he was constantly exposed to inspirational group singing of the church choirs and congregations, both during regular services and at revivals and camp meetings. Then there was the influence of his grandmother, Mary Hall Jones, who lived with his family, had been a slave for thirty years, and was a repository of slave songs that she constantly sang. It is to her that Hall owes his name as it was her family name. He never used "Francis." Two brilliant concert artists—Sissieretta Jones (Black Patti), a stellar operatic singer, and Joseph Douglass, an accomplished violinist and grandson of Frederick Douglass—left indelible impressions on the young Johnson, who vowed, one day, to play like Douglass. And so, at age sixteen, he gave up his ambition to be a painter and decided to become an instrumental musician. In three years' time, he was able to give his first violin recital at age eighteen.

Academic Preparation

Hall Johnson's elementary and secondary education was acquired at the Baxter School, Athens's elementary school for colored children, and at Knox Institute and Industrial School, one of two quality accredited private high schools established by the American Missionary Association circa 1866. These schools, begun with all-white faculties, aimed to educate and train blacks in order to eventually incorporate a teaching staff composed of blacks. In 1903, he graduated from Knox Institute at the age of fifteen and enrolled at Atlanta University. When his father was appointed president of Allen University in Columbia, South Carolina, in 1904, Johnson transferred to Allen and completed his bachelor's degree in 1908.

Now fully committed to a music career, he entered the University of Pennsylvania School of Music in the fall of that year. Here, he pursued graduate study in theory and composition, and continued his violin studies, privately, at the Hahn School of Music with Frederick Hahn, a former member of the Boston Symphony. At the same time, he maintained his own private studio, an arrangement made necessary by the death of his father in 1909. Upon his graduation from Penn in 1910, he won the Simon Haessler Prize for the best composition for orchestra and chorus, the first formal recognition of his extraordinary compositional talent.

The Instrumental Years, 1910–1925

In 1905, while still a student at Allen University, Hall Johnson and Polly Celeste Copening of Lenoir, North Carolina, met at an engagement in Blowing Rock. Their friendship blossomed into love, and in 1912, shortly after his graduation from the University of Pennsylvania, they were married. Two years later, they settled in New York City at the peak of the Harlem Renaissance.

New York was a cauldron of Negro artistic and political activity in 1914, as the Negro strove to achieve a degree of freedom, equality, and self-expression prohibited by the institution of slavery. While some writers attempt to limit the "Renaissance" to literary expression between 1920 and 1940, distinctive black voices were manifest from 1900 to 1968, not only in politics and literature, but in art and music as well. The phrase *Harlem Renaissance* is generally associated with W. E. B. Dubois, who believed that an educated black elite should lead blacks to liberation and that equality could be achieved only by teaching black racial pride with an emphasis on the African cultural heritage. Dubois's contemporary, Alain Locke, articulated a similar philosophy in his book *The New Negro*.

After almost three hundred years of repression, black genius erupted in the literature of Paul Laurence Dunbar, Sterling Brown, James Weldon Johnson, Countee Cullen, Langston Hughes, Zora Neale Hurston, Richard Wright, Ralph Ellison, James Baldwin, Gwendolyn Brooks, Le Roi Jones, Nikki Giovanni, and Toni Morrison; in the art of Hale Woodruff, Edward Burra, Jacob Lawrence, John Biggers, Lois Jones, Aaron Douglas, and William Johnson; in

the music of Paul Robeson, Roland Hayes, Marian Anderson, Hall John-
son,*[3] William Dawson,* William Grant Still,* Jester Hairston,* Leonard
De Paur,* Hazel Harrison,* Hazel Scott,* Everett Lee,* Robert McFerrin,*
Leontyne Price,* Shirley Verrett,* Harry Belafonte,* Eubie Blake, Duke
Ellington, Cab Calloway, Count Basie, Ethel Waters, and Lena Horne; and
in the political activism of Marcus Garvey, Adam Clayton Powell Sr., Wal-
ter White, Stokely Carmichael, Rap Brown, Bayard Rustin, James Farmer,
Martin Luther King Jr., Rosa Parks, Ralph Abernathy, Andrew Young, and
Jesse Jackson (names are listed in approximate chronological order within
each category).

The acceptance of jazz, and the association of it with the black musicians
who developed it, created a demand for black instrumentalists in pit bands
and dance bands in New York. Hall Johnson immediately found work in the
orchestra at Jardin de Danse and later with Castles in the Air, the orchestra
of dancers Vernon and Irene Castle, conducted by James Reese Europe.[4] His
work with the Castles took him on tour with their show, *Watch Your Step*. He
also joined Reese's Clef Club Orchestra (an orchestra comprised of black
union musicians).

Around 1916, Johnson's musical activity introduced him to a gifted cellist
named Marion Cumbo. The two formed a string trio with a West Indian pianist and played chamber music for their own enjoyment. When the pianist
left New York, Johnson and Cumbo were joined by Felix Weir, first violinist,
and Arthur Boyd, second violinist, and thus, the Negro String Quartet was
born (Johnson played the viola). Between 1920 and 1927, the group, later renamed the American String Quartet, played professional engagements in
New York, the District of Columbia, and Pennsylvania. At the same time,
Johnson maintained a studio in New York where he taught theory, composition, and violin.

The all-Negro show *Shuffle Along*, written by Noble Sissle and Eubie
Blake, created a sensation on Broadway. With Johnson in the orchestra,
the show ran for a year on Broadway, and toured for another two years. The
Harmony Kings, one of the featured acts, performed black spirituals and
folk songs every night, in a manner that, to Johnson, lacked authenticity.
He believed that a larger group was needed to capture the sounds he remembered from his childhood. He decided during the run of that show that
he wanted to give to the world the melodic, rhythmic, and emotional richness of the folk songs and spirituals of his people. *Runnin' Wild* (1924), the
successor to *Shuffle Along*, was the last major orchestral job that Johnson
ever did.

The Birth of the Hall Johnson Negro Choir, 1925–1930

On Tuesday, September 8, 1925, in his apartment at 148 West 142nd Street, Hall Johnson met for the first rehearsal with eight singers, carefully selected for their vocal talent, their experience with Negro folk music and spirituals, and their interest in the preservation and performance of Negro music. They were Marguerite Avery and J. Mitchell, sopranos; Consuela Carr and Ruthena Matson, altos; Mack Reeves and Morris Caver, tenors; and George McClean and Service Bell, basses. In his essay "Notes on the Negro Spiritual,"[5] Johnson writes of the origin of the choir:

> Its principal aim was not entertainment. We wanted to show how the American Negro slaves—in 250 years of constant practice, self-developed under pressure but equipped with their inborn sense of rhythm and drama (plus their new religion)—created, propagated and illuminated an art-form which was, and still is, unique in the world of music. The slaves named them "spirituals" to distinguish them from their worldly "everyday" songs. Also, their musical style of performance was very special. It cannot be accurately notated, but must be studied by imitation.
>
> Even then, in 1925, I saw clearly that, with the changing times, in a few years, any spirituals remaining, would be found only in the libraries—and nobody would know how to sing them. I also knew that I was the only Negro musician born at the right time and in the right place ideally suited for years of study of the Negro musical idiom as expressed in the spirituals. I started right in. I had always been a composer and—here was virgin soil. I assembled a group of enthusiastic and devoted souls and we gave our first concert on February 26, 1926.

Johnson soon realized that eight singers did not produce the choral sound he wanted and quickly doubled the number to sixteen singers. While the original group had two singers for each part, the larger group represented a shift in choral balance with only seven women and nine men as confirmed by photographs taken in 1928. Despite his assertion in his personal résumé that his group was "automatically named the Hall Johnson Choir," existing concert programs indicate that until 1928, Johnson had not definitely decided to use that name. On March 16, 1926 (Johnson seems to have mistaken the date in his 1965 essay), the choir made its first public appearance in concert at the International House in New York under the name Harlem Jubilee Singers. The program consisted of twelve spirituals in arrangements by Johnson, along with dramatic readings by Blanche

Berry in original dialects. A newspaper article from the same period calls the group the Jubilee Singers:

This initial performance of Johnson's newly formed group is documented by a detailed, but undated review from an unidentified Afro-American newspaper, found in Johnson's papers. The group consisted of sixteen singers, mostly of Southern birth, and all with beautiful natural voices. The objective of the group was to present religious Negro songs in a less formal style than was customary on the concert stage, and to retain the rare improvisational style of their original creation. The group had been singing for less than a year, but exhibited a zest and spontaneity that predicted a successful career.

The review, titled "Hall Johnson's Jubilee Singers," singled out a number of singers who had already attracted attention as soloists, including Service Bell, baritone; Marguerite Avery, dramatic soprano; Morris Caver, tenor; G. W. McClean, baritone; and Augustus Simmons. Hall Johnson, "organizer and director of the Jubilee Singers," was "well-known" as a composer whose novel arrangements have attracted favorable attention. The reviewer noted that Johnson had already written an operetta based on Negro life.[6]

The following year, after two years of nightly rehearsals, the choir, now thirty-two strong, appeared at the famed Roxy Theatre for two weeks, in February 1927. This was a signal opportunity, as the Roxy Theatre, though new, was second only to Radio City Music Hall in size and reputation. Apparently, the appearance was a great success as there is evidence that the Hall Johnson Negro Choir appeared regularly for the celebration of Lincoln's birthday through 1932. The notation, "Week of Lincoln's birthday, 1930," along with a list of singer's names, addresses, and phone numbers, appears in Johnson's papers.

It is easy to overlook the fact that when *The Green Pastures* opened on Broadway, February 26, 1930, for a run of 640 performances, plus an extended road tour, the concert performances and other activities continued concurrently with the run of the play. This was possible only because the choir, at times, numbered as many as three hundred singers, divided into the *Green Pastures* Choir, the Concert Choir, and the Reserve Choir. When the *Green Pastures* Choir was opening in Cincinnati on February 7, 1932, the Concert and Reserve Choirs were opening in *Let Freedom Ring* at the Roxy Theatre in New York, two hundred strong. The following reviews describe the choir's Roxy appearance and the controversy that arose when Hall Johnson wrote the show, prepared the group of two hundred singers, and wrote special music for the observance "Let Freedom Ring," but was pushed aside to let Fred Waring conduct the performance. The complete reviews are preserved in the

Hall Johnson Collection, but because of copyright restrictions, are only sum-marized here in my own words.

Review: *National News*—February 18, 1932[7]

"Impressions"
Edward Perry began his review by citing Mr. Roxy, the former theater manager, for establishing the practice of staging elaborate productions in the theater, and affirming that the current production is a significant one. He stated that the production was both an earful, and an eyeful, with Mr. Hall Johnson's chorus of two hundred, Mr. Hemsley Winfield's New Negro Art Theatre Dance Group, Fred Waring's Synco-Symphonic Orchestra, Miss Patricia Howman's ballet dancing, the Roxy Ballet Corps, and the thirty-two Roxyettes. Perry commented that although he came to hear Johnson's two hundred voices lifted in praise of Abraham Lincoln, he was also delighted by the fine ballet.

From Africa to the Cotton Fields
The reviewer characterized Hall Johnson as "one of the present geniuses of the Negro race . . . a gifted and imaginative composer and arranger of Negro folk music . . . intellectual without being highbrow. . . . he can, like magic, do marvelous things with a choral group . . . and is one of the most dynamic and musically enlightened American conductors." Johnson's choir, led by Waring, sang gloriously in a Lincoln Memorial scene called *Let Freedom Ring!* depicting the history of the Negro from Africa to the cotton fields of the South. The scene ended on a victorious note with a reading of the Emanci-pation Proclamation.

A Black Mammy and Mr. Fred Waring
Among the songs of sorrow and of joy performed by the choir, the reviewer was most affected by "Strange Lands, Strange Things," and "Mississippi Bound."

Perry lauded Johnson for elevating the spiritual to a high place among the great folk music of the world, and for preserving the essence of its creators rather than superimposing the polished manner of a German or French art song. He closed his review by demanding to know why Mr. Johnson was not on the conductor's podium for his choir's scene, as Mr. Waring's unfamiliar-ity with the music was unpleasant and alarmingly bad as a conductor of the Negro chorus, and could have been forgiven only if he had a "Black Mammy" crooning this music in his ear.

A second review, more prestigious and more precise, appeared on the same day.

Review: *New York Evening Post*—February 18, 1932[8]

"In the World of Music"
Henry Beckett, an admirer of Hall Johnson, was no more complimentary of Waring in his review. He noted that Waring had the difficult task of beating time for a two hundred–voice choir, trained by Hall Johnson, and of performing a scene conceived, composed, and arranged by Johnson, and was clearly out of his element. He advised his readers to keep this in mind when they go to the theater expecting to hear the kind of vital singing that the Hall Johnson Choirs do. Waring, who specialized in "superficial jazz novelties," was unable to replace Johnson, an authority in the music of the Negro, any more than Johnson could succeed with Waring's collegiate orchestra. Beckett also noted that *Let Freedom Ring!* a Lincoln Memorial work, revealed Johnson's taste and imagination and suggested that the full version (the work had been cut to conform to the time restraints of the theater) should be presented subsequently, under Johnson's hypnotic leadership.

On December 20, 1927, the choir, now thirty voices strong but still not called the Hall Johnson Negro Choir, appeared in "a concert of Negro music," at the Renaissance Casino under the name Hall Johnson's Carolina Choir. As a rule, the choir sang only special arrangements by Johnson. Very soon after it began to perform publicly, the repertoire was expanded to include authentic Negro folk songs, work songs, and composed secular songs, generally from the blues idiom, music theater, or (later) from cinema.

The year 1928 was a seminal one for the vibrant Hall Johnson Negro Choir. As fate would have it, in January, the choir was invited by Cobina Wright, a wealthy music patron, former singer, music editor, and syndicated critic, to entertain at a party for the famed composer, Maurice Ravel. Ensconced at 1511 Steinway Hall, 109-113 West 57th Street, she and the guests were so impressed with the choir's performance that with a new manager, William C. Gassner, a concert was arranged on February 29, at the Pythian Temple, and a month later, on March 20, at New York's prestigious Town Hall. The unparalleled speed with which the choir rose to prominence was certainly facilitated by the endorsements of several of Cobina Wright's guests, who just happened to be among the world's most highly esteemed musical artists. While the letters are distilled here, they are preserved in the Hall Johnson Collection. They are addressed either to Mrs. Wright, or to Mr. Gassner, who requested the letters. I have summarized the contents of each letter here.

Deems Taylor, composer and music critic, spoke of the genuine fervor of the choir, of the "*excellent voices, remarkable intonation, its expert training, and sincerity* [my emphasis]."[9]

Eugene Goossens, an eminent conductor, admired the choir for its excellent rhythm, color, and expression. He described the conductor as knowledgeable, and characterized the work of the choir as a cultural contribution of real value. A great future for the ensemble was predicted.[10]

Walter Damrosch, a symphonic, choral, and operatic conductor, praised the work of Johnson with the group and described their singing as having fine precision, a beautiful tone quality, and a deep inner emotion that sweeps the audience along.[11]

Symphonic conductor and violinist *Willem van Hoogstraten* was lavish in his praise of the Hall Johnson Negro Choir. In his words, "*I have received one of the deepest impressions musically that I can ever recall. . . . I have hardly ever heard such a direct expression of the source from which art is created* [my emphasis]." He thanked the choir for having given him "one of the rare moments when one abandons one's self completely to the sure beauty of art."[12]

Maurice Ravel, the famed French Impressionist composer, openly displayed emotion while listening to the choir, and said that he was struck by the beauty of the voices, the rhythm, musicianship, and precision.[13]

The final letter is from *E. Robert Schmitz*, president of Pro Musica Incorporated, an advocacy group for music whose membership roster included Bela Bartok, Alban Berg, Ernest Bloch, Frank Bridge, John Alden Carpenter, Alfred Casella, Manuel De Falla, Vincent D'Indy, Arthur Foote, Eugene Goossens, Percy Grainger, Howard Hanson, Arthur Honneger, Charles Ives, Zoltan Kodaly, Darius Milhaud, Pierre Monteux, Serge Prokofieff, Maurice Ravel, Ottorino Respighi, Albert Roussel, Carlos Salzedo, Arnold Schonberg, Albert Spaulding, Edgar Varese, and Anton von Webern. Schmitz, too, wrote enthusiastically of the singers, calling them "marvelous." He expressed amazement at the range and quality of the soprano voices (doubtless, referring to the high obbligatos in Johnson's works), and of the vitality in the conducting and the singing. He was taken by the combination of the human, and the artistic, displayed by the choir.[14]

Now named the Hall Johnson Negro Choir, the group had finally arrived. The program of a second Town Hall Concert on December 20 included eighteen selections. Sixteen of these were spirituals, and two were blues. The male sextet from the choir performed one group in the center of the program.

The critical acclaim that followed the choir's concerts at the Pythian Temple and at Town Hall was unanimous and instantaneous. Manager William Gassner summarized it thusly:

> The New York critics who covered their first concert on February 29th vied one with the other in praising their authentic "down south" quality, their remarkable

diction, and extraordinary rhythm. W. J. Henderson, the dean of the critics and probably the outstanding authority on the voice wrote in the *New York Sun:* "Mr. Johnson's choir has been taught to sing the songs of its people as Negroes sing them when they do it spontaneously. There is embullient (sic) energy and swift reaction to the melodic pattern in every delivery. These colored brothers and sisters let loose their voices with few reservations and with revelations of deep personal interest."[15]

In Boston, the choir was reviewed by the critic for the *Boston Transcript*, the distinguished composer Horatio Parker, who reported that listening to the Hall Johnson Choir was like hearing the spirituals and work songs in the making. Providing a scholarly analysis, he pointed to thudding rhythms, minor keys, vocal counterpoint, spontaneous outbursts, and the "rapturous refrain." He identified several elements that appeared consistently: the heavenly home, the personal Jesus, and the Lord. The concert was for the choir "instant expression."[16]

Reviews in the remaining New York papers were also quite laudatory:

* The *New York Times* reported that Negro spirituals are rarely sung with the spirit of their creators with the fidelity of the Hall Johnson Negro Choir.
* The *Herald Tribune*, identifying the number of singers as twenty, admired the choir for its intonation, individuality, resonance; its camp meeting fervor and emotion; its diction, precision, phenomenal sense of rhythm, and a "polyphonal publication of traditional songs."[17]
* The *Evening World* painted a much clearer picture of the audience response, reporting that "Town Hall fairly rocked . . . with frantic applause. . . . They sang with spontaneity, fervor and unconcealed relish that carried all before them."[18] The review also spoke of the religious intensity and the power of the spirituals and the deft humor of the secular numbers.
* The *Morning Telegraph* identified the choir as one of the best appearing at that time, with admirable unity of thought and expression, pitch and phrasing. The choir was also lauded for capturing the emotional appeal of each song.

This unbridled praise for the choir created an instant demand for its services as a professional concert presenter. It was immediately invited to appear that season in concert at Lewisohn Stadium on a program with the New York Philharmonic. The reception was so enthusiastic that it returned to the summer concert series for the next five years, and after an interval, for three additional summers. Concert appearances throughout New York; Philadelphia; and Washington, DC, kept the singers quite busy. With their new celebrity came many more singers and the choir grew to 150 voices. From this total number, Johnson established several groups: a concert choir of 16 voices, a *Green Pastures* choir of 30 voices, and a reserve choir of 84 voices. There were also several chamber-sized units: the Swanee Six, the Whispering Trio, and the Over Jordan Sextet.

The Ascendancy of the Professional Choir, 1930–1951

Between 1930 and 1951, the Hall Johnson Negro Choir reigned supreme and unchallenged as America's premiere professional choir. None of the other choirs that might have vied for this title were to come along until almost two decades later: the Roger Wagner Chorale in 1947; the Robert Shaw Choir in 1948; the Gregg Smith Singers in 1962; and the Norman Luboff Choir in 1963. The choir's fame rested on its achievements in four performance areas: concerts, music theater, radio, and cinema.

In 1928, in addition to the successful appearances at the Pythian Temple, Town Hall, and Lewisohn Stadium, it returned to Town Hall for a second concert on December 20. This was followed in 1929 with its movie debut in two shorts with the Duke Ellington Orchestra. The first, *Black and Tan*, featured Fredi Washington, and the second, *St. Louis Blues*, starred Bessie Smith, in her only movie role. Then, in 1930, the Mark Connelly biblical play, *The Green Pastures*, was produced on Broadway and became the perfect vehicle for the choir. Not only did Hall Johnson conduct the music, but he also arranged all the spirituals and wrote several original pieces for the production.

The spirituals and original music were interpolated between the dramatic episodes. As the play did not use an orchestra, the focus was entirely on the drama and the choir, which both sang and acted throughout. The all-Negro play won a Pulitzer Prize and was an instant success on Broadway, perhaps because of its stereotypical characterizations of blacks and because of the beautiful music and singing of the choir. Hall Johnson won the Harmon Award (1931) for his music, which was immediately published for solo voice in a single collection by Carl Fischer. *The Green Pastures* opened to glowing reviews on February 26, 1930, at the Mansfield Theatre, and ran for 640 performances. In addition to its all-black cast, it provided employment for thirty singers. When the show closed on Broadway, it toured for several years. The first road tour was from Chicago to the West Coast; the second, from Boston to the Midwest; the third, through the South.

The excellence of the Hall Johnson Negro Choir did not go unnoticed by the recording industry. RCA Victor released the first recordings of the choir in 1930, *Selections from the Green Pastures*, comprised of six spirituals: "Ezekiel Saw de Wheel"; "Swing Low, Sweet Chariot"; "Hold On"; "Good News"; "Standin' in de Need of Prayer"; and "Religion Is a Fortune" (this recording is currently available on CD: DOCD-5566). It is obvious that Victor named the album as it did to trade on the popularity of the Broadway play, which was enjoying a most successful run. However, it took a great deal of audacity to name an album after a Pulitzer Prize–winning play *and not include a single musical selection from the show in it*. It would be reasonable to assume that the producers of *The Green Pastures* would not permit RCA Victor to do a "cover" recording of hits from the play and that the rapid withdrawal of the recordings from circulation may have well reflected pressure from the play's producers because of the possibility that the advertising was "deceptive." Nonetheless, the quality of the singing was excellent as confirmed by a review from one of New York's most esteemed critics, cited in Ingres H. Simpson's excellent study of Hall Johnson.

Writing for the *New York Times*, Compton Parkenham called the recordings a welcome relief from the pseudo-sophisticated "concoctions" being presented as the right thing in colored art, and found it difficult to believe that the spontaneous outbursts had been carefully rehearsed or that the fervor of religious inspiration resulted from obeying the iron hand of the highly entertaining leader. He pronounced the recording "in every way, excellent."[19]

The following year, Victor recorded the choir again. This time, the recording contained three of the choir's most popular secular numbers: "St. James Infirmary Blues," "Eastman," and "Water Boy." The release of the second recording was delayed until 1938. Once again, the recording was soon dropped from the Victor catalog because of economies mandated by the war as vinyl was only available at a premium. These performances are also included on the document CD 5566: *Negro Choirs, 1926–1931*.

When the New York production of *The Green Pastures* closed, Hall Johnson decided to test both his literary and musical talents and write his own musical play. In the fall of 1932, he started to rehearse sections of a work he called *Run, Little Chillun*, with a large group of singers. As no backer had been found for the show, the only way Johnson could feed them and keep them working at the height of the depression was to do a concert tour and earn sufficient money. So, he took twenty of his best singers, leaving the others rehearsing with assistant conductor, Juanita Hall, and embarked on his first transcontinental tour. Critical and audience response was just as enthusiastic as it had been for the Town Hall concerts as the two reviews which follow indicate.

Review: *San Francisco Call Bulletin*—Undated[20]

"Negro Choir Remarkable"
The critic of the *San Francisco Call Bulletin*, Marie Hicks Davidson, described the singing of the Hall Johnson Negro Choir as "ensemble singing such as San Francisco has rarely heard." She specified that the group consisted of twelve men and eight women and that the program consisted of spirituals, work songs, and blues. She pointed to the uniqueness of black music as a distinctly American cultural entity, even if incorporated into symphonic music by Dvorak and Bloch. Individual soloists were singled out as possessing voices of the quality of singers whose names were emblazoned in lights across the country. The intonation, tone quality, precision of attack, and diction were all said to have been superlative. In concluding the review, the critic noted that the concert was so unique and so well received that the management had arranged for a repeat concert on the following Sunday.

Review: *Los Angeles Record*—Undated[21]

"Enthusiasm Greets Negro Choir"

"Second Concert Sunday"
The choir's concerts in Los Angeles Philharmonic Auditorium received the highest critical acclaim. In his review of the first concert, Llewellen Miller reported that the "Hall Johnson Negro Choir gave the audience . . . one of the most exciting and stimulating evenings music lovers could hope to have." He challenged his readers to attend the second concert if they wanted a new and vivid experience, which has not been duplicated, to hear this superbly trained group. In describing the singing of the choir, Miller said it was "rendered with gusto, intricate harmony, brilliant clarity of tone and pitch . . . as complete and satisfying as a little symphony orchestra." The reviewer singled out the conductor as having a remarkable musical brain, with restrained gestures, sensitive and eccentric. He closed his review with this unreserved praise: "It is impossible to be too enthusiastic in praise of this group. Its singing is like a bright symphony with gay cries and croonings breaking through the ground-swell of the blended, mellow voices."

By 1933, Johnson had completed the book and music for a new form, the Negro folk drama, *Run, Little Chillun*. In view of the splendid success of *The Green Pastures*, Johnson was able to find a backer quickly (Robert Rockmore), and on June 12, 1933, *Run, Little Chillun* opened at the Lyric Theatre. Johnson was the music director of the large cast which included seventeen principals; a chorus of twenty-five singers; a dance chorus of twenty-seven; a small orchestra; and groups of pilgrims, novitiates, and church members. There was some controversy among reviewers of the folk drama as it represented a radical departure from the all-black productions previously seen on Broadway such as *The Green Pastures* and *Shuffle Along*. It avoided the expected stereotypes: the plot was lofty rather than comedic; the characters were human and complex rather than simple; the music was serious and not jazzy; the music represented both folk and operatic idioms. Of four major serious music productions produced during the period (*Four Saints in Three Acts*, *Porgy and Bess*, *The Green Pastures*, *The Emperor Jones*) all about black people, *Run, Little Chillun* was the only work written by a black author and composer. With a "thumbs up" from a majority of the critics and a favorable audience response, it ran for four months at the height of the financial depression. (A more detailed discussion will take place in chapter 3, "The Music of Hall Johnson.")

After three successful road tours, by 1935, a new audience of New Yorkers was ready to enjoy *The Green Pastures*, and its first revival opened at the 44th Street Theater on February 26, with Hall Johnson conducting his choir. This time, the run was shorter and the play closed after seventy-three performances.

The long Broadway run of *The Green Pastures*, an even longer national tour, and the attention the play received as a recipient of the Pulitzer Prize were sufficient to convince Warner Brothers that it would also make a successful movie. So, in December 1935, Johnson and his *Green Pastures* choir, expanded to fifty singers, left New York for Hollywood with tickets purchased by the studio. Shortly after their arrival, he learned that his wife, Polly, whom he had left in New York with a cold, had contracted lobar pneumonia and died. Despite the personal tragedy, Johnson and the choir completed *Green Pastures*, and became the toast of Hollywood. In rapid succession, the choir made three other films in 1936: *Hearts Divided*, *Banjo on My Knee*, and *Follow Your Heart*. Even two politically incorrect cartoons were spun off from *The Green Pastures*: *Sunday Go to Meetin' Time* and *Clean Pastures*, seeming to confirm the old adage, "Imitation is the truest form of flattery."

In 1937, when famed Russian composer Dmitri Tiomkin chose the Hall Johnson Choir for his blockbuster *Lost Horizon*, it created something of a sensation. The film starred Ronald Colman and was advertised as "The Mightiest of Motion Pictures," a phrase that proved to be true when it received nine Academy Awards. When Tiomkin was questioned about his choice of the Hall Johnson Choir for such an important film, according to Jester Hairston, Johnson's assistant conductor, Tiomkin said, "I don't see faces, I hear sounds."

Lost Horizon was also a life-changing event for Jester Hairston as Hall Johnson "became ill" during the production of the movie, and Hairston had to assume the responsibility of directing the choir and completing the film. Hairston's successful association with Tiomkin resulted in a relationship that lasted for twenty years, as Hairston collaborated with him in many subsequent movies and ultimately formed his own integrated studio choir. The question of Johnson's "illness" must be addressed in any authoritative historical account of his life. Based on an interview with Elijah Hodges of the Hall Johnson Choir who actually shared a house with Johnson for several years, Johnson was subject to fits of depression (my term) that caused him to go on alcoholic binges which would sometimes last for weeks. It was such a binge that resulted in Hairston taking over the choir during the filming of *Lost Horizon*. It is also apparent that at some point, Johnson became a virtual teetotaler, as I cannot ever recall seeing him take a drink or smell of alcohol during the period in which I knew him, from 1959 to 1970. There is, however, evidence that the problem persisted at least through 1940, and perhaps longer.

Between 1936 and 1943, the Hall Johnson Choir appeared in films made by Hollywood's best directors, with Hollywood's greatest stars. Frequently, they appeared on camera and in character as no movie about the South was complete without a plantation and its singing "darkies." In other films, they were heard off camera or only on the soundtrack as in the cartoons *Clean Pastures* and *Sunday Go to Meetin' Time*. While most frequently, the choir sang spirituals or black folk music, they proved their versatility and skill in the Oscar-winning *Lost Horizon* and *Slave Ship*, both filmed in 1937 and both with exotic scores. Other evidences of their stylistic acumen may be found in their collaboration with Al Jolson (*Wonder Bar*), Bing Crosby (*Road to Zanzibar*), Roy Rodgers (*Heart of the Golden West*), Gene Autry (*Carolina Moon*), and Ethel Waters (*Cabin in the Sky*). Some members of the choir were also selected for bit parts.

As the decade of the 1930s approached its close, the spirit of the Harlem Renaissance had spread across America, and Hollywood was challenged to stop making movies that stereotyped and denigrated blacks and other minorities. Even a director of the prominence of David O. Selznick was concerned about the social milieu of the period while casting *Gone with the Wind*.

Prior to 1968, he had been concerned with the "Negro problem," and had kept a keen eye on the black press to discern the temper of the times. The filming of *Gone with the Wind* had also aroused the interest of black actors and black organizations. The usual dichotomy existed with some seeing the production as a wonderful opportunity for the employment of black actors, while others opposed it as demeaning to the race and a glorification of slavery, and as incitement to hatred and lynching. Selznick let it be known that he would hire a respected Negro, knowledgeable in the arts, as a consultant on the treatment of the Negroes, on casting, and on dialect. Selznick knew of Hall Johnson from his work in *The Green Pastures* and *Slave Ship*, and seriously considered Johnson for this role, but ultimately chose someone else.[22]

The Hall Johnson Choir made only three more films of the politically incorrect genre: *My Old Kentucky Home, Way Down South, Swanee River,* and *In Old Missouri*. The industry adopted new standards and new story lines and found new ways to use the choir, though less frequently and less often on camera. A detailed discussion of the choir's films occurs in a later chapter.

Roosevelt and the New Deal ushered in a brief period of artistic plenty with the creation and funding of the Federal Theater Project (FTP) of the Works Progress Administration, between 1935 and 1939. Designed to reemploy unemployed theater workers, the FTP provided funds for a West Coast revival of Johnson's folk play, *Run, Little Chillun,* in 1938. The show opened in July at the Mayan Theater with Hall Johnson directing singers from the Hall Johnson Negro Choir and from the Los Angeles area. Performers were paid the munificent sum of $1 per day and had to be unemployed to qualify for admission to the cast.

With the decline in movie work, it was necessary to find another means of attracting singers and maintaining group unity. So, in 1941, Johnson organized the Festival Chorus of Los Angeles with four stated objectives:

1. To build a great chorus
2. To foster exceptional solo talent
3. To work for the establishment of a Negro symphony
4. To acquire a building for the group

Johnson wanted to assemble a large group of volunteer singers that would study and perform black spirituals and folk music, give occasional performances, and nurture young and promising solo singers and instrumentalists. This was consistent with the activities of the large choir in New York, and between the two groups, many fine artists were encouraged and helped, including Harold Blair, Alfred Brown, Sarah Brown, Cecil Cohen, George Goodman, Louise Hawthorne, Charles Holland, David Johnson, Luther Johnson, Oci Johnson, Alonzo Jones, Georgia Laster, Robert McFerrin, Marian Nettles, Louise Parker, Kenneth Spencer, John Swift, Shirley Verrett, Coletta Warren, and Louvenia White.

Hardly had Johnson begun his work with the Festival Chorus of Los Angeles when he was called back to New York to assist in the preparation of the Broadway revival of his folk play, *Run, Little Chillun*. Perhaps it was an indication of the temper of the times, but the run of the show was disappointingly short. The revival opened at the Hudson Theater on August 11, 1943, and closed two weeks later, on August 26.

Radio Appearances for American Audiences

The choir made many guest appearances on local and national and international radio shows. On November 17, 1932, it made a stellar appearance on Radio's Biggest Show, NBC's *Maxwell House Radio Hour*. Jester Hairston conducted. The press was ecstatic on the following day.

The *New York Daily News* entertainment column reported that "Captain Henry's Show Boat steamed into NBC . . . to the cheers of a thrilled throng. The lazy laments of the *Hall Johnson Choir* . . . stole the show with unhappy hymns that were richly received."[23] In the same paper, columnist Ben Gross offered a similar opinion: "Last night's radio program [was] the most satisfying in many months. . . . Certainly my evening would have been a four-star one with the premiere of Captain Henry's Show Boat on WFAF. And what a cast." The cast was listed by Gross and featured the sensational black baritone, Jules Bledsoe, the Hall Johnson Choir, Mabel Jackson, Molasses and January, and the Don Vorhees Orchestra.[24]

The payment sheet for the Hall Johnson Negro Choir's appearance on the *Maxwell House Radio Hour* on November 17, 1932, shows the size of the group used (twenty singers), and the compensation for a network show: $12 per singer, $25 for the conductor, and $20 for the accompanist (author's allocation). Jester Hairston conducted.

In an appearance comparable to their *Maxwell House* radio appearance, the Hall Johnson Choir was showcased on the Ivory Soap Series *The Gibson Family* on May 12, 1935. The announcer began the show as follows: "Ladies and Gentlemen, tonight we bring you the thirty-fifth performance of *The Gibson Family*—radio's most popular musical comedy—one full hour of entertainment featuring new songs and music every week. . . . Tonight we offer you a very special attraction—Hall Johnson and his famous choir—supported by that great cast of radio stars you have chosen as your favorites."[25]

On February 6, 1937, Hairston conducted another guest appearance of the radio choir on *The Oldsmobile Show*. The singers were in character as a church choir on Cobb's Paducah Plantation, with Hairston as the choir director and

Clarence Reese as baritone soloist. Hairston, Reese, and Delsey all had lines and were paid at a higher scale. From the script preserved in the Hall Johnson Collection, it appears the choir sang "Jubilo" with the orchestra and "Sleep Kentucky Babe" a cappella, and that Reese sang "Lonesome Road."

In the summer of 1944, the Hall Johnson Choir performed on New York's "Christian Station," WMCA, in the inaugural season of a historic series, *New World A'Coming*. Based on the work of nationally known journalist Roi Ottley, the show was narrated by African-American actor Canada Lee and showcased the work of other leading black artists. It was a powerful and politically incisive program that aired political and racial issues in the U.S. military and on the home front. Duke Ellington wrote the theme song. The lineup of artists appearing on the show can only be described as awesome and included Duke Ellington, Billie Holiday, Lester Young, Paul Whiteman, Eddie Heywood, Noble Sissle, Louis Armstrong, Jazz at the Philharmonic, Teddy Wilson, and Lionel Hampton, among others. The series lasted from 1944 to 1957. The Hall Johnson Choir appeared on June 25, 1944, in a segment called "The Story of Negro Music." Other musicians on this session were Slam Stewart, Edmund Hall, Arthur Trappler, Art Tatum, Ben Webster, Vic Dickenson, Benny Morton, Roy Eldridge, and Charlie Shavers.

So impressed with the choir was the management of WMCA that it offered Johnson a weekly series on the station. Beginning on July 2, only a month later, the Hall Johnson Choir appeared in a thirty-minute concert on Sunday afternoons at three o'clock, in cooperation with the Citywide Citizen's Committee of Harlem. This series was "designed to portray Negro interpretation of life as expressed in song." A script for the initial show is extant in the Hall Johnson Collection. Recordings of sixteen works performed by the choir on the WMCA series and four works performed on WNYC Radio were rediscovered in 2004. Provided that the quality of the sound has been adequately preserved on the 78 rpm disks, these performances will be transferred to CD for early release.

The great successes of the Hall Johnson Choir in the decade of the 1930s led RCA Victor to record the Hall Johnson Choir again in 1940 and 1941. After more than a decade of concertizing, two successful Broadway shows (written especially for and around the choir), and the release of more than a dozen films in which the choir appeared, the time was right to make a new series of recordings from its extensive repertoire. While the completed recordings were excellent, it is not clear when or if the entire set was released as the outbreak of World War II destroyed all plans for the promotion and sale of them. It was not until October of 1998, almost fifty years later, that Document Records remastered and released these recordings on a compact disc The disc, DOCD 5608, *1940s Vocal Groups, Volume 2*, includes eleven of the Hall Johnson Choir's most popular concert selections and performances by the Southern Gospel singers, the Jubileers, and the Galilee Singers.

United States Steel sponsored the Hall Johnson Choir in a production of *The Green Pastures* on its "Theatre Guild on the Air," April 21, 1946. Johnson conducted the performance, which starred Juano Hernandez as "De Lawd," with Avon Long, Richard Huey, and Maurice Ellis.

Appearances on the Voice of America

Hall Johnson's competency in both German and French made him a natural for appearances on the Voice of America, and on December 27, 1949, he appeared in a broadcast beamed to Germany that included an interview in German and the performance of selected repertoire by the choir. An English translation of the interview follows. The host of the show was David Berger.[26]

Q: Were you always interested in music?

A: Yes. Both my father and mother had had some musical training and there was always a musical atmosphere in the home. I have a brother and three sisters and we all had musical training, but I was the only one to take it up as a profession.

Q: Were you interested primarily in singing and folk songs from the beginning?

A: No. Although I have always loved songs and singing, my early musical education was along instrumental and theoretical lines. I earned my living by playing and teaching the violin and viola, but my chief interest has always been composition. From my earliest childhood, I heard the old Negro songs constantly and, as my musical appreciation developed, I began to realize what a wonderful treasury of music this was and how little known and appreciated.

Q: And is that how you came to organize your choir?

A: Yes, I thought musical audiences would enjoy hearing these old songs done in concert pretty much as they had been done for a couple of centuries by the people who created them.

Q: And you have not been disappointed.

A: Not at all. The response has always been wonderful.

Q: Hadn't these songs been collected and sung in public before your time?

A: Oh, yes. Quite a few collections had been published, but the songs had never become very popular on the concert stage.

Q: How do you account for that?

A: Well, to begin with, the basic structure of the Negro folk song is always very simple. Reduced to elementary, academic rules, most of these songs appear, on paper, rather dull and extremely repetitious. The emotional fervor of actual performance in the peculiar native style is needed to bring them really to life. The singers of an earlier period—mostly male quartets from the Negro schools—sang the dull, unimaginative arrangements which were the only ones available at the time, and while these were well received, due largely to the natural beauty of blended voices, they did scant justice to the merits of the songs themselves.

Q: And that is why you started your choir? How long ago was that?

A: We organized on September 8, 1925, for the purpose of collecting and preserving the best of the Negro folk songs while developing and presenting them in the style of their primitive creators.

Q: And just what are the principal characteristics of this style?

A: First of all, you might say the most noticeable feature of the majority of Negro folk songs is the steady and very pronounced rhythmic pulsation which underlies the whole structure. In the primitive, a cappella singing—where there are no instruments to supply this feeling of "beat"—this is achieved by a more marked accent on the proper syllable. Then there are naturally certain favorite harmonies, embellished by unique twists and turns of the melody and, through it all, an absolute freedom of improvisation which is difficult to imitate.

Q: And has the popularity of this type of music increased or diminished?

A: It has increased to the point of a new danger. Whereas, in the earlier days, the songs were so undeveloped as to sound dull and flat, they are now overdeveloped and decorated to the point of distortion.

Q: And why has this happened?

A: Well, the American people love choral singing and at present there is very little good *original* choral music being written in this country. Hence, the choral *arranger* steps in and seizes upon every tune that will lend itself to group treatment. Negro songs, especially the religious folk songs or spirituals, are naturally first in line. In the desire to provide brilliant display pieces for concert and radio consumption, the simple devout songs are subjected to all sorts of cheap technical devices by professional arrangers from all over the world. These men are clever musicians and are perfectly familiar with every type of music except the authentic music of the Negro. It has never occurred to them that this highly specialized idiom should be studied seriously if their work is to ring true. The transfigured "Negro spiritual" comes out, of course, a weird conglomeration of styles—neither religious nor racial. Real students, however, are not deceived.

Q: How many singers do you use?

A: That depends upon the occasion. Our first rehearsal, nearly twenty-five years ago, was with a double mixed quartet. That number soon proved inadequate for the arrangements and we began to use sixteen to thirty people in our concerts—fifty for outdoor performances.

Q: Is that the largest number you have ever used?

A: No. In 1932, we did a Lincoln's Birthday spectacle in the Roxy Theatre with two hundred people and in 1935, I assembled a group of nine hundred for a music festival at the New York Polo Grounds.

Q: Where do you recruit your singers?

A: Mostly from among people with jobs or homes who do not wish to travel constantly. Our rehearsals are very exacting and we try to keep the same singers year after year.

Q: Are all your singers highly trained musicians and vocalists?

A: All have been taught to read music. The amount of vocal training varies. Occasionally, a very rough, untrained voice is preferable or even necessary for certain folk effects.

Q: And where did you receive your own musical training?

A: My advanced studies were pursued in Philadelphia at the Hahn School of Music and at the University of Pennsylvania. Later, in New York, I studied with Dr. Percy Goetschius, at the old Institute of Musical Art, now the Juilliard School of Music. I find that constant experience is the best teacher of all.

Q: And where did you acquire your facility with foreign languages?

A: Facility? I wouldn't claim that—even in my native English. I got my first idea of French and German phonetics, while I was still very young, from my own father. He was an avid student and possessed a fine library. Since then, I have done a lot of reading, working at long intervals with private teachers whenever I had the time and the money. I have never had much conversational experience.

Q: How interesting. Now let's get on with some music. What is the first song to be?

A: A very familiar one, "Go Down Moses." In one of the old collections this song has fifty-odd printed verses, but we sing only two. ["Go Down Moses"].[27]

*And now, a bright spiritual of exhortation. ["Walk Together Chillun"]

*The next song varies in musical form from the type which usually has a solo line for the leader [that is] answered immediately by a choral refrain. It is more like an old ballad, looking to a happy hereafter as the only relief from present tribulations. ["City Called Heaven"]

*This next song is definitely in the style of the spiritual, but is not an authentic folk song. I wrote it in 1932 for our musical drama *Run, Little Chillun*, which had a great success here and on the West Coast. The play was named from the song. ["Run, Little Chillun!"]

*Now, we come to a song which is not religious at all; it is a work song. Notice the sharp escape of breath when the digging instrument forcibly strikes the search. ["I Got a Mule"]

*And now a "blues" song. Usually about frustrated love, this type of song is more often found in cities than in rural districts and is always done to accompaniment either of guitar or piano. This is one of the best known and is a general favorite everywhere. ["St. Louis Blues"]

*And now the same solo voice is heard in the lament of a very old and no longer useful slave who is forgotten and left behind on a deserted plantation. ["I Cannot Stay Here by Myself"]

*Suppose we conclude with a lively old spiritual, which tells the story of the ancient warrior Joshua, exactly as it is narrated in the Bible. ["Joshua Fit de Battle of Jericho"]

Shortly thereafter, in early 1950, the same program was transcribed for broadcast to France, with the interview in French, hosted by a Mr. Erville. Both the German and French texts of the interviews are preserved in the Hall Johnson Collection. Johnson was a hit with both the Voice of America staff and the Voice of America audiences, and a flood of letters from the foreign listeners came in to Voice of America. So on February 2, 1950, Johnson returned to the Voice of America for a show called *The We Answer Show*, in which he thanked the listeners and answered selected questions from the letters received.

Letters continued to arrive from the German and French audiences in such quantities that the Hall Johnson Choir was asked to return for a special concert on March 3, 1950. Following the special concert, the foreign interest in American folk music only intensified. In April of the same year, Johnson received an invitation from the Voice of America to prepare two programs on the evolution of American folk music to be broadcast to the audience he had developed, and to be illustrated by recordings of the Hall Johnson Choir. (These programs are included in chapter 4, in the Essays of Hall Johnson section.) Johnson articulates the project in his response.

Memorandum for Voice of America Program
181 West 135th Street
New York, New York

April 12, 1950

To: Messrs. Berger and Lamprecht
Representing the Voice of America

Gentlemen:
According to our conversation of yesterday, April 11, I understand that you wish me to prepare for your broadcast series a program which will give a fairly comprehensive idea of the Folk Music of the United States of America. The details of the agreement are to be as follows:

1. I am to select and prepare for recording all such musical material as may be necessary for purposes of illustration.
2. This material may be in the form of already recorded compositions alternating with new performances of living artists, these latter being absolutely necessary in order to get interesting and authentic versions of some of the more distinctive material, especially that in choral form.
3. I am to engage, rehearse and *pay* all performers necessary for this program. I am also to purchase any records or reference books needed.
4. I am to take charge of and pay all expenses connected with the recording on tape of any and all hitherto unrecorded material, but the assembling, combining and unifying process for the final disc and the actual recording of same is to be done by the Voice of America.
5. I am to prepare or to have prepared all explanatory matter necessary by way of introduction and narration for the continuity and interest of the program. This script will be in English and will be translated into any other required language by the regular departments of the Voice of America.
6. In addition to producing this script, I am also to read it for the final recording.
7. It is understood that this program is to be in the form of two broadcasts of the duration of one-half hour each. It is also promised that in all my activities in connection with its preparation, I am to have ample advice and aid from the experienced people connected with your regular work.
8. To cover all expenses attendant upon my obligations under this agreement, I am to receive from the Voice of America the sum of two thousand dollars ($2,000.00), one-half of which ($1,000.00), is to be paid on the signing of this agreement and the balance of $1,000.00 to be paid

when all the desired, but hitherto unrecorded material has been recorded on tape—whether or not the final disc recording has been completed by you.

If the foregoing is also your understanding, your signatures on the lines marked accepted will be considered as legally binding.

Hall Johnson

P.S. Appended hereto is an outlined sketch of the proposed program with my personal suggestions as to what it should contain and how it should be divided. H.J.[28]

In 1945, the choir was cast in a new Broadway show called *Blue Holiday*. The show opened at the Belasco Theater with a cast that included Ethel Waters, Mary Lou Williams, the Katherine Dunham Dancers, the Hall Johnson Choir, and an ingénue, soon-to-become famous Eartha Kitt (Billy Taylor was in the pit orchestra). With such a cast, the show seemed destined for sure success but closed in a week.

Despite the unquestioned ascendancy of jazz, an offspring of the spiritual, over its progenitor, Hall Johnson was unwilling to give up on his dream of using the spiritual as material for not only "art spirituals," but for extended sacred forms. In 1946, Hall Johnson composed his Easter cantata, *Son of Man*. Although Johnson calls this work a cantata, it is in reality a passion, constructed of appropriate spirituals and original music and integrated by the use of a narrator. Naturally, Johnson needed a large chorus to perform the monumental work, the first of its type. For this purpose, he organized the Festival Negro Chorus of New York City. With an administrative skill that can only be characterized as extraordinary, he organized the Festival Chorus on January 9, 1946, and had the group of three hundred voices ready for the premiere of his cantata at New York City Center on April 15 of the same year. Encouraged by his amazing success, he renamed the Festival Chorus, the Interracial Festival Chorus, which, with the inclusion of a number of white choirs, grew to five hundred voices and repeated the performance of *Son of Man* at Carnegie Hall on Good Friday evening, March 28, 1948, at 11:30 p.m. The roster of participating choirs and conductors reads like a choral Who's Who, and includes Harold Aks, Howard Dodson, George Kemmer, and Robert Shaw.

The inception of this grand cantata, compared by one distinguished composer to Handel's *Messiah*, could only be confirmed by Johnson himself.

However, there is a strong probability that the idea originated with a book entitled *The Son of Man: The Story of Jesus* by German author Emil Ludwig that was found in Johnson's personal library. This work, a historical rather than theological narrative of the life of Jesus, was first published in German in 1928. It seems more than coincidental that the English translation was published by Garden City Publishing Company in New York in 1945, only a year before Johnson wrote and premiered his work on the same subject and with the same name.

Triumph in Berlin

In 1951, the Hall Johnson Choir was chosen by the U.S. State Department to represent the United States at the International Festival of Fine Arts in Berlin, Germany. Following three concerts in Berlin, the choir appeared in Hamburg and Nürnberg, and concluded its tour with a performance in Vienna, Austria. For this important tour Johnson took a group of fifteen men and ten women, including the distinguished baritone Robert McFerrin and contralto Louise Parker.

The program consisted of spirituals, selections for men's voices, and secular songs. Each concert opened with a performance of our National Anthem. All were a cappella and in arrangements by Hall Johnson. The program booklet contained the full texts of all the songs in English and in a German translation by Else Richter.

The European press received the performances of the Hall Johnson Choir enthusiastically as the notices below indicate. The choir's first performance was on September 20 at the Festival of Fine Arts in the famed Titania-Palast, the hall that hosted the world's greatest artists when they visited Berlin. The Berlin press was ecstatic. While copyright restrictions require that all reviews be summarized in my own words, the complete reviews are preserved in the Hall Johnson Collection at Rowan University.

Berlin Reviews

Nacht-Depesche—*September 21, 1951*[29]

Chorus of Intoxicating Voices

Titania Palast Reverberates from Applause

There was tornado-like applause after each selection, and at the end, the hall resounded with rhythmic applause. Hall Johnson, the conductor, took bow after bow, and when he announced the selections in German, sometimes with a struggle, he was also applauded. His power and spirituality shine on the chorus, which responds with disciplined attention and controls every voice, each of solo quality. Each beautiful solo voice immediately blends back into the ensemble, which supports the soloists with an organ-like cushion of sound. With surprising technique, flawless articulation and true religiosity, the group demonstrates high art to the very last bow. Among the unbelievable highlights were "I Cannot Stay Here by Myself," "Water Boy," and "In Dat Great Gittin' Up Morning." Every voice in this choir is always more intoxicating.

The choir is a gift to the Berlin Festival and its vocal revelations may be enjoyed again on Saturday.

Der Abend—September 21, 1951[30]

Dark Skin and Voice

Although the skins of some Negroes in the group have grown lighter, their heritage has remained alive. The Hall Johnson Choir, named after its conductor, exists in the world of spirituals, which it performs uniquely as to content, expression, and form. While they might disappoint in other repertoire, they are on the right track with these songs, which conjure up visions of slavery and reflects the origins of this impassioned music.

Neue Zeitung—September 22, 1951[31]

Sorrow, Joy, Piety

Hall Johnson Choir at Titania-Palast

The Negro choir from the United States consists of fifteen women and ten men, each a thoroughly trained soloist with internationally cultivated vocal quality. With simple costumes, they represent a variety of types, faces, and temperaments, and sing a cappella, but with orchestral colors. Dr. Hall Johnson, the leader, possesses a high education, impeccable ear, and creative talent as demonstrated by his dramatic oratorio, *Green Pastures*.

The American Negro music is something primitive and without comparison as it springs from a unique blending of ethos, theatricality, and rhythm indigenous to the race. Its content is always religious. The music is filled with coarse gutturals and some, with high soprano obbligatos.

The religious concept of Negroes is naive, connected with everyday life, and confident of the hereafter. All this could be primitive and artless, were it not done with such unbelievable musicality, vocal virtuosity, and intensity of feeling underlain by a dint of tragedy from centuries of living in slavery.

Der Tagesspiegel—*September 22, 1951*[32]

The Hall Johnson Choir at Titania-Palast

The Hall Johnson Choir, twenty-five colored singers, will long be remembered. For they, too, are America, with looks as fascinating as their art. Theirs is not music tainted by movie and Broadway habits, with unsatisfying concessions made to conform to general taste, for from it erupts the elemental nature, perfected by beautiful and ideal vocal sound, powerful in its outcry, touching in its lament, and driven by basic rhythms.

From its triumphant Berlin debut, the choir traveled to Hamburg for a concert at the Amerika-Haus.

Hamburg Reviews

Die Welt—*September 26, 1951*[33]

American Negro Chorus

Guesting in Hamburg for the first time, after appearing in the Berlin Festival, the famous Hall Johnson Negro Choir impressed its audience with its individuality and fascinating power. The spirituals and secular songs, with strangely vibrating rhythms, far-flowing melodies of a small limited compass, circled a tonal center as if in a magic spell. Frequently, the melody is given to a soloist, most with phenomenal ranges, while the choir emphasizes or embellished with recitations or spontaneous outbursts. There is a closeness and intensity of a controlled power of the highest harmonic fundamental sound that offers an inexplicable treasure of emotion, strong and tender, an expression of pure humanity.

The choir also took its spirituals to the great University of Hamburg.

Hamburger Echo—*September 26, 1951*[34]

Choir Parade from the U.S.A

Hall Johnson Choir at the University

After a late opening and a few faultily tuned spots, the famed Hall Johnson Choir turned the evening into a triumphal success. Negro spirituals and folk songs are popular but these arrangements, specially written by the conductor, were extraordinarily difficult for the voice and in it harmonies, providing good reason to admire the singers for their virtuosity. The performance, not to be measured by German professors, was loved for its wild exuberance, sentiment, and religious fervor.

Hamburger Abendblatt—*September 26, 1951*[35]

Famous Negro Choir

University: Hall Johnson Choir

One must put aside European choral traditions when listening to these exalted singers from America where they even sing in Philharmonic concerts. They have evolved their own style and music into an artistic value. In their refined naturalism, plasticity, magical and quasi-instrumental colors and sound mixtures, and hummed chords, they are similar to Russian choruses.

One feels something of basic Americanism as they sing of sorrow, of hopes and the religious ethos of their country. Their secular singing is also refreshing as the "St. Louis Blues" is not easily forgotten. It is possible that Ravel found here his inspiration for the blues of his violin sonata. The performance was, throughout, a triumph of the elemental and the artistic.

Morgenpost—*September 27, 1951*[36]

Negro Choir Delights

Under the auspices of the Amerika Haus, the Hall Johnson Choir performed spirituals and blues, to roaring applause, in the Great Lecture Hall for eight hundred delighted listeners for almost two hours. The group, started in 1927, boasts thirty singers, attired in tuxedos and gowns, and ranging in coloration from black to almost completely white. Though the choir sings primarily spirituals, it performs on radio and television. While they are headquartered in New York, all America is their workplace.

From Hamburg in the north of Germany, the choir traveled to Bavaria, in southern Germany, to the city of Nürnberg, for a major concert at the "New Theater." Here, a situation occurred which was to have a radical negative impact on Johnson's future with the choir. The choir showed up for the concert forty-five minutes late, and the concert began one hour late. In a letter of explanation to Robert Breen, producer of the Berlin tour, it is not absolutely clear whether or not Johnson was on the bus with the choir as he asserts that "he" was on time. Needless to say, Breen and the other sponsors were quite upset.

In a letter dated February 10, 1952, Johnson offered explanation and justification for the lateness, asserting that there were two problems which contributed to the delay. The choir had a noon concert that was some distance away from their quarters. Following this concert, they had to have lunch and rehearsal. As the choir was (for some reason) singing a new program, the mu-

sic had to be rehearsed until the choir could perform it satisfactorily. The rehearsal was longer than their schedule allowed. After the rehearsal, the choir
members had to return to their various residences, dress for the concert, and
wait for the bus to return and transfer them to the Neue Theater. The bad
situation was further aggravated by the fact that when they arrived to pick up
Bertha Powell, soloist in "St. Louis Blues" and "I Cannot Stay Here by Myself," they found her ill and had to take certain steps to make it possible for
her to perform that evening. The patient German audience waited, and the
concert was a great success as the following reviews indicate.

The negative effect on Johnson's future with the choir and the State Department was significant as he was denied State Department funding for the
International Paris Festival in 1952 and the conductorship of the *Porgy and
Bess* choir scheduled for a European tour in the fall of 1952. (For details of
this matter, refer to the letters to Robert Breen included in chapter 4's section on Hall Johnson's letters.) Ultimately, Johnson's inability to find work
for 1952 to attract and employ singers spelled disaster for his "professional"
choir, a disaster from which he was not to recover.

Nürnberg Reviews

Fraenkisch Tagespost—October 5, 1951[37]

The Hall Johnson Choir

Dr. Hall Johnson's chorus of male and female Negroes of all shades is a wonder
to be heard as he, almost invisibly, draws from ordinary voices suggestive effects
that can only be compared to the Don Cossacks Chorus under Serge Jaroff. In
fact, the Hall Johnson Choir surpasses them artistically, for their music is conceived and sung from their natural feeling. In unity of sound they can hardly
be surpassed. Their crescendos are organ-like with exemplary phrasing and
tone quality. Even more important is their superlative and nuanced delivery of
the text.

Unidentified newspaper—October 5, 1951[38]

Cultivated Originality

At its guest performance in Nürnberg, the acclaimed Hall Johnson Choir convincingly justified its reputation only recently confirmed at the Berlin Festival.
The many listeners, who waited forty-five minutes for the performance to begin, enjoyed Negro spirituals and secular songs in an original, natural yet cultivated performance with great virtuosity. The small group displayed outstanding

natural talent, especially the men who revealed basses with abysmally deep bass voices, and baritones and tenors whose voices reached great heights. The arrangements of Dr. Hall Johnson were commanding and impressive.

Nordbayerische Zeitung—October 5, 1951[39]

The Hall Johnson Choir

Amazed at the high level of musical culture and the choir's repertoire, a packed Neue Theater audience thanked the choir and its intelligent leader, Dr. Hall Johnson. The spirituals and folk songs demonstrated the power source of all folk song, the human soul. The performance displayed fine discipline, artful registration of sound, and excellent soloists. The singers have at their disposal a balance technique, marred only occasionally by imperfections of pitch that may be attributed to an excess of exuberance.

Nuernberger Zeitung—October 6, 1951[40]

The Hall Johnson Choir Sings

The Hall Johnson Choir, known in Germany for its appearances at the Berlin Festival of 1951, is the most famous Negro Chorus in the world. Founded in 1925, its fame rests on broadcast, theater, and film performances. Despite waiting for a full hour at the Bucher Saelen, we were more than compensated by a ninety-minute program of the most impressive kind. The twenty-five member choir boasts outstanding talent, complete balance, cleanest intonation, rhythmic force, superb diction, and precision. A varied program of spirituals and work songs evoked spirited ovations from the audience. Arrangements by the conductor were commendable.

On the last leg of its tour, the choir traveled to Vienna, Austria, for a concert in the famed Brahms Hall.

Vienna Reviews

Die Presse—October 7, 1951[41]

Spirituals in Brahms Hall

An impromptu audience, an a cappella choir of dark-skinned men and women, a unified vocal entity all made for a successful concert that evoked an enthusiastic response from a critical audience that included U.S. High Commissioner Walter Donnelly, his wife, and many leading personalities from the Viennese society. It was a victory of American Negro music, the sole native folk art of that country that arouses the joy and enthusiasm of the entire world, the spiritual. The program consisted almost entirely of spirituals, an art form of unequaled intensity that has found its way from deep distress to faith and music where it now ranks with hymns and choruses of the highest quality. Dr. Johnson's modest and precise conducting of "The Crucifixion" illuminates the passion story with unprecedented intensity. "Deep River," on the other hand, was surprisingly weak, illustrating the dangers of such "concert" versions. Solo performances may be more appropriate for some spirituals. "I Cannot Stay Here by Myself," the lament of an old deserted slave, is a drama in itself that blends the primitive and the artistic convincingly. The highest art of Dr. Johnson and his group becomes evident in their unbelievable precision, enabling the finest dynamic nuances, and in their art that can attain any vocal or instrumental effect, in greatest joy.

Neue Wiener Tageszeitung—October 7, 1951[42]

Hall Johnson's Negro Choir

Sensational Success of Negro Singers in Vienna

by Fritz Skorzeny

The Hall Johnson Negro Choir's performance hit Vienna like a bomb. Vienna, justifiably proud of its own first class choirs, with great joy judged the performance of the ensemble as excellent, and unique. Without regard to their appearance, the singers attain this rating through their high art. The selection of repertoire, striking musicianship, heart-rending soloists, instrumental precision, cultured falsettos and vibratos, and tenderness and force all come from the same ensemble. The peerless taste of the director, Dr. Hall Johnson, is shown in his original work, "Pilate! Pilate! Pilate!"

Wildly applauded, this was a performance that the audience wanted never to end. The choir's complete master of the basic elements—rhythm and melody—enable the singing to be most effective and captivating.

Wiener Kurier—October 8, 1951[43]

Negro Choir and Concert Pianist

by Max Graf

Directly from an unusually successful performance at Brahms Hall, the Hall Johnson Choir, directed by Dr. Hall Johnson, is no stranger to Vienna. Those who saw the film *Green Pastures* will recall a youthful and fervent religious group, the same group of ten men and fifteen women, trained superbly for the presentation of spirituals by director Dr. Hall Johnson. These melodies reflect the life of the Negro race, which has made such a valuable contribution to American musical life. These songs are touching and moving, revealing to the childlike a glimpse of heaven as a release from their earthly misery. An overtone of sadness pervades the heavenly vision, but is overcome by faith in God.

In the secular songs, the guttural tones of the soloist are a natural expression of the love of life of the Negro. In each song the rhythm of the singers could actually be felt by the audience. Stormy applause was evoked by the performance, which presented, in artistic form, "the spirit of a whole race, the land in which it lives, and the heaven to which it aspires."

From Vienna, the choir flew back to New York City via Paris. The singers quickly dispersed, looking for employment in other shows. Hall Johnson, as director of a State Department–sponsored production, was asked to make an oral report on November 9, 1951, in German, on the Voice of America, to be beamed to Germany. The translation that follows touches upon the cultural and political ramifications of this most successful tour.

America Today[44]

Hall Johnson Report on German Tour

Hello, this is David Berger.

Many of you probably had the opportunity to hear the renowned Hall Johnson Negro Choir giving its concerts in different cities of the Republic. Today, we'd like to hear from Mr. Johnson, personally, the impressions he brought back after a three-week stay with you.

DB: Mr. Johnson, I believe, this was your first travel to Germany, right?

HJ: Correct, it was my first and I liked it immensely.

DB: Good. And then you had the opportunity to use your knowledge of German?

HJ: Oh yes, I heard and spoke German all day long. I had planned, of course, to take the opportunity and study German systematically, but had no time; I was too busy.

DB: That I can imagine. You did give not less than ten concerts in twelve days. How did you like Germany?

HJ: I shall never forget the first sight of some of the magnificent cathedrals. And then, between the cities, the magnificent panorama of the landscape, meadows and fields, pastures and herds, beautiful trees and farmhouses. Much reminded me of the fairy-tales by Grimm.

DB: What significance had your German visit as far as music is concerned?

HJ: I was excited that I could be, at least for a short time, in the country, which was the cradle of so many immortal composers. I received my first musical education from teachers of German origin. My violin teacher was a pupil of Hans Sitt and Adolph Brodsky in Leipzig and later played with the Boston Symphony under Arthur Nikisch. My teacher in composition, Dr. Percy Goetsches, spent many years as a student and teacher at the Conservatory of Music in Stuttgart. Therefore, I can say that the influence of German music was always very strong in my life.

DB: How did the Negro spirituals fare?

HJ: According to reviews and judging by audience reactions, very well. Seemingly, many listeners were familiar with some of them, most likely from records or performing artists.

DB: Did the choir perform in concert halls only, Mr. Johnson?

HJ: Oh, no. One of our best concerts, we gave for the workers in the turbine factory of the Berlin Electricity Association. At noon, there gathered about two thousand workers in the huge assembly hall of the factory, to listen to our songs. . . . And then, we stopped on the road to freshen up, sometimes there formed small groups of farmers around our bus. We were just as new to them as they were to us, and of course, this get-together had to be celebrated with a beautiful old song. No concert audience could compare with such listeners— or could have given us such an emotional reception.

DB: There. You have beautiful recollections, Mr. Johnson. Now, we would like to know your general impression of the Germans that you met.

HJ: I like to emphasize that even in the short time which I spent among them, I noticed, just like everyone, most likely, who has visited Germany for the first time, the overall courtesy. Wherever, in shops, train stations, restaurants, and in the streets. I don't mean the superficial kind, which one expects in such places, but a warm cordial smile, and a real wish to be of help. Naturally, that made our stay especially pleasant. And hospitality: Well, had we accepted all invitations, we would still be in Germany.

DB: One more question, Mr. Johnson. Do you believe, aside from the musical and personal experience which you and your public had over there, something special has been attained by your visit to Germany?

HJ: That is not easy to answer, Mr. Berger. I'd say that everything that brings people together in a friendly way is worth it. Through our music we were enabled to meet many people we would never have met. The message, which music brings to the people, is always immediate and effective. Especially with the folk song, which was born of deepest emotions of sorrow and joy of humans, and therefore all human kind.

DB: Mr. Johnson, do you have any disappointments or regrets with your visit in Germany?

HJ: No. No disappointments, only ONE regret . . .

DB: Regret?

HJ: Yes: The whole visit was much too short.

DB: Thank you, Hall Johnson.

To the accolades of the European press must be added those of the sponsors of the Berlin Festival which followed on the heels of the choir as it returned to the United States:

Evaluations from the Sponsors and Hosts

The American National Theater and Academy[45]
  October 16, 1951

Dr. Hall Johnson
634 St. Nicholas Avenue
New York, N.Y.

Dear Dr. Johnson:
  You will doubtless receive expressions of appreciation from more important people, but I want to tell you how grateful I am personally for your participation and that of the choir in the Berlin Festival. *You already know that none of the American contributions was more successful than yours* [my emphasis].
  Splendid reports continue to come into Washington and I hope the satisfaction of having accomplished this mission far exceeds any difficulties which may have been involved.
  Please give my admiration to all the members of the Choir. I trust that at some future time we shall be working together again.
  Sincerely yours,

Robert C. Schnitzer
General Manager
Berlin Arts Festival

United States High Commissioner for Germany[46]
November 5, 1951

My dear Dr. Johnson:

The Berlin Festival 1951 has just come to its very successful conclusion, and I am certain that the American contributions to the program did much to bring to the German public a sound and worthwhile view of American culture and American life.

The concerts which you presented during the Berlin Festival weeks will long be remembered as superb and moving artistic experiences by all those who were fortunate enough to attend them [my emphasis]. The public and critical response to your work are ample proof of the appreciation felt by your audiences.

I should like to thank you and the members of the choir for your extremely valuable assistance in making it possible to carry out the program of the Berlin Festival 1951 with such success, and to let you know how much your cooperation has meant to me and my staff.

Sincerely yours,

John J. McCloy
Unites States High Commissioner for Germany

Department Of State[47]
October 30, 1951

My dear Dr. Johnson:

On behalf of the Department, I wish to thank you and the members of the Hall Johnson Choir for taking part in the Berlin Arts Festival.

It was a privilege to have a musical group of such stature appear with other Americans and contribute so significantly to the success of this event [my emphasis]. The acclaim given the choir by German audiences was evidence of how greatly its performance helped to extend appreciation of American music and American artistry abroad.

Sincerely yours,

J. Manuel Espinosa, Chief
Leaders and Specialists Branch
Division of Exchange of Persons

For those familiar with the history of the cold war era, the political and propaganda significance of the festival and of the participation of a black group is obvious. Robert Breen devotes a rather extensive article to the subject in the October 14, 1951, issue of the *New York Herald Tribune*. The summary below confirms the rationale for the U.S. participation, as well as the popularity of the Hall Johnson Negro Choir. The complete article is preserved in the Hall Johnson Collection.

Cold War Propaganda Value: *New York Herald Tribune*— October 14, 1951[48]

"U.S. Part in Berlin Festival Lauded as Anti-Red Move"

"Spirit of Freedom in Production Called American Secret Weapon"
In this article, Robert Breen articulates the rationale for the State Department sending some 150 actors, singers, and musicians to the Berlin Arts Festival, for the first time, at the cost of the government. The whole purpose was to counterbalance the artistic activity of communist East Germany. As the Soviets were fighting the battle for minds with culture, the Western nations decided to fight back with culture in an effort to win the propaganda war. The selection of participating groups, allegedly, was based entirely on quality.

Breen reported that the participation of the United States created significant excitement in Europe, as well as many requests to book American acts while they were in Europe for the festival. He said that the Hall Johnson Choir might have spent several months giving concerts in Europe had they not had bookings in the United States subsequent to the festival.

The Berlin Arts Festival provided a wonderful culminating experience for the Hall Johnson Choir and its director.

Concert Touring in the United States

While there is a natural tendency to focus on the big events in the career of the Hall Johnson Choir—the Broadway shows, the movies, and the festivals—the scope of the choir's concert touring should not be overlooked. Between the two Town Hall concerts in 1928 and the International Festival of Fine Arts in 1951, the choir toured extensively, not only in New York and the surrounding states, but all over the United States. Thanks to the careful collection of reviews by the choir's manager, William C. Gassner, the scope of the touring and the acclaim that was heaped upon the choir is confirmed for all history by the following press excerpts:[49]

- *San Francisco Chronicle*: "Negro Singers Delight Hearers"
- *Los Angeles Record*: "Enthusiasm Greets Negro Choir"

- *Rocky Mountain News* (Denver, Colorado): "Hearers Forget Icy Blow as Negroes Sing"; "Hall Johnson Compared with Svengali in Control of Choir Voices"
- *San Francisco Examiner*: "Hall Johnson Choir Pleases"
- *Chicago Herald and Examiner*: "Negro Choir Is Feature of Day's Music"
- *San Francisco Call Bulletin*: "Negro Choir Remarkable"
- *Bellingham Herald* (Washington): "Chorus Scores Hit"
- *Tulsa Daily World*: "Negro Singers Stir Audience"
- *Rochester Evening Journal*: "Johnson Choir Singing Stirs Audience"
- *Lawrence Daily Journal-World*: "Negro Choir Was Unusual Success"
- *Harrisburg Telegraph*: "Johnson Choir Gets Ovation"; "Immense Crowd Fills State Education Forum for Splendid Concert"
- *Fresno Tribune* (California): "Negro Choir Wins Acclaim of Large Fresno Audience"
- *Los Angeles Times*: "Negro Choir Fascinates Philharmonic Audience"
- *Toledo Blade*: "Fine Concert Opens Series"
- *Toledo Morning Times*: "Spirituals Are Pleasing at Civic Music Concert"; "Audience Laughs Aloud and Turns Sad over Southern Harmonies"
- *Tucson Arizona Daily Star*: "Hall Johnson, Choir, Brings Gotham Unit to City"
- *Evening News* (Harrisburg, Pennsylvania): "Hall Johnson Choir Pleasing"
- *Chicago Daily News*: "Hall Johnson Choir Gives Splendid Song Concert"
- *Seattle Post Intelligencer*: "Negro Choir Delights"
- *St. Louis Star and Times*: "Johnson's Choir Gives Spirituals 'All Dressed Up'"
- *St. Louis Globe*: "Hall Johnson Choir Gives Fine Concert"; "Enthusiastic Audience Hears Negro Spirituals Sung Artistically"

Despite the fact that the foci of the Hall Johnson Choir's activity were on the East and West Coasts, it is clear from the headlines above that the choir also performed in the Midwest and in the center of the country. These rare reviews of these concerts, at the time found in the newspapers of every major city in which the choir appeared, provide the only enduring evidence of the choir's renown, the best description of the response it evoked from audiences, and the most objective evaluation of its concert performance over a ten-year period. All have been preserved in Hall Johnson's memorabilia.

Reviews of Major East and West Coast Performances

The choir's initial appearance with the New York Philharmonic at Lewisohn Stadium was in 1928 on the heels of their sensational Town Hall debut. The following two reviews describe the second of eight successive appearances:

New York Times—*July 23, 1929*[50]

Johnson Negro Choir Delights at Stadium

The appearance of the Hall Johnson Negro Choir at Lewisohn Stadium thrilled the audience, which called them back for three encores. In two groups of Negro spirituals, the singers, twenty-five in number, revealed beautiful voices and interpretations marked by simplicity and fervor. The selections performed were (in the order performed) "Go Down Moses"; "Wade in de Water"; "In Bright Mansions Above"; "Honor, Honor"; "Some o' Dese Days"; "Swing Low, Sweet Chariot"; "My God Is So High"; "Po' Moaner Got a Home at Last"; "Scandalize My Name"; and "Religion Is a Fortune." Willem van Hoogstraten conducted the Philharmonic Symphony.

New York Herald Tribune—*July 23, 1929*[51]

Hall Johnson Choir Singers Meet Encore Storm at Stadium

by Eudora Garrett

The lightning and thunder that preceded the concert made it seem like a scene from *Porgy and Bess*, as the Hall Johnson Negro Choir made the first of two appearances on the Lewisohn Stadium Summer Concert Series. The playing of the Philharmonic under Willem van Hoogstraten was pleasing, but it was the black singers of the Hall Johnson Choir that generated unbridled applause from the brave audience that defied the weather to listen. At the conclusion of the two groups on the program, the cheering crowd demanded six encores, which were happily offered by Johnson and the choir. The encores provided the best work of the choir and had the audience yelling out the names of their favorites for the group to sing. The perennial "Water Boy" was the favorite and displayed the fine solo talents of Benjamin Ragsdale.

New York Times—*March 18, 1932*[52]

Negro Choir Delights Audience

The Town Hall appearance of the Hall Johnson Negro Choir confirmed, once again, its extraordinary abilities. It achieves two ends—it ably demonstrates the unique contributions of the race to music performance and literature in America, and it displays a choral virtuosity characteristic of the finest professional groups. The arrangements of Mr. Johnson are a significant contribution to musical culture, and his conducting is peerless, comparable only to that of the choirmaster of St. John Lateran's in Rome, evoking extraordinary tonal color, balance, and nuance.

New York Herald Tribune—*March 18, 1932*[53]

Hall Johnson Negro Choir Gives Recital

Hall Johnson and his choir of about forty singers are the foremost performers of spirituals and black folk songs in the eastern United States. The choir displayed the expected excellence conceptual unity, responsiveness to the conductor, and sensitivity to the various moods of the music. This was accompanied by impeccable diction, artlessness, spontaneity, and gusto. Without seeming overpolished, the choir maintains an element of sophistication of interpretation, all due to the training and astute leadership of its director.

Two years after the choir's New York debut, it made its first appearance at Philadelphia's Robin Hood Dell with the Philadelphia Orchestra in the summer of 1930. The review summaries that follow mark the fifth successive appearance of the choir at the Dell.

Philadelphia Evening Bulletin—*August 4, 1934*[54]

Johnson Choir Returns to Dell

Negro Singers Get Enthusiastic Reception in
Rendition of Old Favorites to 6,000

Give St. James Infirmary

Some six thousand people greeted the Hall Johnson Negro Choir on its return to the Dell last evening to sing a concert of spirituals and work songs. While it has become a tradition of the conductor to say that each encore is a request from the Philadelphia Orchestra, after several encores shouted from the audience, Mr. Johnson brought the concert to a close by announcing the program for the following night.

Philadelphia Evening Public Ledger—*August 4, 1934*[55]

Hall Johnson Choir at Dell

by Samuel L. Laciar

A capacity crowd was on hand last evening to hear the Hall Johnson Negro Choir, one of the star summer attractions. The choir, which shared the program with the Philadelphia Orchestra, once again proved its excellence in that unique and difficult idiom for which it is famous, the Negro spiritual and work song. No musical ensemble in the world is so completely under the control of its director, or more highly disciplined. The original musical effects, the use of the natural rather than the tempered scale, the faultless rhythm, all hallmarks of the group, were present throughout, and under the control of the musical personality of Mr. Johnson. In the opening group, "Hope I Join de Ban'" and "Gospel Train" were so beautifully sung that an encore was demanded, for which the choir sang "Little David, Play on Your Harp." For its second group, the choir sang "Go Down Moses"; "Lord, I Don't Feel Noways Tired"; and "Joshua Fit de Battle of Jericho." The audience demanded and received four encores.

The Philadelphia Record—*August 4, 1934*[56]

Hall Johnson Choir Gives Dell Recital

Hans Kindler Is Guest Conductor in First Half of Program

by Elsie Finn

The depression doesn't exist for the Hall Johnson Negro Choir, for each time it visits Philadelphia, its audience grows. The crowd last evening filled Robin Hood Dell to capacity. The enthused and insistent audience cheered every selection and refused to leave their seats until the choir sang the famous "St. James Infirmary Blues."

Hall Johnson, who has led the group to international acclaim, was generous with encores, but the encore group only left the audience clamoring for more. The sheer perfection of the singing of the choir makes the name "Negro Choir" inappropriate, as that would imply that they are singing the spirituals in a secular manner. Johnson's arrangements are professional and polished, as are the soloists. The highly trained group thrilled the listeners with their orchestral effects and rhythmic stability, and they are the preeminent singers of this repertoire.

Unidentified Philadelphia paper—*August 4, 1934*[57]

Negro Choir in the Dell

Audience of 7,000 Demands Nine Encores from Johnson's Singers

Last evening, seven thousand fans applauded so wildly and insistently after the performance of the Hall Johnson Negro Choir at Robin Hood Dell that the group was forced to sing nine encores. The audience, only slightly smaller than on the previous night, numbered well over seven thousand and waxed so enthusiastic that it appeared the singers would never be allowed to leave the stage. The many encores allowed Johnson to make several of his characteristic speeches.

Even though that portion of the reviews which deals with the orchestral performance has not been included, it is significant that in all cases, both in New York and Philadelphia, the reviewer relegated less space and attention to the performances of the New York and Philadelphia orchestras as the headlines imply.

The filming of *The Green Pastures* in 1936 and of *Lost Horizon* in 1937 made the Hall Johnson Choir an even hotter concert property than ever before. The choir was kept quite busy with East and West Coast concerts in 1938 before the opening of the revival of *Run, Little Chillun*, under the auspices of the FTP. Its April appearance at the Wilshire-Ebell Theater in Los Angeles indicates the nature of the response elicited from critics and audiences alike.

Los Angeles Evening Herald and Express—April 26, 1938[58]

Audience Acclaims Hall Johnson Choir

by Carl Bronson

The renown Hall Johnson Choir, a veritable pipe organ of sound, gave the capacity crowd packed into the Wilshire-Ebell Theater a musical experience that will long be remembered. The musical arrangements represented an advanced stage from the spirituals of the 1930s. The incredible male singers pushed the limits of the vocal range, with the encouragement of Hall Johnson, to achieve something distinctly racial. The variegated women's voices were able to create every possible timbre. This new registration concept was inspired and achieved by the leader, Hall Johnson.

On occasion, the voices separated into male and female units to sing numbers like "Mos Done Traveling," "Good News," "Crucifixion," "Goin' Down Dat Lonesome Road," "Casey Jones," and "Scottsboro Prison Camp." Virtually every number was acclaimed and the group could have sung all night if left to the crowd.

Los Angeles Times—April 26, 1938[59]

Hall Johnson Choir Wins Wilshire-Ebell Audience

by Isabel Morse Jones

One thousand or more people jammed Wilshire-Ebell Theater to hear the fifty voices of the Hall Johnson Choir in a program of folk music. Although some twenty-five selections were performed, there was no indication of the audience leaving until the group had sung its traditional closer, "The Little Black Train," and the curtains were closed.

The music was primarily religious, except for the famous "St. Louis Blues," demonstrating the faith of the singers in every song. The uniqueness of the Hall Johnson Choir results from Johnson's skillful orchestration of the voices, the blend, the melodies, and the rhythms all combining to present impressionistic colors. Johnson's significance as an American composer can hardly be overestimated, as his work reveals learning, intelligence, and discrimination. One finds not a single false or insincere note in the choir's repertoire.

These spirituals remain the basic source material for all American composers, and Johnson preserves their essence but adds to them advanced harmonies much as the Negro had added the characteristics of American civilization.

New York Times—July 6, 1938[60]

Negro Folksongs Stadium Feature

Hall Johnson Choir Appears on Program for First Time in Four Seasons

Bertha Powell Soloist

Orchestra Offers Works by Rimsky-Korsakoff, Nicolai and Tchaikovsky

For the first time in four seasons, the Hall Johnson Choir appeared at Lewisohn Stadium, sharing the program with Alexander Smallens and the New York Philharmonic Symphony. As before, the group was "totally under the hypnotic power of the slender hands and supple wrists of its director." Though displaying technical superiority and a rich tone, "it seemed somewhat dispirited, partially, because of the over-sophistication of some of the arrangements." Johnson has, at times, employed "harmonic elaboration and tricky effects . . . of an instrumental nature," unsuited for Negro folk song. "These stunts, borrowed from Broadway, rob the spirituals of both simplicity and depth."

The best solo performance was that of Bertha Powell in the lament, "I Cannot Stay Here by Myself."

New York Herald Tribune—July 6, 1938[61]

Hall Johnson Choir Is Heard at the Stadium

Negro Ensemble Appears with Philharmonic in 2 New Numbers

The Hall Johnson Choir returned to Lewisohn Stadium last evening after a five-year absence, to share a program with Alexander Smallens and the Philharmonic Symphony. Singing much of their familiar repertoire, the choir presented two new works, "Crucifixion," for men's voices, and "Scottsboro," for mixed voices. As in previous appearances, the Negro choir exhibited superb training, fine intonation, a warmth of tone, carefully modulated dynamics, and the ability to accurately convey the contrasting moods of the music. Contralto Bertha Powell was impressive with a resonant voice, poignantly and expressively used.

New York World-Telegram—*July 6, 1938*[62]

Hall Johnson Choir Aids Stadium Concert Program

by Robert C. Bagar

Alexander Smallens and the Philharmonic Symphony Orchestra shared last night's Lewisohn Stadium concert with Hall Johnson and his Hall Johnson Choir, which has not appeared here since 1933. The choir presented two new works, "Crucifixion" and "Scottsboro," plus a generous serving of more familiar works. The expert training of the group was reflected in its precision and tonal shading. The finest moment of the concert was Bertha Powell's moving rendition of the slave lament "I Cannot Stay Here by Myself." Miss Powell was also the soloist in "Scottsboro," a new piece for full choir that didn't live up to its name despite the fact that the audience demanded that it be repeated. The work song "I Got a Mule" evoked ample applause from the delighted audience.

New York Sun—*July 6, 1938*[63]

Negro Spirituals Sung at Stadium

Hall Johnson Choir Heard by Large Audience

The Hall Johnson Choir returned to Lewisohn Stadium after an absence of five years and was greeted by an audience of six or seven thousand people. On the program with the Philharmonic Symphony, Mr. Johnson led the singers in a dozen spirituals and work songs and was required by the audience to repeat several of them. Two new arrangements were featured, "Crucifixion" and "Scottsboro," the latter being a protest song inspired by the notorious criminal case in the South, focusing on the injustices committed by the courts on Negroes. The audience demanded that it be repeated.

The choir demonstrated its usual strengths in performance: conceptual unity, conviction, and tonal variety, aided by rapt attention to the leader's commands. One cannot escape noting the sophistication of some of the arrangements, but there is no question of their effectiveness. Outstanding among the soloists was the work of contralto, Bertha Powell.

Hollywood Citizen-News—*August 26, 1938*[64]

Choir Gains Plaudits in Concert

by Richard D. Sanders

A large audience enjoyed the artistry of the Hall Johnson Choir in a concert of folk song at the Wilshire-Ebell Theater. The crowd demanded a number of encores, some called from the audience, and refused to leave until the last note was sung. "Johnson is, without a doubt, a genius," molding ordinary voices into an instrument of great expression. Greater even than the singing are the choral arrangements, which capture uniquely the features of the racial music and develop them through the use of new colors, blends, and antiphony to orchestral proportions. The spirituals provided great stylistic variety.

The consistency of the critics in confirming the uniqueness and preeminence of the Hall Johnson Choir is inescapable in view of the documentation provided herein. When the concert group had movie, stage, or other long-term commitments, singers were drawn from the reserve group to fill conflicting engagements due to public demand.

The Final Years, 1952–1970

The glorious Berlin-Vienna Tour was a fitting conclusion to two decades of unrivaled supremacy enjoyed by the Hall Johnson Choir. It ended even more rapidly than it began. When the choir returned from Vienna, many of the singers auditioned for other shows that offered good employment at union scale. Virgil Thompson considered the Hall Johnson Choir for his production of *Four Saints in Three Acts*, but concluded that most of the singers were too old. Some of the younger singers did join the cast and played for two weeks in New York in 1952, and flew to Paris for a two-week run. A larger number joined the *Porgy and Bess* troupe, which opened at the Dallas State Fair immediately after the closing of *Four Saints*. With Leontyne Price and William Warfield as stars, the *Porgy* tour was to last for four years. This is relevant because Gassner, Hall Johnson's agent, attempted to arrange a European tour in 1952 without Johnson's expressed approval and was subjected to a severe rebuke in a letter dated December 1951:

> My most recent cause for dissatisfaction has to do with your recent visit to the State Department in Washington. . . . Then I brought up my regular old argument—that the choir was not in adequate shape, and there was no way of knowing, under the circumstances, just when it would be. I hastened to

add that *I would not again go abroad or anywhere else with a group which did not represent my very best effort.* I repeated what I have said to you *so often,* that I cannot get results from a group of people who come together at the last minute simply because there is an engagement—and they want to work. . . . Like any other layman, you naturally think, when you see me standing before a group of singers, that they ought to sound wonderful. . . . When you promise (or even intimate) that I can deliver an engagement of such pretensions, knowing as you do my serious problem with the choir personnel (so recently discussed), you are putting me in a position which is quite false and dangerous now, at this moment, and still more so if I should be unable to deliver when the time arrives.[65]

Johnson's anger was more than justified as the event, "Masterpieces of the 20th Century: A Great Cultural Exposition of the Arts," scheduled from April 28 to June 1, 1952, in Paris, France, boasted some of the greatest artists of the century in the areas of symphony, opera, ballet, chorus, drama, art, literature, and philosophy. Although it is not clear just how Hall Johnson learned that his choir had been scheduled to participate in this festival, it is likely that at some point he received a copy of the extant oversized poster found in his memorabilia. The poster depicts a photograph of the Hall Johnson Choir in the center of the showcased acts in the festival: the Boston Symphony, Charles Munch, Pierre Monteux, the New York City Ballet Company, George Balanchine, Bruno Walther, and Igor Stravinsky. The long list of other participants included the Halle Orchestra, the Orchestra Dell'Academia Della Santa Cecilia Rome, L'Orchestre de la Suisse Romande, L'Orchestre National de la Radiodiffusion Francaise, the Paris Conservatory Orchestra, the R.I.A.S. Orchestra, the Royal Opera House of Covent Garden, the Vienna State Opera, the Paris Opera, the Chorale of St. Guillaume, the Sheffield Chorus, and the Chorus Dell'Academie Della Santa Cecilia. Articles about the forthcoming festival began appearing in the major New York papers as early as November 29, 1951 (*New York Times*). In January of 1952, even Eleanor Roosevelt, former first lady of the United States, wrote an article for the *New York World-Telegram* praising this international cultural cooperation. The array of talent would have been daunting even if the Hall Johnson Choir had been a resident professional choir with state or private funding. Johnson did indeed attempt to acquire funding for the Paris event, but the best he could do was to get an offer from Bob Breen of payment for the transatlantic round-trip travel, in exchange for three Paris concerts; this offer did not cover food, lodging, or per diem for the singers. Breen's cable arrived on January 14, 1952, and a response was requested the same day. Without funds in hand and the availability of top talent, the choir was withdrawn from the festival.

Johnson had first been approached about making a movie out of *Run, Little Chillun* in 1939, on the heels of its fantastic success as a play on the West Coast. This interest was effectively killed by the intervention of the federal government, which resulted in charges of communist infiltration, the abrupt termination of the FTP, and the destruction of the opportunity for an extensive road tour by claiming federal "ownership" of all the sponsored plays.

Johnson was approached again in 1952, by producer Harry Joe Brown, to whom he wrote on January 29:

Dear Mr. Brown,

It was a pleasure to hear from you. Of course I remember Warner's [Warner Brother's] explanation for the delay. My delay in responding to your letter was certainly not due to any lack of interest. However, there are a number of other things cooking which I thought would be clear before [now], or I would have written immediately. Now things are beginning to shape up.

It looks now as if the choir and I will be tied up for the next few months but that should not materially affect any plans you may form concerning plays. Mr. Rockmore, the original producer, will retain 50% of the rights. I am sure he will not make any unreasonable difficulty and I cannot think of any other legal obstacle.

There is one thing however which will be difficult to explain but is nonetheless extremely important. You mention three times in your short letter the name of Mr. ——. I have no way of knowing to what extent you may be considering this gentleman's cooperation in a possible production of *Run, Little Chillun*, but I think I should make it quite clear now that his inclusion (in any capacity whatever) would make such production simply impossible and render any further discussion between us unnecessary.

Please believe me, this attitude is not based on any personal prejudice on my part. It is simply a business measure—and a very final one—so I thought that the sooner you knew it, the better. The details are not important now—at this date—but they can be learned from any newspaper which reviewed the 1943 revival of the play *Run, Little Chillun* in New York.

This is a rather unpleasant subject to have to bring up at this moment, and I regret that it is necessary. However if you are still interested in a possible production with that one condition, I shall be glad to continue correspondence about the details and promise to reply very promptly, now that I am a bit clearer about my future plans.

Thank you again for your interest.

Very sincerely yours,

Hall Johnson[66]

One cannot say with certainty who the person was that Johnson vehemently refused to work with. However, his reference to the 1943 revival of the show would lead one to believe that this person was Clarence Muse, whose direction of the New York revival had resulted in the demoralization of the cast, an unsuccessful run, and the loss of his job as stage director. (A different reason for this failure is given in some reports, that is, that all of the top black voices had been engaged at the time and were performing in a production of *Carmen Jones*.) Whatever the reason, for the second time, *Run, Little Chillun* was not to be translated into film.

Hollywood had discontinued making movies about the old South that required large contingents of slaves, field workers, and plantation choruses. The studios also found it much more economical to use studio singers who did not have to be credited and were skilled musicians who only had to be paid by the Screen Actor's Guild and the American Federation of Television and Radio Artists (AFTRA) scale. As even token racial integration was still in the future, there was little demand for a black professional choir. So with the dispersion of his top talent, Hall Johnson returned to Pasadena, California, in 1952, where he remained for five years and occupied himself with teaching and conducting.

The Jubilee Singers

On August 20 of that year, he received a commission from the Irwin Parnes Concert Agency to arrange an extended work based on spirituals to be performed by the Jubilee Singers in Europe and South America. Parnes represented a galaxy of first-rank concert artists including Mischa Elman, Percy Grainger, John Brownlee, Claudio Arrau, Lawrence Tibbett, Roland Hayes, Richard Tucker, Marjorie Lawrence, and Dorothy Maynor. He paid Johnson the sum of $500, and Johnson set to work on a job that had to be completed for a 110-concert tour starting on October 12—only seven weeks away. The approximately thirty-minute work for male voices and orchestra was called *Spiritual Moods* and was premiered at the Theater Municipal in Tunis on November 29 of that year. All performance rights were reserved to the Jubilee Singers. Members of the quartet were Robert-Perrin Bradford, tenor; Starling Hatchett, tenor; George Goodman, baritone; and Daniel Andrews, bass. The work created a sensation as described by Matthew Kennedy, the director of the group, in a letter to Hall Johnson dated July 12, 1953: "A few nights ago, we had the pleasure once more of performing *Spiritual Moods*—this time with the Buenos Aires Symphony. The reception was fantastic! There was such insistence by the public that it was necessary to repeat it from the beginning to the conclusion of 'Joshua.' Everyone here says they never witnessed such an ovation; one gentleman says the only similar demonstration that he can recall took place 30 or so years ago for Caruso.

"July 16: The Cordoba performance evoked an even bigger demonstration!"[67]

On February 1, 1955, Johnson was admitted to Cedars of Lebanon Hospital in Los Angeles for an unspecified illness and for an unspecified duration. Later that year, he received a second commission from the Jubilee Singers. Irwin Parnes, the manager of the Jubilee Singers, had been so delighted with Johnson's wonderful work that had made the international tour such a grand success and which had been written in twelve weeks for a paltry $500, that the music director of the group again wrote to Johnson, this time only three weeks before the tour. Needless to say, Johnson was annoyed by the ridiculously short amount of time allotted and at the suggestion that the earlier fee should again apply, as this excerpt from his response indicates:

> Dear Mrs. Myers [director],
>
> I was thrilled to hear of the fine reception given the *Spiritual Moods* I wrote for you in 1952, and delighted to know that you want me to do another similar composition. . . . But the three years in between have brought changes in my situation which will make it absolutely impossible for me to prepare this composition for you except at a cost greatly exceeding the amount you paid me for the first work.
>
> In an ordinary business commission . . . I would ask for a job like this $3,000 to $5,000, and best of all, three months time instead of three weeks. As it is, on account of my sincere friendship for you and my great admiration for your work, I am willing to do this—for you—for $2,000 and in the very uncomfortable space of three weeks. By working night and day, I can get it ready in three weeks—but I won't be able to do anything else within that period.

The manuscripts of both works have been preserved and may be published at some future date.

The Sprites and Sprouts
Earlier that same year (1955), the Disney Studios engaged Johnson to provide a group of singers for the *Mickey Mouse Club* television series. Johnson describes the creation of this group thusly:

> In May 1955, the Music Director of the Walt Disney Studios suggested [that I] prepare a group of Negro boys and girls to appear from time to time in the daily *Mickey Mouse Club* program, then under consideration. I enlisted the help of

Mrs. Wathea Jones, who is not only a specialist in child-training, but an accomplished singer and thorough musician. Together, we assembled and began to develop the group now known as the Hall Johnson Sprites and Sprouts. The Sprites are children of 4 to 9 years old; the Sprouts have an age limit of 15.

This group has been in regular rehearsal for the past year and in addition to several T.V. Appearances with the *Mickey Mouse Club*, has been heard from time to time in concert. The group includes youngsters of at least four different national origins, as, quite naturally, they specialize in the folk songs of many nations—in addition to the patriotic and popular songs of our own country.

These children are being given an excellent foundation in phonetics for both speaking and singing. Along with their musical talents, they are combining interest in dancing and the drama. Most important of all, however, is the emphasis placed upon living and working together in the spirit of true brotherhood.[68]

Johnson was assisted in coaching this group by Wathea Sims Jones.

The Belafonte Affair

In 1957, Johnson returned to New York to work with the Harry Belafonte Enterprises. Belafonte, one of the country's premiere folk singers, always toured and recorded with a male backup group and instruments. His interest in collecting, singing, and recording authentic folk music of Africa and of America was genuine. He had two primary objectives: (1) to record commercial hits to sing on his tours and (2) to record a comprehensive anthology that would trace the evolution of black music from Africa to the present day. (It was my good fortune to record with Belafonte from 1960 to 1968 and to verify much of this account firsthand. One of the results of our association was the 2001 release *The Long Road to Freedom*.) Because of Hall Johnson's reputation as an authority on folk music and as a composer and arranger, Belafonte thought that Johnson would be ideal as conductor for his recording sessions. He did not, however, consider the clash in cultures and work approaches of a conductor who had begun in 1925 with singers who would rehearse long hours without compensation in a Salvation Army hall, and modern, well-educated singer-musicians who belonged to AFTRA, the recording union, and had to be paid for every minute of rehearsal. These singers were normally expected to read the music from sight without previous rehearsal. The endless talking that Hall habitually did in his rehearsals cost thousands of dollars in studio rental, singer salaries, and engineer salaries. Hall Johnson wouldn't be hurried. Belafonte wouldn't be bankrupted. So, this alliance was destined to fail from the start. When the author's personal association with Belafonte began in 1960, his primary conductors were Leonard De Paur, a student of Hall Johnson; Howard Roberts; and Robert De Cormier. Even after observing union practices in the recording of *The Long Road to Freedom*, with Leonard De Paur, the project was so expensive that RCA shelved it for over thirty years. It was finally purchased by BMG and released in a six-CD set in 2001.

Johnson reestablished his studio on St. Nicholas Avenue and resumed coaching and teaching theory and composition. He also continued to arrange and compose, and to meet weekly with a "workshop chorus" of fewer that two dozen singers, most of whom were remnants of a previous epoch. The names Alice Ajaye, Roger Alford, and Joshua Cato come to mind.

Final Film Offer for *Run, Little Chillun*

In 1959 and 1960, Johnson once again undertook negotiations with backers who were interested in making a movie from his folk drama *Run, Little Chillun*. These negotiations were delayed because of the difficulty of determining whether or not Johnson owned the rights to the work since it had been produced by Robert Rockmore on Broadway. On September 21, 1959, Arthur Landau, who represented the Hollywood producers, wrote to Hall Johnson to complain about the long delay in establishing Johnson's ownership of *Run, Little Chillun*. Johnson had been sent documents to negotiate which would give the Hollywood producers the film rights to the play. Landau indicated that the company was impatient to get started on the film and to give Johnson the expense money that he had requested. Apparently, Johnson had traveled to Hollywood to confer with the producers, and it only remained for Johnson, upon his return to New York, to legally arrange with his lawyer for the transfer of rights. Landau requested an immediate letter from Johnson, detailing his progress in effecting the necessary transfer.

Unknown to Landau, Johnson's letter was already in the mail to him, and it appears below:

> A.L.
> Enclosing documents which I have been waiting for. Have carbon duplicate of Rockmore's letter, but not of Davis'. Have here also a photostatic copy of 1941 B.A. [Basic Agreement] with the special added features of the Meter Davis contract attached, including sundry correspondence among and between all parties. None of it has any value now—as Mr. Davis' letter so plainly states, but will send it all if you wish to plough through it—or can send the 1948 B.A. alone since the Guild says that's the one for this deal. Just let me know how

much of this you want. Rockmore has no rights other than motion picture—
or he would have come up with claims before now.

As to the other information you desire, from the D.G. [Dramatists' Guild],
it would be much better and clearer if you wrote them yourself requesting it. It
is too complicated for me. Some time ago, I gave them your name and address—as my agent, and asked them to send you a copy of the present B.A., but
they demurred—under some sort of explanation (which was not quite clear to
me)—that it did not affect the present deal. Ask them also to clarify to you the
conflict you seem to feel in the "separation of rights," that you mention. They
have not told me to adhere to the present B.A. for anything. They merely said
that whatever rights given to Barry, should apply to his [?] film only. I have not
discussed any theater production with them. Am sure it is better for you to
write them direct.

As to Wesley's suggested figures, they seem OK to me although I must say
that only the third one is really interesting. I should like to say here and now
that I would rather not do any presentation that would be too skimpy in the
number of singing voices. The modern recording devices do make the voices
more resonant (even unnaturally so) but they do not give the depth and full-
ness of a greater number of voices. Let's economize on anything but that. That
is the one and only department in which *Run, Little Chillun* can hope to top all
other films—the group singing.

Question: Is the initial $4,000 in the nature of an advance—to be deducted
from the final purchase price—and so, subject to division with Rockmore? This
is important to me at this moment. Please mention this when you write
next,—and let me know whether you want the full Meyer Davis text, or only
the '41 B.A.

Thanks for your promptness and "on-the-jobness." I do not see Belafonte.
Think it is better to wait until we have a little sample to show him.

Hall

Upon receiving Johnson's letter, Landau fired back a detailed response on
September 25, 1959, just four days later.[69] He explained the delay by saying
that Hall's letter had gone to his old address. Once again, Landau indicated
that Barry, the producer, was ready to move, but that his lawyer would not
execute the contract until several details were clarified.

According to Landau, Edward Colton, of the Dramatists' Guild, was check-
ing copies of the old contracts (for the Broadway production in 1933 and the
revival in 1945) with Meyer Davis, George Jessel, and Robert Rockmore, to
see what rights had been assigned them for backing, financially, the live productions. Johnson was told either to acquire copies of these agreements and
send them to Landau, or better, to have these gentlemen sign a quitclaim
agreement and give up their rights. (With regard to this last suggestion, one

must wonder if Landau was really serious to even suggest that these gentle-men, all interested in making more money, would even consider giving up their shares of the theater, radio, movie, and publishing rights to a play that was about to make some real money as did *The Green Pastures*.) Barry, the pro-ducer, did not want to commit to the project until he was certain exactly what these rights would cost and what rights remained from the old contracts. He would not even pay Johnson's $4,000 advance until all this was absolutely clear.

Landau felt that Robert Rockmore, himself an attorney, should take the lead in expediting and clarifying these details and, if inexperienced in con-tractual matters, hire an attorney who knew how to handle such a problem. Johnson was told to seek Rockmore's assistance and, further, to specify how much money he wanted and whether it should be all cash, a percentage of the profits, or a combination of cash and a percentage. He would try to get that amount for Johnson.

In conclusion, Landau said, "The boys are ready to go at once. Your money, as agreed, is ready," but also stated that the producer would make no payments until all the required information was submitted to him. "I believe you have a hit play and so do the boys. The very minute Barry gets the contract terms and copyright clearances, and the information on the Meyer Davis, Jessel and Rockmore papers, it will then be full speed ahead."[70]

This tragicomedy continued, unrelieved, despite the fact that in Decem-ber of 1959, the Madison Avenue law firm of Zissu, Marcus, Ebenstein, and Stein was retained to unravel the problems, apparently without success. In Landau's handwritten note of January 3, 1960, it is clear that the time had come and gone for this project, as he stated, "I cannot seem able to learn any-thing from Wesley Barry or Ed Kay. They claim the attorneys here and New York, and those at the Guild seem lost as to how to write the contracts to conform with your original play arrangements."[71] Landau said that he didn't feel it was fair to keep Johnson waiting so long, but once again, he asked that Johnson send him the details.

This process was still ongoing and the matter was still unresolved when ill-ness overtook Johnson, then seventy-two years old. Like Moses, Johnson was never to enter the promised land, only to see it. The dream of making the film was never to materialize.

The only possible explanation of this tragic injustice to Johnson is that it was a cruel and overt demonstration of American racism. A single letter to Johnson from his idol, the great Will Marion Cook (the pioneer of the black musical comedy), written on August 29, 1941—only three years before his death—confirms this opinion.

Will Marion Cook Comments on Racism
A.S.C.A.P
c/o Miss M.S. Brooks
Asheville, North Carolina

Dear Hall,

Have lost my pen, so must use pencil.

Your addressing me as Mr. Cook is a bit formal; then too, there are many Wm. Cooks—only one—I hope!—Will Marion! True, you are a bit young to say Will, but you can, with strain, say "Dad!" In France, they called me, "Mon Pere," and so on.

You too, Hall, have done your Share; in fact, plenty. And you would have done much more if the damned Jews had not restricted you, as they do all the others—except me. I'm a fighter! Born of African and Indian parentage, been in revolutions, have no sense! Just a damned fool who cares not where he sleeps, what he eats, or where he goes—just as long as he carries on in his own "phool" way. And now, it looks as tho' I'm about to cash in plenty! *The Jews may yet make a monkey of me but will take lots of cunning, twisting, and stealing.* I've plenty of protection, lawyers, Miss Brooks—*and a few Great and Real Jews* [my emphasis]—to back me up.

I'm working plenty, under a tremendous strain—both financially and physically. Have as yet made no contracts! Have no agents! No Managers! Have no contracts yet because my projected school shall give away all I earn so that gov't shan't take one mill tax to feed England,—nor one penny to feed "no goods" who won't and never did work. I'll give as it comes in—so the contracts are rather hard to figure out; especially since my lawyer Mr. Shumlin of Song Writers is away—and when he returned to New York, I was too busy to see him (doing a million things, mostly badly). But soon as finances are OK and dates set—I'll need you buddy, if I want to "Ring the Bell." . . .

When I get a full estimate of all expenses [for a proposed Madison Square Garden extravaganza]—and get a real Business Manager, not a kike, nor a Broadway Ghoul Agent, but a real Business Manager appointed by real business men of note whom I've worked for in the past 60 years—(or their sons or grandsons), when all this is ready, then I'll call upon two or three men to take over and help, . . . not me, but a grand Race even if they seem sluggish—evil—jealous, all the "-ishes" of an inferior people, but with the hopes, yes prospects of a Superior people. You and I know, Hall—*the white man is nearly finished. He's had his fling* [my emphasis].[72]

Unquestionably, Dad Cook's words seem racist and politically incorrect. But they accurately reflect the feelings of a classically trained black artist, an Oberlin graduate and a violin virtuoso trained by the renown Joachim in Europe, whose mother and father had graduated from Oberlin around 1865 and who had suffered derogation and exploitation for some fifty years. He felt that the same things were happening to Johnson and that he understood why.

We find confirmation of Cook's allegations in the following letter from the office of George Jessel, dated February 6, 1943, in relation to producing a revival of Johnson's *Run, Little Chillun* on Broadway. If one considers that Johnson wrote both the book and the music and, further, that Connelly and Bradford became rich from their authorship of *The Green Pastures*, Jessel's offer to Johnson is an insult.

In a letter dated February 6, 1943, speaking of a Broadway revival of Johnson's *Run, Little Chillun*, Lou Cooper of the Jessel office sent Johnson an option check in the amount of $100 and told him he would receive a straight *5 percent* of the gross of the show, and the same should there be a second road company. He advanced the notion that this would be, for Johnson, "a lot of money."

Unfortunately, Johnson was desperately in need of money and accepted the first offer thrown to him, without hesitation. Despite the record-breaking success of *Run, Little Chillun* on the West Coast, it was doomed to fail in the New York revival. While Johnson had written and arranged all the music for *The Green Pastures*, he possessed no rights to the show as it was owned by the producers and by Connelly and Bradford. *The Green Pastures* opened on Broadway in 1930, and by the time the road tours were completed in 1935, it had been optioned to be produced as a movie. It encountered no difficulties with the Guild and was filmed in 1936. We know that Connelly and Bradford had made over $290,000 from the stage production by 1935. The amount they made from the movie rights is unknown. With *Run, Little Chillun*, which opened in 1933, Johnson was the whole show. He should have owned the play and the music, and he should have done the musical direction if filmed, as he did on Broadway. This was unheard of in the theater. There had been George and Ira Gershwin, Lerner and Lowe, Rodgers and Hammerstein—all duos—but Johnson wrote his drama and music and had a hit great enough to be thrice offered a film contract; this was, in the opinion of the power-structure, too much of an achievement for a black man between 1933 and 1960. While the Hollywood producers were very sincere as the letters indicated, the difficulties experienced in New York with the Dramatists' Guild (the controlling agency) and with the affected lawyers were a perfect application of the old slavery technique: "Keep that fool a-running." In this cruel practice, a vicious slave master would choose his most imposing male slave (perhaps also the one with the most leadership potential). He would give the slave a note and tell him to run as fast as he could and take the message to the master of the next plantation. When the next plantation owner opened and read the note, it would simply say, "Keep this fool a-running." This would be repeated until the slave fell dead from exhaustion or was punished savagely when he could run no farther. With a unionized theater and Dramatists' Guild, the requirements for all shows to move from stage to screen were the same. Yet somehow, between 1939 and 1959, *Run, Little Chillun* could not clear all the obstacles to allow its filming. It is possible that Johnson allowed Rockmore, Davis, and Jessel to usurp his ownership rights to an inordinate degree. However, as Rockmore, the original producer, would have received 50 percent of the income, he would have had no economic reason to obstruct efforts to make a film of *Run, Little Chillun*. As fate would have it, Rockmore was to live only a few years more, and I, with no knowledge of his historical significance at the time, was actually soloist with a De Paur Chorus, at his funeral.

In June of 1961, Johnson suffered a light stroke and was briefly hospitalized in Sydenham Hospital at 123rd Street and Manhattan Avenue in New York. When he was released, his two sisters, Alice Foster and Susan Jordan, came from California and took him back to Pasadena to recover. Fortunately, his recovery was swift and he was able to return to New York before the end of 1962. He suffered little permanent damage from his stroke and was able to walk, speak, and write normally, but with a bit more deliberation. A comparison of his handwriting before and after his stroke would reveal more irregularity and undulation in his post-stroke script.

When Johnson returned to New York, he received an important commission from the great contralto, Marian Anderson. In August 1961, Anderson recorded an album of twenty standards of the spiritual repertoire with Franz Rupp for RCA Victor. Subsequently, she asked Hall Johnson to write and arrange a second album of new and different works for her to record. Johnson wrote an album that he called *Jus' Keep On Singin'*. He worked with Miss Anderson and accompanist John Motley, and the team recorded the songs for RCA at Webster Hall in September 1964. Both of these albums are now available on a single CD (09026-61960), *He's Got the Whole World in His Hands*. The interpretations on both albums are authoritative. However, as these works were recorded at the end of Anderson's long career, she was not in the glorious vocal estate that her earlier spirituals recordings demonstrate.

In a letter dated November 9, 1962, a fourth commission was offered Johnson, this one by a quartet organized by Irwin Parnes—baritone Robert McFerrin; his wife, Sarah; Helen Thigpen; and an unnamed tenor. With the customary inconsideration (inadequate time, problematic task), Sarah McFerrin blithely informed Johnson that their quartet had two sopranos, a tenor, and a baritone, and that they were requesting arrangements that would accommodate an alto-less quartet with sufficient expedition that they could begin rehearsals and do a debut of the program in Philharmonic Hall, in Los Angeles in the early spring.

Johnson's reply was exactly what one might expect from a seventy-five-year-old who had just recovered from a stroke. Both his speech and his writing were slower and required effort. He wrote the following:

> Dear Sara,
>   News exciting. I can't help—never quartet—at least six [voices]. Not enough voices. Have tried. Only one success— "'Buked" ["I've Been 'Buked and I've Been Scorned"], because so close. Sorry . . .
>   H. J.

It is easy to see that Johnson's writing style had become very concise, almost cryptic, because of his stroke. He made it clear that writing for a quartet would not achieve a desirable result, although the record shows that his *Spiritual Moods* for the Jubilee Singers and orchestra created a sensation. The reasons for his refusal were two: his deteriorating health and the fact that arrangements for two sopranos, tenor, and bass are intrinsically unsatisfying for the lack of an alto part, even more so if a cappella or accompanied only by piano. Johnson suffered another unspecified illness in July of 1967. Then seventy-nine years old, he was hospitalized in Prospect Hospital, 730 Kelly Street, Bronx, New York, for a period of three weeks—from July 15 to August 4. The following year, under the care of Dr. Robert Scher, Johnson made outpatient visits to the hospital on June 3 and 4, July 1, October 7, and December 16.

Independence of Spirit

Hall Johnson demonstrated a decidedly independent streak early in life. His early aspirations to become a painter at a time when Booker T. Washington was urging Negroes to pursue practical careers was unusual, even had he been white. His interest in violin study as a black kid in a small Georgia town was different. Then, after successfully breaking into the professional black orchestral circle in New York, to give it all up and start in a totally new area—professional choral work—was a clear indication that he thought "outside the box." So was the creation of the new forms represented by *The Green Pastures*, *Run, Little Chillun*, and *Son of Man*.

Unlike so many professionals, then and now, Hall Johnson was uncompromising. He always strove for perfection and demanded that those under him have the same objective and be willing to go to great lengths to accomplish it. Thus, his rehearsals seemed endless because he would routinely talk about a phrase or a work until you captured the concept, and then he would repeat that phrase or work until you rendered it precisely. The same meticulous standard was applied to his individual song coaching. This was completely different from most rehearsals and recording sessions where an acceptable level is sought, but may be far from the best that could be done. Time and money rule the conduct of the contemporary conductor. Hall Johnson *never* rushed and was quoted as saying, "They waited for me on Broadway, they waited for me in Hollywood, and they are going to wait on me tonight." The only other classical composer who behaved in that manner (in my experience) was Paul Hindemith, who worked with a chorus of Yale University master's candidates for one hour on a single page of the Monteverdi *Lagrime*. In the popular realm, Harry Belafonte had that kind of obsession for getting a performance *just* right, and I once observed him record a single work twenty-seven times.

Little attention has been given to the fact that Hall Johnson, a Negro composer, conductor, and violinist, was able to sustain himself for sixty years—through reconstruction, segregation, and the Great Depression—exclusively through professional activity. At no time in his life did he fall back on a "day job" or employment by schools, colleges, or churches (although he did acquire a teaching certificate). But it was not always easy. He made many sacrifices; never owned a home; and spent many years living with family members, friends, at the Y.M.C.A., and finally at his apartment at 654 St. Nicholas Avenue, which had originally been leased by his brother, George Decker Johnson, and his wife. A March 27, 1959, Social Security Administration document noted in the following paragraphs shows how frugal his existence really was, especially in the final decade of his life.

In response to what appears to have been a denial of Social Security benefits for 1957, the chief payment officer indicated that Johnson's case had been reconsidered and that earnings of less than $1,200 that year made him eligible for payments the entire year.

Apparently, 1957 was Johnson's worst year, for he tripled that amount in 1960, reporting a gross income of $4,522, and for 1961, a gross income of $5,182. Despite his genius and hard work, he never had the "big pay day" that he so deserved. While so many of his colleagues affiliated themselves with universities or churches, Johnson's personality and need for creative and personal freedom led him to eschew such alliances. In this way, he was able to focus all his energy and attention on the project at hand. This undivided effort allowed him to perform feats reminiscent of classical composers like Mozart: to prepare twenty-five arrangements and original selections for the

Broadway debut of *The Green Pastures*, between his choir's second Town Hall concert in November 1928 and the opening on February 26, 1930, or to write the book and music of *Run, Little Chillun* in the year between the close of the Broadway production of *The Green Pastures* and the opening of *Run, Little Chillun* on June 12, 1933. Thus, the freedom from the institutional demands seems to have provided the milieu necessary for his abundant creativity and the legacy he left. It was, however, not without a price, as there were times when he literally didn't know where his next dollar was coming from. There is no question that his talents were purchased too cheaply, whether because of the racism of the time or because of the lack of a good personal representative. At the same time Johnson was earning $2,800 for scoring and conducting *The Green Pastures* between 1930 and 1935, Marc Connelly and Roark Bradford together were making $296,563,[73] and George Gershwin was making $2,000[74] weekly for his informal radio show. So, pastures were green for all—except Hall:

Royalties to Mark Connelly and Roark Bradford—Authors	$296,563
Hall Johnson—"Choir Director"	$2,800

Religious Beliefs

Based on an examination of his musical and literary output, Hall Johnson seemed a deeply religious man. Save for an early musical comedy, *Fi-yer* modeled on the successful productions of Will Marion Cook—and a few work, blues, and secular art songs, virtually everything that Johnson wrote was faith based. This is clearly reflected in the titles of his major works: *The Green Pastures, Run, Little Chillun,* and *Son of Man.* Obviously, religion is the essence of the spiritual, and each of these works incorporated spirituals as the primary musical form.

And yet, there is no evidence that Johnson was ever a member of any church, traditional or nontraditional, as an adult. One might find some justification in the fact that his work as conductor of a professional choir required frequent travel and performance on Sunday, but certainly, after 1951 and the choir's return from its tour of Germany and Austria, this was not the case. Despite his African Methodist Episcopal background, correspondence with his sister Alice Foster confirms that his interest in organized religion was confined to Scientology. After years of dialogue with Alice, Johnson actually began a book that was a hybrid of religion and philosophy, which, unfortunately, was never finished and, thus, never published.

The most striking discovery about Johnson's religious convictions is the extent to which they were custom made. An examination of his personal Bible to determine what passages he deemed most significant reveals something even more astounding. In addition to a number of highlighted passages that, it may be assumed, confirmed his beliefs, a number of carefully deleted (crossed out) passages appear, indicating that Johnson found these portions of the scripture unacceptable. To most Christians, to cross out or delete a single word from the inspired holy scripture would be an act of unspeakable blasphemy. That Hall Johnson would do this, in many places, gives some insight into his mind. In the earlier discussion of the creation of *Run, Little Chillun*, two important aspects of Johnson's personality and mentality were mentioned: (1) the duality of his personality, comprised of both a spiritual and a hedonistic side as represented by his membership in both Hope Baptist Church and the New Day Pilgrims and (2) a god-like concept of his own powers, which permitted him to believe that he could write both the book and the music of a great Broadway play and have it successfully produced in 1933.

An examination of Johnson's Bible reveals that he paid little attention to the Old Testament, but studied the New Testament in great detail. It is impossible to postulate what he might have been thinking, but the passages that he highlighted and the passages that he deleted seem to relate to the mental and personality traits already identified. The following passages are representative of the many that he highlighted:[75]

Verily I say unto you, Whatsoever ye shall bind on earth shall be bound in heaven: and whatsoever ye shall loose on earth shall be loosed in heaven. . . . For where two or three are gathered together in my name, there am I in the midst of them. (Matthew 18:18, 20)

Woe unto you scribes and Pharisees, hypocrites! for ye make clean the outside of the cup and of the platter, but within they are full of extortion and excess. Thou blind Pharisee, cleanse first that which is within the cup and platter, that the outside of them may be clean also. (Matthew 23:25–26)

But rather seek ye the kingdom of God; and all these things shall be added unto you. (Luke 12:31)

For the wrath of God is revealed from heaven against all ungodliness and unrighteousness of men, who hold the truth in unrighteousness. . . . Because that when they knew God, they glorified him not as God, neither were thankful; but became vain in their imaginations, and their foolish heart was darkened. (Romans 1:18, 21)

And if Christ be in you, the body is dead because of sin; but the Spirit is life because of righteousness. (Romans 8:10)

Every man's work shall be made manifest: for the day shall declare it, because it shall be revealed by fire; and the fire shall try every man's work of what sort it is. . . . If any man's work shall be burned, he shall suffer loss: but he himself shall be saved; yet so as by fire. (1 Corinthians 3:13, 15)

For we must all appear before the judgment seat of Christ; that every one may receive the things done in his body according to that he hath done, whether it be good or bad. (2 Corinthians 5:10)

The passages below are representative of those Johnson deleted from the biblical text:

Be ye therefore perfect, even as your Father which is in heaven is perfect. (Matthew 5:48)

Take my yoke upon you and learn of me; for I am meek and lowly in heart: and ye shall find rest unto your souls. (Matthew 11:29)

Watch and pray, that ye enter not into temptation: the spirit indeed is willing, but the flesh is weak. (Matthew 26:41)

It is the spirit that quickeneth; the flesh profiteth nothing: the words that I speak unto you, they are spirit, and they are life. (John 6:63)

I am the light of the world: he that followeth me shall not walk in darkness, but shall have the light of life. (John 8:12)

He that hath my commandments, and keepeth them, he it is that loveth me; and he that loveth me shall be loved of my Father, and I will love him, and will manifest myself to him. . . . If a man love me, he will keep my words: and my Father will love him, and we will come unto him, and make our abode with him. (John 14:21, 23)

And be not conformed to this world: but be ye transformed by the renewing of your mind, that ye may prove what is that good, and acceptable, and perfect, will of God. (Romans 12:3)

What? know ye not that your body is the temple of the Holy Ghost which is in you, which ye have of God, and ye are not your own? For ye are bought with a price: therefore glorify God in your body, and in your spirit, which are God's. (1 Corinthians 6:19–20)

And what agreement hath the temple of God with idols? for ye are the temple of the living God; as God hath said, I will dwell in them, and walk in them; and I will be their God, and they shall be my people. (2 Corinthians 6:16)

For the flesh lusteth against the Spirit, and the Spirit against the flesh: and these are contrary the one to the other: so that ye cannot do the things that ye would. (Galatians 5:17)

Be not deceived; God is not mocked: for whatsoever a man soweth, that shall he also reap. For he that soweth to his flesh shall of the flesh reap corruption; but he that soweth to the Spirit shall of the Spirit reap life everlasting. (Galatians 6:7–8)

Whom we preach, warning every man, and teaching every man in all wisdom; that we may present every man perfect in Christ Jesus. (Colossians 1:28)

For the word of God is quick, and powerful, and sharper than any two-edged sword, piercing even to the dividing asunder of soul and spirit, and of the joints and marrow, and is a discerner of thoughts and intentions of the heart. Neither is there any creature that is not manifest in his sight: but things are naked and opened unto the eyes of him with whom we have to do. (Hebrew 4:12–13)

There is no way of knowing at what point in his life Johnson made these redactions or if he continued to reject such a significant body of Christian dogma throughout his life. One can only observe that the struggle between the body and the spirit is a major theme in many of the passages, and that this struggle is manifested in his musical play of 1933, *Run, Little Chillun*. His personal struggles with alcoholism and lifestyle choices persisted well into his senior years and lead one to conclude that his religion was custom made.

Struggle with Alcoholism

Johnson's "illness" during the filming of *Lost Horizon* has already been identified as a prolonged bout with alcoholism. Had it occurred in 1936, during the filming of *The Green Pastures*, one might logically assume that it was depression related and due to the untimely death of his wife in December 1935. That is, however, not the case. Despite the fact that I knew several of the original Hall Johnson Choir members personally, in the 1960s, we never discussed Johnson's problem with alcohol. Subsequent research indicates that the problem was periodic, but severe as early as 1931, four years before the death of his wife. In a letter dated March 26, 1932, a potential client who had contacted Johnson's manager about bringing him to Texas for a workshop at her school, told Johnson of her grave reservations about the venture because of her rude treatment in New York and because of his drunken behavior at the Harmon Awards, with a candor unequalled by any other correspondent.

In a lengthy letter, Mrs. Manet Fowler[76] made the following points: Johnson was totally unknown in Texas.

Although she had sponsored Nathaniel Dett, Carl Diton, Marian Anderson, and Roland Hayes, she had certain concerns about Johnson that had to be discussed. Among those concerns was Johnson's unspeakable behavior at the Harmon Awards where he was so drunk that he couldn't stand up. She said, further, that such behavior before the leading musical figures in New York had disgraced every black professional present. The assessment of Hall Johnson by those in the profession, she said, was that he was a great musician, but he was a "whiskey-head." She feared "that anytime you got up before a chorus of people in Texas, with your hair all disheveled, your eyes flaming, and your face distorted, gradually disrobing yourself, as I have actually seen you do here, driving the disgust deeper with the vilest profanity, you would be evicted from that place."

Mrs. Fowler also addressed the question of the Hall Johnson "hangers-on": "You can thrive a little while longer on the sentimental mush . . . of the parasites that feed on you mentally and physically. . . . Your deportment along this line is becoming a millstone . . . dragging you backward at such a pace . . . that perhaps some white man takes your ideas and purchases happiness with them."

It is apparent that the writer was speaking about more than Johnson's drinking; Mrs. Fowler was also addressing what she considered to be an immoral lifestyle. This becomes clearer as the letter continues, and Fowler gives the only impressionistic snapshot of Johnson's relationship with his wife, clearly indicating that she knew them both quite well. After telling him that she would incur his hatred because she must speak the truth, she continued,

> You made a remark in my presence once that I was just like your wife, wanting you to be something else, and not tolerating you as you are. . . . I shall never forget an expression I saw on your wife's face the night you introduced me to her and she clung to you with a sort of childlike simplicity . . . you did look so grand, so worthwhile, and she, trying to fool herself, even as you have done, to make herself believe she was happy—but withal, hungry for that real something that only a faithful, manly husband can give . . . and you cuddled her and said . . . in a tone that I have not heard . . . before or since . . . "my wife." There was something . . . that made me know that despite all the evil temptations that clutch at your throat, you are capable of the highest form of love.

Not yet having completed her analysis of Johnson's problems, Mrs. Fowler expressed regrets that Johnson's work removed him from the surveillance of a wife, which he sorely needed to make him conform to the conventions of polite society. She went on to recall an appointment to audition for Johnson where she was met at the door of his apartment at ten o'clock at night by a man in bedroom slippers and a lounging robe. She had been forced to entertain herself for forty minutes at the piano while a female guest also moved in and out of the bedroom. Ultimately, she said, she was forced to make some excuse and leave without being heard. She concluded her letter, "Now the right kind of wife there would have planned these things. . . . You can't be husband, wife, gigolo, musician, poet, business man and a thousand other things at the same time. It's impossible."

Manet Fowler's letter has been summarized and quoted here after some deliberation because it is difficult to read, even with some redactions, without realizing that it may hold the key to understanding the creation of *Run, Little Chillun*. It offers the possibility, even the probability, that there were *two Hall Johnsons: one with the primordial urges of the New Day Pilgrims, the other with the conventions and restraints of the members of the Hope Baptist Church.* Certainly it is more than a coincidence that Mrs. Fowler's most articulate and exacting confrontation occurred less than a year before the opening of *Run, Little Chillun*, making it appear that the play may indeed have been autobiographical, with the struggle between the two religions being a metaphor for the struggle between the bad and the good in Hall Johnson.

Despite Mrs. Fowler's excoriating letter of 1932, over the next several years, she and Hall Johnson resolved their differences and again became friends. She was instrumental in the selection of Hall Johnson as conductor of the Convention Chorus for the National Association of Negro Musicians sixteenth annual convention, August 25–29, 1935, in New York City. In 1943, she sought and received help from Johnson in creating a school song for her private School of Afro-American Arts, Mwalimu. Johnson wrote original music for her text, which was in the Yoruba language. Mrs. Fowler also collaborated with Johnson in the transcription of several of his arrangements into Braille. In a letter of January 8, 1961, she attempted to convince Johnson that they should publish some of his art songs for this purpose. She closed her letter "with my love and continued interest in your good work," a clear indication that they had regained the warm friendship they once enjoyed. The two art songs Johnson selected were "Dear, Would You Know" and "Song of the Mother." While it is not known if they were ever published, copies of the transcriptions into Braille are preserved in the Hall Johnson Collection.

At least one other person—Charlotte Osgood Mason (aka Charlotte van der Veer Quick Mason)—who was in no way dependent upon Johnson, illustrated her concern for Johnson in the summer of 1928 by warning him of the dangers of his lifestyle. Mrs. Mason, who insisted on being called "God-mother," was a wealthy white widow who extended patronage to a number of gifted black artists of the Harlem Renaissance, including Langston Hughes, Zora Neale Hurston, Alain Locke, and Louise Thompson.[77] In her undated letter to Johnson,[78] Mrs. Mason told him that she had learned from Alain Locke and Langston Hughes of his progress with the choir and that she was looking forward to the appearance of the choir at Lewisohn Stadium, saying it could be like "a bright jewel." She also informed him that the French papers were praising his work with the chorus of *Blackbirds*,[79] an all-Negro show playing on Broadway. In the latter part of the letter, she took a serious tone and admonished Johnson to keep up his courage and "keep off the horde of human beings who sit on the tail of your flight and continually pin down your wings. This is the real thing that stands continually in your road, eats up your vitality, eats up your inspiration and curtails your financial possibilities." Despite her concern and good advice, there is no indication that the Godmother ever made any financial contribution to Johnson's success.

Johnson clearly continued to drink throughout the making of *Lost Horizon* in 1937 until the summer of 1939 when he entered a sanitarium for treatment. This is confirmed by a letter to him from Jester Hairston:

> I am so glad that you are well again and back to your old self again. When I came down there a few weeks ago I came to your house to see you and stayed until four in the morning. . . . You were pretty high, but I can't see why Mays didn't tell you I was there. . . . Am glad you went to that place I tried to get you into last year. They are really good and I'm sure you won't be bothered with it [the alcoholism] again.
>   Your daughter,
>   Hester [Jester]

The truest confirmation, however, is to be found in Hall Johnson's own words. With his customary thoroughness, Hall gave a detailed account of his illness on four scribbled and barely decipherable pages:[80]

Introduction
Have for many years been periodic drinker.
Have studied question.—Don't like, and have never liked liquor.
Believe it has helped me in lots of ways—change of consciousness.
Have always started and stopped deliberately, approach to life and people.
Have never been afraid of habit—bringing out and suppressing different qualities.

In my case, the cause has been purely mental and I have always believed the cure to be.
Have taken it in seasons, never when a big job was in progress.[81]

Samaritan [rehabilitation hospital]
Friends plead to try cure—I refused—didn't need it—would stop when I got ready.
They visit Institute—have stuff—to me, emphasizing physical basis of disease. I disagreed.

First Trip to Samaritan
Did need some sort of physical treatment. Was there from February 20–24. Describe treatment: Mrs. A's talk: "Must have cooperation. No cure without patient's consent. Made me promise to report return of urge—atmosphere of sympathy—radio . . . after treatments.

In between Visits
After getting my strength back (from the drastic treatment) I was glad that I had had the treatment. At first had revulsion of feeling at the thought of liquor but this wore off to natural distaste. Had always been obliged to "tune up" gradually anyhow—later I realized that I could drink again if I wanted to. This condition lasted nearly three months. I did not want to drink but I knew that I could and would drink when I got ready.

Finally
The third week in June, in San Diego, I began gradually to drink again. The details of what followed appear in H's statement and it is not necessary for me to repeat them here. They are true as I remember them myself. Naturally, I would have a slightly different angle on what happened and here it is.

Second Visit
On Monday eve, June 19th, we got back home from San Diego. I had been drinking pretty steadily for the past three days but I had three months of building up so my resistance was pretty good and when I went to bed drunk that night, I was feeling fine physically and had no thought so far about stopping my drinking spree or being stopped. The next morning, Tuesday the 20th, I waked up very clear—attended to the business that came up, including a conference with J.C., my assistant. I had every intention of going to L.B. that evening—where the company was playing. Imagine my shock when the three men walked in and asked me to go to the Institute with them. I refused point blank. In the first place, I was not ill, in the second place, I was not ready to stop drinking for the time being and I knew by their own admission, that they could not help me against my will. I knew that I was going on with my spree

until I got ready to stop. I knew that I was not in financial position to go even if I had wanted to. I remembered how they had piled on extra charges on the previous occasion in spite of the fact that their pamphlet states emphatically that the one price of $150 covers everything. No extra charges. My last visit had cost me $212. I was loud and firm in my arguments, but to no avail. The three men waited patiently until I had stretched out on my bed. Then they came in and overpowered me by brute force—three against one—dragged me through the door of my home—through the yard, and forced me into their car. In doing this, they struck my head against the top of the car and also twisted my arm to force me to go in when I refused to lower my head. All the way to the Institute, I tried to explain the situation to them. That it was not only an infringement of my privacy in my own house, but absolutely useless as I was not going to stop drinking and the "cure" would do me no good. When we got to the hospital, I put up the same struggle about getting out of the car and they forced me out just as they had forced me in. By that time, I had learned that struggling was of no use. So for the sake of my own dignity (and to prove that I was able to do it) I went upstairs unaided and into the room.

Once in the room, I began my protests again, telling them that I didn't want my "cure," that I was going on drinking, that their "cure" was no cure—that they had no right to drag me over their against my will, etc. They let me talk on without replies of any consequence. Then I saw that protests and resistance were not going to help me any at the moment. If I had ever thought otherwise, that hope was completely dispelled when four grim-looking men walked in the room together. I decided that my best . . . [The account breaks off here.]

While the above narrative breaks off abruptly, Johnson provides a second narrative, much more detailed and illegible.

Friday, June 16—Began to get drunk late in the evening at Douglass. Got to hotel about daylight Saturday. Got up and went to matinee. Hotel late—Went shopping—shirts, watches—night show late—talk in—both busses with company who were leaving for L.A. Dinner at Douglass—treating everybody— other table went to Lincoln. I ordered more food—didn't eat—stayed till 3:00 o'clock—stopped woman, refused to pay for food—got to Pacific Hotel at 4:00 A.M. (Sunday 18) Got up about 1:00. . . . Went to see Mrs. Brown—Went to Tijuana with me asleep in car. When we crossed line coming back, I woke up and wanted to go back to Tijuana, but Junior wouldn't. I was too drunk.

Monday, June 19—Left San Diego about noon (was very drunk in battery place and asleep in gas place) with the car, but slept most of the way. When we got to Long Beach, Junior would not let me get out of the car. He went in to the rehearsal and Crawford came out and talked to me at the car. In about 1/2 hour, we came on in to L.A. I was fussing in between naps because Junior wouldn't let me go into the rehearsal and stay in Long Beach. Got to our house about 7 o'clock. I didn't want to get out of car, resisted, was still very drunk. Junior went into dining room and sat down and went to sleep—The bags were taken . . . while I was still asleep in the car. I finally came out of car and lay across the bed. Junior called Mays [the housekeeper]—but got Des Verney. Mays was out. Junior went to Good Samaritan [rehab hospital]. When he went in—Ames was in lobby. She asked Junior what was the news—he replied—it's rather bad. She took him into her office in the back. She asked if I was drinking again. He said yes. She asked when did it start? He told her, "On San Diego trip." He had just got back and didn't know what to do. He asked, could she tell him anything he could do. She said, I should have come back to them when I felt the urge coming on. Of course, being in San Diego made that impracticable even if I had wanted to. Ames wound up by suggesting another treatment. Junior said he did not know what to say about that, but that he would call Miss Shaw and find out what was best to do. She said alright. Junior left. He is blurred about what followed.

The next morning—Somebody called from Samaritan. At first, they asked for Crawford, but I told them Crawford was not here.—Asked Junior how I was. Junior told them. Then they asked Junior if he thought I would come along with no trouble. Junior replied he did not know. They then said they would send a couple of men over in a half hour. Meanwhile, Myrtle Anderson called to say that Miss Shaw wanted Junior to come out in the street and call her. She also said something (which Junior couldn't recall just now) but which gave him the idea that . . . the men were coming so he told Anderson that he knew it, as the men had already called. And so it was unnecessary to call them. (Also Crawford, my assistant musical director in the choir, had been here and had received a mysterious phone call which we will investigate later. I transacted my business with Crawford and he left.)

After a while, three men came to the door—asked where I was—Junior told them I was in the bathroom. They came in and waited 1/2 hour until I came out. They had already asked Junior if I was dressed. He told them no. Then one man came in the back of the house and talked to me. He asked (according to Junior) how I was and if I didn't want to go along with him. I told him no. (He had already asked me if I remembered him.) I asked him if he wanted a drink. I remember no further conversation but only that this man finally went back in the front and left me in the kitchen, where I had another drink. I went into the bathroom—I came in there—looking pretty exhausted—and he helped me across the hall into the bedroom where I lay across the bed. The three men, seeing my condition, thought this was their opportunity. I evidently was already partly dressed (with Junior's help?). I had on a business suit, trousers and socks. Jr. put my shoes on when they were taking me off the bed. They finally forced me off the bed in spite of my struggles—kicking, biting, etc. They dragged me through the door in spite of my cries and struggles and forced me in the car (a two-door sedan Chevrolet 35?) All three of them . . . I refused to bend down to get in so one of them got in and pulled me in while the other two pushed me in—striking my head against the top of the car and twisting my arm. I was still yelling protests, and struggling. I asked for Junior to come along—they told him and he said he would follow along in his own car. I kept up conversation with my captors—did not go to sleep. . . . When we got to the hospital, two of them pulled while the third one pushed me, struggling, out of the car. Dr. Nicholas came out to the car and watched this. By this time, I saw the futility of struggling and walked up the stairs and to the room unassisted—refusing their attempts to support me. Junior followed me up. A nurse brought pajamas—By this time, there was only one man in the room—Junior's not certain whether or not he was one of the original three. The nurse started to undress me. I protested—saying that I didn't want anyone to undress me but Junior. He took off my shoes and finally got down to my underwear which I refused to take off. They [3] stood around in the room for some little time. After about 20 minutes of this [during which time] I was lying silently across the bed with the other 3 sitting around in the room.

(Junior forgot to mention in it's proper place that Ames had asked him in their conversation if he thought it was something mental that was worrying me. Junior said no—he didn't think so. Then Ames said that Miss J. had the theory that I was worried because I wished to be white. Junior denied this vigorously—saying that if that was so, I wouldn't be giving so much of my time to the development of my own people. Ames agreed that the theory didn't sound plausible.)

Junior left—saying that he supposed that was all he could do. The reply was, "Yes, I suppose we can handle him alright now." On the way out he saw one of the men who had taken me over—They merely waved "So Long!" Nobody had talked to him about the case or asked him anything—either about authority or expense. From the beginning of the visit of the three men (which was my first knowledge of the whole matter), I had been protesting loudly that I didn't want any "cure," that the whole business was a fake, which everybody knows, and that I was not going to stand for much imposition and brutality.

Junior came [went] back home—and went to Long Beach for the show. The next day (Wednesday, June 21st) Mays called the hospital to see if I wanted anything brought over as they were planning to visit me. They came over in the afternoon and found me angry and sick from the treatment—The night before I had been very well although quite drunk. While they were there, I had a severe vomiting spell although it had been some little time since my last treatment. Junior left to go to Pasadena for the show.

Here, Johnson's account stops. There is no explanation for the existence of two versions, save for the possibility that at the time he wrote the accounts, he might have been angry and considering suing Good Samaritan Hospital. The purpose of including the two detailed accounts is to establish how severe Johnson's addiction was and how destructive it had to be to his professional activities. It is miraculous that during these bouts of alcoholism, his assistants and the solid membership of the Hall Johnson Choir kept the ship afloat. We know that when he went on a binge during the filming of *Lost Horizon* in 1937, Jester Hairston, then assistant conductor, took over and the choir completed the movie very successfully. In 1939, during the episode recounted above, Joseph Crawford, assistant conductor for the production of *Run, Little Chillun*, took over and the choir, largely a local group under FTP, seems not to have missed a beat.

The young man constantly referred to in the narrative as "Junior" was Elijah Hodges, who joined the choir at the age of eighteen and who lived in the same house as Hall Johnson for five years, during which time he served as driver for Johnson. They were so inseparable that the choir gave Hodges the appellation "Junior." At this writing, Hodges, now eighty-six, still lives in California, and although he has recently suffered a stroke, when asked if Johnson gave up alcohol after the 1939 stay at Good Samaritan, the answer was a clear-minded, unqualified "no!" I met and did some work with Hodges in New York in the 1960s, during the same period I met Johnson. Hodges continued to be close to Johnson until his death. It is his opinion that Johnson never gave up alcohol completely. This opinion is shared by Madeline Preston, who knew Johnson well from 1948 until his death and indicated that while not a teetotaler, he had mastered the art of drinking in moderation.

The Burden of Interpersonal Demands

Hall Johnson was a "sweetheart" in the sense that he genuinely wanted to befriend everyone who needed help and appeared to offer friendship and admiration in return. It is difficult to imagine how expensive this attitude was in terms of time and money during the years of the Depression and even afterward. Given Johnson's almost instant fame with the success of the Hall Johnson Choir's debut in Town Hall and at Lewisohn Stadium, as well as the phenomenal success of the choir on Broadway in *The Green Pastures*, virtually all of his associates, friends, hangers-on, and parasites thought that he was "rich." About one-third of Johnson's correspondence was from management, producers, or publishers and related to his work as a conductor and composer. Of the remaining two-thirds, at least 75 percent included requests for either his time or his money.

From 1931 until the start of World War II, the period when the choir did most of its touring, choir members were constantly penniless on tour and had to "borrow" money from Johnson to eat and sleep, a situation exacerbated by the Great Depression and by the relatively small salaries paid choral singers. Typically, when Johnson toured with his concert choir of thirty singers, he would have a list with the names and amounts borrowed from him that included at least half of the group. Unfortunately, many of the loans were never repaid. In 1939, on one of the many occasions when Johnson was running short of money, he asked Jester Hairston to collect some of the money owed him from the California group he was conducting. Hairston responded,

> Enclosed is all the money I could muster from Joe and Busch this pay. Busch said he owed you $5.00, which is enclosed. He is also sending Alford $2.50 which he owed him and $2.00 for Sis Mays. That makes $9.50 from him. James said he could not send but $2.00 of his indebtedness to you this pay, because he is bringing Mays up here this coming Sat. He is coming to L.A. Sat. night after the show and will probably call you Sunday and explain his situation. So all in all, I am enclosing $7.00 for you and $4.50 for Mays and Alford. As soon as Lancaster gets his check, I shall send what he gives me. As for me, I would make the difference and send you, but the old income people got me for almost half of my check this week and I had to send my folks back east the rest. . . . If . . . you just have to have a little more money before you get your check on the first, I may be able to borrow it from Mr. Teevin or somebody. At least, I will make every effort to get it for you.[82]

After the choir members, there were "friends" who were down on their luck or unemployed who were sure that Johnson could easily afford to help them out, sometimes repeatedly. Examples of two such requests follow:

- From Ronnie: "It's lucky I got the job because I have a rent bill of $84.50. That's for two months. My brother and myself were to pay half and half. I paid my part last month in January, but he conked out, so now he decides to give me the apartment. However, I think I'll be able to go through with everything after I get my $84.50 paid."
- From Edna: "Your letter came in the midst of great turmoil and was sort of a glimmer of light in the darkness. I dare not hope too much. I realize my position and appreciate what you are trying to do for me. But here goes the sad news: From L.A. to Denver—Coach—$25, Tourist—$39, First Class—$49.29. . . . If you can help me in any way at all, I will never forget it and will repay you as soon as possible."

Then, there were those who were seeking employment in Johnson's next movie, next theatrical production, or in any capacity whatsoever.

In reference to the film production of *The Green Pastures*, Hodges wrote, "I received your letter and also the money. It came just in time because my rent was due and I did not have another cent left. I had been borrowing money from Leonard [De Paur] and he did not have any more to loan me. I'm asking you if you can afford it, would you let me have a little more the next time, because . . . my rent has gone up, and my sister is charging me for my meals. . . . I hope you can give me some definite idea as to how soon you will have me out there."

Some of Johnson's associates even sought employment for their relatives: "My daughter is studying almost daily in the Weigester Studio in Steinway Hall . . . and we would be pleased if she could in some way assist herself . . . there is a brother in college. Should you need a singer and would like to try Evelyn out, you will find her with her aunt in Brooklyn at this address. . . . Mrs. Johns."

There were frequent demands from those seeking assistance with their professional careers: performers seeking letters of recommendation or prestigious references and choral directors asking for a gift of a single copy of music rather than whether or not they might buy it.

George Van Hoy Collins, director at Fayetteville State College, wrote, "I talked with you on the phone concerning an SATB arrangement of your beautiful 'Fix Me Jesus.' You kindly consented to send me a manuscript. I was so thrilled when I heard Marian Anderson do it on the Bell Telephone Hour." To add insult to injury, the following year, Collins wrote, "I have misplaced the copy of 'Fix Me Jesus' that you sent me. *Please* send me another one." And again, two years later, Collins wrote, "Please tell me where I can get a simple arrangement of 'Rock A My Soul in the Bosom of Abraham.'"

Johnson was also subjected to many requests from "creative" musicians, some whose compositions existed only in their heads and just needed Johnson to write them out and arrange them effectively. Others wished to bring their works to him for evaluation and comment. Dr. Drazin wrote, "I have several songs, among them, some 'spirituals,' all originals, my own composition. The words are all on paper; the musical notes . . . are in my head only, and not reduced to writing. . . . I had visualized them being sung by some person like Paul Robeson." One of his former students wrote, "I've another tune I'm ready for you to look over entitled 'One Look at You Makes Me Dream.' This is a big musical production type of number, very felicitous, torchy and flexible."

Almost weekly, Johnson received requests that he attend concerts of all sorts involving friends, students, associates, or acquaintances. For example,

Dorothy Rooks (Maynor) wrote, "Please come over to this program. The music will be good and I want you to hear Miss King (Juanita)." Ms. Porter wrote, "I have a friend who has written a piece called 'Congo' (the orchestration is done by William Grant Still) and he wants to get an interview with you in regard to your doing it on one of your programs sometimes." Similarly, Ms. Cutler wrote, "I understood you were to have been down to Daly's last night to see our show 'Haiti.' I waited outside with several of the girls and didn't see you. . . . I shall be expecting a call from you."

Among the several other categories of people who made requests on a regular basis were those who wished a commitment to meet with them socially. There was no end to the requests for visits, lunch, dinner, or even more intimate liaisons. In the face of these constant and multiple assaults on Johnson's time and money, it is truly amazing that he was able to accomplish all that he did. Certainly, he paid a price for failing to process both his mail and appointments through a personal representative or private secretary so that his energies could have been used much more exclusively for his creative work.

Personal Relationships

After the death of Johnson's wife, Polly Celeste Copening Johnson, in December 1935, he remained single for the rest of his life but had several long-term relationships that were significant.

Jester Hairston

Perhaps the most important of these was his relationship with Jester Hairston, a relationship that proved, in many ways, to be even more important than that with his wife. Hairston, talented, ambitious, and with a music school education, came to New York in 1929, where he met Hall Johnson and joined the Hall Johnson Choir, which had already established its eminence with a successful Town Hall debut and a triumph at Lewisohn Stadium. When *The Green Pastures* opened in 1930, Hairston immediately became Johnson's primary assistant conductor. For the next ten years, he was invaluable to Johnson, who was battling with alcoholism. It was the talent, training, and loyalty of Hairston that enabled him to rescue the Hall Johnson Choir on their second critical film assignment, *Lost Horizon*, when Johnson went on an alcoholic binge. Although Dmitri Tiompkin was so impressed with Hairston that he used him as choral director for his films for the next twenty years or so, Jester remained loyal to Johnson and served as both assistant conductor and conductor for productions of *The Green Pastures* and *Run, Little Chillun*, as well as for concerts and radio appearances of the choir as needed. In many ways, Johnson was to him a father figure for whom his love, admiration, and respectful esteem never wavered, even when Johnson was hospitalized for his drinking in 1939. The following excerpt from an undated letter (circa 1940) from Hairston reveals the depth of his feeling for Johnson:[83]

1654 E. 23rd Street
Los Angeles, California

Dear Brother Johnson,
    It's so seldom that I get a chance to sit down and have a heart to heart talk with you that I am taking this method to tell you how deeply grateful I am to you for the check you gave me today over and above the three days we worked. My gratitude goes far beyond this act of kindness on your part I assure you, for had it not been for you I certainly would not have known the things in this business which I have learned under your direction.
    I am well aware of my limitations as an artist, but I have tried to show you my appreciation for what you have done for me during these many years of our association by my sincerity in my work when you trusted me with anything. All this may seem to you like a "going away" speech, but I was so overcome this evening as I thought about the many little things you've done for me that I just had to sit down and put it in a letter to you. You are my great friend as well as my teacher and inspiration, Bro. Johnson and my constant prayer is that I shall never give you cause to doubt my appreciation nor my determination to help you in my humble way to carry on the great work which you are doing.
    Again, I thank you from my heart for the honor to help direct this lovely play[84] and hope that it will be an even greater success than *Run, Little Chillun*.
    Your daughter,
    Hester [Jester]

Among his own future accomplishments, Hairston was to marry his beloved Marge, form his own interracial studio choir (which performed in numerous films), create a catalog of dozens of arrangements of spirituals and black folk songs, act in twenty-eight movies and two television series, and become one of the world's most popular choral clinicians.

Any scholar who examines the considerable body of correspondence of Jester Hairston found in the Hall Johnson Collection will be puzzled that the letters he addressed to Hall Johnson for the first ten years of their association most frequently started, "Dear Mother," and ended with "Your daughter, Hester."

After Hairston married in the early 1940s, he began to use the appellation "Brother Johnson" but continued to sign his letters "Hester." In the final years of their association, which existed until Johnson's death, most letters were signed simply "Hairston." As evidenced in a 1966 letter, Jester—always a soul of great humility—returned to the master-disciple relationship that had existed during the first years of their acquaintance. Although Hairston was now world famous, the letter reflects that Hall Johnson was still his true mentor, model, and teacher:[85]

July 22, 1966

Dear Bro. Hall:
    Please believe me when I say that my failure to respond to your sending the scripts and the album is not due to sheer disinterest. . . . I am here at the College of the Pacific Music Camp for the 18th year. . . .
    I am so much richer by having known and studied with you, Bro. Johnson. My work all over the world would not have been half as effective had it not been for the wonderful lessons I learned all those years at your feet. And every time I stand before a choir of young people, I try to inspire them as you inspired me, with something more than a mere singing of the notes. You taught me how to reflect the Divine Presence of God through the music, and the more experience I accumulate from year to year, the better I am able to project God. . . .
    Good luck, maestro. Marge sends her love to you also.
    Yours,
    Hester

After carefully examining all the correspondence from Hairston, there is no evidence to suggest that their relationship was anything but the most ideal friendship, and that the usage of "mother" and "sister" was a type of slang, used between friends to designate a special closeness. This usage apparently persisted into the fifties, as I recall that the same usage was in vogue among fraternity brothers of Alpha Phi Alpha at Howard University between 1947 and 1951. Similar usages are evident in black urban slang today, however, the actual words tend to be expletives.

Wathea Sims Jones

In November 1940, Johnson accepted as a "pupil" Mrs. Wathea Sims Jones, a gifted public school music teacher. According to Johnson, "Wathea Sims Jones was a regular attendant at my classes during the last four years of my work in Los Angeles [1940–1943]. Miss Jones took choral classes in oratorio, opera, classic and folk music, for a total of 568 hours of formal instruction." She also studied voice privately with Valdemar Banke, under Johnson's "sponsorship."[86] Correspondence confirms that the two remained close friends until 1969, one year before Johnson's death.

A significant amount of correspondence in the 1940s and 1950s is preserved that indicates that her relationship with Johnson was far more than just a friendship and that she loved Johnson deeply. At some point in the early 1940s when Johnson was still in Los Angeles, Mrs. Jones gave birth to a son whom she named Jan Hall Jones. Her letters to Johnson always included references to Jan and indicated that he, too, had a special relationship with Johnson. Of all the correspondence Johnson received, the only letter from a small child is a letter from Jan Hall Jones, which follows:[87]

3716 Lomitas Drive
Los Angeles 32 Calif.
Nov. 7, 1951

Dear Hall:
   I'm doing fine in violin, reading, spelling and arithmetic.
   Thank you for the pictures. I am happy with those pictures. It's so good to go to Berlin. I liked those maps and programs.
   Here is a picture of me in the Painted Desert, Arizona, this summer. When are you coming to see us?
   Your friend,
   Jan Hall Jones

An actual birth announcement, in mint condition, established the date of birth as June 23, 1943, in Queen of Angels Hospital, Los Angeles, California, so Jan Hall wrote the above letter when he was eight. Wathea and Marvin Jones were listed as parents. Even though the evidence is only circumstantial, a number of facts seem to suggest that Jan Hall might indeed have been Hall Johnson's son: (1) The child was obviously named after Hall Johnson, and Johnson's grandmother was named Mary Hall Jones. (2) Jan Hall chose to study violin (as Hall Johnson did) and demonstrated special talent early, appearing on the Carlton Moss Show around the age of eight. (3) In addition to writing the above letter to Hall Johnson, the child sent Father's Day cards to Hall Johnson on at least three occasions, which are preserved in the Hall Johnson Collection. (4) The child demonstrated a predisposition toward alcoholism at a young age and came home drunk at three o'clock in the morning when only fourteen years old. (5) Jan Hall revealed behavioral problems when he ran away from home at age fourteen to avoid being sent to a private institute. (6) In each case of problematic behavior, Mrs. Jones informed Hall Johnson, frequently suggesting that Jan Hall might be more obedient to his discipline than hers. (7) Johnson frenquently visited the child and the mother when in California. (8) Johnson sent gifts to the child and vice versa. (9) While the date of her marriage to Mr. Jones is not established, it is clear that the marriage was short-lived. (9) Mrs. Jones professed her love for Johnson in a letter to him, which is preserved in the Hall Johnson Collection.

An extensive search reveals that after her retirement from the public schools, Mrs. Jones moved from Los Angeles to Lytle Creek, California, where she lived at 13880 Pollard Drive until her death in 1996 at the age of eighty-five. She became an ordained minister and was loved and highly regarded in this community. A letter from Mrs. Jones to Helen Duesberg, dated August 20, 1969, reveals that she had visited Hall Johnson in 1967 when he was ill, with the idea of assisting Mrs. Duesberg (who was then living with the seventy-nine-year-old Johnson) with his care. However, Johnson—in his only unkind act known to me—hurt Mrs. Jones terribly by ordering her out of the doctor's office. "Get that woman out of here," he said to Duesberg, after which Mrs. Jones vowed never to come to Johnson's aid again unless he personally asked her to. There is no further mention of Jan Hall after 1964, and no trace of him could be found through online search mechanisms. In a personal interview with one of Hall Johnson's grand-nephews, who would have been a contemporary of Jan Hall, the nephew revealed that he knew Jan but that he could not recall having seen or heard from him since the 1960s.[88] It was finally established that Jan Hall had died as a young man in San Francisco under unexplained circumstances.[89] The relevant letters are preserved in the Hall Johnson Collection.

David Wells
In the summer of 1942, Johnson began an association with David Wells, a young man of about twenty who had been deferred from military service to work for an outfit called Basic Magnesium Incorporated, in Las Vegas, Nevada. Their association is traced through a flurry of correspondence that began in November 1942 and ended in July 1944. During that brief period, David wrote more than thirty-five letters to Hall Johnson, which revealed him as bright, ingratiating, and parasitic. From their meeting in Los Angeles, David, a trumpet player, left to work in Las Vegas for a few months before entering U.S. Army Air Force Cadet Training in Kearns, Utah; at Montana State University; and finally in Santa Ana, California. At some stage in his flight training, David was injured and, after several months in the hospital, honorably discharged. In 1943, Johnson returned to New York for the ill-fated revival of *Run, Little Chillun*, and not a moment too soon. During the brief association, the young man was able to get Johnson to part with considerable money and a two-year-old automobile despite the fact that the failure of *Run*,

Little Chillun left Johnson in debt and virtually penniless. An examination of the correspondence shows a request for money, or some kind of assistance, in almost every letter. David even requested the considerable sum of $80 so that he could get married (a union that lasted barely a year). Johnson's affection for the young man is expressed in an art song that he composed from a poem of San Francisco poet Dwight Strickland, entitled simply, "David."

David[90]
I know Heaven, Heaven, Heaven's
Never really out of reach.
When it's summer, summer, summer.
And I'm lying on the beach,
Looking upward, upward, upward
To the star bright night above,
I hear David, David, David
Singing little songs of love.

In a pasture wide as Heaven,
Surely all will be forgiven;
I can sleep, you can sleep, we can sleep.

There's a comfort sweetly ringing
In the sound of David's singing,
That the shepherd tending stars
Will tend his sheep.

So in winter or in summer,
In the town or on the beach,
I know Heaven, Heaven, Heaven's
Never really out of reach.

Looking upward, upward, upward
To that star-bright night above,
I hear David, David, David
Singing little psalms of love
And I can sleep,
You can sleep,
We can sleep.

Madeline Preston
In 1948, Johnson met Madeline Preston, a beautiful young soprano from suburban Mamaroneck, New York, who came to the auditions for *Son of Man*.

Preston was accepted in the group and soon after began a relationship with Johnson that lasted approximately five years. During this time, they actually lived together both in New York and in California. Among Hall Johnson's letters is a greeting card to Ms. Preston, which says,

> Christmas Greetings for My Wonderful Wife
> This greeting at Christmas is bringing
> A wish that is full of good cheer
> With love for my Wonderful Wife
> Who is all that is precious and dear.

The card was signed, "Always—through sunshine or shadow—Your H.J."

When questioned about their "marriage," Ms. Preston unhesitatingly replied that they were never married but had lived together for a number of years. She added that because of the age difference, Johnson frequently introduced her as his granddaughter.

Preston traveled with the choir to Berlin and Vienna, but as the Hall Johnson Choir had no firm professional obligations after the European tour, Miss Preston joined the Katherine Dunham organization and continued an association with Ms. Dunham to the time of our interview in 2002.

Aurelia Walkes

In the midfifties, Johnson had a very close friendship with a young lady named Aurelia Walkes in New York City. Because of their proximity, there is relatively little correspondence that would provide any biographical data about Ms. Walkes or clarify the nature of the relationship. It is known that she was an excellent soprano who sang in Johnson's workshop choir. In the 1960s, Ms. Walkes appeared to have been in her twenties. I was unable to locate her or find anyone who had made contact with her in recent years.

Helen Duesberg

The final extended relationship was with a mature woman named Helen Duesberg. A naturalized citizen from Estonia, Ms. Duesberg was hired (by me) as organist of Friendship Baptist Church in 1959. Shortly thereafter, she met Hall Johnson and began to study composition with him. From this, there developed a relationship that endured until his death. Since Johnson was advanced in age, Ms. Duesberg was able to learn from him and also be useful in practical ways, including music copying, house cleaning, and other tasks generally performed by a girl Friday. However, there was definitely a special relationship that Ms. Duesberg, who lived with her daughter in Arizona at the time of our interview, preferred not to discuss. She apparently was the last person to see Hall Johnson alive, having left his apartment shortly before the fire that killed him started.

Ronnie

Johnson also maintained a relationship with a young man from the early 1960s who was known only as "Ronnie." He was present at Johnson's apartment on more than one occasion when I visited Johnson. A young man of perhaps twenty-five, Ronnie was obviously uneducated, not especially articulate, and seemed to fulfill the role of an errand boy who really liked Johnson and wanted to do anything he could to help him in his final decade. In the letters to Johnson preserved in his memorabilia, Ronnie addresses Johnson as "Poppa" and asks several times, in an ingratiating manner, for money for seemingly legitimate reasons. (At the time, Johnson was in California recovering from a stroke that occurred in February 1962.) One letter had a return address at a "Work House" and another at a New York jail. Johnson did attend a court hearing relative to Ronnie's incarceration but was asked by the young man not to come to any other court proceedings, apparently because he was so well-known. Ronnie's importance as a member of Johnson's "extended family" is established by his mention in several letters of Wathea Jones. In at least one of these, she mentions that she had sent gifts, including one for Ronnie.

Professional Friends and Associates

If one studies the history of the nineteenth century art song, one learns not only of Franz Schubert, but of the friends and associates who helped create a musical and social milieu. Thus, we know of Vogl, of Schober, of Schwind. This is no less true in studying so significant a figure of the Harlem Renaissance as Hall Johnson, whose life touched so many major talents between 1915 and 1970. All held Johnson in high esteem for his unique abilities and achievements. The Afro-American artists included in this group are as follows (in general, listed in order of historic contributions):

James Reese Europe—First black musician to receive a New York ticker-tape parade; director of Castles in the Air orchestra and Clef Club Orchestra

Will Marion Cook—Pioneer and composer of first black Broadway musical comedy; violin virtuoso

Eubie Blake—Pianist and composer of *Shuffle Along*

Noble Sissle—Collaborator with Eubie Blake and James Reese Europe in musical comedy songs

Jester Hairston—Noted conductor and arranger for Hollywood and school choirs; actor and song writer

Leonard De Paur—Famed conductor and arranger; founder and director of the De Paur Infantry Chorus; conductor of anthology, *The Long Road to Freedom*

Robert McFerrin—First black male artist on Metropolitan Opera roster

Marian Anderson—World-renown contralto and concert artist

Dorothy Maynor—Legendary lyric soprano and concert artist

William Warfield—Concert bass-baritone, actor, and recording artist; world-famous "Porgy"

Kenneth Spencer—Internationally known basso

Jules Bledsoe—Concert singer and musical theater artist

Eva Jessye—Choral director of the original *Porgy and Bess* choir

William Dawson—Famous choral arranger and conductor of the Tuskegee Institute Choir

John Work—Famous arranger and choir director at Talladega College

William Grant Still—Famed black composer

F. Nathaniel Dett—Pianist and composer

Hazel Harrison—First internationally known black female concert pianist

Langston Hughes—Negro poet laureate

Katherine Dunham—Dancer and choreographer

Duke Ellington—Jazz composer, pianist, and band director

Fredi Washington—Actress and dancer

Bessie Smith—Legendary blues singer

Bill Robinson—Dancer and actor

Ethel Waters—Singer and actress

Sammy Davis—Singer, actor, and entertainer

Ossie Davis—Actor

Richard B. Harrison—Actor; "De Lawd" in *The Green Pastures*

Clarence Muse—Actor and director

Edward Boatner—Composer, arranger, and voice teacher

Harry T. Burleigh—Singer, composer, and arranger

Roland Hayes—International concert tenor

Brock Peters—Broadway and movie actor

Betty Allen—International concert mezzo-soprano

Muriel Rahn—International concert mezzo-soprano

Harry Belafonte—Folk singer, actor, and entrepreneur

Lawrence Brown—Accompanist for Paul Robeson
Clarence Cameron White—Composer and professor
Abbie Mitchell—Concert soprano; original Serena in *Porgy and Bess*
William C. Handy—Composer and publisher
Ralph J. Bunche—Assistant secretary general, United Nations
Zelma George— Alternate U.S. delegate to the United Nations General Assembly from 1960 to 1961
Dorothy Candee—Concert soprano
Alan Garcia—Concert tenor, Hall Johnson Choir, De Paur Infantry Chorus, and the Collegiate Chorale
John Carter—Composer, *Cantata on Spirituals*; Guggenheim Fellow
Naomi Pettigrew—Concert soprano, Town Hall Debut
William Shores—Concert baritone; MA from Juilliard School of Music
Frederick Wilkerson—Voice professor, Howard University
Fela Sowande—Composer, Lagos, Nigeria
Georgia Laster—Concert mezzo-soprano
Marion Cumbo—Concert cellist, American String Quartet
Bruce Nugent—Dancer
Frances Walker—Concert pianist
Lola Hayes—Concert singer and voice teacher, New York City
Charles Higgins—Concert tenor; choral conductor
Adele Addison—International concert and operatic soprano
Frances Kraft Reckling—Harlem music retailer
Charles Holland—International concert and operatic tenor
John Morrison—Concert tenor and soloist, Riverside Church, New York City
James Wilson—Concert tenor
John Miles—Concert tenor
Barbara Conrad—International concert and operatic mezzo-soprano
Cecil Cohen—Concert pianist; professor, Howard University

The list of white musical and theatrical personages who were associates of Johnson is even more impressive (listed chronologically):

Fiorello La Guardia—Mayor of New York City, 1931
David O. Selznick—Hollywood producer
Lauritz Melchior—Wagnerian tenor, Metropolitan Opera
Samuel Chotzinoff—General music director, National Broadcasting Company
Russell Potter—Institute of Arts and Sciences, Columbia University

Carleton Sprague Smith—Director, National Arts Foundation

H. Augustine Smith—Choral director, Boston University College of Music

Oscar Hammerstein, II—Broadway composer and lyricist

Newbold Morris—Mayoral candidate, New York City, 1949

Millard Bloomer—President, National Arts Foundation

Robert Breen—Executive secretary, the American National Theatre and Academy

Channing Tobias—Director, Phelps-Stokes Fund

Robert Schnitzer—General manager, Berlin Arts Festival

John J. McCloy—U.S. high commissioner for Germany

Walter Donnelly—U.S. high commissioner for Austria

Max T. Krone—Dean, Institute of the Arts, University of Southern California

Leopold Stokowski—Conductor

Jack Lavin—Walt Disney Productions

Donald D. Engle—Martha Baird Rockefeller Fund

Benjamin Steinberg—Director, New World Symphony

Robert Wagner—Mayor of New York City, 1963

Wanda Toscanini—Arturo Toscanini's wife

Maxwell Anderson—Playwright

Ruth Bernhard—Photo artist

Howard McKinney—Historian, Rutgers University

Denishawn—Dance Artist

Henry Beckett—Music critic, *New York Evening Post*

William C. Gassner—Concert manager

Irwin Parnes—President, Concert Agency

John Finley Williamson—Director, Westminster Choir College

Robert Rockmore—Broadway producer

George Jessel—Broadway producer

Meyer Davis—Broadway producer

Marc Connelly—Playwright; director

Virgil Thompson—Composer

Fred Waring—Conductor

John Lindsay—Mayor of New York City, 1966

Eleanor Roosevelt—Former first lady of the United States

Guy Fowler—Metro-Goldwyn-Mayer Pictures, Hollywood, California

Jascha Zayde—Concert Pianist; staff member at WQXR radio station, New York

Charles Wakefield Cadman—Composer; conductor

Horatio T. Parker—Critic, the *Boston Transcript*
Willem van Hoogstraten—Guest conductor, New York Philharmonic
Walter Damrosch—Conductor
Alexander Smallens—Conductor
Hans Kindler—Conductor, National Symphony, Washington, DC
Lorna Cook De Varon—Conductor, New England Conservatory

The many motion picture stars that Johnson worked with are detailed in an exhaustive list in the chapter on films.

Organizational and Promotional Skill and Breadth of Concepts

Little if any attention has been paid by scholars to these aspects of Hall Johnson's personality. Perhaps this is because it is impossible to observe these characteristics with any kind of perspective save from above. That is, you are only aware of these qualities if you can examine his whole life through the evidence provided by all of his personal papers and memorabilia. His conceptual breadth is evident on several levels. First, it never occurred to him that he was anything but a "renaissance man," so he excelled as painter, photographer, violinist, violist, arranger, orchestrator, conductor, composer, teacher, and linguist. Second, his approach to composition and arranging was not limited by the approach of his predecessors. His works demonstrated flawless thematic organization and a textural and structural expansion hardly found in choral music until the works of Boito, Mascagni, and Gustav Holst. For example, four, six, and even eight parts in the male voices are not uncommon, with the total texture expanding to thirteen parts. Such writing is significantly more challenging, however, when performed a cappella, than similar scores in opera in which the parts are doubled and undergirded by the orchestra. Third, each of his extended works—*The Green Pastures, Run, Little Chillun,* and *Son of Man*—represents a departure from the norm structurally and requires a highly skilled choir of considerable size because the singers are almost entirely unaccompanied. Fourth, despite the fact that the Hall Johnson Negro Choir began with only 8 voices, it grew to 16 voices in a few weeks, to 150 voices within five years, and ultimately to 300 voices. What he heard in his mind and ear was the sound of an immense group as was finally realized in the Carnegie Hall performance of *Son of Man*, which used five hundred voices. Johnson described this as "a great chorus." Actually, he envisioned an even larger group in 1935, after singing for eight seasons at Lewisohn Stadium. A poster from that year reads, "The first public demonstration will be *A Grand Negro Chorus of 2,000 Voices*, singing on July 10, 1935, at the New York Polo Grounds." There is no documentation of the number of voices that actually assembled on that day. Fifth, Johnson's dream even had a national dimension. In 1950, he undertook the establishment of the National Choral Plan to Help Children through Music: Sing Out, America! He explained it thusly, "Naturally, the success of the whole plan depends upon *numbers: thousands* of people singing together in every large city in the country."[91] His objective closely paralleled that of Lowell Mason's one hundred years earlier.

One needs only to look at the scope of these projects to imagine how much organizational skill would be required for the successful completion of any one of them. One of his earliest efforts was to create the Alliance for the Development of Afro-American Music. Only the objectives are articulated here. The detailed proposals are available in the Hall Johnson Collection at Rowan University.[92]

The Alliance for the Development of Afro-American Music

Present Situation: Summer 1937

All of my life has been devoted to the study, collection, arranging, and general preservation of Negro folk song. After twelve years of public work in this field, the following facts are obvious:

1. The Negro race in America has the finest equipment of folklore, including stories and songs, to be found concentrated in any *one* part of the globe.
2. The Negro race in America is immensely gifted as performers, singers, actors, writers, etc., and *they* should present this material.
3. Owing to lack of organization and untoward economic conditions, Negroes have not been able to develop and control this mine of artistic material.
4. Hence, it has been exploited, in the main, by white producers who have developed it only so far as it served *their* needs—and the demands of *their* public. Another limiting factor has been the lack of genuine understanding, on the part of the white producers, of the Negro material and the Negro temperament.
5. It is highly desirable that this wealth of native beauty should be formed out carefully and scientifically by *Negroes* who are prepared to do this. The American stage needs the stories and the fine actors so to be produced. The whole world needs the message of peace, hope, and faith in God and humanity which the Negro songs and Negro singers will deliver.

6. The time has arrived when these results may be brought about quite easily and simply through a scientifically planned organization under expert leadership.

In the summer of 1935, I started an organization for this purpose among the Negro singers and musicians of New York City and surrounding towns. Its central group was a chorus of approximately a thousand voices which made one appearance at the New York Polo Grounds in July of that year. When I came to Hollywood soon afterwards to work on the *Green Pastures* film, this movement was still too young to continue to grow without my leadership, and it is now in a period of "suspended animation," though not at all dead.

After a year and a half of residence in California, I am convinced that here is an even more favorable opportunity to work out these ideas. There are hundreds of Negro singers with splendid voices connected with the numerous churches. These people are intelligent and progressive. They already have a spirit of organization which needs only one thing, a real leader to whip it into shape and direct its course toward a definite goal. The local leaders of small groups are anxious to collaborate and cooperate in such a mass organization. They see readily that it will also build themselves and their own individual groups, each of which would preserve its own particular existence and function while being a constructive part of the whole. At the present moment there are rehearsals going on for conventions, conferences, and annual affairs of all sorts. One rehearsal alone has a group of over seven hundred.

The big idea of the moment is to teach all these groups a fine program of Negro folk songs, trained and directed by their own directors under the same technical and interpretive process, bring them all together, and give a huge demonstration at the end of the summer in a place like Hollywood Bowl. Everything is ready for such a step. The chorus would number by that time at least two thousand singers—every individual, an active and responsible part of the whole.

For this occasion, the organization should be announced so as to give great publicity to its *name* and its *objects*. This would be *world news*. By that time, the organization, in fact, would be about three months old and already working smoothly.

Immediately following this presentation, rehearsals should be started for a large mid-winter offering to take place in the Shrine Auditorium or Pan-Pacific Auditorium, or some such place. Smaller groups should be presented in Negro plays and operas or operettas, financed and supported by the organization. There is a fine collection of Negro plays and operas in manuscript which will never see performance through any other method.

In due time a large plot of ground should be bought in the right location and a home for the organization erected, including among other things, a theatre auditorium, studio rooms, a library-museum for racial writings and historical objects, a picture gallery, etc. Then groups could be organized in other cities until the organization reaches the proportions of a national movement, all under one program.

This organization should be known as:

I. The Alliance for the Development of all Through Music (ADAM)

The Book of Adam

The membership to be grouped and to function after manner of a huge book—following a pure decimal system.

Each separate, individual worker is	A Word
Ten words (under two leaders)	A Sentence
Ten sentences (100 words)	A Paragraph
Ten paragraphs (1000 words)	A Page
All the workers in one town	A Chapter
All the workers in one state	A Volume

***

It is to be the main duty of each worker to multiply himself into a sentence—each sentence, into a paragraph, etc.

The officers will gain and keep their positions *only on the basis of work done*, results shown (musical and financial).

Each sentence shall have a "Cap" and a "Period" who shall report monthly to the "Head" of its Paragraph which shall report on the 1st day of every month to the "Title" of its Chapter.

At a fixed assessment per word, a steady sum will be raised monthly, the expenditure of which will be decided by a monthly Council of Paragraphs (Heads only—each representing 100 people.)

Musical directors to be chosen by each paragraph (with the approval of the general music director) and paid by each paragraph—at an hourly rehearsal rate—not to exceed a fixed sum per hour.

Every word shall be able to know at all times the activities and financial status of the organization.

The membership is to include not only musicians, but painters (visual artists), writers, dancers, swing-bands, and all craftsmen and business men interested in the development of the race.

There should be an advisory board consisting of non-musicians, including representative men and women in other professions.

The organization is to have no religious or political program.

III. The Alliance for the Development of Afro-American Music

The Alliance for the Development of African-American Music aims to unite under one constructive program all who believe that the American Negro should make his contribution to the culture of the civilized world, and that he should be, not only the chief apostle, but the chief beneficiary of this contribution. As Negro music is inextricably bound up with stories, plays, dances, and pictures, a scientific development of Negro folk songs must inevitably foster the growth of all related branches of literature and art; while the educational, social and economic advantages accruing to everyone who participates, in whatever capacity, must justify the existence of the organization as an Alliance for the Development of All, through music.

The recruitment and auditioning of the large number of singers for the required festival choirs in Los Angeles and in New York required extensive planning, organization, and clerical resources. While there is ample evidence that Hall Johnson personally composed and prepared for mailing the materials for many of his projects, one must assume that he enlisted many of his singers for the tasks of typing, duplicating, and stuffing envelopes. The Carnegie Hall performance alone required communication with twenty-five choral groups and their directors to secure their participation, as well as the planning and notification of these groups about music, rehearsals, and stage arrangements. For the original music, it required the duplication and distribution of parts to choirs before they arrived for rehearsal. It required the acquisition of rehearsal space for the combined festival choir, raising the funds for the rental of the hall, and the printing of programs and tickets. The production of *Run, Little Chillun*, only a year after the close of *The Green Pastures*, required, in addition to writing the play and music, the identification of a funding source; theater rental; and the acquisition of a producer, director, singers, dancers, and instrumentalists. While some of these details are routinely taken care of by the producer and director, the writer generates all the copy and ultimately has to be pleased with the result. A copy of the organizational plan for the New York chapter of Sing Out, America follows.

IV. Sing Out, America! A Nation-wide Choral Plan to
Help Children Through Music

First Public Announcement on Labor Day 1950
First Public Demonstration on Columbus Day 1950
Pre-announcement Report of Workers to July 1, 1950
Groups already preparing in the New York Area

A. Large organizations controlling many groups
   1. N.Y.C. Department of Community Education—Mr. Mark A. McCloskey
      (Afternoon and evening sessions in the public school buildings)

2. United Neighborhood Houses of Greater N.Y.—Miss Helen Harris (52 centers throughout the five boroughs)
3. Police Athletic League of N.Y.C.—Lt. Frank Day (Specially directed toward underprivileged and delinquent youth)
4. Salvation Army, N.Y.C. organization—Lt. Col. H.R. Smith
5. Columbia University Teachers College (Summer Sessions)—Prof. H.R. Wilson (Several hundred choral directors from many different states)
6. Baptist Educational Center (Many groups)—Miss C.D. Stokes
7. Harlem Y.M.C.A.—Men: Mr. Henderson; Boys: Mr. Cook
8. Riverside Church Youth Guild—Miss Gertrude Fagan
9. Cathedral of St. John the Divine (Youth Groups)—Canon Edward West
10. Free Synagogue (Youth Groups)—Rabbi Edward Klein

B. Individual centers already active
1. Manhattanville Neighborhood House—Miss Young
2. Morningside Community Center—Miss Williams
3. Salvation Army Red Shield Club—Hall Johnson
4. St. Philip's Episcopal Church—Rev. Shelton Bishop
5. Convent Avenue Baptist Church—Mr. Howard Mann
6. Calvary Methodist Episcopal Church—Miss Louvenia White
7. Church of the Master—Miss E. Knighten
8. St. Augustine Presbyterian Church—Rev. Edler G. Hawkins
9. St. Paul Baptist Church—Mrs. Etta J. Stroud
10. Camp Minisink, Fort Jervis, N.Y.—Miss Gladys Thorne
11. Camp Wo-chi-ca, Fort Murray, N.J.—Miss Leslie Spence
12. P.S. 101, East Harlem District—Miss Vereda Pearson

C. Scores of individuals leading Neighborhood Rehearsals in N.Y. and N.J.

Groups Beginning Work on September 1st

N.Y.C. Board of Education—Mr. George H. Gartlan, Director of Music
B'nai Brith Youth Organization—Dr. Daniel Raylesburg
Columbia University Choral Department—Dr. Harry R. Wilson
Yorkville Community Center—Mrs. Ross Harris
Brownsville Youth Organizations—Mr. Milton J. Goell
Henry Street Settlement Music School—Miss Grace Spofford

Most Enthusiastically Cooperating

Metropolitan Conference of Temple Brotherhoods—Mr. Harry M.Weinberger, Pres.
Community Church of N.Y.C.—Rev. John H. Holmes, Rev. D. Harrington
National Urban League—Mr. Julius Thomas, Director Industrial Relations
United World Federalists, Inc.—Mr. Bernard Hennessy, Projects Director
Citizens Committee on Children for N.Y.C.—Miss Charlotte Carr

To get a true idea of how grandiose Johnson's idea is, one needs only to multiply the complex organization he has outlined for New York by twenty-five major cities in America. In addition to Johnson's professional pursuits in music, he had an idealism that saw music as a force for (1) strengthening racial unity and promoting racial harmony, (2) developing Negro talent and increasing opportunities for study and employment, (3) raising funds for music scholarships, and (4) providing exposure and contacts for gifted individual performers. Along with this was mixed a liberal sprinkling of patriotic fervor that revealed itself in music written during World War II.

What seemed to most observers a wild fantasy was to Hall Johnson a desirable and achievable vision. He really believed that group singing could change the world and spent a great deal of time planning a program that would make this dream a reality. Only the introductory section of his detailed proposal follows. Its breadth of concept is evident.

Sing Out, America! A Federation of Singing Cities

Some Salient Points

The aim of this program is to make a better world for children, and better children for the world.

All to be done through the agency of music—unaccompanied group singing of uplifting songs, not highly trained singing of complicated music, but strong, simple songs which anyone can learn quickly.

To be used not only for special meetings of Sing Out, America! but on any occasion, by any group of people, anywhere.

No production expense for meetings because all singing is without instrumental accompaniment, and all service given without pay.

Helping children through music, a blameless, uncontroversial idea.

No one can find any fault or refuse to help.

Literally, everyone may contribute in a pleasant, inexpensive opportunity for service for everybody—using spare time activity only—not regular business hours.

Extra talents only—not professional skills unless voluntary.

All service voluntary and without pay of any kind.

Any *necessary fulltime* services paid for as running expense.

All expenses met by sale of songbooks.

No money donations solicited at any time.

Persons who like to make donations may buy songbooks in quantity for children's groups, settlement-houses, charitable institutions, etc.

Profits from sale of songbooks to be devoted *exclusively* to improvement of children—*both* local delinquency problems, and world-wide child relief.

Financial reports of profits, disbursements, and distribution of funds to be published periodically.

Finally, and most important of all—Sing Out, America! must be, now and always, carefully protected from identification with the name of any individual or group of individuals. It must be, and remain, a Federation of *Impersonal Cities*, united in a single effort to make a better world for *all* the world.

In pursuit of his vision, Johnson approached some of the most prestigious personages in New York, including Samuel Chotzinoff, Russell Potter, H. Augustine Smith, and Oscar Hammerstein II. All were impressed with the idea and were encouraging though skeptical. In a letter dated December 13, 1948, Chotzinoff, general music director for NBC, kindly refused to be involved. He complimented Johnson for having idealistic and ambitious objectives for his "world chorus," but thought that the practical method of achieving these objectives without a large and expensive organization was not at all clear to him. Broadcasting, in his view, was not involved.

Russell Potter of Columbia University, on the other hand, viewed Johnson's proposal quite favorably, as indicated in a letter dated January 22, 1949. He thought that such a festival would be a "natural for radio" and that it should be sponsored nationwide by the National Association of Broadcasters, with the festivals being organized by member stations and broadcast locally and by short wave to foreign countries. He wished Johnson well with the project.

H. Augustine Smith, director of church music at Boston University and father of the massed choir movement in America, was delighted with Johnson's idea. Smith, who had conducted a massed choir of fifty thousand voices, called the plan "a triumph," one that he had always had in mind and ideal for radio, for millions of people could be reached with the festival. In a letter of July 26, 1949, he indicated that he would watch for Johnson's wide introduction of the plan to the nation.

Oscar Hammerstein II thought that Johnson had a wonderful idea, but said pointedly that he did not see how anyone could accomplish this. He wished him luck and admired his courageous spirit.

The most practical response came on January 23, 1950, from Charlotte Carr, director of the Citizens' Committee on Children of New York City. Ms. Carr thought that it was unrealistic to attempt to raise money without the formation of a committee with a celebrity head. With a committee, Johnson would be able to seek foundation support. Apologizing for dragging Johnson out of the clouds, she thought that it would be a miracle if he were to raise any money and suggested that it might be necessary for him to incorporate.

She also commented that although he had interested a number of people in his project, he should employ a business manager if he wished to have any success in financing his enterprise.

History was to confirm the prophetic nature of Charlotte Carr's advice, for although Hall Johnson pursued his dream into the 1960s, it was never realized. In 1963, Johnson made his final overtures to leaders of the National Urban League and the Student Non-Violent Coordinating Committee and to Dr. Martin Luther King Jr. of the Southern Negro Leadership Conference. Johnson's requests were given a low priority at the height of the civil rights struggle.

Influence on Choral and Vocal Music and Musicians in America

It is difficult to overestimate Johnson's influence on the appreciation, the acceptance, and the performance of black vocal music in America. While the Fisk Jubilee Singers are credited with introducing the Negro spiritual to America and to Europe between 1871 and 1881, the Broadway production, the touring company, and the movie of *The Green Pastures* reached more people in aggregate in one week than the Fisk Singers could have reached in a lifetime. The choir's singing of spirituals was so successful in popularizing them that Carl Fischer published all of the *Green Pastures* spirituals in easy arrangements for solo voice the year the show opened. With some thirty motion pictures that featured the choir, frequently singing spirituals, the genre became accepted and loved by black and white Americans, despite the fact that the films were politically incorrect from a social point of view. Led by Al Jolson, many white performers, who had only sung black comic music as black-face minstrels, added spirituals to their repertoire, even when not in makeup. The Hall Johnson Choir's films include several examples of this. In *Big Boy*, Al Jolson sings "I Got Shoes" and "Go Down Moses"; in *Dimples*, Shirley Temple sings "De Gospel Train"; in *The Vanishing Virginian*, Kathryn Grayson sings "Steal Away to Jesus"; and in *Dixie*, Bing Crosby sings "Swing Low, Sweet Chariot." On the concert stage, a group of spirituals became mandatory for black artists, and the arrangements of Hall Johnson became the arrangements of choice among the leading spiritual arrangers, including (listed chronologically) Harry T. Burleigh, John Work, Nathaniel Dett, Edward Boatner, Roland Hayes, Florence Price, and Margaret Bonds. Between 1925 and 1970, choral spirituals became staples of most high school and college choral concerts. They also became a significant category in the catalogs of the major music publishing houses. While Johnson's voluminous output was divided among several publishers, others had series by a single arranger, including Harry Burleigh, William Dawson, Leonard De Paur, Jester Hairston, Howard Roberts, and myself, Eugene Thamon Simpson.

Hall Johnson also influenced generations of later composers and arrangers through the manner in which he developed the spiritual. Beginning with the simple homophonic arrangements of *The Green Pastures*, he consciously developed the choral form by greatly increasing the texture from four to thirteen parts; expanding the structure; using single, double, and polyphonic obbligatos; and using the voices orchestrally. In his solo voice arrangements, Johnson developed Burleigh's simple chordal accompaniments into art accompaniments that utilized developed introductions, contrapuntal material, exchange of melody between voice and piano, descriptive devices, dissonance, and virtuosity. He was the first choral arranger to use folk material as a basic for original creation in the original portions of *Green Pastures*, *Run, Little Chillun*, and *Son of Man*. In so doing, he influenced a number of composers like John Carter, and perhaps even George Gershwin and Louis Gruenberg.

Equally, if not more, important is the large number of choral directors and concert artists who studied with, sang with, or were simply inspired by contact with Hall Johnson and/or his choir. This list, by no means comprehensive, includes the following:

1. Jester Hairston—First choral assistant with the Hall Johnson choir; replaced Hall Johnson during the making of *Lost Horizon* and spent twenty years as choral director for Dmitri Tiomkin; founder of the first interracial studio choir; arranger of countless spirituals; one of America's foremost choral clinicians and cultural ambassadors
2. Leonard De Paur—Former assistant conductor to Hall Johnson; founder and director, De Paur Infantry Chorus; international touring and recording artist with the De Paur Chorus, for RCA and Mercury labels, and with Leontyne Price, Shirley Verrett, Harry Belafonte, and others; former community relations director, Lincoln Center for Performing Arts
3. John Motley—Director of music, City of New York; director of the All-City Chorus (twenty-five years); Victor recording with Marian Anderson; international tour as accompanist for Miss Anderson
4. Eugene Thamon Simpson—College music educator and administrator; director, Virginia State College Choir, Bowie State College Choir, and Rowan University Chamber Choir; choral director, 1958 All-Army

World Tour Show; performances through the United States, Europe, Russia, the Far East; TV appearances on *Ed Sullivan Show*, *Camera Three*, *Ragtime Years*

5. Carroll Buchanan and George Hill—Cofounders, Carr-Hill Singers, who performed as a high-level community choir in Queens, New York for forty years
6. Arthur Bryant—Founder and director, Arthur Bryant Choir
7. Louvenia Pointer—Director, Great Day Chorale; conductor, NYA Radio Workshop Choir; assistant conductor, *Green Pastures*
8. Hamilton G. McClain—Choral arranger published by Hope Publishing Company and Broadman Press
9. Juanita King—Dramatic soprano with active career on Broadway, radio, and opera; founder and director, Juanita King Singers
10. Ulysses Elam—Choral director and arranger with numerous publications
11. Ulysses Chambres—Choral director and assistant director, *Green Pastures*
12. Reginald Nathaniel Parker—Concert organist, composer, and choirmaster, New York and Norfolk, Virginia
13. Joseph Crawford—Assistant conductor, Los Angeles production of *Run, Little Chillun*, 1939
14. Herbert Wyatt—Pianist and assistant conductor, eastern road tour of *The Green Pastures*
15. George Van Hoy Collins—Choral conductor, Fayetteville State College, Fayetteville, North Carolina
16. Charles Henry—Concert singer; manager, Dixie Artists Bureau
17. Meredith Birche—Conductor, Maryland Boys Choir
18. James Bell—Concert singer
19. Marguerite Avery—Concert artist, dramatic soprano, Town Hall Debut
20. A. Leon Casher—Founder/director, the Casher Philharmonic Choir of Mobile, Alabama
21. Vera Little—Concert and operatic singer, United States and Europe
22. Louise Parker—Concert singer, contralto; college professor, Temple University
23. Hope Krieger—Concert singer, soprano, United States and Europe
24. Gwendolyn Sims—Concert singer, soprano, United States and Europe
25. Betty Allen—International concert artist, mezzo-soprano
26. Benjamin F. Dean—Choral director, Richmond, Virginia

27. Robert McFerrin—Concert and operatic baritone; first black male to appear at the Metropolitan Opera (*Rigoletto*)
28. Dr. Calvin Dash—Concert singer; college professor
29. Edward Broadnax—Concert singer, bass
30. Alston Burleigh—Concert singer
31. Louise Hawthorne—Concert singer, soprano
32. Allen Brown—Concert pianist
33. Oland Gaston—Concert pianist
34. David Johnson—Concert violinist
35. Harold Blair—Concert singer, tenor
36. Oci Johnson—Concert singer, mezzo-soprano
37. Alonzo Jones—Concert singer, baritone
38. Coletta Warren—Concert singer, coloratura soprano
39. Shirley Verrett—International concert and opera star, Metropolitan Opera, La Scala, Covent Garden, Paris Opera, and others
40. George Goodman—International concert bass-baritone, Town Hall Debut
41. Benjamin Gray—Concert pianist
42. Georgia Davis—Concert mezzo-contralto
43. Doris Mayes—International concert mezzo-soprano
44. James Wilson—Concert tenor
45. Thomas Carey—Concert baritone, United States and Europe; professor, University of Oklahoma
46. Kenneth Spencer—Concert bass, United States and Europe
47. Charles Holland—Concert tenor, United States and Europe
48. John Morrison—Concert tenor and soloist, Riverside Church
49. John Swift—Concert baritone

Honors and Awards
Hall Johnson received a number of awards throughout his busy life, albeit, far too few. To judge by his personal résumé, he seems only to remember those awarded late in life and the *honorary doctorate* bestowed upon him in 1934 by the Philadelphia Music Academy (now the University of the Arts), whose president was Frederick Hahn (Johnson's violin teacher). On June 6, 1934, at the sixty-fifth annual commencement exercises, Johnson and Robert Braun received the doctor of music degree, and the gala concert accompanying the ceremony featured the now famous Hall Johnson Choir. Although the regular graduating class had only five members, the repertoire performed by the students was of the highest quality and included the following:

"Overture to Die Meistersinger"—Wagner
"Piano Concerto in C: Allegro"—Beethoven
Contemporary songs—Marie Foster Kennedy
"Rondo Capriccioso"—Mendelssohn
"Violin Concerto in D: Allegro"—Mozart
"Etude in D Flat"—Liszt
"Ballade in A Flat"—Chopin
"Egmont Overture"—Beethoven

The recognition of his special genius began in 1910 when he graduated from the University of Pennsylvania and was awarded the *Simon Haessler Prize* for the best composition for orchestra and chorus. It was sixteen years before Johnson won another award. Both in 1926 and 1927, he won the *Holstein Award* for composition given by Casper Holstein, through *Opportunity Magazine*, to a young Negro who showed great artistic promise. Four years later, in 1931, Johnson received the *Harmon Award* for his musical arrangements in *The Green Pastures*. The William E. Harmon Awards for Distinguished Achievement among Negroes had been granted since 1926, and were administered in cooperation with the Commission on Race Relations and the Federal Council of Churches in the fields of literature, music, fine arts, science, business, religious service, and, in alternate years, race relations. The awards presented in 1931 consisted of a gold medal and a cash prize of $400. The ceremony was held at St. James Presbyterian Church, 141st Street and St. Nicholas Avenue, on Race Relations Sunday, February 8, 1931. The choral selections for the ceremony were all chosen from arrangements of Hall Johnson, and performed by sixty members of the Hall Johnson Choir, including the *Green Pastures* choir.

"Go Down Moses"
"Hold On!"
"City Called Heaven"
"Religion Is a Fortune"
"My God Is So High"

The award recipients were

Albon L. Holsey, *Harmon Award in business*;
Langston Hughes, *Harmon Award in literature*;
Hall Johnson, *Harmon Award in music*.

In 1932, a *Bust of Hall Johnson*, created by American sculptor Minna Harkavy was placed on exhibition at the Bing Galleries in Paris. The sculpture had been loaned to the museum by the Russian government, which owned it. The holder of the rights to the photograph of this bust could not be located, but the photograph may be viewed in the Hall Johnson Collection at Rowan University.

The May 26, 1962, edition of the *Saturday Review* featured "The Hands of Hall Johnson" photograph on its cover with the caption, "Hall Johnson Conducting." Out of fifty photographs chosen for exhibition in New York's Museum of Modern Art, this photo of the hands conducting had been chosen, and thereby immortalized. The photo was taken by Ruth Bernhard.

The following month, New York's mayor, Robert Wagner, bestowed upon Johnson the *Distinguished Service Award*. That same year, the Voices of Friendship Chorale, under my direction, performed two all–Hall Johnson choral concerts in Johnson's honor. These were the first all–Hall Johnson concerts ever performed by a group other than the Hall Johnson Choir. The first concert was on Sunday, January 28, at Union Congregational Church, 58 138th Street, New York City. Soloists were (in order of appearance on the program) Roger Alford (of the original Hall Johnson Choir), Rose Battle English, Bernice Hall, John Miles, Barbara Atkinson, Norbert Simmons, Oliver Gibson, and John Morrison. The second performance was in the Borough of Brooklyn at the Bethany Baptist Church, Sunday, May 6, 460 Sumner Avenue.

On February 17, 1963, the Association for the Study of Negro Life and History presented Johnson with the *Heritage Award* at a grand luncheon at the Hotel Americana. Founded in 1915 by Dr. Carter G. Woodson, the association had as its objective the study of the history of Afro-American's achievements and the highlighting of these achievements through annual awards. On this occasion, in addition to the Heritage Award that went to Johnson, four other awards were presented:

Carter G. Woodson Award	Dr. Charles Wesley
Harriet Tubman Award	Mrs. Daisy Bates
Ira Aldrich Award	Mr. Frederick O'Neal
Mary Bethune-Eleanor Roosevelt Award	Mrs. Margaret Smith Douglas

Music for the occasion, all arrangements of Hall Johnson, was performed by the Arthur Bryant Choir. As Hall Johnson was in California, his award was received by his long-time friend, Dr. Eva Jessye, who delivered the following acceptance speech:[93]

Madam Chairman, Worthy President, Honored Guests, Ladies and Gentlemen:

It is a great distinction indeed to be permitted to represent the great Hall Johnson. I wish first to assure you that musicians of color everywhere are grateful for the recognition given their esteemed colleague on this occasion. Were the Honoree present in person this afternoon, he would in stature tower above most of us, but would in spirit be of the humblest. He would no doubt reply briefly, in the halting measures so characteristic of the man who has given fullest expression to our folk music, as well as composition in the classical vein. I repeat, he would no doubt reply in terse sentences, but those who know him best would hear heartbeat behind the words; they would hear determination, indication, devotion of a lifetime to the exploration and preservation of our musical heritage . . . as expressed in titles of our beloved spirituals he has so lovingly highlighted with his incomparable genius with keen awareness of the significant times in which we live, we would hear his heart say to his people: Though "We've Been 'Buked and We've Been Scorned"—"Hold On"—"Keep Yo Hand on the Plow"—For "We Are Seeking for a City," "A City Called Heaven."

And to this organization, particularly to this organization to which we are deeply indebted today, he would say: "Walk Together, Chillun, Don'tcha Git Weary"—"I Don't Feel Noways Tired."

And never forget, we—"Ain't Got Time to Die!"

In the name of Dr. Hall Johnson, I thank you.

In October of the same year, Robert Wagner, mayor of New York City, appointed Johnson to the Citizen's Advisory Committee to the Office of Cultural Affairs (October 28). The Uptown Musicians and the Harlem Opera presented Johnson with a citation, *The World's Greatest Choral Director*, on April 10, 1966, and on March 12, 1970, Johnson's eighty-second birthday, Mayor John Lindsay presented Johnson with New York's highest honor, the *George Frederic Handel Award*. One week later, Marian Anderson, Barbara Conrad, William Warfield, Camilla Williams, and Marion Cumbo headlined a tribute to Johnson at which John Motley conducted portions of Johnson's *Son of Man*, and Johnson received a plaque in honor of his contributions to music.

In late 1967, Johnson's friends and associates became mindful of his declining health and financial condition. Under the leadership of the New Urban League of Boston and with the cooperation of Lorna Cook De Varon and the New England Conservatory, the Friends of Hall Johnson Committee organized a *Salute to Hall Johnson*, which took place in Jordan Hall on February 16, 1968, at three o'clock in the afternoon. The proceeds of this event all went to benefit Hall Johnson. In the spring of 1969, the Virginia State College Choir, with me as conductor, released *The Hall Johnson Song Book*, the first volume in a projected Black Heritage Series. The album was chosen by the *Choral Journal* as one of the twelve best albums by college choirs of that year, and evoked a laudatory response from Johnson.

There were other impressive honors offered to him that may or may not have been accepted. On September 11, 1934, the *Etude Music Magazine*, at that time the premiere music magazine in America, published a "Historical Portrait Series" of the "best known musicians and outstanding figures in the music world." The magazine advised Johnson that he had been selected to appear: "This series is appearing alphabetically and we have now come to your name, which, on account of your achievements in the world of music, we deem it worthy to include. . . . Would you be good enough to send us your photograph at your earliest convenience, together with brief biographical data?"[94]

On February 24, 1949, he was appointed to membership on the nation's most prestigious arts advocacy organization. Director Carlton Sprague Smith informed him, "Enclosed is an acceptance letter for membership on the Music committee of the National Arts Foundation. I would appreciate it if you would sign and return it to the Foundation. I look forward to some early collaboration."[95]

In 1950, Johnson was recognized by Marquis' "Who's Who in America" for inclusion in volume 26. It appears that he accepted the invitation to become a biographee but did not purchase a copy, as he received a letter stating, "Dear Biographee . . . We are giving subscriptions placed by our biographees . . . a priority on this windfall supply of the current Who's Who, feeling doing so to be appropriate and logical."[96]

On an unspecified date in 1951, Johnson received an engraved invitation that read as follows:

The Editorial Board of
This I Believe
Edward R. Murrow
Ward Wheelock
Edward P. Morgan
extends an invitation to
Mr. Hall Johnson
to appear as guest on
Edward R. Murrow's
This I Believe Program
R.s.v.p.

The enclosed material stated "You have been invited to be a guest on *This I Believe* because you have been recommended to the Editorial Board as the decent living, decent thinking person who will have great value in promoting the moral and spiritual values in practical philosophies of life."⁹⁷ Starting in January of the coming year, the show was to be aired on 175 U.S. radio stations twice daily, with 39 million listeners per week, and to be printed in 175 U.S. newspapers with a circulation of 16 million per week. It was also to be broadcast on 140 Armed Forces Radio stations, the Voice of America, and in newspapers of ninety-seven foreign countries. Johnson was to prepare a statement of his private beliefs of about six hundred words, submit it in writing, after which he would be contacted by the show to schedule the recording of his beliefs. Johnson did not return the acceptance form, as it remains unexecuted among his papers. Apparently, Johnson was consumed with the preparation of his choir for its appearance at the International Arts Festival in Berlin, which took place in the early fall of that year. By this act of omission, he missed an opportunity to offer his philosophy to the world, along with other honorees, including Helen Keller, Edward R. Murrow, Albert J. Nesbitt, William O. Douglas, Edward P. Morgan, Constance Warren, Herbert H. Lehman, Dore Schary, and other great figures of the day. With Johnson, nothing would have take priority over representing his country and presenting his songs to the world.

There were other honors bestowed upon Johnson by individual poets, writers, artists, and friends, some famous, others little known. Among these was a set of nine poems by his dear friend Langston Hughes, personally and individually autographed, with the simple dedication, "For Hall Johnson, these poems of the Harlem night."

1. "To Midnight Nan ay Leroy's"
2. "Mulatto"
3. "Harlem Night Club"
4. "To a Little Lover-Lass, Dead"
5. "Brass Spitoons"
6. "Cold Winter Blues"
7. "Nude Young Dancer"
8. "Dream Variation"
9. "Star Seeker"

These autographed copies are a part of the Hall Johnson Collection.

On Thursday evening, April 9, 1970, the Church on the Hill A.M.E. Zion Church at 975 St. Nicholas Avenue, Reverend Ulysses Jackson, pastor, climaxed a week-long celebration of its twenty-first anniversary with a concert by the Virginia State College Choir, under my direction. Dr. Johnson had promised to attend and we were honored to see him, now eighty-two years old, in the audience. He sat on the front row, obviously relishing in the performance. While the spirituals on the program were all by William Dawson as they were to be recorded by the choir the following week, for the first encore, the choir performed his great original spiritual, "Ain't Got Time to Die," with the late Sylvester Graves as soloist. A standing ovation followed during which Johnson was acknowledged and graciously shared the applause. We thanked him for coming and the choir members were thrilled to meet him, as they had recorded an album of his music the preceding year. Exactly three weeks later, on April 30, 1970, Hall Johnson was dead of smoke inhalation in his apartment at 634 St. Nicholas Avenue. An inveterate smoker despite the pleading of his friends and disciples, Johnson apparently fell asleep with a lighted cigarette in his hand. The cigarette fell onto the mattress, and he never awakened from his sleep. Most of the damage to his apartment and to his memorabilia seems to have been from water (of the firemen) rather than from fire. We are grateful that so many of his books, his recordings, and musical scores have survived for posterity. We are grateful also for the generosity of his sisters, Alice Foster and Susan Jordan, in donating his memorabilia to Rowan University to establish the Hall Johnson Collection as a permanent memorial and research repository. It is with equal gratitude that we acknowledge the generous gift of his sister-in-law, Bessie Johnson (Mrs. George Decker Johnson), which provides a permanent endowment for the collection, of which I am the founding curator.

Notes

1. Karl Kobald, *Franz Schubert and His Times* (New York: Alfred A. Knopf, 1928), 129.

2. The primary source of biographical data on William Decker Johnson is the digitization project of the University of North Carolina–Chapel Hill, *Documenting the American South*, in the sections indicated:

   a. James T. Haley, *Afro-American Encyclopedia* (Nashville, TN: Haley & Florida, 1895), "African Methodist Episcopal Clergy," "Johnson, William Decker," 591.
   b. Richard R. Wright, *Centennial Encyclopedia of the African Methodist Episcopal Church* (Philadelphia: Book Concern of the A.M.E. Church, 1916), "Rev. William Decker Johnson, D.D.," 137.
   c. Horace Talbert, *The Sons of Allen* (Xenia, OH: Aldine Press, 1906), "Rev. William Decker Johnson," 245–46.

3. Asterisk (*) indicates my addition to the usual limited list of Afro-American artists.

4. James Reese Europe is the only Afro-American musician to ever receive a ticker-tape parade in New York City; it followed the triumphant return of his highly decorated 369 U.S. Colored Infantry Band from Paris, after World War I.

5. Hall Johnson, "Notes on the Negro Spiritual" (unpublished essay, 1965). Reprinted by permission of the Hall Johnson Collection (Rowan University, Glassboro, NJ).

6. Reference here is made to the early operetta of Johnson's, *Fi-yer!*, which was never performed in its entirety. There are several extant recordings of the title song, and several selections from the work have been recorded by the Rowan University Chamber Choir on *The Best of the Hall Johnson Centennial Festival* album.

7. Edward Perry, "Impressions," *National News*, February 18, 1932. Courtesy of the New York Public Library, Schomburg Center for Research.

8. Henry Beckett, "In the World of Music," *New York Evening Post*, February 18, 1932.

9. Deems Taylor, letter to Mrs. Cobina Wright, February 6, 1928. Courtesy of the Hall Johnson Collection (Rowan University, Glassboro, NJ). All rights reserved.

10. Eugene Goossens, letter to Mrs. Cobina Wright, February 7, 1928. Courtesy of the Hall Johnson Collection (Rowan University, Glasboro, NJ). All rights reserved.

11. Walter Damrosch, letter to Mrs. Cobina Wright, February 8, 1928. Courtesy of the Hall Johnson Collection (Rowan University, Glassboro, NJ). All rights reserved.

12. Willem van Hoogstraten, letter to William Gassner, August 14, 1928. Courtesy of the Hall Johnson Collection (Rowan University, Glassboro, NJ). All rights reserved.

13. Maurice Ravel, letter to Cobina Wright, April 1, 1928. Courtesy of the Hall Johnson Collection (Rowan University, Glassboro, NJ). All rights reserved.

14. E. Robert Schmitz, letter to William Gassner, August 14, 1928. Courtesy of the Hall Johnson Collection (Rowan University, Glassboro, NJ). All rights reserved.

15. W. J. Henderson of the *New York Sun*, quoted in a publicity brochure prepared by William C. Gassner, manager of the Hall Johnson Negro Choir, undated.

16. Horatio Parker of the *Boston Transcript*, quoted in a publicity brochure prepared by William C. Gassner, manager of the Hall Johnson Negro Choir, undated.

17. William C. Gassner, publicity brochure for the Hall Johnson Negro Choir, undated. Courtesy of the Hall Johnson Collection (Rowan University, Glassboro, NJ).

18. Gassner, publicity brochure.

19. Compton Parkenham, "Newly Recorded Music," *New York Times*, October 26, 1930, sec. 8, 10.

20. Marie Hicks Davidson, "Negro Choir Remarkable," *San Francisco Call Bulletin*, Fall 1932 (clipping undated).

21. Llewellen Miller, "Enthusiasm Greets Negro Choir," *Los Angeles Record*, Fall 1932 (clipping undated).

22. Leonard J. Leff, "*Gone with the Wind* and Hollywood's Racial Politics," *Atlantic Monthly*, December 1999.

23. *New York Daily News*, November 18, 1932.

24. Ben Gross, "Big Town Song Book," *New York Daily News*, November 18, 1932.

25. Radio Announcer Script, *The Gibson Family*, Ivory Soap Series, May 12, 1935.

26. Courtesy of the Voice of America. All rights reserved.

27. A song title in brackets indicates that the named song was played at this point in the radio program.

28. The scripts for both shows are included in chapter 4, "Literary Expression," in the Essays of Hall Johnson section.

29. "Chorus of Intoxicating Voices: Titania-Palast Reverberates from Applause," *Nacht-Depesche* (Berlin), September 21, 1951.

30. "Dark Skin and Voice," *Der Abend* (Berlin), September 21, 1951.

31. "Sorrow, Joy, Piety: Hall Johnson Choir at Titania-Palast," *Neue Zeitung* (Berlin), September 22, 1951.

32. "The Hall Johnson Choir at Titania-Palast," *Der Tagesspiegel* (Berlin), September 22, 1951.

33. "American Negro Chorus," *Die Welt* (Hamburg), September 26, 1951.

34. "Choir Parade from the U.S.A.," *Hamburger Echo* (Hamburg), September 26, 1951.

35. "Famous Negro Choir: University: Hall Johnson Choir," *Hamburger Abendblatt* (Hamburg), September 26, 1951.

36. "Negro Choir Delights," *Morgenpost* (Hamburg), September 27, 1951.

37. "The Hall Johnson Choir," *Fraenkisch Tagespost* (Nürnberg), October 5, 1951.

38. "Cultivated Originality," unidentified newspaper (Nürnberg), October 5, 1951.

39. "The Hall Johnson Choir," *Nordbayerische Zeitung* (Nürnberg), October 5, 1951.

40. "The Hall Johnson Choir Sings," *Neurnberger Zeitung* (Nürnberg), October 6, 1951.

41. "Spirituals in Brahms Hall," *Die Presse* (Vienna), October 7, 1951.

42. Fritz Skorzeny, "Hall Johnson Negro Choir: Sensational Success of Negro Choir in Vienna," *Neue Wiener Tageszeitung* (Vienna), October 7, 1951.

43. Max Graf, "Negro Choir and Concert Pianist," *Wiener Kurier* (Vienna), October 8, 1951.

44. Courtesy of the Voice of America. All rights reserved.

45. Courtesy of the U.S. Department of State. All rights reserved.

46. Courtesy of the U.S. Department of State. All rights reserved.

47. Courtesy of the U.S. Department of State. All rights reserved.

48. Robert Breen, "U.S. Part in Berlin Festival Lauded as Anti-Red Move," *New York Herald Tribune*, October 14, 1951.

49. Gassner, publicity brochure.

50. "Johnson Negro Choir Delights at Stadium," *New York Times*, July 23, 1929.

51. Eudora Garrett, "Hall Johnson Choir Singers Meet Encore Storm at Stadium," *New York Herald Tribune*, July 23, 1929.

52. "Negro Choir Delights Audience," *New York Times*, March 18, 1932.

53. "Hall Johnson Negro Choir Gives Recital," *New York Herald Tribune*, March 18, 1932.

54. "Johnson Choir Returns to Dell," *Philadelphia Evening Bulletin*, August 4, 1934.

55. Samuel L. Laciar, "Hall Johnson Choir at Dell," *Philadelphia Evening Public Ledger*, August 4, 1934.

56. Elsie Finn, "Hall Johnson Choir Gives Dell Recital," *Philadelphia Record*, August 4, 1934.

57. "Negro Choir in the Dell," unidentified Philadelphia paper, August 4, 1934.

58. Carl Bronson, "Audience Acclaims Hall Johnson Choir," *Los Angeles Evening Herald and Express*, April 26, 1938.

59. Isabel Morse Jones, "The Hall Johnson Choir Wins Wilshire-Ebell Audience," *Los Angeles Times*, April 26, 1938.

60. "Negro Folk Songs Stadium Feature," *New York Times*, July 6, 1938.

61. "Hall Johnson Choir Is Heard at the Stadium," *New York Herald Tribune*, July 6, 1938.

62. Robert C. Bagar, "Hall Johnson Choir Aids Stadium Concert Program," *New York World-Telegram*, July 6, 1938.

63. "Negro Spirituals Sung at Stadium," *New York Sun*, July 6, 1938.

64. Richard D. Sanders, "Choir Gains Plaudits in Concert," *Hollywood Citizen-News*, August 26, 1938.

65. Hall Johnson, letter to William Gassner, December 1951. Courtesy of the Hall Johnson Collection (Rowan University, Glassboro, NJ). All rights reserved.

66. Hal Johnson, letter to Harry Joe Brown, January 29, 1952. Courtesy of the Hall Johnson Collection (Rowan University, Glassboro, NJ). All rights reserved.

67. Matthew Kennedy, letter to Hall Johnson, July 12, 1953. Courtesy of the Hall Johnson Collection (Rowan University, Glassboro, NJ). All rights reserved.

68. Hall Johnson, excerpts from program notes for the Sprites and Sprouts. Courtesy of the Hall Johnson Collection (Rowan University, Glassboro, NJ). All rights reserved.

69. Arthur Landau, letter to Hall Johnson, September 25, 1959. Courtesy of the Hall Johnson Collection (Rowan University, Glassboro, NJ). All rights reserved.

70. Landau, letter to Hall Johnson, September 25, 1959.

71. Arthur Landau, letter to Hall Johnson, January 3, 1960. Courtesy of the Hall Johnson Collection (Rowan University, Glassboro, NJ). All rights reserved.

72. Will Marion Cook, letter to Hall Johnson, August 29, 1941. Courtesy of the Moorland Spingarn Research Center (Howard University, Washington, DC). All rights reserved.

73. "Pastures Green for All," *New York Times*, April 28, 1935, p. 2X.

74. This figure was quoted by Beverly Sills in the 2003 New Year's Eve PBS telecast of the New York Philharmonic Orchestra, *Live from Lincoln Center*, featuring

Gershwin's *Porgy and Bess*, with the Harlem Interfaith Choir, Loren Maazel, conducting.

75. All Bible verses are taken from the King James Version.

76. Manet Harrison Fowler was an African-American dramatic soprano concert artist and teacher from Forth Worth, Texas, who garnered favorable reviews in the *Fort Worth Record*, *Chicago Evening Post*, *Dallas Gazette*, *Shreveport Sun*, and *Chicago Defender*. In August 1930, she produced and directed her original pageant, *The Voice*, for the Golden Anniversary of the Negro Baptists of America, performed in the Chicago Coliseum with a cast of two thousand. Among her assisting staff were music notables William Henry Smith, Florence Price, Margaret Bonds, William Henry Dyett, and William Dawson. The Fowler letters are preserved in the Hall Johnson Collection (Rowan University, Glassboro, NJ).

77. Emily Bernard, *Remember Me to Harlem: The Letters of Langston Hughes and Carl Van Vechten, 1925–1964* (New York: Yale University Press, 2001), 71–72.

78. Charlotte Osgood Mason, undated letter to Hall Johnson. Courtesy of the Hall Johnson Collection (Rowan University, Glassboro, NJ). All rights reserved.

79. *Blackbirds of 1930*, a Broadway musical comedy with an all-black cast and score by black pianist and composer Eubie Blake. This letter from Charlotte van der Veer Quick Mason is the only authoritative evidence that Johnson prepared the chorus for this highly successful production. The letter is preserved in the Hall Johnson Collection (Rowan University, Glassboro, NJ).

80. Courtesy of the Hall Johnson Collection (Rowan University, Glassboro, NJ). All rights reserved.

81. This statement is belied by what actually happened during the filming of *Lost Horizon*, the winner of nine Academy Awards. Johnson's drinking caused him to be taken off the movie, and Jester Hairston, his assistant conductor, served as choral director for the remainder of the film.

82. Jester Hairston, undated letter to Hall Johnson. Courtesy of the Hall Johnson Collection (Rowan University, Glassboro, NJ). All rights reserved.

83. Jester Hairston, undated letter to Hall Johnson. Courtesy of the Hall Johnson Collection (Rowan University, Glassboro, NJ). All rights reserved.

84. Undoubtedly, this reference must be to *Fi-yer* as it is the only other musical play that Johnson wrote. Unfortunately, it is not named, and there is no documentary evidence—that is, programs, reviews—that *Fi-yer* was ever produced.

85. Jester Hairston, letter to Hall Johnson, July 22, 1966. Courtesy of the Hall Johnson Collection (Rowan University, Glassboro, NJ). All rights reserved.

86. This information is found in a letter of recommendation for Mrs. Jones, written by Hall Johnson, and included in chapter 4, "Literary Expression."

87. Jan Hall Jones, letter to Hall Johnson, November 7, 1951. Courtesy of the Hall Johnson Collection (Rowan University, Glassboro, NJ). All rights reserved.

88. Interview with Jeffrey Fields, son of Celeste Robinson, heir to the Hall Johnson Estate, March 2003.

89. In what could only be described as an act of fate, I was able to locate the eighty-seven-year-old sister of Wathea Sims Jones, a Mrs. Robert Brown (Lela), who, in an interview on May 6, 2003, confirmed the death of Jan Hall, but not the cause of death.

90. Dwight Strickland, "David," Carl Fischer Music. Used by permission. All rights reserved.

91. Hall Johnson, "National Choral Plan to Help Children through Music" (unpublished proposal). Courtesy of the Hall Johnson Collection (Rowan University, Glassboro, NJ).

92. Courtesy of the Hall Johnson Collection (Rowan University, Glassboro, NJ). All rights reserved.

93. Eva Jessye, acceptance speech, February 17, 1963. Courtesy of the Hall Johnson Collection (Rowan University, Glassboro, NJ). All rights reserved.

94. *Etude Music Magazine*, undated letter to Hall Johnson. Courtesy of the Hall Johnson Collection (Rowan University, Glassboro, NJ). All rights reserved.

95. Carlton Sprague Smith, undated letter to Hall Johnson. Courtesy of the Hall Johnson Collection (Rowan University, Glassboro, NJ). All rights reserved.

96. *Marquis' Who's Who in America*, undated letter to Hall Johnson. Courtesy of the Hall Johnson Collection (Rowan University, Glassboro, NJ). All rights reserved.

97. Edward R. Murrow's *This I Believe*, undated letter to Hall Johnson. Courtesy of the Hall Johnson Collection (Rowan University, Glassboro, NJ). All rights reserved.

~

CHAPTER TWO

The Hall Johnson Choir: Star of the Silver Screen

Eminence among Movie Choirs

One reliable source recalls an incident in which Hall Johnson held a choir beyond the curtain time because of his dissatisfaction with the prerehearsal. When informed that the audience was growing impatient, he replied, "They waited for me in Hollywood, they waited for me on Broadway, and they are going to wait for me tonight."[1] To the uninformed, this statement may appear immodest, and even arrogant, but an examination of the true history of Hall Johnson and his choir, not heretofore available, proves this to be a simple statement of fact. The Hall Johnson Choir was the only choir in the history of the American cinema to become a movie star. If we apply the criteria to the choir that are applied to any actor—billing, number of movies made, scenes on camera, and integration into the plot—this conclusion is inescapable. This is all the more amazing because it happened three decades before an African American could eat in a restaurant, use a rest room, or live in a hotel that was not segregated.

The singularity and eminence of the Hall Johnson Choir's position as a cinematic star becomes evident if we search the film history of other leading professional choirs of the twentieth century. The Robert Shaw Chorale appeared in no movies and in two television documentaries. The Mormon Tabernacle Choir (world renown, but actually a church ensemble), the Roger Wagner Chorale, the Albert McNeil Jubilee Singers, and the Jester Hairston Singers—none are credited with even one motion picture. While preliminary research for the 1988 Hall Johnson Centennial Festival credited the

Hall Johnson Choir with only twelve movies, current research has confirmed a film legacy of thirty-seven movies, seven of which are "shorts."

The movie career of Hall Johnson and his choir extended from 1929 to 1946. He worked for the major motion picture studios including RKO, 20th Century Fox, Warner Brothers, Columbia, United Artists, MGM, and Paramount. The directors and producers of these movies include the biggest names in the business: Frank Capra, Marc Connelly, Buddy De Silva, Walt Disney, Sol Lesser, Vincent Minelli, Jack L. Warner, and Darryl F. Zanuck, among others. Many of the actors with whom Johnson worked have become legends. This chapter will provide a complete listing of studios, producers, directors, and principal starring actors and actresses with whom the Hall Johnson Choir worked, along with a synopsis of the plot of each movie and a brief discussion of the choir's role and repertoire.

In many of the full-length films, the Hall Johnson Choir was given star billing in the opening credits, sometimes in larger letters than the actors. In a number of cases, the choir opened and closed the film, sometimes on camera and sometimes off camera, but under the credits as they rolled. In the majority of films, the choir was integrated into the plot.

One must ask how the Hall Johnson Choir came to be so famous and so much in demand between 1929 and 1943. The answer is historical, sociological, and musical, involving the introduction of the "talkie" (sound movies), the vitality and emotional gamut of the Negro spiritual, the excellence of the Hall Johnson Choir (fostered by a conductor every bit as demanding as Toscanini), and the vestigial remnants of slavery, which were legally retained in the South until 1964. Most of these movies were set in the South, during and just after slavery. Any realistic portrayal of this *Gone with the Wind* mythology had to include a large body of plantation slaves who were field hands and house slaves, and who comprised the wonderfully resonant plantation choruses, dancers, and banjo pickers. These movies were so popular in the South because they perpetuated the stereotypes that Southern whites wanted to hold on to: that Negroes were lazy, Negroes were stupid (or childlike, if you prefer), Negroes were funny (watch Stepin Fetchit), Negroes could dance (watch Bill "Bojangles" Robinson), and Negroes were happy in poverty and slavery. Clearly, these films buttressed the self-concept of white superiority and reminded blacks of their history of subjugation and denigration. The Shirley Temple movies were exceptions to this rule as they integrated the children at play and attributed to black characters qualities of humanity and nobility. Thus, the Hall Johnson Choir added pathos, joy, and comedy to these movies, and at the same time, introduced the beauty of the Negro spiritual to moviegoers all over America.

This chapter documents, for the first time, the extent to which the Hall Johnson Choir was a major force in cinematic history from the very beginning of sound films to the midforties, when social pressures for integration made it politically incorrect to market movies with the stereotypical plantation environs and characters. There is perhaps no stronger proof of this than the fact that the 1945 New York revival of *Green Pastures*—which had a triumphal Broadway run in 1930—lasted only one night, because of protests by the NAACP (National Association for the Advancement of Colored People). Even in the 1980s, protests by the Black Professionals Organization was a major factor in preventing the production of *Porgy and Bess* by the Hollybush Opera Theater at Rowan University, despite my white paper attesting to the work's significance to the arts and for black singing artists (I portrayed Porgy on the New York City Opera's float in the 1964 Macy's Thanksgiving Day Parade). In many of the movies in the Hall Johnson Choir's film legacy, the choir actually appears on camera as characters: slaves, field workers, church members, or as a performing group. In a few instances, the voices of the choir are used, especially in the cartoon shorts and in *Dumbo*. In several movies, only the male voices, or even a small group of men, are used. The only virtually complete library of these films is available for viewing and research in the Reserved Hall Johnson Collection at the Rowan University Department of Music.

The Chronology of the Hall Johnson Film Legacy

In this age of DVDs and wide-screen high definition TV sets, it may be useful to clarify several terms used in the following section. A movie "short" is literally defined by the word as it is a short film, generally fifteen to twenty minutes in length as contrasted with a full-length film of at least an hour and fifteen minutes. In an earlier generation, shorts were a staple of the movie industry and were most often cartoons of the Bugs Bunny genre. The movie *Clean Pastures* is an example of this. Another term that may be foreign to some is *politically incorrect*. When the term is used in reference to films, it is simply a euphemistic way of saying "racist." These films intentionally portrayed various races in a negative, stereotypical manner. In America, and especially during the period in which the Hall Johnson Choir worked in Hollywood, blacks were the most frequent targets of stereotypical portrayals. But other races or cultures—Asians, Italians, Jews, and Arabs— were also frequently victimized. In the mid-1940s, under pressure of groups like the NAACP, movie studios were forced to withdraw these films from distribution. (However, if one looks at the entertainment industry today, the stereotyping of blacks is, in my opinion, worse than it was in 1930 because recorded music and television are so pervasive. The vulgarity, sexism, self-loathing, and misogyny that spews from the mouths of the most salable black Hip Hoppers and comedians is far more denigrating and abusive than *Amos and Andy* or *The Green Pastures*.) Among the Hall Johnson Choir's films, *The Green Pastures*, *The Clean Pastures*, *Sunday Go to Meetin'*, and *Song of the South* easily fit into this category and for many years were unavailable for purchase or distribution in the United States. (I purchased the *Green Pastures* and *Clean Pastures* shorts from a collector through eBay, and I bought *Song of the South* in Israel.) Today, a number of these films are back in the video stores, perhaps reflecting the same change in racial attitudes in the country as the nooses that are appearing publicly from Jena, Louisiana, to Columbia University, my alma mater.

In several instances in the following list, two names appear for a single film. The two Duke Ellington films at the top of the list are shorts that are a part of a larger video. Thus, the name of the video and the particular short are provided to facilitate easier purchase by interested researchers. In the case of *Dimples* and *It Happened in New Orleans*, the studio released the films under one name, and then changed the name on a subsequent release thinking that they would sell better. Finally, with *Saint Louis Blues*, where the name of the two leads appears, this indicates that there are other movies by that name with a different cast, and the only easy way to distinguish between them is by cast or year of release, which may be harder to come by initially. Where Duke Ellington's name appears, the film was based on a musical suite by the same name, so he was both star and composer.

1929	*Black and Tan* (short); aka *Jazz Classics*—Duke Ellington/Orchestra
1929	*St. Louis Blues* (short); aka *Hollywood Rhythms* (Jazz Cocktails)
1930	*It Happened in New Orleans* (*Rainbow on the River*—1936)
1930	*Big Boy*
1931	*Pardon Us*
1934	*Wonder Bar*
1935	*Little Sinner* (short)
1936	*Dimples*; aka *The Bowery Princess*
1936	*Hearts Divided*
1936	*Banjo on My Knee*
1936	*Road Gang*
1936	*Sunday Go to Meetin' Time* (short; politically incorrect cartoon)
1936	*Follow Your Heart*

1936	*The Green Pastures*
1936	*The Song of a Nation*
1936	*Lost Horizon*
1937	*The Clean Pastures* (short; politically incorrect cartoon)
1937	*Slave Ship*
1937	*Deep South* (short)
1938	*Jezebel*
1938	*My Old Kentucky Home*
1939	*Stanley and Livingstone*
1939	*Way Down South*
1939	*Zenobia*
1939	*Swanee River*
1939	*St. Louis Blues* (Lamour and Nolan)
1940	*In Old Missouri*
1940	*Carolina Moon*
1941	*Dumbo*
1941	*Lady for a Night*
1941	*The Vanishing Virginian*
1941	*Samson* (short)
1941	*Meet John Doe*
1941	*Road to Zanzibar*
1942	*Tales of Manhattan*
1942	*Heart of the Golden West*
1942	*Syncopation*
1942	*Syncopated Sermon* (short; politically incorrect cartoon)
1943	*Dixie*
1943	*Cabin in the Sky*
1946	*Song of the South*

Major Movie Stars the Hall Johnson Choir Appeared With

The list of major stars the Hall Johnson Negro Choir appeared in films with has been extracted from the casts of the films listed above. It is both extensive and impressive, and includes the following: Bobby Breen, May Robson, Charles Butterworth, Louise Beavers, Alan Mowbray, Eddie "Rochester" Anderson, Shirley Temple, John Boles, Jack Holt, Karen Morley, Bill "Bojangles" Robinson, Stepin Fetchit, Dick Powell, Marion Davies, Charlie Ruggles, Arthur Treacher, Claude Rains, Edward Everett Horton, Barbara Stanwyck, Joel McCrea, Walter Brennan, Buddy Ebsen, Helen Westley,

Frank Morgon, Robert Kent, Delma Byron, Marion Talley, Michael Bartlett, Nigel Bruce, Louis Alberni, Henrietta Crosman, Clarence Muse, Rex Ingram, Oscar Polk, Frank Wilson, Abraham Greaves, George H. Reed, Ronald Coleman, H. B. Warner, Jane Wyatt, Sam Jaffe, Evelyn Venable, John Farrell McDonald, Grant Richards, Bernadette Hayes, Spencer Tracy, Nancy Kelly, Cedric Hardwicke, Richard Greene, Charles Coburn, Ralph Morgan, Steffi Duna, Oliver Hardy, Harry Langdon, Billie Burke, Alice Brady, James Ellison, Hattie McDaniel, Don Ameche, Andrea Leeds, Al Jolson, Felix Bressart, Jack Chandler, Leon Weaver, Frank Weaver, June Weaver, June Story, Marjorie Gateson, Joan Blondell, John Wayne, Ray Middleton, Phillip Merivale, Blanche Yurka, Edith Barrett, Kathryn Grayson, Spring Byington, Natalie Thompson, Douglass Newland, Leigh Whipper, Louise Beavers, Gary Cooper, Edward Arnold, Charles Boyer, Rita Hayworth, Ginger Rogers, Henry Fonda, Charles Laughton, Edward G. Robinson, Paul Robeson, Ethel Waters, Thomas Mitchell, Cesar Romero, Elsa Lanchester, George Sanders, J. Carol Naish, Roy Rogers, Smiley Burnett, George Hayes, Ruth Terry, Sons of the Pioneers, Adolphe Menjou, Jackie Cooper, Bonita Granville, George Bancroft, Ted North, Todd Duncan, Connee Boswell, Mona Barrie, Charlie Barnet, Alvino Rey, Harry James, Benny Goodman, Gene Krupa, Lena Horne, Louis Armstrong, Kenneth Spencer, Bill Bailey, Butterfly McQueen, Ruby Dandridge, Duke Ellington, and Bessie Smith.

The Role and Scope of the Hall Johnson Choir in Its Films

Black and Tan (Short)—1929

This nineteen-minute film represents the cinematic debut of Duke Ellington and the Hall Johnson Choir. The rather thin plot line serves as a vehicle for the display of the musical talents of the Duke Ellington Orchestra, the Hall Johnson Choir, and the dance talent and beauty of Fredi Washington.

The film opens with Duke and his lead trumpet player rehearsing his "Black and Tan Fantasy." They are interrupted by two piano movers who have come to repossess his piano. This is averted when Fredi Washington enters and offers the movers a bottle of gin to leave the piano. She also tells Duke that they have been hired for an appearance at the Cotton Club. Duke warns her that her heart condition may make the appearance dangerous for her. During the performance, Fredi collapses on stage and in the final scene she dies with Duke reprising the "Black and Tan Fantasy" assisted by the Hall Johnson Choir.

The choir is integrated into the action of the final scene as the singers stand in stark relief at the foot of the dying Fredi's bed, raise their hands toward the heavens in gestures of supplication, and sing the opening lines of the old spiritual "Same Train, Leaving Tomorrow." When Duke and his trumpeter begin the "Black and Tan Fantasy," the choir joins him in a wordless instrumental wail that adds gravity to the scene as Fredi expires and the movie comes to an end. The Hall Johnson Choir appears in the opening credits as a featured performer and the quality of its performance heralds the bright future that lay ahead.

St. Louis Blues (Short)—1929

This poignant short, produced by W. C. Handy for Gramercy Studios is the only movie in which the legendary Bessie Smith appears. Implicit in the plot is the fact that Bessie is a prostitute who returns to her hotel room to find her pimp with another woman. She attacks the woman and drives her from the room. Bessie begs Jimmie not to leave her but he pushes her down, kicks her, and departs. Bessie retires to the hotel night club where she sits alone at the bar and sings the immortal "St. Louis Blues." The Hall Johnson Choir, seated around the room as patrons, accompany her in an elaborate arrangement by composer W. C. Handy. The orchestra interrupts Bessie's lament with a hot jazz chorus during which dancers fill the floor and Jimmie returns for a flashy dance solo. Jimmie and Bessie are reunited, but only long enough for him to get all her money and leave again. Bessie and the choir sing the final chorus in the original tempo and the movie ends, leaving her alone and dejected.

In this film, the Hall Johnson Choir is integrated totally and effectively into the plot as the singers appear as extras in the film without a visible conductor. It makes an essential contribution to the musical arrangement and complements the soloist in a natural manner that advances the dramatic intent. The recorded sound is remarkably good.

It Happened in New Orleans—1930

This delightful movie showcases the extraordinary singing talents of child star Bobby Breen, who is ably supported by Louise Beavers, Charles Butterworth, Alan Mobray, and May Robson. After being lovingly raised by an exslave named "Mammy," when his father is killed in the Civil War and his mother dies in a fire, Phillip is forced to leave his New Orleans home and live in New York with his Yankee grandmother. In New York, an evil aunt does her best to turn the grandmother against the lad so that she and her daughter can inherit her estate. Cantankerous Grandma tries her best not to like the boy but is ultimately charmed and won over by his singing, his banjo strumming, and his dancing. With the help of the butler, the plotting of the aunt and her daughter is revealed and the grandmother takes Phillip back to New Orleans to get the Toinette, the ex-slave who raised him from infancy.

Although the voices of the Hall Johnson Choir are only used in three scenes, the choir receives the most prominent billing of any cast members save for Bobby Breen. The choir first appears in a production number, "Waitin' for the Sun to Rise," where they are cast as plantation workers in this post–Civil War drama. Breen (Phillip) joins them for a solo in the middle of the number. Later, in New York, the choir provides off-camera support for Breen when he reminisces about the South and performs "Swanee River" for his grandmother. In the final scene of the movie, the choir reappears as field workers and reprises "Rainbow on the River" as Phillip, Toinette, and Grandma leave the plantation to return to New York. Whenever the choir appears on camera, it is as a character that supports both plot and action.

Big Boy—1930

Big Boy is a remake of a Broadway musical that Al Jolson opened at the Winter Garden Theatre in 1925. After a Broadway run of several months, the show toured until 1927 and was made into a movie in 1930. While Jolson devoted his life to performing minstrel roles in "blackface," this is the only role in which he portrayed, rather than imitated, a Negro character singing, dancing, and telling jokes. Simply put, *Big Boy* is the story of a thoroughbred colt that is raised by Gus, a black stable hand, to enter and win the Kentucky Derby. There is a plot to "fix" the race by substituting a crooked jockey for Gus. In the end, Gus outsmarts the crooks, rides Big Boy, and wins the Derby.

Though the film takes place in the twentieth century, the men of the Hall Johnson Choir appear with Gus in a great flashback scene in which Gus appears as his grandfather and leads the black stable hands in the performance of "Dixie," and two Negro spirituals: "I Got Shoes" and "Go Down, Moses." The singers appear in character and act, sing, and dance as the drama demands. The Hall Johnson Choir is not credited in this film.

Pardon Us—1931

In this, their feature film debut, Stan Laurel and Oliver Hardy are joined by Walter Lang and Wilfred Lucas in this romp about prison life. The movie opens with bootleggers Stan and Ollie being arrested for selling beer to a prohibition agent. Their prison roommate is the infamous "Tiger" who engineers a prison break in which they are caught up. To facilitate their escape, Stan and Ollie disguise themselves in blackface and mix with the black plantation workers. They are discovered when they repair the warden's car and are sent back to prison where they inadvertently foil Tiger's next escape attempt, become heroes, and are pardoned.

Although the Hall Johnson Choir is not credited in this film, its appearance represents an extended and significant part of the film. The choir is featured in two scenes in the very middle. In the field scene, the choir appears as cotton pickers. As they work, they sing three well-known spirituals: "Keep A-Inchin' Along," "Hand Me Down My Silver Trumpet," and "Down the Jubalee." In the quarters scene, the workers sing "Swing Along Chillun," "Gonna Ride That Train," and "Lazy Moon" with Ollie as the featured soloist. Without these six numbers, this fifty-six-minute feature film would be a short. The choir truly becomes a "starring" character, as important as the two lead actors.

Wonder Bar—1934

This delightful musical is based on Al Jolson's 1931 Broadway hit. Set in a lavish Paris night club, Jolson, the lead singer and proprietor, is assisted by Ricardo Cortez, Dolores Del Rio, Kay Francis, and Dick Powell. The musical numbers and dances are organized as a variety show with Jolson functioning as master of ceremonies and star singer. It is held together by a plot in which everyone loves the wrong person: Inez loves Harry, Harry loves Liane, Al and Tommy love Inez. When Inez kills Harry after an argument, Al disposes of the body by secreting it in the car of a man planning to drive off a cliff.

The Hall Johnson Choir does not appear in the film until the finale of the revue. This is the most elaborate, demanding, and musically satisfying performance of the choir in its entire filmology. With Jolson as soloist, the twelve-minute scene "Goin' to Heaven on a Mule" is a vocal concertato, starting with the soloist alone and layering the textures until it rises to a hair-raising ending. With staging and choreography by the great Busby Berkeley, all performed by the large choir, the Negro's vision of heaven unfolds in music and in action. While all of the racist stereotypes are there—Gabriel, tap dancing, possum pie, pork chops, and watermelon—the final tableau with a galaxy of singers clad in white robes and angel's wings has rarely been equaled. Despite its outstanding contribution, the Hall Johnson Choir is not credited in this film.

Little Sinner (Short)—1935

The Little Rascals shorts were staples of the Saturday afternoon matinee fare. In Little Sinner, Spanky succumbs to the call of the wild when his father gives him a new fishing rod, and he cuts Sunday School to go fishing. Accompanied by Porky and Alfalfa, Spanky has some bad luck when he loses his bait and is chased away from his first stream by an old man who says that fishing is forbidden on Sunday. As Spanky and his buddies search for another place to fish, they encounter a large black congregation having a baptismal service. The ecstatic screams and the shouting of the worshippers, coupled with long white robes on the novitiates, scare the socks off the kids who run back to the church, having learned their lesson.

The Hall Johnson Choir, cast as a part of the large congregation at the baptismal service, give splendid renditions of "Moaner Found a Hiding Place," "Oh Lord, Won't You Save Me," and "I'm Leaning on the Lord." The choir is not credited in the film titles.

Dimples—1936

Dimples (aka *The Bowery Princess*) is one of many delightful movies made by the greatest of all child stars, Shirley Temple. Temple is cast as a street urchin who is used as a diversion by her grandfather (Frank Morgan) as he picks pockets and engages in other nefarious activities. When Dimples performs at the home of a rich old dowager, the lady takes a fancy to her and offers to raise Dimples as her own daughter. The dowager's son offers Dimples the part of Eva in a play based on *Uncle Tom's Cabin*, and she scores a triumphant success.

The Hall Johnson Choir is credited in this film and first appears on camera with Dimples as she rehearses the old spiritual, "De Gospel Train." The choir reappears in the film's most dramatic moment, as "Little Eva" lies dying and sings "Swing Low, Sweet Chariot." Although he is not credited, famed baritone Robert McFerrin has the wonderful baritone voice heard in the solo; McFerrin was destined to become the first Afro-American male singer to perform with the Metropolitan Opera. "Dixiana," the finale of the movie, is sung by the all-male Minstrel Chorus, on stage, and the men of the Hall Johnson Choir, off stage.[2]

Hearts Divided—1936

Napoleon Bonaparte sends his brother Jerome on a good will visit to the United States prior to the Louisiana Purchase. After pretending to be a French tutor, Jerome falls in love with a beautiful Baltimore socialite. When Napoleon learns of the affair, he insists that his brother give up his beloved so that he can fulfill an arranged marriage. Marion Davies, Dick Powell, Claude Rains, and Arthur Treacher star.

Although the Hall Johnson Choir is given equal billing with the stars in this tasteful musical film, it is only used in two scenes. The choir appears on camera in the slave quarters when the heroine brings a lost black child back to his mother. It sings the first chorus of "Nobody Knows de Trouble I See" superbly. The choir sings again, off camera, near the end of the film when the three senators propose. It can be heard softly in the background intoning "Steal Away to Jesus."

Banjo on My Knee—1936

This musical comedy with a rather convoluted plot stars Walter Brennan, Tony Martin, Joel McCrea, and Barbara Stanwyck. McCrea and Stanwyck marry as the movie opens, but he is forced to flee their houseboat on his wedding night because he thinks he has killed a man in a fight. With the marriage still unconsummated, McCrea ends up in the Navy, and Stanwyck in New Orleans as a waitress. A comedy of errors ensues when McCrea returns to port and allows his hot temper to wreck his own surprise party. The couple is finally reunited when Stanwyck returns to the boat prior to leaving for Chicago with Tony Martin, a friend who had worked with her as a singer in New Orleans.

The Hall Johnson Choir is credited in the titles of this film. Although the choir appears in only one scene, it performs Hall Johnson's complex arrangement of "The St. Louis Blues" spectacularly. Integrated into the plot, the male singers appear as stevedores unloading freight from river barges, and the women as homemakers on the balconies of their quarters, which overlook the dock. Heartbroken that she had stubbornly left her husband's home and come to New Orleans, Stanwyck goes down to the banks of the Mississippi River to decide what to do with her life. As she sits on a bench, the choir sings the "St. Louis Blues." When she is joined by Tony Martin (who has fallen in love with her), they talk as the choir softly reprises the number. One reviewer described the performance as one "rendered to perfection by the marvelous Hall Johnson Choir." The movie received one Academy Award nomination.

Road Gang—1936

In this B movie, Donald Woods is a reporter who sets out to expose the abysmal conditions, injustice, and political corruption of the prison system. To silence him, he is framed and sent to the penitentiary where he witnesses and experiences the dehumanizing brutality first hand. He is finally rescued through the intervention of his girl friend and succeeds in bringing the prison administration down.

Male singers from the Hall Johnson Choir, identified only as "black prisoners," perform off camera in two scenes. In the first scene, a prisoner is lashed twenty times with a whip as the men plaintively sing "Swanee River."

In the second scene, a prisoner is hung by his wrists over night. The singers intone "Swing Low, Sweet Chariot," as you view a tableau that is vividly reminiscent of the crucifixion of Christ. The singing is beautifully done, and the spiritual features an extraordinary tenor soloist.

Sunday Go to Meetin' Time (Short)—1936

This politically incorrect cartoon, so called because of its overtly racist characterization, has been withdrawn from public purchase and exhibition since the 1960s. Produced by Warner Brothers, cartoons of this type were immensely popular to segregationists as they portrayed blacks with every conceivable negative stereotype. In this seven-minute film, Nicodemus is dragged away from his dice game and made to go to church by his wife. He slips away from church, steals a chicken, and is accidentally struck on the head and made unconscious. Before Nicodemus awakes, he dreams that he is in hell where he is tormented by fire and devils. When he comes to, he hastily returns to church as he has learned his lesson.

This is one of several animated films in which the voices of the Hall Johnson Choir are used. The film opens with a black preacher standing at the door of his church, singing with a magnificent bass voice "To the Chapel Come Ye Sinners One and All." He is supported by the choir. Although neither the choir nor soloist is credited, the soloist is probably Jules Bledsoe or Kenneth Spencer. When the service begins, the Hall Johnson Choir sings the spiritual "I Got Shoes." When Nicodemus is cast into hell, the choir sings an original song, "You Got to Give the Devil His Due." When he returns to church, the choir reprises "I Got Shoes." In each instance, the music underscores or describes the action of the film and contributes significantly to its effectiveness.

Follow Your Heart—1936

This delightful musical features opera star Marion Talley as a young and gifted singer torn between a career in opera or that of a homemaker. Though discouraged by her mother who had already experienced the life of a professional singer, she is tricked into singing the lead in a touring production and falls for a singing career and the leading tenor. The show, essentially a Broadway revue, is so successful that the troop heads for New York and the big time. The cast includes Michael Bartlett, Nigel Bruce, and Henrietta Crosman.

The Hall Johnson Choir is cast as plantation workers in this post–Civil War confection designed originally to be toured to similar venues throughout Kentucky. The singers are integrated into the revue as a unit and perform three numbers in their set with tableau staging. At the opening performance of the music production, the choir sings a medley comprised of three songs: "I Work All Day on the Levee," "It's All over Me," and "He's Keeping Me Alive." The first features a marvelous baritone soloist, the second an equally polished tenor. In a subsequent touring performance, the choir sings "Work in the Morning" to the tune of the spiritual "Wade in de Water," accompanied by a solo dancer, orchestra, and percussion in a jazz tempo. The choir is on camera for each of the selections.

The Green Pastures—1936

Adapted from Marc Connelly's Pulitzer Prize–winning Broadway play of the same name, *The Green Pastures* is a politically incorrect white man's version of a black man's concept of heaven in exaggerated Negro dialect, undergirded by wonderful spirituals and glorious singing by the Hall Johnson Choir. The Old Testament stories are told from the viewpoint of an elderly black Sunday school teacher, who presents the biblical prose in a conceptually and linguistically simple manner. *De Lawd* is a Southern Baptist preacher; heaven is a place with big choirs, big cigars, and frequent fish fries; Noah is a skipper who needs two kegs of liquor on his ark; and Moses is a "conjure man." It elegantly makes a point of the prevailing social assumption of the day: "simple stories for simple folks." Actors like Eddie "Rochester" Anderson, Rex Ingram, and Frank Wilson, as well as the singing of the Hall Johnson Choir, bring dignity and believability to lines that might otherwise seem ludicrous.

The design of *The Green Pastures* is similar to the contemporary Broadway music except that the chorus, rather than the solo voice, is the main musical protagonist. It alternately reflects the action or creates the mood for each scene. Hall Johnson selected from the broad repertoire of traditional spirituals those appropriate for the scenes (nineteen in all), arranged them, and conducted them for the original Broadway production and for the movie. In the film, the choral spirituals were used just as orchestral music is used in films—as background to the drama. While members of the choir appeared on camera in many scenes as church members, revelers, Israelites, and others, they did not appear as the singing choir. The music was obviously recorded and blended with the dramatic movement, frequently using only short portions of a work. This film includes the most extensive sampling of spirituals found in any movie (here listed by scene):

Opening Titles
   "Walk Together Chillun"
   "Cert'ny Lord"

The Heaven Tableau Scene
   "Rise and Shine"
   "Cert'ny Lord"
   "My God Is So High"
The Creation
   "Hallelujah, Been Down into the Sea"
The Creation of Adam
   "In Bright Mansions Above"
The Creation of Eve
   "Don't Let Nobody Turn You Round"
   "Run Chillun, Run to Your Hidin' Place"
God Goes to Earth
   "No Hidin' Place"
Noah's Flood
   "The Ole Ark's A'Moverin'"
The Ark on Mt. Sinai
   "Witness"
Earth's Second Chance
   "Go Down, Moses"
The Exodus
   "Lord, I Don't Feel Noways Tired"
Joshua Replaces Moses as Leader of the Israelites
   "Joshua Fit de Battle of Jericho"
God Repents of His Creation of Earth
   "Death's Gonna Lay His Cold Hands on Me"
The New Covenant with Man
   "You Shall Gain the Victory"
   "Oh! Rise and Shine"
The Crucifixion
   "Hallelujah, God of Mercy, God of Life"

The Hall Johnson Choir is credited in the film's opening titles, and Hall Johnson is credited separately as arranger and conductor.

The Song of a Nation (Short)—1936

It is inexplicable why this wonderful Technicolor tribute to Francis Scott Key has been withdrawn from circulation. It tells the story of Key and how he came to write the "Star Spangled Banner." The movie opens with a party at the home of the Keys where he is revealed as a rabid advocate of the war against the British, a position that alarms his wife and many of his guests. He boards a British ship to negotiate for the release of a captured American doctor. While aboard, the British attack Fort Henry and Francis fears that it will not withstand the bombardment through the night. As the dawn approaches and he sees the American flag still unfurled, he pens the immortal words, "Oh say can you see . . ." When he returns to shore, his friend takes the poem to the local Baltimore paper, and the public reception is instant and enthusiastic. When his estranged wife hears the anthem, she returns to him.

It is a happy coincident that the Hall Johnson Choir was chosen to provide the choral music for this film as Johnson had composed a number of patriotic songs and was himself decidedly patriotic. The choir sings off camera in two scenes of the film. It hums the "Star Spangled Banner" as Frances hurriedly pens the words. In the final scene, a crowd fills the lawn of Francis Scott Key to sing the anthem for him. The choir voices the anthem in Hall Johnson's own arrangement, but only on a neutral syllable, for reasons that cannot be justified.

Lost Horizon—1936

This epic, dubbed "the Mightiest of All Motion Pictures" represented Columbia Pictures' magnum opus in 1936 and required an investment equal to half the value of the studio. Directed and produced by Frank Capra, it had a huge cast led by Ronald Coleman, John Howard, Thomas Mitchell, and Jane Wyatt; a great story written by James Hilton; the great Hall Johnson Choir; and the top composers and arrangers, including Robert Russell Bennett, Jester Hairston, Hall Johnson, and Dmitri Tiomkin. In the complex plot, an airliner crashes high in the Tibetan mountains. Among the survivors are a British diplomat, his brother, and a consumptive prostitute. Miraculously, they are rescued by mysterious mountaineers who take them through the snow to a fertile valley where the temperature is always perfect, life span is tripled, war and hatred are unheard of, and people devote their time to the pursuit of wisdom and self-improvement. Upon his arrival in Shangri-La, Conway learns that he has been brought there intentionally to replace the High Lama who governs the community. Conway agrees to assume this responsibility as he has fallen in love with the beautiful Sandra. His brother, however, convinces him that the High Lama is insane and that what he has been told is untrue. Conway leaves with his brother for the outside world, becomes hopelessly lost, and is finally rescued and returned to England as an amnesiac. When his memory returns, he heads back to Shangri-La and the arms of his beloved Sandra.

The Hall Johnson Choir is listed prominently in the opening credits of this film. Composer Dmitri Tiomkin, himself a Russian, was said to have an

especial affinity for the quality of Negro voices. He employed the choir in-
strumentally in this film by having them sing with the orchestra using neutral sounds. The choir sings off camera under the opening credits. The choir
is used again in the welcome scene as the rescued travelers enter Shangri-La.
The third usage of the choir is at the death of the High Lama. Only in the
magnificent funeral scene is the choir used on camera as it performs the powerful processional music. During the production of this film, Hall Johnson became ill and Jester Hairston, his assistant conductor, took over the preparation of the choir and conducted it when necessary, thereby establishing a
long association with Dmitri Tiomkin.

The Clean Pastures (Short)—1937
This short Warner Brothers cartoon bears little resemblance to the successful movie of the preceding year, *The Green Pastures*, except in the most obvious ways: the cast is all black, the dialogue is ethnic, and all of the common stereotypes are grossly exaggerated, including the slurred speech, the big
lips, the dice parlors, the tap dancing, and the jazz rhythms. In five minutes,
Leon Schlesinger manages to convert a Pulitzer Prize–winning play into a politically incorrect and racist romp that deserves to be withdrawn permanently
from circulation. The only thematic idea preserved from the movie version
is the idea of God going down to earth to put a stop to all the wickedness. In
Clean Pastures, God sends St. Peter to Harlem where he tours the "Kotton
Club" and meets some famous "black" performers: Cab Calloway, Fats Waller,
Al Jolson(!), and Louis Armstrong. One can find no redeeming features in
this cartoon unless one agrees with the truism that "imitation is the sincerest form of flattery."

This is an animated film and the male voices of the Hall Johnson Choir
are only heard in the final scene where a line of "swinging" couples strut their
stuff to a hot version of "Oh, Dem Golden Slippers." Warner Brothers is as
consistent with its sexism as with its racism as the remainder of the choral
singing in the film (done by studio singers) also uses only male voices.

Slave Ship—1937
In this interesting adaptation of the William Faulkner novel *The Last Slaver*,
Captain Lovett resolves to quit the slave trade and fire his crew so that he can
make a new start. The crew, reluctant to give up the big money made in the
trade, mutinies and attempts to make one more big haul. As they approach
the Virginia port, they spot a Coast Guard vessel approaching. Fearful of being boarded and hanged for what is now a capital offense, the mutineers throw
the entire shipment of slaves into the ocean. With the help of the cabin boy

and the captain, the mutineers are captured by the Coast Guard and the captain is exonerated of any guilt and allowed to marry his fiancée. Warner Baxter, Wallace Beery, Mickey Rooney, and George Sanders star.

The Hall Johnson Choir appears as the slaves in the climactic scene of the movie. With an innate prescience, the slaves sense that they are about to be sacrificed and sing against a most effective orchestral counterpoint music, which is composed and yet a cacophony of wails. Written by the distinguished composer Alfred Newman, this music in style and complexity is a far cry from anything else sung by the choir in its entire filmology. The choir is not credited for its fine work.

Deep South (Short)—1937

This film is no longer available from any source. Produced by RKO Pictures and directed by Leslie Goodwins, it featured the acting talents of Willie Best, Daisy Bufford, and Clarence Muse, and the singing of the Hall Johnson Choir. I found no mention of this film, a short, in any listing except that of the Internet Movie Database. It was discovered quite accidentally while reading one of the thousands of letters in the Hall Johnson memorabilia. Apparently, a number of the singers were given bit parts. In the absence of a summary of the plot, the letter provides considerable insight into the film. Addressed to Hall Johnson, it was written by Paul Smellie, a former member of the Hall Johnson Choir living in New York City.

> Dear Dr. Johnson,
> On Sunday (yesterday) I saw *Deep South*. It is truly a "swell jog." The music was played up to good advantage. As I tried to analyze your choral arrangements and anticipated the entrance of the different voices, my mind ran back to the good old days at Coachman's Hall.—"Dat Suits Me," "Ain't Gwine Lay My 'Ligion Down,'" etc.
> Also interesting, was that I recognized quite a few of the players: Oliver Hartwell plastering the log cabin (hardest work I ever saw him do, smile). Winifred Gordon in the front pew in the church, Mr. Broadnax sawing the log (did he lose any weight?), Mrs. Ball [Olive] passing the good word, Anabelle Walker riding the gig with the little "chippy," Ernest Baskette building the roof of the cabin (he always contrives to be top-man), and Bessie Guy pulling the lazy man away from the festive board. There were others whose names I do not remember. Although I saw Jester Hairston in *Green Pastures*, I did not see him in *Deep South*. It was quite a treat seeing them all again. I wished it were possible to see you too.
> It seems to me that the George Randall Co. should advertise [the movie] better than they did. It was only by merest chance that I saw the picture. I just

met Gilbert Allen and he had not known anything about it. However, may I say that it was well received. Even before the fadeout was finished the audience broke into a vociferous applause.

Whenever I see the Hall Johnson Choir advertised, I shall continue to enter the theater to sing my bass line with the group, and to remember my run with the "Little Chillun."[3]

Jezebel—1938

Set in New Orleans, a decade before the Civil War, Jezebel was a vehicle for a virtuoso performance by the young Bette Davis, which won her a second Oscar in a three-year period. It was said to have been her studio's way of compensating her for giving the role of Scarlett O'Hara to Vivian Leigh in *Gone with the Wind*, which was filmed the following year. Julie (played by Davis) is a wealthy Southern belle who is engaged to a wealthy banker (Henry Fonda). Strong headed, impulsive, and selfish, Julie defies convention and forces Press (Fonda) to take her to the cotillion ball in a red, rather than white, ball gown. She and Press were scandalized and Press, disgusted at her continuous childish behavior, leaves her and goes to New York for a year. An epidemic of yellow fever rages in New Orleans, and Julie and her aunt leave town for their plantation north of the city. When the epidemic is at its height, Press returns to the plantation with his beautiful new wife. Julie is crushed and sets out to precipitate a duel between Press and another admirer, George Brent. The plan goes awry when Press is called to New Orleans, and his younger brother is challenged to a duel by Brent in which Brent is killed, but not before blaming his death on Miss Julie. When Julie learns that Press has come down with yellow fever in New Orleans, she goes to the city to nurse him back to health, risking her life in order to prove that she has become a worthy, mature woman who repents of all the evil she has done.

The Hall Johnson Choir is not credited in this film but plays a significant role. The choir is first heard off camera, when Miss Julie arrives at Halcyon, the "Big House," singing "Oh My Pretty Quadroon," under the action. The choir is heard again humming in the background when Press returns from New York. During this visit, the choir entertains, on camera, with the performance of "Ring-a-Round Miss Suzie," complete with group dancing. As the social evening reaches a dramatic climax with the two men, Press and brother Ted, agreeing to meet in a duel on the following morning, the choir underscores the callous and heartless nature of Julie by joining her in the singing of "Raise a Ruckus Tonight." At the very end of the movie, as Julie rides away with Press to the island for those infected with the fever, the high voices of the choir join the orchestra in the symphonic postlude Max Steiner has written for the final credits. The movie received two Academy Awards and three additional nominations.

My Old Kentucky Home—1938

An engaged couple of Kentucky blue bloods become estranged when Larry is accidentally blinded in the New York apartment of his protégée, a beautiful girl who loves him. The situation is aggravated by salacious press reports. When Larry recovers from the accident, he is advised that he will gradually become permanently blind. Larry decides it would be unfair for his fiancée, Lisbeth, to marry a man who would soon be blind, and he breaks off the engagement without explaining why. He returns from New York to Kentucky but still does not tell his former fiancée of the future that lies ahead for him. Larry's mother plans a centennial celebration, which is to be broadcast over the radio and at which she will make him the new president of their company. Gail, the other woman, confesses to Larry's ex-fiancée that Larry is going blind but was never involved romantically with her. Remarkably, a new medical break-through restores Larry's sight, and he is reunited with Lisbeth, his true love. Bernadene Hayes, Grant Richards, and Evelyn Venable star.

Not only is the Hall Johnson Choir credited in the film, but the name also appears in bolder fonts than any other members of the cast. The choir is used to sing the title song "My Old Kentucky Home," both at the beginning and the end of the movie.

The movie opens with the choir singing under the titles and appearing on screen, being conducted as a choir, in the very first scene. The conductor is not Hall Johnson but an actor, probably a member of the choir. The title song appears several times, like an idée fixe, both under the action, off camera, and on camera. They are always cast as plantation workers, never as slaves. They provide the musical entertainment for the centennial program, and as a plantation choir, they always appear in a singing formation and with a conductor. When the choir next appears on camera, it is rehearsing for the radio performance. The action stops as the choir sings the title song, which is to serve as a commercial for the company's products, "Old Kentucky Home Foods." As the action resumes, the choir begins to rehearse "My Darling Nelly Gray." When the action stops again, the choir performs the first chorus of "Old Black Joe," led by the marvelous bass Kenneth Spencer, who studied with my own teacher, Paola Novikova. There follows at another break in the action a chorus of "My Darling Nelly Gray" and one of "Massa's in de Col', Col' Ground." On the centennial broadcast, the choir sings the title song again and closes the movie with a reprise. This is a perfect example of the choir being integrated into the plot as it becomes a participant in the action, is discussed by other characters, and appears on camera most of the time.

Stanley and Livingstone—1939

A top reporter for the *New York Herald* (Henry Stanley) is sent to Africa by his editor to find the missing Scottish missionary, Dr. David Livingstone. After a year's journey, he locates Livingstone, who is happily attending to the health and spiritual needs of an African tribe. Stanley returns to London a changed man, but the Society of Geographers refuses to believe that Livingstone is alive and that he drew the maps of the region that Stanley brings back. During the hearings to determine the truth of Dr. Stanley's story, a telegram arrives from Zanzibar confirming that Livingstone has died and bearing a message for Stanley, asking him to return to Africa and continue his work. Stanley accepts the challenge. The strong cast is headed by Walter Brennan, Charles Coburn, Cedric Hardwicke, and Spencer Tracy.

The singers of the Hall Johnson Choir are used very discretely in this film in five scenes. When Stanley and his party pass white slave traders with a long column of slaves headed for the coast, the voices can be heard, in the background, singing an expressive and mournful wail on a monosyllable that is reminiscent of their role in *Slave Ship*. The choir next appears in the choir rehearsal scene when Dr. Livingstone leads a large group of natives in a rousing performance of "Onward Christian Soldiers." This assemblage, to have any dramatic verisimilitude, is not supposed to sound like a polished group, yet the identifiable element so characteristic of Hall Johnson's choral arrangements, the high obbligato, is sung by the soprano during the final chorus. This is the only time in the movie when the choir sings text. In the festive farewell sing as Stanley prepares to leave Africa for London, the male voices accompany the dancing of a multitude of natives with a strong modal melody. The movie ends as the men of the choir offer a full-throated "Onward Christian Soldiers," sung in a soaring unison. The choir is not credited in this film.

Way Down South—1939

Set in antebellum Louisiana, this delightful movie is the only film that unites the talents of three significant figures of the Harlem Renaissance: Langston Hughes, Clarence Muse, and Hall Johnson. Hughes and Muse wrote all of the original songs, and Hall Johnson did the choral arrangements and performed them with his choir.

In this film, a young lad inherits one of the wealthiest plantations in Louisiana upon the accidental death of his father. As the boy is not of age, the plantation is overseen by an evil executor who attempts to sell all of the slaves and convert the property into cash so that he can go to Paris with his mistress. The lad manages to outwit the executor, and a judge removes the evil man from his position the day before the sale is to take place. The slaves rejoice and return to the plantation where they enjoy security and relative freedom. Bobby Breen, Alan Mobray, Ralph Morgan, and Clarence Muse head the cast.

The members of the Hall Johnson Choir are cast as plantation slaves and are central to the plot and to the movie. They are on camera during almost every scene in which they sing. As the film credits roll, a vibrant rendition of "Peter Go Ring Dem Bells" is heard, and the opening scene shows the field hands picking cotton and singing. The singers next appear in the cane fields where they perform an elaborate production number, "Good Ground," which includes soloists, dancing, and rhythms reminiscent of the "Charleston." The flogging of one of the slaves inspires the singing of "Nobody Knows de Trouble I See."

In the dinner scene at Café Papa Doudons, the choir provides background for Bobby Breen when he sings "Louisiana" and "Some Folks Do" off camera. The most musically and dramatically effective scene is the worship scene, which takes place after the slaves learn that they are all to be sold. The choir gives superb performances of three spirituals: "I Couldn't Hear Nobody Pray," "Didn't My Lord Deliver Daniel," and "Sometimes I Feel Like a Motherless Child." Breen solos admirably in the last work. The choir concludes the movie with a rousing "Jubalee" when they learn that they will not be sold. The choir is credited in the opening titles. The movie received one Academy Award nomination.

Zenobia—1939

Perhaps the most significant thing about this film is the absence of Stan Laurel because of a contract dispute. Oliver Hardy is assisted by Billie Burke, Stepin Fetchit, Harry Langdon, and Hattie McDaniel, but they cannot make this inane story into a winner. Hardy, a country doctor, is called to treat an ailing carnival elephant. The elephant, Zenobia, becomes attached to the doctor and refuses to be separated from him. The elephant's owner sues for alienation of affection. The lawsuit plays right into the hands of the town's richest and snobbiest woman, who does not want her son to marry the doctor's daughter. All is resolved in the courtroom trial and Zenobia's infatuation with the doctor ends when she gives birth to a baby elephant to which she transfers her affection.

While the Hall Johnson Choir is credited in the titles of this film, it only appears in one scene. The choir provides entertainment at the engagement party given by the groom-to-be's mother. Neatly arrayed at the entrance of the palatial plantation manor entrance, the choir sings "In the Evening by the Moonlight" as the guests enter, and later, they back up the bride-to-be as she sings the same tune.

Swanee River—1939

Swanee River is the only Technicolor movie that Al Jolson made and features Don Ameche as Stephen Foster in a romanticized and sanitized biography of his life. Foster is in love with a wealthy Kentucky debutante and decides, against the advice of his and her parents, to choose music composition as a career. Inspired by the music of the slaves, he begins to write songs and eventually meets and teams up with E. P. Christy (Al Jolson) of the Christy Minstrels. When the Civil War breaks out, Foster is labeled a Confederate sympathizer because all of his songs extol the virtues of the South. He and his wife move to New York where his drinking leads to alcoholism and his ventures into classical composition lead to the decline of his career. When his wife leaves him, Foster's health rapidly declines and he becomes a virtual pauper. When Jane (his wife) learns of his poor health, she returns and inspires a final composition, "Swanee River," which the Christy Minstrels introduce to the world on the night of his death. Felix Bressart, Andrea Leeds, and George Reed share the lead roles in this touching musical.

The Hall Johnson Choir, which had performed so superbly in Jolson's earlier musical, *Wonder Bar*, does an equally outstanding job in this film. Fully credited in the titles of this film, the choir sings, under the opening titles, Foster's famous tune "Ring, Ring De Banjo." In the opening scene of the movie, Foster stands mesmerized on the banks of the river as the slaves unload cargo and sing Hall Johnson's arrangement of "Mule Song (Heah Come the Heavin' Line)." The most touching moment in the film is the grave scene in which the choir stands at "Uncle" Joe's graveside and sings "Old Black Joe." There is little doubt, based on the acoustical evidence, that the choir also joins the Christy Minstrels in "Swanee River," the finale of the movie. The movie received one Academy Award nomination.

St. Louis Blues—1939

This film is no longer available from any source. The participation of the Hall Johnson Choir is confirmed by newspaper reviews and by soundtrack listings that appear in the Internet Movie Database.

In Old Missouri—1940

This film is no longer available from any source. The participation of the Hall Johnson Choir is, however, confirmed in the listings of the All Movie Guide.

Carolina Moon—1940

This film is no longer available from any source. The participation of the Hall Johnson Choir is confirmed, however, by the existence of a Gene Autry CD, which credits the choir for its collaboration with Autry in the title song, "Carolina Moon."

Dumbo—1941

One of the most beloved of the Disney animated films, *Dumbo* is the story of a baby elephant with huge ears who suffers ridicule and ostracism by the other circus members. When his mother tries to come to his defense, she is chained and separated from him. His only friend is Timothy Mouse, who encourages him to celebrate his diversity. After indulging in a vat of booze, Dumbo gets drunk and wakes up with his friend in a tree. Here he encounters some jive-talking birds who convince him that the only way he could have gotten there was to have flown. Dumbo and Timothy Mouse fly back to the circus where he becomes the star attraction and is reunited with his loving mom.

The Hall Johnson Choir is not credited in the film titles but their contribution in the film as the jive-talking birds in the tree scene is documented by a number of sources including the soundtrack listing and in the *Dumbo* CD album credits. Members of the choir speak the dialogue and sing the delightfully jazzy tune "When I See an Elephant Fly." The film received two Academy Awards, two Academy Award nominations,[4] and one Cannes Festival Award.[5]

Lady for a Night—1941

John Wayne and Joan Blondell head the cast of this rather weak comedic drama. Jack (Wayne) and Jenny (Blondell) are in love and are co-owners of a gambling boat moored in the port of New Orleans. Jenny's aspirations to be a lady lead her to marry a broke blue blood who happily shares his good name in order to eradicate a gambling debt. Her membership in the family is opposed by her in-laws, who resort to attempted murder to be rid of her. When Jenny plans a lavish party, her wicked sistert-in-law tells all the invited guests not to come. When Jack learns of this, he applies pressure and blackmails the guests into attending. At the party, Jack is accidentally poisoned by drinking a beverage meant for Jenny, and Jenny is indicted and convicted of murdering him. As Jenny is about to be sentenced, the younger sister-in-law breaks down and confesses that her older sister poisoned her brother, just as she poisoned the younger sister-in-law's lover many years before.

The Hall Johnson Choir is credited in the opening titles of this film but makes only a single appearance in the middle of it. Before the big party, the choir stands in a free formation in front of the plantation manor and sings the spiritual "Ezekiel Saw de Wheel" in its entirety. The performance includes several solos and much improvised dancing. It is accompanied by a banjo.

The Vanishing Virginian—1941

The *Vanishing Virginian* is part of a movie genre that seems to have virtually disappeared. It is a tale of a Lynchburg district attorney (Frank Morgan) who has successfully run for election nine times but loses on the tenth attempt. Basically a character study, it paints the hero as a perfect father, perfect husband, perfect friend, and perfect public citizen, who is rewarded by having a perfect wife and family. As the movie progresses, we see glimpses of his talented daughter (Kathryn Grayson); his faithful servant, Josh; and his selfless wife (Spring Byington). The single exciting moment in the film comes when Josh, a leftover former slave, rescues the hero's young daughter from the charge of a raging bull. The final scene confirms the thesis of the Virginian as a perfect man when he displays perfect equanimity upon losing the election and opens his front door to receive the acclaim of a crowd of people who apparently had voted for him again.

The Hall Johnson Choir is not credited in this film but appears in a single scene, the funeral for Uncle Josh. In an arrangement credited to Jester Hairston, assistant conductor of the Hall Johnson Choir, the choir sings the spiritual "Steal Away to Jesus," with Kathryn Grayson as soloist. The singers are cast as the church choir.

Samson (Short)—1941

Written by Jester Hairston, *Samson* is a musical short based on the biblical story that provides a vehicle for the talents of the Hall Johnson Choir. The single extant copy was made available to Hall Johnson by the family of the late Jester Hairston. The movie begins with a church service in which the preacher tells the story of Samson to the congregation. In the ensuing action, Samson meets and talks with the Lord before going down into the valley. In the valley, he meets and marries Delilah, is deceived by her, and is delivered into the hands of the Philistines. The crowd in the temple taunts him and praises Dagon. God goes down into the valley to rescue Samson, who brings down the temple as his sight and strength are restored.

In the opening scene, the choir is cast as the congregation and sings the spirituals "Witness" and "Go Down in the Lonesome Valley" before the preacher delivers his sermon. As Samson walks toward the valley, the choir hums off camera "Nobody Knows de Trouble I See." In the third scene, Samson is captured by the Philistines (led by Jester Hairston) and delivered to the temple. Here the choir is cast as a Philistine mob and sings original music: "Dagon, Dagon"; "Deliver Our Enemies into Our Hands"; and "Come On Samson!" When God comes down to rescue Samson, the choir sings the spiritual "Didn't My Lord Deliver Daniel." The picture and sound in this short are excellent. An estimated one minute of the beginning of the film is missing as there are no credits, and the opening section of "Witness" is missing.

Meet John Doe—1941

The last of Frank Capra's "social statement" films, *Meet John Doe* begins with the firing of a young reporter (Barbara Stanwyck) by a major paper that is losing circulation. As her final act, the reporter writes a letter to the paper saying that she, John Doe, in protest against the country's poor treatment of little people, will commit suicide from the top of city hall on Christmas Eve. The letter creates a sensation and a long line of men professing to have written the letter show up at the paper on the next day. With the competing paper calling the letter a fraud, the reporter and publisher agree to create John Doe by hiring a transient who agrees to say that he wrote the letter in return for financial compensation. John Doe (Gary Cooper) is given a weekly radio broadcast on which he delivers inspirational messages written by Ms. Mitchell (the reporter). Millions embrace the message and start fan clubs all over the country. When the publisher tries to co-opt the movement and capture the 20 million club members' votes for him as a third party candidate for president, John Doe revolts but his credibility is destroyed before he can tell the truth at a convention of club members. Doe decides that he must commit suicide to reestablish his credibility, but on Christmas Eve, Ms. Mitchell, who has fallen in love with Doe, convinces him that they can rebuild the idea and the trust together. Edward Arnold and Walter Brennan perform admirably as the villain and the sidekick.

The Hall Johnson Choir is credited in the closing titles. All singing is done off camera. The soundtrack listing of the Internet Movie Database indicates that the following five works are sung by the choir:

1. "Battle Hymn of the Republic" (Steffe-Howe)
2. "Take Me Out to the Ball Game"

3. "Oh Susannah"
4. "Silent Night"
5. "Ode to Joy"

My examination of the film, however, found the following five songs:

1. "Battle Hymn of the Republic" (Steffe-Howe)
2. "Oh Susannah"
3. "America (My Country 'Tis of Thee)"
4. "Silent Night"
5. "Ode to Joy"

This appears to be careless scholarship on the part of Internet Movie Database, for even if "America" was cut from the film copy now available, that does not account for the addition of "Take Me Out to the Ball Game." The choir is first heard as the crowd in the John Doe Club convention scene as it sings "The Battle Hymn of the Republic," "Oh Susannah," and "America." In the Christmas tree scene that occurs on Christmas Eve, the women of the choir sing "Silent Night." In the final scene, the choir sings Beethoven's "Ode to Joy." The movie received one Academy Award nomination.

Road to Zanzibar—1941

The *Road to Zanzibar* is one of four movies designed to exploit the comedic talents of Bob Hope and the singing talents of Bing Crosby. Consequently, the plot is thin and at best zany, if not ridiculous. As the movie begins, Fearless (Bob Hope) and Chuck (Bing Crosby) are appearing with a South African Circus. When they accidentally start a fire that burns down the circus, they are forced to flee the police. To earn enough money to pay for their passage back to the United States, Fearless and Chuck perform in a variety of African venues. Just as they have saved the amount necessary, Chuck spends all their money on a fraudulent map of an African gold mine. Fearless sells the same map to two drunken men who pursue them and force them to take the first boat leaving the city. When they arrive at the next port, Fearless and Chuck are deceived by two American girls who take some of their money and get them to agree on a safari to Zanzibar to see a dying father. Enroute, they experience the beauties and dangers of Africa and learn that the ladies are taking them "for a ride." In the end, Chuck and Donna (Dorothy Lamour) fall in love and all the problems are resolved.

The Hall Johnson Choir is not credited in this film but sings very effectively as the group leaves on safari. In the version of the film currently available, the choir of male voices only, cast as bearers, sings a wonderful and extended work by Jimmy Van Heusen called "African Etude." The treatment is unique, for after the choir sings the opening chorus, it is joined on the second chorus by what is called a partner song of a contrasting style, "The Road to Zanzibar," sung by Chuck (Bing Crosby). Here the choir resorts to harmonies in the style of the old Stan Kenton group, the Four Freshmen, which are based on the interval on a fourth. The same music is sung briefly by the bearers alone, when the girls and the bearers leave Fearless and Chuck in the jungle alone.

Tales of Manhattan—1942

Tales of Manhattan is not one movie but six short films, each with a different cast and plot, strung together by the tale of a cursed tailcoat that belongs to the hero of each film. Perhaps the most significant feature of the movie is the participation of a parade of the greatest stars of the period, including Eddie Rochester Anderson, Charles Boyer, W. C. Fields, Henry Fonda, Rita Heyworth, Charles Laughton, Thomas Mitchell, Paul Robeson, Edward G. Robinson, Ginger Rogers, and Ethel Waters. Only the final tale involves the Hall Johnson Choir.

In that final story, a mobster robs a casino and heads for Mexico by plane with the loot. Bad weather causes the plane to crash, and as it is going down, the cursed tailcoat is throw out with all of the money in its lining. The coat lands in the yard of a poor black couple (Paul Robeson and Ethel Waters). They find the money and consider it the answer to their prayers. The wife insists that they give it to their minister and share it with the entire community. The congregation gathers and everyone gets money to buy what he or she has prayed for, save a sick old man who might have prayed for all the money. When consulted, he remembers that all he prayed for was a scarecrow. The people rejoice.

All of the singing of the choir is off camera and is designed to underscore the drama. Under the opening scenes, the choir hums the spiritual "I've Been 'Buked." After the couple meet with the preacher and decide to share all the money, the choir sings "Good News, the Chariot's Comin'" and "In Dat Great Gittin' Up Mornin'." After brother Christopher confirms that he did not pray for the money, the choir concludes the film with an original number, "Make Way for the Glorious Day," featuring the glorious bass voice of Paul Robeson.

Heart of the Golden West—1942

The plot of this Roy Rogers vehicle is very basic. A group of cattlemen are enraged when the single trucking company doubles the rates for transporting their stock to market. Roy Rogers solves the problem by arranging to transport the stock on a large riverboat. Faced with the loss of the contract, the owner of the trucking company decides to steal the cattle. Roy and the cattlemen finally catch up to the rustlers, subdue them, and recover their cattle. The movie ends with the boat load sailing away toward the market.

The Hall Johnson Choir is credited in the titling of this film as is Hall Johnson for his choral arrangements. The choir is first heard off camera in the Indian scene where it combines with the tom-toms and sings "Cowboys and Indians." The choir is not heard again until the latter portion of the film. In the river boat scene, the choir sings a medley of three songs. "Oh My Children" features a wonderful contralto soloist in an arrangement that is both interesting and intricate. The boat is moored and some singers appear to be workers on the boat and others on the shore. The second song, "Who's Gonna Help Me Sing," is led by Roy Rogers and backed up by the choir. The last song of the medley is the familiar spiritual "Every Time I Feel the Spirit." At the end of the film, choir and company sing "Here Comes the River Robin" as the boat disappears into the distance.

Syncopation—1942

An excellent film, Syncopation traces the development of jazz from Africa to America and gives short glimpses of the amalgamation of African rhythms with the melodic and harmonic structures typical of European music. Beginning with the slaves in Africa, it jumps to New Orleans where it tells the story of Basin Street, black musicians, and New Orleans jazz. Here Rex Tearbone (Todd Duncan), trumpeter, is the main black protagonist. It shows the migration of jazz from New Orleans to Chicago, where the main protagonist becomes Johnny (Jackie Cooper), a white trumpeter. The remainder of the film deals with Johnny's struggle to develop the Chicago jazz style and to develop an audience for it. Cameo appearances by jazz greats Charlie Barnet, Benny Goodman, Harry James, Gene Krupa, and Alvino Rey add much to the authenticity of this film.

The Hall Johnson Choir sings original background music—"Slave Market," written by Johnson—of which only a snippet remains in the film version currently available. The film goes almost immediately to the opening scene in twentieth-century New Orleans, possibly to make it more politically correct. Here the choir sings "Many Thousands Gone (No More Auction Blocks for Me)." The only other appearance of the choir is in the church scene where young Rex blows his trumpet, and the choir, as a part of the congregation, gives an exciting rendition of the spiritual "Blow Your Trumpet, Gabriel."

Syncopated Sermon (Short)—1942

A cartoon-length short produced by Vitaphone, a subsidiary of Warner Brothers, *Syncopated Sermon* opens with a token white singer performing "Sing, Brother Sing," with the Hall Johnson Choir, on camera, providing the background responses. After the opening number, the film is all black. It is set in a church where the singers are seated with the congregation, but all together. With Hall Johnson conducting from the pulpit, the choir sings four spirituals: "City Called Heaven"; "Cert'ny Lord"; "Steal Away"; and "In Dat Great Gittin' Up Mornin'." There is no plot; this is essentially a video concert by the choir. It has special historical significance as it is the only film in the Hall Johnson filmology that shows the great man conducting. There is considerable doubt as to whether or not the conducting movements are properly synchronized with the singing, but, unquestionably, one is able to observe his conducting style, which was unique indeed. The film titling reads, "The Hall Johnson Choir with Willard Robison."

Dixie—1943

A rather tepid musical, *Dixie* is primarily a vehicle designed to display the vocal talent of Bing Crosby and has little dramatic interest. The story of Dan Emmett traces his development as a song writer and as a minstrel. While Crosby sings many tunes, none but "Dixie" bears any stylistic or textual resemblance to minstrel songs. Minstrel costumes alone fail miserably to convey the vitality and spirit of this music that Al Jolson demonstrated so effectively in *Swanee*. Emmett leaves Kentucky to pursue his career in New Orleans. He meets "Bones" and they collaborate on the first Minstrel Show. He returns to Kentucky, marries his old girl friend, and heads for the big time in New York where he sells all of his songs except "Dixie." He is lured back to New Orleans where the new Minstrel Show is a big success.

The Hall Johnson Choir sings only once in this film. In the river boat scene when Emmett is leaving for New Orleans, the Hall Johnson Choir gives a performance of the spiritual "Swing Low, Sweet Chariot"—first with a superb tenor soloist and in the second chorus, with Dan Emmett (Bing Crosby)—in what is easily the most moving moment of the film. The harmonization is not typical Hall Johnson because of the low range of Bing Crosby's voice. The harmony frequently has to be written above the solo voice, but it is very beautiful and well performed by the men of the choir.

Other principles in the cast are Dorothy Lamour and Billy De Wolfe. The Hall Johnson Choir is not credited in the film titles or in the soundtrack listing, which even omits the name of the spiritual it sings.

Cabin in the Sky—1943
One of the best films ever made in the "all black" genre, Cabin in the Sky has an all-star cast, including Eddie Rochester Anderson, Louis Armstrong, Stepin Fechit, Lena Horne, Rex Ingram, Kenneth Spencer, and Ethel Waters. Based on a successful Broadway musical of the same name, it is basically a story of the eternal conflict between good and evil as played out by the characters in a love triangle, Petunia (the faithful wife), Joe (the errant husband), and Georgia Brown (the seductress). Despite his best efforts, Joe is lured to the Paradise Club where he is shot in a gambling dispute. While delirious, he dreams that he has died and that God gives him six months to live so that he can redeem himself and avoid hell. Lucifer Jr. and God's general are both struggling for his soul. With Lucifer's help, Joe wins the lottery, breaks up with his wife through a misunderstanding, and falls right into the arms of Georgia Brown. Once again he gets into a fight with the gambler who had shot him, and both he and his wife are killed. Petunia qualifies for admission to heaven, but Joe seems destined for hell until Petunia is able, through her prayers, to get God to relent. Joe comes out of his delirium a changed man.

The Hall Johnson Choir is credited in the film titles and does a great deal of singing, mostly off camera and as support for the soloists. The choir is heard off camera as the opening credits roll. The scene immediately cuts to a church where Joe is expected to join. The singers appear as part of the congregation and sing the spiritual "Little Black Sheep," and the invitational hymn "'Tis the Old Ship of Zion," led by the magnificent bass Kenneth Spencer as the preacher. When Ethel Waters (Petunia) sings the title song, "Cabin in the Sky," she is joined by the choir. In the dream sequence, Domino (the gambler) returns to the Paradise Club where he makes a grand entrance and sings, "Jes' Because My Hair Is Curly," in collaboration with the choir. The choir returns in the final scene, after Petunia and Joe have been allowed to enter heaven's gates, and sings "Hallelujah!" and then reprises the title song, "Cabin in the Sky," when Joe awakes. The movie received one Academy Award nomination.

Song of the South—1946
The release of Song of the South in 1946 created much controversy as it was opposed by the NAACP and the black press for its stereotypical portrayal of

Afro-Americans. Despite its sympathetic depiction of Uncle Remus as a wise and kind old former slave, the dialect of the title character and of Br'er Rabbit and his friends is no different than that of many racist cartoons and full-length movies that preceded it. So sustained and severe were the protests that the film was eventually withdrawn from exhibition and sale in the United States. I was fortunately able to acquire a copy that had been released in Israel and still had Hebrew subtitles.

Song of the South is the last movie the Hall Johnson Choir made. It is significant to note that when Hollywood could no longer make such movies—those that pictured blacks as lazy, stupid, servile, humorous, and talentless except in singing and tap dancing—without protest, it stopped including all but a token number of them in its productions. The plot line is rather simple. The wife of a couple contemplating divorce returns with her son to her mother's baronial Georgia plantation. Her son misses his father and is distraught until he meets Uncle Remus, who cultivates his friendship and relates to him by telling him "Br'er Rabbit" tales with a moral. The mother disapproves of their close relationship and forbids Uncle Remus to see the boy. Uncle Remus decides to leave the plantation and find work in Atlanta. Seeking to stop him, the boy runs through a cow pasture and is injured by a bull. His life is saved when Uncle Remus returns to his bedside. The parents reunite, and the father agrees to stay on the plantation for good.

The cast includes James Baskett as Uncle Remus, Bobby Driscoll as Johnny, and Hattie McDaniel as Aunt Tempy. Disney uses two choirs in the film—a studio choir and the Hall Johnson Choir. The Hall Johnson Choir sings in three scenes, all totally integrated with the unfolding of the plot. In the introduction to Uncle Remus, Johnny visits the quarters to seek out Uncle Remus. The choir sings "Dat What Uncle Remus Say." In a following scene, the workers are walking to the fields as they sing "Let the Rain Pour Down." Their most effective singing is done in the death scene after Johnny is injured by the bull. The choir stands in front of the manor and sings the mournful spiritual "All I Want." The choir is not credited in the titling of the film or in the main film database listing of the cast. It is, however, credited in the soundtrack listing.[6] The movie received one Academy Award and one Academy Award nomination.

Summary

In evaluating the cinematic achievements of Hall Johnson and his choir, one must bear in mind that all were accomplished between 1929 and 1946. The choir's entire movie career was completed one year before Jackie Robinson integrated professional sports; two years before Truman desegregated the

armed forces; eight years before *Brown vs. Board of Education*; nine years before the Montgomery bus boycott; seventeen years before Martin Luther
King spoke his eternal words, "I Have a Dream"; and eighteen years before
the Civil Rights Act of 1964. The choir appeared in every movie genre:
comedies, dramas, action films, musicals, race films, and cartoons. The choir
appeared with the greatest stars of the period and worked for the biggest studios and the best-known directors. In many cases, the Hall Johnson Choir
was credited, sometimes in titles larger than the rest of the cast. The choir
sang spirituals, work songs, popular songs, and composed movie music. In
many movies, the choir was on camera for at least a portion of the film, frequently in character as an element of the plot.

It has frequently been alleged that African Americans have no history of
achievement because so much of it has not been documented by white or
black historians. This contention has been permanently and completely in-
validated by the data unearthed by the current research.

Notes

1. John Motley, New York conductor, student, and close associate of Hall Johnson
for many years. Motley co-conducted many performances of Johnson's cantata, *Son of
Man*.

2. Parts to the "Dixiana" arrangement are preserved in the Hall Johnson Collection at Rowan University, Glassboro, NJ.

3. Paul Smellie, undated letter to Hall Johnson. Courtesy of the Hall Johnson
Collection (Rowan University, Glassboro, NJ). All rights reserved.

4. Internet All Music Guide, www.allmusic.com.

5. Internet Movie Database, www.imdb.com.

6. In a 1959 letter to Disney Studios, Hall Johnson steadfastly denies making this
film, but it is obvious from the evidence that unspecified singers from one of his several choirs did the film, probably directed by one of his many former assistant conductors, but unknown to him as he was in New York at the time. The related correspondence is included in the letters section of chapter 4, "Literary Expression."

CHAPTER THREE

~

The Music of Hall Johnson

Methodology Employed in Listing

Considerable thought has been given to the most effective manner in which to organize this material so that it clearly presents the following: arranged works, composed works, published works, works unpublished but registered with ASCAP (American Society of Composers, Authors, and Publishers), works existing only in manuscript, works in print currently, works out of print, and works available on rental from the Hall Johnson Collection. Additionally, a determination had to be made as to which works could be annotated in a comprehensive treatment like this.

Clearly, the annotation of individual compositions and arrangements would comprise a separate volume in itself. However, the importance of the extended works, which include many of the smaller compositions, requires full and extensive treatment—for their musical significance, their theatrical and historical significance, and the role they played in shaping Hall Johnson's life. It would seem that the basic data on the individual compositions can best be presented in a chart that includes the following fields: name; major work in which the composition or arrangement was included (whether play or movie); medium; publisher and key (for solo works); whether arranged or original work; and availability in the Hall Johnson Collection.

It must be kept in mind that some of these works did double or even triple duty. Doubtlessly, many of the twenty-five works that Hall Johnson selected for inclusion in the 1930 production of *The Green Pastures* had been arranged for the Hall Johnson Choir's concerts, which began in 1926. This same rule applies to the inclusion of spirituals in the many movies the choir performed in. Consequently, the number of spirituals arranged especially for motion pictures is small. Then, too, the choir sang many movie scores that included no spirituals at all.

The concert solo arrangements resulted primarily from requests by concert artists for the same. Similarly, the provision of orchestrations for some of the most popular spirituals also was a response to such requests, beginning with the commission of *Spiritual Moods*, in 1951 by the Jubilee Singers, and ending with the orchestration of "Ain't Got Time to Die," for the Philharmonic Hall appearance of Gwendolyn Sims in 1966. These orchestrations can be rented from the Hall Johnson Collection.

Following the chart of Hall Johnson's complete works is a section detailing Johnson's extended works. Each of the extended works is listed with pertinent information about opening/closing dates, total number of performances and locations, revivals, production details, and principal cast members. There follows a historical perspective, a summary of important reviews, a synopsis where appropriate, and a discussion of the work's formal structure.

The following information will be helpful in understanding and accurately interpreting the chart:

Column 1   The name of the individual work

Column 2   The major work for which it was written or in which it is included

Column 3   Medium: SATB = indicates mixed voices; TTBB = indicates male voices; Voice/Piano = indicates solo voice with piano accompaniment. Upper case letter = major key; lowercase letter = minor key

Column 4   Publishers: HB = Handy Bros.; MS = Manuscript; CF = Carl Fischer; EMI = EMI Music; CPPB = CPP Belwin Music; GS = G. Schirmer; RMC = Robbins Music; ASCAP = ASCAP registration; EBM = Marks Music. Where no entry appears in column 4, the work appears on concerts of the Hall Johnson Choir, was not published, and is not extant.

Column 5   Indicates whether the work is an arrangement or original

Column 6   The score is in the Hall Johnson Collection if an "X" appears in the column.

The Complete Works of Hall Johnson

Name	Major Work	Medium	Publisher Key	Arrangement or Original	Hall Johnson Collection
St. Louis Blues	Banjo on My Knee	SATB	HB	Arrangement	X
Cold Winter Blues	Fi-yer	SATB	MS	Original	X
Cotton Song	Fi-yer	SATB	MS	Original	X
Death Is a Liar	Fi-yer	SATB	MS	Original	
Don't Cry, War Will Soon Be Over	Fi-yer	SATB	MS	Original	
Elegy (A Negro Sorrow Song)	Fi-yer	SATB	MS	Original	X
Fi-yer	Fi-yer	Voice/Piano	CF-f	Original	X
Fi-yer	Fi-yer	Voice/Piano	MS-f	Original	X
Good Times	Fi-yer	SATB	MS	Original	X
Goopher Song	Fi-yer	TTBB	MS	Original	
He'll Bring It to Pass	Fi-yer	SATB	MS	Original	X
Howdy-Do Miss Sylvie	Fi-yer	TTBB	MS	Original	X
Howdy-Do Miss Sylvie	Fi-yer	SATB	MS	Original	
Hush-a-bye Tune	Fi-yer	Voice/Orch.	MS	Original	
In His Own Good Time	Fi-yer	SATB	MS	Original	
John Henry Green Hits Broadway	Fi-yer	SATB	MS	Original	
July Sun Chorus (picnic scene)	Fi-yer	SATB	MS	Original	
Lullaby	Fi-yer	SATB	MS	Original	
Mother to Son (No Crystal Stair)	Fi-yer	Voice/Piano-c	CF	Original	X
No Crystal Stair (Mother to Son)	Fi-yer	Voice/Orch.-c	MS	Original	X
Pastor's Aid Song	Fi-yer	SATB	MS	Original	
Pull Together Sisters	Fi-yer	Chorus	MS	Original	
Simmon Tree	Fi-yer	SATB	MS	Original	X
The Banjo Dance	Fi-yer	Solo/SATB	MS	Original	X
The Cotton Strut	Fi-yer	SATB	MS	Original	
What You Goin' ter Do	Fi-yer	Duet	MS	Original	
You Ain't Livin' Unless You're Lovin'	Fi-yer	Voice/Piano	MS	Original	X

(continued)

Name	Major Work	Medium	Publisher Key	Arrangement or Original	Hall Johnson Collection
Don' Cry, War Will Soon Be Over		SATB	MS	Original	
He'll Bring It to Pass	Green Pastures	Voice/Piano	ASCAP	Arrangement	X
Cert'ny Lord	Green Pastures	SATB	CF	Arrangement	X
City Called Heaven	Green Pastures	SATB	EMI (CPPB)	Arrangement	X
City Called Heaven	Green Pastures	Voice/Piano-f	Robbins	Arrangement	X
City Called Heaven	Green Pastures	Voice/Piano-g	MS	Arrangement	X
Death's Gonter Lay His Cold Icy Hands on Me	Green Pastures	SATB	CF	Arrangement	
De Blind Man Stood on de Road	Green Pastures	SATB	CF	Arrangement	
De Ole Ark's a-Moverin'	Green Pastures	SATB	CF	Arrangement	
Dere's No Hidin' Place	Green Pastures	SATB	CF	Arrangement	
Don't You Let Nobody Turn You	Green Pastures	SATB	CF	Arrangement	
Go Down Moses	Green Pastures	SATB	CF	Arrangement	X
Hail de King of Babylon!	Green Pastures	SATB	MS	Original	
Hallelujah!	Green Pastures	SATB	CF	Arrangement	
Hallelujah, King Jesus!	Green Pastures	SATB	CF	Original	X
I Can't Stay Away	Green Pastures	SATB	CF	Arrangement	
In Bright Mansions Above	Green Pastures	SATB	CF	Arrangement	
I Want to Be Ready	Green Pastures	SATB	CF	Arrangement	
Joshua Fit de Battle	Green Pastures	SATB	CF	Arrangement	
Joshua Fit de Battle	Green Pastures	SATB	EMI	Arrangement	
Joshua Fit de Battle	Green Pastures	SATB	MS	Arrangement	X
Joshua Fit de Battle	Green Pastures	TTBB	MS	Arrangement	
Lord, I Don't Feel Noways Tired	Green Pastures	SATB	CF	Arrangement	X
March On!	Green Pastures	SATB	CF	Arrangement	
My God Is So High	Green Pastures	SATB	CF	Arrangement	
My God Is So High	Green Pastures	Voice/Piano-Eb	MS	Arrangement	X
My God Is So Hgh	Green Pastures	Voice/Piano-Db	MS	Arrangement	X

My Lord's a Writin' All de Time	Green Pastures	SATB	CF	Arrangement	
My Soul Is a Witness	Green Pastures	SATB	CF	Arrangement	
Oh Mary, Don't You Weep	Green Pastures	SATB	CF	Arrangement	
Oh! Rise and Shine	Green Pastures	SATB	MS	Arrangement	X
Run, Sinner Run	Green Pastures	SATB	CF	Arrangement	
Some o' Dese Days	Green Pastures	SATB	CF	Arrangement	
When the Saints Come Marchin'	Green Pastures	SATB	CF	Arrangement	
You Better Min'	Green Pastures	SATB	CF	Arrangement	
Amazing Grace	Run, Little Chillun	SATB	MS	Arrangement	
Credo	Run, Little Chillun	SATB	MS	Original	X
Done Written Down My Name	Run, Little Chillun	SATB	GS	Arrangement	
Do You Love My Lord?	Run, Little Chillun	SATB	MS	Arrangement	
Great Gittin' Up Mornin'	Run, Little Chillun	SATB	MS	Arrangement	X
Hymn to the Rising Moon	Run, Little Chillun	SATB	MS	Original	X
I'll Never Turn Back No' More	Run, Little Chillun	SATB	EMI	Arrangement	X
Nobody Knows de Trouble	Run, Little Chillun	SATB	EMI	Arrangement	
Nobody Knows de Trouble	Run, Little Chillun	Voice/Piano-F	MS	Arrangement	X
Nobody Knows de Trouble	Run, Little Chillun	Voice/Piano-Ab	MS	Arrangement	X
O, Jesus, Come Dis-a-Way	Run, Little Chillun	SATB	MS	Arrangement	
O Lord Have Mercy on Me	Run, Little Chillun	SATB	GS	Arrangement	
O Lord Have Mercy on Me	Run, Little Chillun	Voice/Piano-d	MS	Arrangement	X
Oh My Lovin' Brother	Run, Little Chillun	SATB	MS	Arrangement	
Processional	Run, Little Chillun	SATB	MS	Original	X
Return, Oh Holy Dove	Run, Little Chillun	SATB	MS	Arrangement	
Run, Little Chillun	Run, Little Chillun	SATB	EMI	Original	X
So Glad ("Ser Glad")	Run, Little Chillun	SATB	MS	Arrangement	
Steal Away	Run, Little Chillun	SATB	CF	Arrangement	X
Steal Away	Run, Little Chillun	TTBB	CF	Arrangement	
Steal Away	Run, Little Chillun	Voice/Piano-G	CF	Arrangement	X
Steal Away	Run, Little Chillun	SATB	MS	Arrangement	X

(continued)

Name	Major Work	Medium	Publisher Key	Arrangement or Original	Hall Johnson Collection
Steal Away	Run, Little Chillun	Voice/Orch.-G	MS	Arrangement	X
Sulamai's Song	Run, Little Chillun	Solo	MS	Original	
Tongola Dance Music	Run, Little Chillun		MS	Original	
Tongola Scene	Run, Little Chillun	Vocal Score	MS	Original	X
Ain't Got Time to Die	Son of Man	SATB	GS	Original	X
Ain't Got Time to Die	Son of Man	Voice/Piano-Eb	GS	Original	X
Ain't Got Time to Die	Son of Man	Voice/Piano-F	GS	Original	
Ain't Got Time to Die	Son of Man	Voice/Piano-Db	MS	Original	X
Ain't Got Time to Die	Son of Man	Voice/Piano-F	MS	Original	X
Ain't Got Time to Die	Son of Man	Voice/Orch.-Db	MS	Original	X
Ain't Got Time to Die	Son of Man	Voice/Orch.-F	MS	Original	X
Ain't Got Time to Die	Son of Man	Voice/Piano-Eb	MS	Original	X
Christ Is Risen	Son of Man	SATB	MS	Original	X
Come On, Brothers and Sisters	Son of Man	SATB	MS	Original	X
Den We'll Break Bread Together	Son of Man	SATB	MS	Arrangement	X
Dey Didn't Know He Was de Son	Son of Man	SATB	MS	Original	X
Hallelujah, King Jesus!	Son of Man	SATB	CF	Original	X
He Is King of Kings	Son of Man	SATB	MS	Arrangement	X
I Feel Like My Time Ain't Long	Son of Man	SATB	MS	Arrangement	X
I Got to Lie Down	Son of Man	Voice/Piano-d	CF	Arrangement	X
I Got to Lie Down	Son of Man	Voice/Piano-e	MS	Arrangement	X
I Got to Lie Down	Son of Man	Voice/Piano-c	MS	Arrangement	X
I've Been 'Buked	Son of Man	SATB	GS	Arrangement	X
I've Been 'Buked	Son of Man	Voice/Piano-F	MS	Arrangement	X
I've Been 'Buked	Son of Man	Voice/Piano-Eb	MS	Arrangement	X
I Will Arise and Go to Jesus	Son of Man	SATB	MS	Arrangement	X
Judas Was a Weak Man	Son of Man	SATB	MS	Arrangement	X
Lament of His Followers	Son of Man	SATB	MS	Original	X

Look What Dey Doin' to Jesus	Son of Man	SATB	MS	Original	X
Lord of Love	Son of Man	SATB	MS	Original	X
Man of Sorrows	Son of Man	SATB	MS	Original	X
March Up the Hill	Son of Man	SATB	MS	Original	X
Mary Come a-Runnin'	Son of Man	SATB	MS	Arrangement	X
Oh de Angel Rolled de Stone	Son of Man	SATB	MS	Arrangement	X
Pilate! Pilate! Pilate!	Son of Man	SATB	MS	Original	X
Pilate! Pilate! Pilate!	Son of Man	SATB	GS	Original	
Po' Little Jesus, Cryin'	Son of Man	SATB	MS	Original	X
Ride On, King Jesus	Son of Man	Voice/Piano-Db	CF	Arrangement	X
Ride On, King Jesus	Son of Man	Voice/Piano-D	MS	Arrangement	X
Ride On, King Jesus	Son of Man	Voice/Piano-Db	MS	Arrangement	X
Ride On, King Jesus	Son of Man	SATB	MS	Arrangement	X
Ride On, King Jesus	Son of Man	Voice/Orch.-D	MS	Arrangement	X
Sabbath Has No End	Son of Man	SATB	MS	Arrangement	X
Take My Mother Home	Son of Man	SATB	CF	Original	X
Take My Mother Home	Son of Man	TTBB	CF	Original	
Take My Mother Home	Son of Man	Voice/Piano-G	MS	Original	X
Take My Mother Home	Son of Man	Voice/Piano-F	MS	Original	X
Take My Mother Home	Son of Man	Voice/Piano-Eb	CF	Arrangement	X
Terror! Darkness!	Son of Man	SATB	MS	Original	X
The Crucifixion	Son of Man	TTBB	MS	Arrangement	X
The Crucifixion	Son of Man	SATB	CF	Arrangement	X
The Crucifixion	Son of Man	Voice/Piano-g	MS	Arrangement	X
The Magdalen and the Master	Son of Man	S-T Duet/Piano	MS	Original	X
The March up the Hill	Son of Man	SATB	MS	Arrangement	X
They Led My Lord Away	Son of Man	SATB	MS	Arrangement	X
They Led My Lord Away	Son of Man	Voice/Piano-F	MS	Arrangement	X
They Led My Lord Away	Son of Man	Voice/Piano-G	MS	Arrangement	X
'Tis Midnight, and on Olive's	Son of Man	SATB	MS	Arrangement	X

(continued)

Name	Major Work	Medium	Publisher Key	Arrangement or Original	Hall Johnson Collection
Weepin' Mary	Son of Man	SSAA	MS	Arrangement	X
Were You There?	Son of Man	SATB	GS	Arrangement	X
When I Was Sinkin' Down	Son of Man	SATB	GS	Arrangement	X
Woe Is Me	Son of Man	Voice/Piano-d	MS	Original	X
You Won't Find a Man Like Jesus	Son of Man	SATB	MS	Arrangement	X
Here Come de Heavin Line	Swanee River	SATB	MS	Arrangement	
Ole Black Joe	Swanee River	TTBB	MS	Arrangement	
Couldn't Hear Nobody Pray	Way Down South	SATB	GS	Arrangement	X
Rain Down Fire	Way Down South	SATB	MS	Arrangement	
Send One Angel Down	Way Down South	SATB	MS	Arrangement	
Sometimes I Feel Like	Way Down South	SATB	MS	Arrangement	
Ain't Dat Good News		SATB	MS	Arrangement	
All Over Dis World		SATB	MS	Arrangement	
Amen		SATB	ASCAP	Arrangement	
Amor Ti Vieta (Fedora)		TTBB/Solo	MS	Arrangement	X
Angels Waitin' at de Door		SATB	MS	Arrangement	
Annabel Lee	(Janowsky-Johnson)	SATB	EM	Arrangement	X
Annabel Lee		SATB	MS	Arrangement	X
April Eve	(Lundquist-Johnson)	SATB	MS	Arrangement	X
Around about the Mountain		SATB	ASCAP	Arrangement	
At the Feet of Jesus (Melody by Toy Harper)		Voice/Piano-C	MS	Arrangement	X
At the Feet of Jesus (Melody by Toy Harper)		Voice/Piano-C	CF	Arrangement	X
Balm in Gilead		SATB	GS	Arrangement	
Before This Time Another Year		SATB	MS	Arrangement	
Belshazzar Had a Feas'		SATB	MS	Original	
Birthday Song		Voice/Piano-G	MS	Original	X

Birth of the Blues		SATB	MS	Arrangement	X
Blind Man Stood on de Road		SATB	CF	Arrangement	
By and By		SATB	MS	Arrangement	X
By Myself	(Individual parts)	SATB	MS	Arrangement	X
Camp Meetin' Friends	(Individual parts)	SATB	MS	Arrangement	X
Camp Meeting in the Promised		SATB	CF	Arrangement	
Camptown Races	(Individual parts)	SATB	MS	Arrangement	X
Carry Me Back to Old Virginia		SATB	MS	Arrangement	
Casey Jones	(Individual parts)	SATB	MS	Arrangement	X
Chain Gang		SATB	GS	Arrangement	
Chloe	(Individual parts)	SATB	MS	Arrangement	X
Come Here, Lord		SATB	MS	Arrangement	
Courtship		Voice/Piano-F	CF	Original	X
Courtship		Voice/Piano-F	MS	Original	X
Covah Her Up	(Individual parts)	SATB	MS	Arrangement	X
Crossing the Bar		Voice/Piano-D	MS	Original	X
Crossing the Bar		Voice/Piano-C	MS	Original	X
Crucible		Voice/Piano-d	MS	Original	X
Crucifixion		TTBB	CF	Arrangement	X
Darkies	(Individual parts)	SATB	MS	Arrangement	X
Dat Suits Me		SATB	MS	Arrangement	
Dat Suits Me		SATB	GS	Arrangement	
David		Voice/Piano	CF	Original	X
Dear Could You Know		Voice/Piano-Db	MS	Original	X
Dear Could You Know		Voice/Piano-Eb	MS	Original	X
De Blin' Man Stood on de Road		SATB	MS	Arrangement	
Dedication	(Franz-Johnson)	SSAA	MS	Arrangement	X
Dedication	(Franz-Johnson)	TTBB	MS	Arrangement	
Deep River		SATB	MS	Arrangement	
De Old Sheep Done Know		SATB	ASCAP	Arrangement	

(continued)

Name	Major Work	Medium	Publisher Key	Arrangement or Original	Hall Johnson Collection
Didn't My Lord Deliver Daniel		SATB	MS	Arrangement	
Did You Read Dat Letter		SATB	MS	Arrangement	
Dinah	(Akst-Johnson)	TTBB	MS	Arrangement	
Dinah	(Akst-Johnson)	Voice/Piano-G	MS	Arrangement	X
Dis Ole Hammer, Killed John Henry		SATB	MS	Arrangement	
Dis Ole Hammer, Killed John Henry		SATB	GS	Arrangement	
Dixie		SATB	MS	Arrangement	
Dixie-anna		SATB	MS	Arrangement	X
Done Written Down My Name	(Individual parts)	SATB	GS	Arrangement	
Don'tcher Let Nobody Turn You		SATB	CF	Arrangement	
Don't Stay Away		SATB	MS	Arrangement	
Do You Think I'll Make a Soldier?		SATB	MS	Arrangement	
Dry Bones in the Valley		SATB	MS	Arrangement	
Elijah Rock		SATB	GS	Arrangement	X
Everybody Loves My Baby		TTB	MS	Arrangement	
Every Time I Feel de Spirit		Voice/Piano-F	GS	Arrangement	
Every Time I Feel de Spirit		Voice/Piano-F	MS	Arrangement	X
Every Time I Feel de Spirit		Voice/Piano-Eb	MS	Arrangement	X
Every Time I Feel de Spirit		SATB	MS	Arrangement	
Ezekiel Saw de Wheel		TTBB	MS	Arrangement	
Fix Me Jesus		SATB	GS	Arrangement	X
Fix Me Jesus		Voice/Piano, Eb	GS	Arrangement	X
Foundling		Voice/Piano-Eb	MS	Original	X
Foundling		Voice/Piano-C	MS	Original	X
Foundling		Voice/Orch.-C	MS	Original	X
Free at Last		SATB	MS	Arrangement	
From a Foxhole		Voice/Piano-Db	MS	Original	X

Title		Voicing	Publisher	Type	
Gimme Yo' Han'		Voice/Piano-F	MS	Arrangement	X
Gimme Yo' Han'		SATB	MS	Arrangement	X
Give Me Jesus		Voice/Piano-Eb	CF	Arrangement	X
Give Me Jesus		Voice/Piano-Db	MS	Arrangement	X
Give Me Jesus		SATB	MS	Arrangement	X
Glory Hallelujah to the Newborn		Voice/Piano-D	MS	Arrangement	
Go Down Death		SATB	MS	Arrangement	
Goin to See My Sarah		TTBB	MS	Arrangement	
Goin' Where De Wind Don't Blow		SATB	MS	Arrangement	
Golden Slippers	(Individual parts)	TTBB	MS	Arrangement	X
Good News		SATB	EMI	Arrangement	
Good News		TTBB	MS	Arrangement	
Gospel Train		TTBB	GS	Arrangement	
Great Day		SATB	GS	Arrangement	
Great God A'mighty	(Individual parts)	SATB	MS	Arrangement	X
Gwinter Hol On to de En'		SATB	MS	Arrangement	
Hallelujah!	(Youmans-Johnson)	TTBB	MS	Arrangement	
Hear the Angels Singin'		SATB	MS	Arrangement	
Heaven Is a Beautiful Place		TTBB	MS	Arrangement	
Heaven Right Now		SATB	MS	Arrangement	X
Heaven Right Now		Voice/Piano-D	ASCAP	Arrangement	
Heaven Right Now		Voice/Piano-C	MS	Arrangement	X
Heaven Right Now		Voice/Piano-Eb	MS	Arrangement	X
Heb'n Bells Ringin'		SATB	MS	Arrangement	
He'll Bring It to Pass		Voice/Piano-Eb	ASCAP	Original	X
He'll Bring It to Pass		Voice/Piano-F	MS	Original	X
He'll Bring It to Pass		Voice/Piano-G	MS	Original	X
He'll Bring It to Pass		Voice/Piano-D	MS	Original	X

(continued)

Name	Major Work	Medium	Publisher Key	Arrangement or Original	Hall Johnson Collection
He Rose		SATB	MS	Arrangement	
He's Got the Whole World		Voice/Piano	ASCAP	Arrangement	
He's Listenin' All de Night Long		SATB	MS	Arrangement	
His Name So Sweet		Voice/Piano-F	MS	Arrangement	X
His Name So Sweet		Voice/Piano-Eb	MS	Arrangement	X
His Name So Sweet		SATB	MS	Arrangement	X
His Name So Sweet		Voice/Piano-G	CF	Arrangement	X
His Name So Sweet		Voice/Orch.-F	MS	Arrangement	X
His Name So Sweet		Voice/Orch.-G	MS	Arrangement	X
His Name So Sweet		SATB	CF	Arrangement	X
Hold-a My Han' Lord		Voice/Piano-Db	MS	Arrangement	X
Hold-a My Han' Lord		Voice/Piano-Eb	MS	Arrangement	X
Hol de Light		Voice/Piano	CF	Arrangement	X
Hol de Light		SATB	CF	Arrangement	X
Hol' de Win'		SATB	MS	Arrangement	X
Hold On		SATB	RMC/EMI	Arrangement	X
Hole in de Bucket		ASCAP		Arrangement	
Honor, Honor		Voice/Piano-Bb	MS	Arrangement	X
Honor, Honor		Voice/Piano-G	CF	Arrangement	X
Honor, Honor		SATB	CF	Arrangement	X
Honor, Honor		TTBB	CF	Arrangement	
Honor, Honor		SATB	CF	Arrangement	
Hope I Join de Ban'		SATB	MS	Arrangement	
Hosanna, I'm Happy and Free		SATB	MS	Arrangement	X
How I Got Over		SATB	MS	Arrangement	
How Long Train Bin Gone		SATB	MS	Arrangement	
How Many Members Gone		SATB	MS	Arrangement	X
I Am Climbin' Jacob's Ladder		SATB	MS	Arrangement	

Title		Arrangement	Publisher	Type	
I Been in de Storm So Long		Piano/Voice-d	ASCAP	Arrangement	X
I Been in de Storm So Long		Piano/Voice-e	MS	Arrangement	X
I Been in de Storm So Long		Piano/Voice-f	MS	Arrangement	X
I Been in de Storm So Long		Piano/Voice-g	MS	Arrangement	X
I Been in de Storm So Long		Voice/Orch.-d	MS	Arrangement	X
I Cannot Stay Here by Myself		SATB	CF	Arrangement	X
I Cannot Stay Here by Myself		Piano/Voice-C	MS	Arrangement	X
I Cannot Stay Here by Myself		Piano/Voice-F	MS	Arrangement	X
I Cannot Stay Here by Myself		Piano/Voice-Bb	MS	Arrangement	X
If I Have My Ticket Lord		SATB	HS	Arrangement	
I Got a Home in Dat Rock		SATB	MS	Arrangement	
I Got a Mule		TTBB	RMC/EMI	Arrangement	X
I Got Shoes		Voice/Piano-Ab	EMI	Arrangement	X
I Got Shoes		Voice/Piano-C	MS	Arrangement	X
I Got Shoes		Voice/Piano-Ab	MS	Arrangement	X
I Got Shoes		SATB	RMC/EMI	Arrangement	X
I Heard a Swallow Cry	(Jackson-Johnson)	Voice/Piano	MS	Arrangement	X
I Heard de Preachin' of de Elders		SATB	MS	Arrangement	
I Know the Lord		ASCAP		Arrangement	
I'll Be There in de Mornin'		SATB	MS	Arrangement	
I Love the Lord		ASCAP		Arrangement	
I'm Callin' Yes I'm Callin'		Voice/Piano-F	MS	Original	X
I'm Goin Down Dat Lonesome Road		Voice/Piano-Eb	MS	Arrangement	X
I'm Gonter Tell God All of My		Voice/Piano-f	CF	Arrangement	X
I'm Gonter Tell God All of My		Voice/Piano-g	MS	Arrangement	X
I'm Gonter Tell God All of My		Voice/Piano-f	MS	Arrangement	X
I'm Gonter Tell God All of My		Voice/Piano-d	MS	Arrangement	X
In Dat Great Gittin' Up Mornin'		SATB	MS	Arrangement	
In My Heart		SATB	MS	Arrangement	
It's All Over Me		SATB	MS	Arrangement	

(continued)

Name	Major Work	Medium	Publisher Key	Arrangement or Original	Hall Johnson Collection
I Want God's Heaven to Be Mine		SATB	MS	Arrangement	
I Want Jesus to Walk with Me		SATB	ASCAP	Arrangement	
I Want to Be Ready		SATB	CF	Arrangement	
I Want to Die Easy		SATB	MS	Arrangement	
I Went Down in de Valley to Pray		SATB	MS	Arrangement	
I Will Arise		SATB	MS	Arrangement	X
Jesus Is Risen from the Dead		SATB	MS	Arrangement	
Jesus, Lay Your Head in de Winder		Voice/Piano-c	EMI	Arrangement	X
Jesus, Lay Your Head in de Winder		Voice/Piano-c	MS	Arrangement	X
Jesus, Lay Your Head in de Winder		SATB	RMC/EMI	Arrangement	X
Jesus Rose, and Gone to Heaven on a Cloud		SATB	MS	Arrangement	
John, De Revelator		SATB	MS	Arrangement	
John Henry		Voice/Piano-Eb	CF	Arrangement	
John Henry		TTBB	MS	Arrangement	
Jubilee		SATB	MS	Arrangement	
Jus' Keep On Singin'		Voice/Piano-F	ASCAP	Original	X
Jus' Keep On Singin'		SATB	MS	Original	
Keep Inchin' Along		TTBB	GS	Arrangement	
Kentucky Babe	(Individual parts)	SATB	MS	Arrangement	X
King Jesus Is a Listening		SATB	MS	Arrangement	
Leanin' on Dat Lam		SATB	MS	Arrangement	
Leanin' on de Lord		SATB	MS	Arrangement	
Le's Have a Union		Voice/Piano-f	MS	Arrangement	X
Le's Have a Union		Voice/Piano-c	MS	Arrangement	X
Le's Have a Union		Voice/Piano-eb	MS	Arrangement	X
Le's Have a Union		Voice/Piano-eb	GS	Arrangement	X
Le's Have a Union		Voice/Piano-c	MS	Arrangement	X

Title		Voicing	Publisher	Type	
Le's Have a Union		Voice/Orch.	MS	Arrangement	X
Let De Heb'n Light Shine on Me		TTBB	GS	Arrangement	
Let Us Break Bread Together		SATB	ASCAP	Arrangement	
Let Your Light Shine Around de Worl'		SATB	MS	Arrangement	
Life		Voice/Piano-G	MS	Original	X
Lindy Lou	(Individual parts)	SATB	MS	Arrangement	X
Little Black Train		SATB	MS	Arrangement	
Little Bright Light		SATB	MS	Arrangement	
Little David Play on Your Harp		TTBB	ASCAP	Arrangement	
Little Voice		Voice/Piano-C	MS	Original	X
Lonesome Road		SATB	MS	Arrangement	X
Lonesome Valley		SATB	MS	Arrangement	
Long Live America	(H. Millard)	SATB	MS	Adaptation	X
Lord, Have Mercy		SATB	MS	Arrangement	
Lord I'm Noways Weary		SATB	CF	Arrangement	
Lord, I Want to Be a Christian		Voice/Piano-F	MS	Arrangement	X
Lord, I Want to Be a Christian		Voice/Piano-G	MS	Arrangement	X
Lord, I Want to Be a Christian		SATB	GS	Arrangement	X
Louisiana Belle	(Individual parts)	SATB	MS	Arrangement	X
Louisiana Hayride	(Individual parts)	SATB	MS	Arrangement	X
Love Is a Plague		Piano/Voice	MS-D	Arrangement	X
Man to Man	(Williams-Johnson)	Voice/Piano	MS	Original	X
March		String Orch.	MS	Original	X
Mary Had a Baby		SATB	GS	Arrangement	
Massa's in de Col', Col' Ground	(Individual parts)	SATB	MS	Arrangement	X
Me and My Pardner		SATB	MS	Arrangement	
Mighty Rugged Road		SATB	MS	Arrangement	
Mississippi	(Individual parts)	SATB	MS	Arrangement	X
Mos' Done Travelin'		SATB	MS	Arrangement	
Mother of Mine	(Burleigh-Johnson)	TTBB	MS	Arrangement	

(continued)

Name	Major Work	Medium	Publisher Key	Arrangement or Original	Hall Johnson Collection
Mother to Son		Voice/Piano-c	MS	Original	X
Mule on de Mount		SATB	MS	Arrangement	X
Mule Song		TTBB	MS	Original	X
Mwalimu Song	(Fowler-Johnson)	Unison	MS	Original	X
My Good Lord Done Been Here		Voice/Piano-C	CF	Arrangement	
My Good Lord Done Been Here		Voice/Piano.-Db	MS	Arrangement	X
My Good Lord Done Been Here		Voice/Piano-Ab	MS	Arrangement	X
My Good Lord Done Been Here		Voice/Piano-Ab	CF	Arrangement	
My Lord's a-Writin' All de Time	(Individual parts)	SATB	MS	Arrangement	X
My Lord What a Mornin'		SATB	MS	Arrangement	
My Way Is Cloudy		SATB	MS	Arrangement	
Nelly Gray	(Individual parts)	SATB	MS	Arrangement	X
Nobody Knows de Trouble		Voice/Piano-Ab	MS	Arrangement	X
Nobody Knows de Trouble		Voice/Piano-F	MS	Arrangement	X
Nobody Knows de Trouble		SATB	RMC/EMI	Arrangement	
Nobody Knows de Trouble		TTBB	MS	Arrangement	
Nobody Knows de Trouble I See Lord		SATB	MS	Arrangement	
None But the Righteous		SATB	MS	Arrangement	
Norfolk Suite II	(Full set of parts)	Orchestra	MS	Original	X
Norfolk Suite III	(Alone in the Night)	Violin/Piano	MS	Original	X
Oh Freedom		Voice/Piano-Bb	MS	Arrangement	X
Oh Freedom		SATB	GS	Arrangement	
Oh Glory		Voice/Piano-D	MS	Arrangement	X
Oh Glory		Voice/Piano-D	CF	Arrangement	X
Oh Glory		Voice/Orch.-D	MS	Arrangement	X
Oh Graveyard		SATB	MS	Arrangement	
Oh, Great Eternal Wisdom	(Lyrics)	SATB	MS	Original	X
Oh Heaven Is One Beautiful Place		Voice/Piano	ASCAP	Arrangement	
Oh Heaven Is One Beautiful Place		Voice/Piano-c	MS	Arrangement	X

Title	Note	Voicing	Publisher	Type	
Oh Heaven Is One Beautiful Place		Voice/Piano-d	MS	Arrangement	X
Oh Heaven Is One Beautiful Place		Voice/Piano-a	MS	Arrangement	X
Oh, Holy Lord		SATB	MS	Arrangement	
Oh Lord Have Mercy on Me		Voice/Piano-d	MS	Arrangement	X
Oh Lord Have Mercy on Me		SATB	GS	Arrangement	X
Oh Mary Don't You Weep		SATB	CF	Arrangement	
Oh Peter, Go Ring Dem Bells	(Individual parts)	SATB	MS	Arrangement	X
Oh, Rise an' Shine		SATB	MS	Arrangement	X
Ol' Black Joe		TTBB	MS	Arrangement	
Ol' Man River	(Kern-Johnson)	TTBB	MS	Arrangement	
On Ma Journey		SATB	ASCAP	Arrangement	
On the Dusty Road (Melody by Toy Harper)		Voice/Piano-C	CF	Arrangement	X
Over Yonder		SATB	MS	Arrangement	
Over Yonder		SATB	GS	Arrangement	
Passing By	(Purcell-Johnson)	TTBB	MS	Arrangement	
Plenty Good Room		SATB	MS	Arrangement	
Polonaise (Chopin in Harlem)		Piano	ASCAP	Original	
Po' Moner Got a Home at Last		Voice/Piano	MS	Arrangement	X
Po' Moner Got a Home at Last		Solo	GS	Arrangement	
Po' Moner Got a Home at Last		SATB	GS	Arrangement	X
Pray (Don't Ever Stop)		Voice/Piano-D	MS	Arrangement	X
Pray (Don't Never Stop)		Voice/Piano-C	MS	Arrangement	X
Prayer Is de Key		SATB	MS	Arrangement	X
Prayer Is de Key		SATB	GS	Arrangement	
Prayer Is de Key		Voice/Piano	GS	Arrangement	
Prayer of the Soul		Voice/Piano-Ab	MS	Arrangement	X
Prison Camp	(Hairston-Johnson)	TTBB	MS	Arrangement	
Quartet in G	(Andante Doloroso)	Vln, Vla, Cello	MS	Original	X
Rain Down Fire	(Individual parts)	SATB	MS	Arrangement	X

(continued)

Name	Major Work	Medium	Publisher Key	Arrangement or Original	Hall Johnson Collection
Religion Is a Fortune		SATB	GS	Arrangement	X
Ride On, Jesus		Voice/Piano-F	MS	Arrangement	X
Ride On, Jesus		SATB	MS	Arrangement	
Ride On, Jesus		SATB	GS	Arrangement	
Ride the Chariot		SATB	ASCAP	Arrangement	
Ring Dem Christmas Bells		SATB	MS	Arrangement	
Rise Up, Shepherd		Voice/Piano-F	MS	Arrangement	X
River Chant		SATB	CF	Arrangement	X
River in the Sky		Voice/Piano-Eb	MS	Arrangement	X
Road to Mandalay	(Speaks-Johnson)	TTBB	MS	Arrangement	X
Roll de Stone		SATB	MS	Arrangement	X
Roll Jerd'n, Roll		Voice/Piano-F	MS	Arrangement	X
Roll Jerd'n, Roll		Voice/Piano-Db	MS	Arrangement	X
Roll Jerd'n, Roll		Voice/Piano-Eb	MS	Arrangement	X
Roll Jerd'n, Roll		SATB	GS	Arrangement	
Roll Jerd'n, Roll		SATB	MS	Arrangement	X
Runnin' Wild	(Mack, J. Johnson-H. Johnson)	SATB	MS	Arrangement	X
Scandalize My Name		SATB	GS	Arrangement	X
Scottsboro	(Individual parts)	TTBB	MS	Arrangement	
Sen' One Angel Down		SATB	MS	Arrangement	X
Serenade for Violin and Piano		Violin/Piano	MS	Original	X
Shortnin' Bread		SATB	MS	Arrangement	
Singin' Roun' the World		Voice/Piano-D	MS	Original	X
Singin' Roun' the World		SATB	MS	Original	X
Sing Out America!		SATB	MS	Original	X
Sing Out America!		Piano	MS	Original	X
Sing You Sinners!	(Harling/Coslow-Johnson; parts)	SATB	MS	Arrangement	X

Title		Voicing	Publisher	Type	
Sinner Man, So Hard to Believe		SATB	GS	Arrangement	
Sinner Please Don't Let Dis Harves' Pass		SATB	MS	Arrangement	
Sleepy Time	(Individual parts)	SATB	MS	Arrangement	X
So Hard to Give up de Wor''		SATB	MS	Arrangement	
Somebody Knocking at Yo' Door		SATB	MS	Arrangement	
Some of These Days		SATB	CF	Arrangement	
Sometimes I Feel Like		SATB	ASCAP	Arrangement	X
Song of the Bayou	(Individual parts)	SATB	MS	Arrangement	X
Song of the Mother		Voice/Piano-Eb	MS	Original	X
Song of the Mother		SATB	MS	Original	X
Soon Ah Will Be Done		SATB	MS	Arrangement	
Soon One Mornin'		SATB	MS	Arrangement	
Spiritual Moods		TTBB/Orch.	MS	Original	X
Spiritual Moods No. 2		TTBB/Orch.	MS	Original	X
Standin in De Need of Prayer		SATB	GS	Arrangement	
Stan' Still Jordan		SATB	MS	Arrangement	
Star Spangled Banner	Song of a Nation	SATB	CF	Arrangement	X
Star Spangled Banner	Song of a Nation	SATB	MS	Arrangement	X
Stay in de Field		SATB	MS	Arrangement	
Stay on the Train	(Individual parts)	SATB	MS	Arrangement	X
Stillness		Voice/Piano	MS-B	Original	X
St. James Infirmary Blues		SATB	MS	Arrangement	
Storm	(Individual parts)	SATB	MS	Arrangement	X
Study War No Mo'		SATB	MS	Arrangement	
Sunshine in a My Soul		SATB	MS	Arrangement	
Swanee River		SATB	MS	Arrangement	
Swing Dat Hammer		Voice/Piano-g	GS	Arrangement	X
Swing Dat Hammer		TTBB	GS	Arrangement	X
Swing Low, Sweet Chariot		SATB	MS	Arrangement	X

(continued)

Title		Voicing		Arrangement	
We'll Anchor By and By		SATB	MS	Arrangement	
We Shall Gain the Victory		SATB	ASCAP	Arrangement	
What Kinder Shoes		SATB	MS	Arrangement	
What Kinder Shoes		SATB	CF	Arrangement	X
When de Train Comes Along		SATB	MS	Arrangement	
When I Lay My Burden Down		SATB	GS	Arrangement	
When I'm Gone		SATB	MS	Arrangement	
Where Shall I Be When the First Trumpet Sounds?		SATB	MS	Arrangement	
Who Built de Ark		SATB	CF	Arrangement	
Who Built de Ark		TTBB	MS	Arrangement	
Witness		Voice/Piano-f#	CF	Arrangement	X
Witness		Voice/Piano-d	CF	Arrangement	X
Witness		TTBB	MS	Arrangement	
Won't Stop Prayin'		SATB	MS	Arrangement	
Workin' on de Buildin'		SATB	MS	Arrangement	
You Better Min'		SATB	CF	Arrangement	
You Can't Stan' There	(Individual parts)	SATB	MS	Arrangement	X
You Go, I'll Go with You		SATB	MS	Arrangement	
You Gonter Reap What You Sow		SATB	MS	Arrangement	
You Got to Die		SATB	MS	Arrangement	
You Hear the Lambs A-Cryin'		SATB	CF	Arrangement	
You Hear the Lambs A-Cryin'		SATB	MS	Arrangement	
You May Bury Me in de East		SATB	MS	Arrangement	
You've Got to Go		SATB	MS	Arrangement	

Extended Works

I. *The Green Pastures*—A Fable

Original Production—New York, New York
Mansfield Theater
Opening	February 26, 1930
Closing	August 30, 1931
Duration of run	Seventy-nine weeks
Total performances	640
Writer	Marc Connelly
Based on	*Southern Sketches*, "Old Man Adam and His Chillun," by Roark Bradford
Producer	Laurence Rivers, Inc.
Director	Marc Connelly
Choral director	Hall Johnson

Opening night cast: Reginald Blythwood, Joe Byrd, Alicia Escamillia, Anne May Fritz, Richard B. Harrison, Wesley Hill, Charles H. Moore, McKinley Reaves, Jazzlips Richardson Jr., J. A. Shipp, Frances Smith, Edna Thrower, Homer Tutt, Howard Washington, the Hall Johnson Negro Choir

Road Tour—Chicago to California
Starting	September 1931
Ending	July 1932
Duration of tour	Forty-seven weeks

Road Tour 2—Boston, the East, and the Midwest
Starting	September 1932
Ending	May 1933
Duration of tour	Thirty-four weeks

Road Tour 3—Roanoke, Virginia, and the South
Starting	September 1933
Ending	February 1934
Duration of tour	Twenty-four weeks

Revival—New York, New York
44th Street Theater
Opening	February 26, 1935
Closing	Date unknown

Total performances   Seventy-three
Producer   Laurence Rivers
Choral director   Hall Johnson

Opening night cast: Laura Anderson, Franklin Brown, Allen Charles, Annie
Mae Fritz, Richard B. Harrison, Randall Homer, Roy McKinley, Charles H.
Moore, Willie Morton, Oscar Polk, Billie Richards, Nonie Simmons, Dinks
Thomas, Irene Watts, Edward Yancey, the Hall Johnson Choir

Revival—Boston, Massachusetts
Colonial Theater
Opening   February 12, 1951
Closing   February 26, 1951

Revival—Philadelphia, Pennsylvania
Forrest Theatre
Opening   February 26, 1951
Closing   March 13, 1951

Revival—New York, New York
Broadway Theater
Opening   March 15, 1951
Closing   April 21, 1951
Total perfomances   Forty-four
Producer   Wigreen Company in association
                                            with Harry Fromkes
Director   Marc Connelly
Choral director   Hall Johnson
Assistant choral director   Louvenia White (Pointer)

Opening night cast: Alice Ajaye, Roger Alford, Alonzo Bosan, Miriam Burton,
Vinnie Burrows, Calvin Dash, Ossie Davis, Avon Long, William Marshall,
Robert McFerrin, Louise Parker, Louvenia White, the Hall Johnson Choir

Road Tour—Plattsburgh, New York
Hartman Theater
Opening   February 22, 1932
Closing   February 28, 1932
Producer   Laurence Rivers
Director   Marc Connelly

Choral director   Hall Johnson
Assistant choral director   Ulysses Chambre
"The Lawd"   Richard B. Harrison

Road Tour—Los Angeles, California
Biltmore Theater
Opening   June 20, 1932
Closing   Date unknown
Producer   Laurence Rivers
Director   Marc Connelly
Choral director   Hall Johnson
Assistant choral director   Ulysses Chambre
"The Lawd"   Richard B. Harrison

The Movie (1936)—Hollywood, California
Directors   Marc Connelly, William Keighley
Writers   Roark Bradford, Marc Connelly, Sheridan Gibnry
Studio   Warner Brothers
Producers   Henry Blanke, Jack L. Warner
Conductor   Hall Johnson
Choral arranger   Hall Johnson
Orchestrater   Hugo Friedhofer
Original music   Erich Korngold
Cinematographer   Hal Mohr
Art directors   Stanley Fleisher, Allen Saalberg
Costume designer   Milo Anderson

Principal cast: Eddie (Rochester) Anderson, Myrtle Anderson, Abraham Greaves, James Fuller, Edna Mae Harris, Rex Ingram, Oscar Polk, George Reed, Al Stokes, Frank Wilson

A Historical Perspective
It is ironic, though characteristic of the "American dilemma," that three of the four major theatrical creations of the 1930s about black Americans and black art, life, and culture should be written by white men. One certainly cannot evaluate these works without being fully cognizant of the social and racial climate in the United States at this time. "This period has been called the 'nadir' of black history because so many gains earned after the Civil War

seemed lost by the time of World War I, and because racial violence and lynching reached an all time high."[1] This milieu gave birth to *The Green Pastures* (1930); *The Emperor Jones* (1933); *Run, Little Chillun* (1933); and *Porgy and Bess* (1935). As each of these works portrays the Negro in stereotypical terms, they have provoked controversy among critics and, especially, among black Americans. It is this very "political incorrectness" that endeared these works to theater goers, the majority of which were certainly white in the 1930s and even today. Yet, in every instance, each work has many redeeming features—a moving musical score; a noble hero or heroine; or a people yearning for freedom, for truth, and for self-worth. And despite the fact that whites have exploited "blackness" in minstrelsy, comedy, jazz, cartoons, and serious theater, hundreds and even thousands of Negroes have found theatrical, musical, and operatic employment that provides extraordinary opportunities for development and expression of their performing and creative talents. Without the musicals mentioned above and similar works, the world would never have enjoyed the talents of Ann Brown, Todd Duncan, Leontyne Price, Paul Robeson, William Warfield, Camilla Williams, Lawrence Winters, and many other great artists.

Marc Connelly's play, *The Green Pastures*, was based on a 1928 book of stories—*Ol' Adam an' His Chillun*—by Roark Bradford, which told selected biblical tales from the first five books of the Bible in the characteristic language and concepts of simple, poor Southern black folks. Despite the deprivations of poverty and segregation, these folk seem to be buoyed and sustained by their religious faith and the promise of a future reward in heaven. Just as Gershwin visited Charleston prior to writing *Porgy and Bess*, Connelly (a white man) traveled to New Orleans to confirm both his concept of his characters and the dialect they were to speak. A part of Connelly's concept of the play was that the dramatic scenes would be underscored and united by a choral group singing spirituals, much in the manner of the chorus in Greek drama. The confluence of this ideal and the Hall Johnson Negro Choir, only recently formed at the time, was to mark a kairos in American culture: a unique theatrical event; a new theatrical form, as only a cappella music was used; a perfect vehicle to introduce and popularize both the spiritual and the Hall Johnson Negro Choir in America and the world.

Even though the cast of *The Green Pastures* was all black, the racism of the period reared its ugly head when financial backers learned that "De Lawd" and all his angels were to be portrayed as black. The show eventually found an angel in the person of Rowland Stebbins, a Wall Street broker. Auditions for the many parts were conducted in Harlem, and Hall Johnson was engaged to select and arrange the spirituals and to conduct his famous choir in the show. Only at the last minute did the casting director locate Richard B. Harrison, who was then teaching drama at A&T College in Greensboro, North Carolina, and living in New York during the winter. It was Harrison's first professional production, but with his training and full head of silver gray hair, he was auditioned and hired for the main role: "De Lawd." After some convincing, Harrison remained to play this role for 1,657 times until he was called by death.

The play won a Pulitzer Prize in 1930, had a national tour, and enjoyed two New York revivals. It was made into a movie in 1936, featuring the Hall Johnson Choir, and was so popular that when it opened at the Radio City Music Hall, it was said to have sold six thousand tickets every hour. For his arrangements and original music and the magnificent singing of the choir, Hall Johnson received the Harmon Award but was totally ignored by the drama critics of the New York press, who credited the writer, the stage director, the producer, and the entire cast, but omitted any mention of Hall Johnson, who was the music director, composer, and arranger. Fortunately, this apparent bias was not demonstrated by the press in any other geographic sections of the United States, and both Johnson and the choir received lavish praise from many critics as the additional reviews included will show.

Reviews

For Hall Johnson, an artistic figure who has gone unheralded by history, it is important to include evidence of the kind and extent of coverage he received while he was professionally active. While copyright law prevents the exact quotation of the available reviews without payment of a prohibitive fee, the relevant details have been extracted and briefly summarized here in my own words. All reviews have been preserved, in their entirety, in the Hall Johnson Collection at Rowan University.

New York Times—*February 27, 1930*[2]

Brooks Atkinson, esteemed critic of the *New York Times*, was lavish in his praise of *The Green Pastures*, describing it as a drama of extraordinary beauty, which excelled in every aspect, whether as a comedy, as fantasy, as folklore, or as a religious play. He praised the play for its emotional depth and the all-Negro cast for a performance of the highest order. Despite the fact that the play was the first Broadway production with music ever to use only an a cappella choir, rather than an orchestra, Atkinson's only reference to the choir and the twenty-five Hall Johnson arrangements it sang was to indicate that the spirituals projected the mood from one scene to the next.

New York Herald Tribune—*February 27, 1930*[3]
The *Herald Tribune*'s critic, Arthur Ruhl, shared Atkinson's enthusiasm for the play and its actors, but took notice of the importance of the spirituals and the singing of the Hall Johnson Choir for bridging the emotional gaps and providing the needed continuity between the thirty scenes. He concluded that the singing of the choir was nearly as important to the overall impressiveness of the work as the performance of any individual actor.

New York Journal—*February 27, 1930*[4]
Writing in the *New York Journal*, John Anderson thought the play provided grand entertainment, but that the playwright fell short and became repetitive toward the end. He praised the Hall Johnson Negro Choir as being both superlative and authentic in its singing of spirituals. He reiterated his praise for the choir at the end of his review by referring to the beauty and effectiveness of the singing. The road tour of *The Green Pastures* took the Hall Johnson Negro Choir to major cities from the East Coast to the West Coast, with performances in Cincinnati, Ohio; Des Moines, Iowa; Los Angeles, California; and Spokane, Washington. Despite the incredible demand of theater audiences around the country for *The Green Pastures*, many cities had to wait two years to see it, as it was only booked in fifteen cities on the original road tour.

Cincinnati Enquirer—*February 7, 1932–February 14, 1932*
The opening in Cincinnati, Ohio, was heralded in a lengthy article by *Cincinnati Enquirer* critic George A. Leighton, in which he discussed the author, the development of the play, the plot, the starring actor, and Hall Johnson, as writer and arranger of the music and conductor of the choir.[5] When the one-week run of the show was extended for a second week, Leighton used the opportunity to write a special article on Hall Johnson and the music of *The Green Pastures*. Speaking of the mingling of the theatrical arts and the a cappella singing of spirituals, Leighton called the show unforgettable and defined the show as a "dramatization of spirituals." He also noted the contribution of Johnson and Stebbins (the producer) for their efforts to introduce the spiritual as an important element in American culture, and averred that Johnson had, through his work in *The Green Pastures*, become a force in contemporary artistic life.[6]

Des Moines Iowa Register—*April 2, 1932*[7]
The significance of the spirituals and the singing of the Hall Johnson Negro Choir received increased attention as the production moved farther west. In Iowa, Clifford Bloom, critic for the *Des Moines Iowa Register*, opined that the

singing of the "Heavenly Choir" was adequate reason to go to heaven. With unusual insight, Bloom perceived that the spirituals, though ostensibly incidental music, were in fact as vitally important to the play as the spoken lines, representing a Negro theology—the consolation and refuge of a people. With uncanny clarity, he expressed Johnson's great aim and achievement thusly: "We heard these spirituals sung as they were intended to be sung . . . but it is doubtful if any of these singing prophets [Roland Hayes, Paul Robeson] have given more significance to them than this kind of group upon which tradition really rests. They sang with a rhythm, simplicity, and plaintiveness of the sorrowful and pious African groping toward the white man's God."

Los Angeles Times—*June 26, 1932*[8]

Isabel Morse Jones, critic for the *Los Angeles Times*, focused almost entirely on the music in her review of *The Green Pastures*, which she headlined, "Green Pastures, Musical Masterpiece of Scoring." She spoke of the power of the spirituals to convey the deepest emotions of man, of the record of faith and atonement they provide, of Johnson's skillful arrangements and the highly trained choir. The play was likened to a "Native Opera," effecting a smooth transition between the dialogue and the chorus. She lauded Johnson's fine professional education and his achievement of a "masterpiece in scoring."

The cross-country road tour of *The Green Pastures* ended in Spokane, Washington, where the critical acclaim for the play was no less enthusiastic than at the previous fourteen venues. The *Review* has graciously consented to the reprint of the entire review.

Spokesman-Review—*July 10, 1932*[9]

Green Pastures Proves Delight

Large Audience Enjoys Performance of Prize Play That Won New York

**Story Is Beautiful Play Woven about Southern Negro;
Also Offers Fine Spirituals**

The outstanding dramatic novelty of a couple of decades, so far as Spokane is concerned, is "The Green Pastures" which held a large audience spellbound at the Post Street Theater last night. The same people and the same production that thrilled New York and Chicago for months and brought to the play a recognition seldom given offerings of the commercial theater are being offered in Spokane. It is impossible in cold type to give any comprehensive idea of what the play has to offer. Were it possible to do this unusual entertainment full justice in a newspaper article, there would not be an auditorium in Spokane large enough to hold the crowds that would clamor to see it at the matinee and night performances today, closing the engagement.

Play Is Beautiful

Roark Bradford inspired the play with his short story studies of the southern Negro in *Ol' Man Adam and His Chillun*. The genius of Marc Connelly made a dignified and reverent play out of it, and the art of Robert Edmond Jones made it a series of beautiful stage pictures. Even that is not the complete story. Fate played right into their hands when it made available that great Negro actor, Richard B. Harrison, for the role of "The Lawd." Mr. Harrison, last night, literally swept the crowd with him in his eloquent, forceful treatment of what is probably the most difficult role ever written. He is, in appearance, a patriarchal Negro preacher, portraying the Old Testament Jehovah, who could be fatherly and benign one moment, and strike the elder sons down in a second, in his indignation and wrath. It is a portrayal not soon to be forgotten. Mr. Harrison is about 75 percent of the acting strength of *The Green Pastures*.

Hall Johnson has made a mighty contribution with his "heavenly choir," heard in something like 27 spirituals, some of them written by him for this production. They appear on stage in some scenes, but most of their singing is offered incidentally from a leaf covered bower that fills the orchestra pit.

Such Harmony Is Seldom Heard

Spokane has seldom heard such precision, such harmony, such volume, and such melody. At last, the real Negro voices are heard in their own real music. Perfectly trained, they are manipulated like a vast pipe organ in the hands of a virtuoso. Their smashing crescendos make the blood tingle, while their softer harmonies fade off into the distance with an effect that is remarkable. Some of their numbers are familiar, but most are new to Spokane.

The Green Pastures has some notable Negro players in addition to Mr. Harrison. In the cast of nearly 100, it is possible to mention only a few. Samuel Davis as Gabriel adds a comedy touch that is refreshing. Tutt Whitney makes a cigar-smoking Noah out of a discouraged Negro person, and Alonzo Fenderson does some fine acting as Moses. Daniel L. Haynes, a heroic type with real acting ability, scores doubly, first as Adam, and again as Hezdrel, the leader of the soldiers. There is a rare pictorial quality about his work.

The 1951 New York revival of *The Green Pastures* was preceded by a two-week run in Boston and a two-week run in Philadelphia. The Boston reviews that follow, most in their entirety, give some indication of how the play had worn during the twenty-year period since the original Broadway production. One can also measure the extent sociological changes in race relations had affected audience and critical response. Finally, in stark contrast to programs and reviews of the 1930 New York opening, the important contributions of Hall Johnson and the Hall Johnson Negro Choir are now acknowledged, again, save for the New York performances.

Christian Science Monitor—*February 13, 1951*[10]

Through the generosity of the *Monitor*, we are able to reprint the entire review, in order to better convey the spirit and milieu of the period.

The Green Pastures Returns

Fable by Marc Connelly in Revival at Colonial

At the Colonial—Revival of [the] play by Marc Connelly, presented by the Wingreen Company in association with Harry Fromkes, directed by Mr. Connelly, production designed by Robert Edmond Jones, musical direction by Hall Johnson. . . .

Marc Connelly's *The Green Pastures* was revived last evening, at the Colonial Theater. Any person who went there with the notion of drawing comparisons between this new production and the original was likely to have abandoned the inclination before the curtain had been up more than 15 minutes. No precious time was to be wasted over futile comparisons. For this presentation of certain Old Testament characters in terms of Louisiana local color is as astonishingly beautiful, as deeply moving, as before. One should accept it as a modern miracle play and then enter into its wonder, sway sympathetically to its rhythms, in a mood of suitable gratitude. . . . To savor this play, one must first enter unresistingly into the minds and hearts of those Negroes of the Deep South who, as Mr. Connelly has explained, "accepted the Bible in terms of their own lives." Real reverence is manifest however whimsical and childish their concepts may appear to the more sophisticated members of the audience. When the curtain first rises upon the vivid scene of the fish fry, titters may be detected in the theater, but they soon subside. It would seem to this critic that the humorous side of the play is now less conspicuous than in the former presentation. Gabriel, as an example, is less comic in his byplay with the trumpet. Noah, too, while quaint, twisted little figure of a country preacher, brings fewer laughs and more respectful response, all of which means that the table has, at least in a measure, given way to the miracle play. The time, our time, Mr. Connelly feels, is ripe for this play to recur with its forceful challenge to men to reform their mistaken ways. If ever there was a play more religiously effective than many sermons, here it definitely is. Anything more poignantly lovely than the scene which shows the children of Israel, it would be difficult to discover in the theater. . . . The Green Pastures Choir, under the direction of Hall Johnson, supports and modulates the whole play by its singing of spirituals. It emphasizes and signals the religious import of the scenes and actions. . . . "Green Pastures" has returned—and that is abundantly well. M.V.

Boston Traveler—*February 13, 1951*[11]

Green Pastures Revived in Inspired Production

"Divine Comedy" is a perfect description of *The Green Pastures*, the revival of Marc Connelly's fable which had its first performance last night at the Colonial, for this 21-year old play is filled with delightful comedy and a stirring spiritual message which carries even more urgency today than in 1930. . . . It is a play of tears and laughter and tremendous reverence. It is written with great affection for an illiterate people in an earlier south to whom religion was as much a part of their daily life as food, and who translated it into their own terms.

The overwhelming spiritual beauty is further enhanced by the spirituals so exquisitely sung by the Hall Johnson Choir. . . . *The Green Pastures* offers an evening of extraordinary entertainment, it brings an inspiring light of hope to a troubled world.

Boston Herald—*February 13, 1951*[12]

The Green Pastures

by Elinor Hughes

To all who made possible the arrival of Marc Connelly's *The Green Pastures* at the Colonial last evening, everyone there present and those who will see this beautiful play during its fortnight in Boston owe a tremendous vote of gratitude. . . . *The Green Pastures* remains substantially the same as it was two decades ago, but Mr. Connelly has done some rewriting to make clearer what he believes is the play's message for people today: the overwhelming need of mankind for a personal God. At one point—and this is what has always been the play's greatest virtue for me—is there the slightest sense of condescension toward the devout faith of a people whose simplicity caused them to translate the Bible story into terms of their own lives. . . . Meanwhile, there is time only to praise the excellent all around performance by the Hall Johnson Choir.

Boston Daily Globe—*February 13, 1951*[13]

Durgin, of the *Boston Daily Globe*, makes the critical verdict in Boston unanimous, calling the production as delightful and touching as ever. He praises the performance of William Marshall as "De Lawd," "and the soaring music of the Hall Johnson Choir . . . which supplied not only admirable singing of Negro spirituals, but account, by their skill for a good deal of the intensity of the shifting moods."

New York Sun—*March 16, 1951*[14]

In New York, *The Green Pastures* was accorded a favorable reception as in Boston, but the *Green Pastures* choir and the spirituals it sang were given short shrift. Writing for the *New York Sun*, Ward Morehouse noted that the production was superbly played, but said of the music only that the choir sang as "rousingly as ever."

New York Herald Tribune—*March 16, 1951*[15]

In a lengthy review, Otis L. Guernsey Jr. found the revival charming, with the imagination in some scenes still burning bright. Though somewhat short on pathos, he felt the show would still captivate newcomers. He acknowledged Hall Johnson and the choir in a single line, without according the singing or the spirituals any special significance.

New York Journal American—*March 16, 1951*[16]

It is difficult to read the New York reviewers without coming away with the feeling that, after the passage of twenty years and after the motion picture version of *The Green Pastures* had been shown around the world, they had "been there, done that." John McClain, the *Journal American* critic, used such clichés as "Timeless Drama," "simplicity," and "durability." He characterized the performance of William Marshall as "De Lawd" as "inspired." With regard to Hall Johnson, his choir, and his spirituals, McClain's comments are limited to a captioned paragraph—"Lots of Spirituals"—and crediting the choir with singing "every spiritual you ever heard."

New York Sun—*March 16, 1951*[17]

Of all the reviewers of the revival of *The Green Pastures*, only one, Ward Morehouse of the *New York Sun*, attempted to explain why the production, though excellent, did not create the excitement it did in 1930. "It's to be remembered that the world has changed . . . the theatre has changed . . . it has had Hitler, Stalin, a great war, a troubling and tottering peace." What he failed to mention was the revolution that was occurring in the area of civil rights. Truman had already desegregated the military, and movies and plays that stereotyped the Negro and portrayed him as childlike and simple had become "politically incorrect." While such vehicles provided employment for Negro singers and actors, many blacks were staging protests that were changing the conscience of the American audiences, both black and white.

The Hall Johnson Negro Choir Town Hall flyer, 1928. Courtesy of the Hall Johnson Collection (Rowan University, Glassboro, NJ).

Dr. William Decker Johnson and Alice Sansom Johnson. Courtesy of the Hall Johnson Collection (Rowan University, Glassboro, NJ).

Young Hall Johnson at his first violin recital, circa 1904. Courtesy of the Hall Johnson Collection (Rowan University, Glassboro, NJ). All rights reserved.

Hall Johnson's family portrait. Courtesy of the Hall Johnson Collection (Rowan University, Glassboro, NJ). All rights reserved.

Graduation portrait, Allen University, 1908. Courtesy of the Hall Johnson Collection (Rowan University, Glassboro, NJ). All rights reserved.

Graduate student at the University of Pennsylvania, 1909. Courtesy of the Hall Johnson Collection (Rowan University, Glassboro, NJ).

The American String Quartet, from left to right: Felix Weir, Marion Cumbo, Hall Johnson, Arthur Boyd, 1927. Courtesy of the Hall Johnson Collection (Rowan University, Glassboro, NJ).

Hall Johnson, "One Man Show." Courtesy of the Hall Johnson Collection (Rowan University, Glassboro, NJ).

*The Angelic Choir on Broadway—The Green Pastures, 1930. Fred Fehl, photographer.
Used by permission/courtesy of Gabriel Pinsky. All rights reserved.*

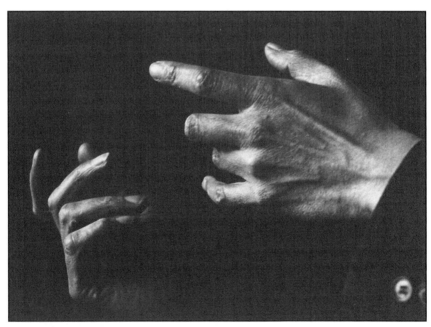

*"The Hands of Hall Johnson," by Ruth Bernhard, 1962. Courtesy of Ruth Bernhard. All
rights reserved.*

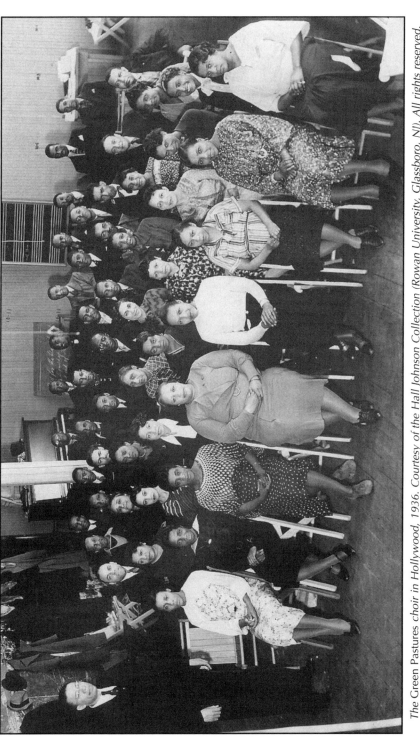

The Green Pastures choir in Hollywood, 1936. Courtesy of the Hall Johnson Collection (Rowan University, Glassboro, NJ). All rights reserved.

The "Swanee Six" male sextet of the Hall Johnson Choir, 1932. James L. Allen, photographer. Courtesy of the Hall Johnson Collection (Rowan University, Glassboro, NJ). All rights reserved.

Hall Johnson's wife, Polly Celeste Copening Johnson, 1912. Courtesy of the Hall Johnson Collection (Rowan University, Glassboro, NJ). All rights reserved.

The Festival Negro Chorus of New York, 1946. Courtesy of the Hall Johnson Collection (Rowan University, Glassboro, NJ). All rights reserved.

Johnson and the Berlin Arts Festival Choir, 1951. Courtesy of the Hall Johnson Collection (Rowan University, Glassboro, NJ). All rights reserved.

The Hall Johnson Choir at Titania Palast in Berlin, 1951. Courtesy of the Hall Johnson Collection (Rowan University, Glassboro, NJ).

Maestro Johnson conducts choir in Vienna, 1951. Courtesy of the Hall Johnson Collection (Rowan University, Glassboro, NJ).

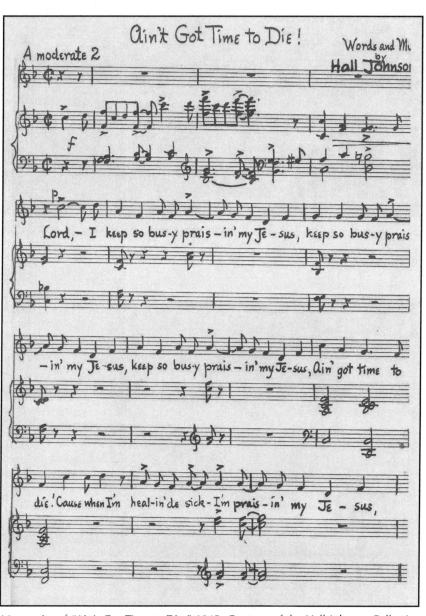

Manuscript of "Ain't Got Time to Die," 1945. Courtesy of the Hall Johnson Collection (Rowan University, Glassboro, NJ).

Run, Little Chillun—*Tongola Scene, 1933. Courtesy of the Hall Johnson Collection (Rowan University, Glassboro, NJ). All rights reserved.*

Hall Johnson's son, Jan Hall Jones. Courtesy of the Hall Johnson Collection (Rowan University, Glassboro, NJ) and Mrs. Lela Brown. All rights reserved.

634 St. Nicholas Ave., #4B,
New York, N.Y. 10030,
August 13th, 1969.

Dr. Eugene Thamon Simpson,
       and the
Virginia State College Choir,
Dear Friends:

A word of congratulation
on Volume One of your Black Heritage Series. I deem it great personal honor that your very first issue
should be selected from my songs.
Please accept my grateful appreciation. The whole idea is tremendous
and will certainly bear fruit in the
right direction.

I have just recently returned
from a visit to the University of Southern
Illinois at East St. Louis. Miss Katherine Dunham, who directs the Dept.
of Performing Arts Training center,

Congratulatory letter for The Hall Johnson Song Book, *1969. Courtesy of Eugene Thamon Simpson. All rights reserved.*

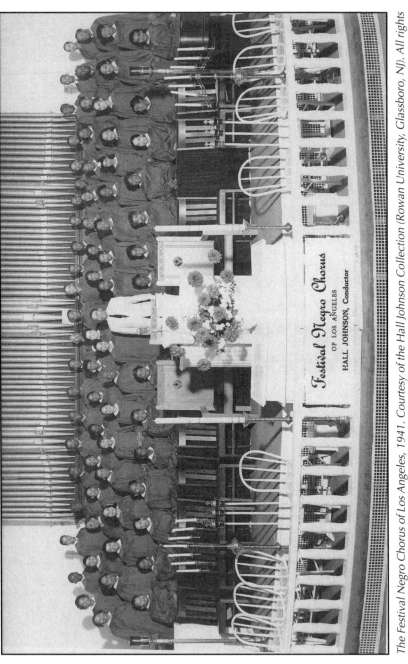

The Festival Negro Chorus of Los Angeles, 1941. Courtesy of the Hall Johnson Collection (Rowan University, Glassboro, NJ).

Synopsis of Scenes

Part I

Scene 1—The Sunday School

Scene 2—A Fish Fry

Scene 3—A Garden

Scene 4—Outside the Garden

Scene 5—A Roadside

Scene 6—A Private Office

Scene 7—Another Roadside

Scene 8—A House

Scene 9—A Hillside

Scene 10—A Mountain Top

Part II

Scene 1—The Private Office

Scene 2—The Mouth of a Cave

Scene 3—A Throne Room

Scene 4—The Foot of a Mountain

Scene 5—A Cabaret

Scene 6—The Private Office

Scene 7—Outside a Temple

Scene 8—Another Fish Fry

The following synopsis is summarized from the Illinois Theater program for the performance of September 7, 1931:

The Green Pastures
a fable, suggested by
Roark Bradford's Southern Sketches,
Ol' Man Adam an' His Chillun
Sunday School Stories from the Old Testament
(told in the idiom of rural southern Negroes)

Mr. Deshee, a Sunday School teacher, takes children to Sunday School where he describes heaven as a place where "De Lawd," a kind-hearted preacher, is enjoying a big fish fry with his angels. De Lawd creates the firmament, the earth, the sun, and finally man. In the Garden of Eden, he creates Eve for Adam and tells them to eat of the fruit of the Garden except for one tree. Adam and Eve disobey and Cain slays his brother Abel. De Lawd mingles among his creatures and observes gambling, drinking, and low morals. He is angered by the prevalence of sin. Noah invites him to a chicken dinner, and De Lawd tells him of his decision to destroy the world with a great flood. He tells Noah to build the ark and fill it with every species so that the world can be repopulated after the deluge. Noah is mocked by the disbelievers who are all destroyed in a forty-day rain. When a rainbow appears, the flood recedes.

The years pass and once again, De Lawd's chosen people are overcome by wickedness and corruption. This time, De Lawd decides to destroy man, completely. When he returns to earth, he finds a single righteous man and repents of his anger. He decides to let Moses deliver the Hebrews from Egyptian captivity and gives him miraculous powers to strike down the first-born sons, to

part the Red Sea, and to lead the Israelites to the land of Canaan. The Israelites reach the Promised Land and Moses relinquishes his command to
Joshua. The suffering and redemptive power of Jesus transform the God of
anger and wrath to a God of love and mercy.

The Music of the Play
All arrangements and compositions are by Hall Johnson.

Act I
"Oh! Rise and Shine"—"When the Saints Come Marchin' In"—"Cert'ny
Lord"—"My God Is So High"—"Hallelujah!"—"In Bright Mansions
Above"—"Don't You Let Nobody Turn You Roun'"—"Run, Sinner Run"—
"You Better Min'"—"Dere's No Hidin' Place Down Here"—"Some o' Dese
Days"—"I Want to Be Ready"—"De Ole Ark's a-Moverin'"—"My Soul Is a
Witness"—"City Called Heaven"

Act II
"My Lord's a Writin' All de Time"—"Go Down Moses"—"Oh Mary, Don't
You Weep"—"Lord, I Don't Feel Noways Tired"—"Joshua Fit de Battle of
Jericho"—"I Can't Stay Away"—"Hail de King of Babylon!"*18—"Death's
Gonter Lay His Cold Icy Hands on Me"—"De Blind Man Stood on de
Road an' Cried"—"March On!"—"Oh! Rise and Shine"—"Hallelujah,
King Jesus!"*

Formal Structure
In considering the musical form used in *The Green Pastures*, one must be
aware that structure in the spirituals of Hall Johnson was an evolving element that developed from the simple to the complex. The arrangements in
The Green Pastures represent the earliest stage of Johnson's style, and the simplicity of structure was appropriate both to the dramatic essence of the play
and to his original concept of what folk arranging should be. Consequently,
the arrangements were all stanza forms of a single part like "Oh! Rise and
Shine," or bipartite (verse and chorus) like "City Called Heaven." He made
these basic forms more interesting through the use of (1) a rhythmic and
moving bass line and (2) single and multiple obbligatos. "Cert'ny Lord"
demonstrates a most effective and expressive use of this device.

As to the structure of the whole work, the similarity to the Greek dramatic chorus has already been alluded to. There is not an exact balance of
song and dialogue, as the play has eighteen scenes, but twenty-five musical

selections. As with the typical Broadway show, several spirituals serve as an overture, and several as a finale. If we add to that number music composed for the scenes for which there was no appropriate traditional spiritual, we easily account for the twenty-five musical selections. Ultimately, the frequency with which the choral numbers appeared was governed by the dictates of the drama. The decision to use only a cappella choral music throughout the play was, at this time, unique in the history of the theater. It is regrettable that this uniqueness could not be preserved in the movie version, as the several orchestral statements composed by Korngold seem totally out of place.

II. *Run, Little Chillun*—A Negro Folk Drama in Four Scenes

Original Production—New York, New York
Lyric Theater

Opening	March 1, 1933
Closing	Date unknown
Total performances	128
Producer	Robert Rockmore
Writer	Hall Johnson
Music (original)	Hall Johnson
Choral arrangements	Hall Johnson
Conductor	Hall Johnson
Assistant conductor	Jester Hairston

Opening night cast (principals only): Olive Ball, Marietta Canty, Edna Commodore, Esther Hall, Bertha Powell, Mattie Shaw, Bennie Tattnall, Nell Taylor, Edna Thomas, Jimmie Waters, Henri Wood, the Hall Johnson Choir

Revival—Los Angeles, California
Hollywood Playhouse, Mayan Theater

Opening	July 1938
Closing	September 3, 1939
Total performances	480 (estimated)
Producer	W. H. Lusher
Music director	George Dilworth
Choral director	Hall Johnson

Opening night cast (principals only): Jess Lee Brooks, Ruby Elzy, Roy Glenn, Florence O'Brien, Prince Modupe, the Hall Johnson Choir

Revival—New York, New York
Hudson Theater

Opening	August 11, 1943
Closing	August 26, 1943
Total performances	Sixteen
Producers	Lew Cooper, Meyer Davis, George Jessel
Director	Clarence Muse
Writer	Hall Johnson
Music	Hall Johnson
Conductor	Hall Johnson

Opening night cast: Edna Mae Harris and the Hall Johnson Choir

A Historical Perspective

Nothing could be more revealing about Hall Johnson, his capacity for creative work, and the facility with which he did it, than the realization that the folk drama *Run, Little Chillun* was written, capitalized, cast, and rehearsed between June 1932 and March 1, 1933. Johnson opened the national tour run of *The Green Pastures* at the Biltmore Theater in Los Angeles on June 20, 1932. Once *Green Pastures* was running smoothly, Johnson left the conducting in the hands of the assistant conductor (as he frequently did once a show was extablished), and then had a mere eight months to accomplish all the work on *Run, Little Chillun*. To further confound observers, Johnson started rehearsals on *Run, Little Chillun* five months before the opening, probably rehearsing each section as he wrote it and without any expectation of performing it, and then took off on a transcontinental concert tour in order to earn enough money to sustain his rehearsal group. In an article based on an interview with Hall Johnson, Hollywood author Martha Ennis relates the story of the creation of *Run, Little Chillun* in an unpublished article, "One-Man Show":[19]

> Back in '32 Hall Johnson was a little W.P.A [Works Progress Administration] all by himself. He had a choir which he had trained himself, the Hall Johnson Choir. It had sung his music in *Green Pastures*, and was doing things over the radio and at the Lewisohn Stadium, and it made such a name for itself that half of Harlem wanted to join. Pretty soon he found himself with a group of about 300 unemployed singers, which is a full house in a one-man training school. So he wrote some music and some sketches for a Negro play to give them something to do.

"I tried to find someone to write the script for it, but they all looked at the sketches and told me I had better do it myself. So I finally had to." The group went to work. He says that they weren't sure what would happen when they got through rehearsing it, but no one else had anything to do, so they rehearsed every day for five months. "It's the only time I ever heard of 300 people rehearsing a play before they had any expectation of having it produced."

Meanwhile, to make ends meet, he took twenty singers out on a transcontinental tour. They had a bus, some tents, and a cook-stove—and a wonderful time. They made most of the big towns from coast to coast and sang to a lot of enthusiastic audiences. The proceeds, after expenses were paid, went back to the gang in New York.

They ran a soup kitchen there, in Coachmen's Hall where they rehearsed, because you can't practice five months on an empty stomach. But when the choir came back, the income ceased, and they were just about at the real worrying point when a lawyer named Robert L. Rockmore became interested in producing the play. Hall Johnson talked to him on the phone. "I'll be over tomorrow to see a rehearsal, and we'll talk afterwards." "You'd better come today. We may not have any place to rehearse tomorrow."

Rockmore would go on to produce the show at the Lyric Theatre where it opened on March 1, 1933.

According to Eileen Southern, "*Run, Little Chillun* . . . represented a milestone in the history of Negro folk opera, in that it was the only one of the successful stage works of the time . . . to be written by a black man."[20] It would be logical to ask the question, "But what about *Shuffle Along* (1921, by Sissle, Blake, Miller and Lyles)?" *Shuffle Along*, while it too had an all-black cast and was created by all-black artists, belongs to another genre, "musical comedy." Hall Johnson, who wrote both the book and the music of *Run, Little Chillun*, without collaboration, was in the category of "serious drama," and his play was in competition with those of Eugene O'Neill (*The Emperor Jones*), Marc Connelly (*The Green Pastures*), and Du Bose Heyward (*Porgy and Bess*). Of the four "operas," *The Green Pastures* was an immediate success, with a long Broadway run, a longer national tour, several successful revivals, and a movie. While Gershwin's *Porgy and Bess* was a popular success but not a critical one, it has endured to become a classic and to finally be accepted as the greatest American opera. The *Emperor Jones*, which premiered at the Metropolitan Opera with Lawrence Tibbett in the title role, was unanimously acclaimed by the critics, yet has not been performed in a major opera house since 1933. It has the handicap of having only one act. The critical opinion on *Run, Little Chillun* was divergent, with some critics lauding it and others decrying it. The drama however received substantial public approval with a four-month run on Broadway at the height of the Depression, and revivals on the West Coast that lasted well over a year. In examining some of the extant reviews, it appears that the success of *Run, Little Chillun* varied with the direction and the cast. The most successful production was in Los Angeles and featured the marvelous singer and actor Jess Lee Brooks as Elder Tongola. The least successful revival was in New York in 1943, and was directed by Clarence Muse. The cast was less than stellar. Given an ideal cast, fine direction, and adequate rehearsal time (typical time for rehearsing a Broadway show is three weeks), *Run, Little Chillun* could become a repertory item in theaters like New York City Opera.

Needless to say, much of the critical dissent over *Run, Little Chillun* was due to the fact that the work represented a departure from all the all-black shows that had preceded it. White audiences were use to black shows that portrayed blacks as comedic, diffident, servile, happy, and willing to sing and tap dance at any time. Spirituals were expected and jazzy music even more preferred. The whole idea that Hall Johnson, a black man, would write a play of conceptual loftiness that juxtaposed good against evil, eschewed cardboard characters, and was devoid of watermelon, fish fries, and dice games surprised and even offended some critics. To add insult to injury, Johnson had the audacity to juxtapose two musical styles, the operatic and the folk, and to hearken back to the black man's primeval origins in the construction of modal melodies ("Mo-ta-me-ko-la"). That this juxtaposition should not escape the viewer, at times, Johnson actually inserted in the play program, the theology of the New Day Pilgrims. "Black people sorely need a new religion based upon and developed out of their own essential nature and not grafted on through contact with other people . . . ineffable joy of life in nature, not tears of remorse and repentance, is the sign of the divine truth. Sin has no existence as fact, but is only a sense of guilt inculcated by a wrong education."[21] It is hard to say whether the death of Sulamai at the end of the play is an indication of Johnson's true feeling, or is a concession to public taste in letting the traditional church win out over cultism. From among the deluge of critical discussion and analysis during the run of the show and its revivals, Burton Rascoe alone provides an analysis which is both thorough and entirely valid.

New York World-Telegram—*September 4, 1943*[22]
In an extended article that Burton called "Reflections on *Run, Little Chillun's* Failure," he lavished almost unbridled praise on the "music drama," which he described as a "rare aesthetic treat," and credited Hall Johnson for bringing to the Broadway stage one of the few original ideas in the past twenty-five

years. Expressing disappointment at the show's failure, he found it revolutionary both in form and content, a "tragedy in choral tableaux," comparable to Ibsen's *Emperor and Galilean*. As Ibsen had failed to achieve the greatness of this theme, so had Johnson.

For Burton, the shortcomings of the play were almost entirely the fault of the direction and the delivery of the dialogue by three of the principles. Noting that the production had been a great success on the West Coast, he pointed to backstage disputes that lowered the morale of the ensemble and killed the spirit and excitement that made the voluptuous Tongola scene so thrilling on opening night. Espousing the stereotype that Negroes are natural actors, like children, he points to the fact that when they are dispirited, they let down their performance standards, and as such, allow the performance to become dull and mechanical.

Burton insisted that the play was intellectually challenging in its social implications, and showed clearly that the social and economic deprivation of the Negro and the imposition of white religion upon the race has caused a sort of spiritual starvation that contrasts greatly with the passion of their more primitive African worship traditions.

In her study on Hall Johnson,[23] Ingres Hill Simpson includes assessments from several reviewers that appeared in well-known periodicals of the time and clearly demonstrate the conflicting opinions about Johnson's work as a playwright.

Commonweal—*April 1933*[24]

The Play

by Richard Dana Skinner

Hall Johnson, head of the famous Hall Johnson Choir, has written a Negro folk-drama which, in spite of some extra-ordinarily fine dramatic material, presents a vast confusion of ideas. Superficially, it is supposed to depict the struggle between age-old nature worshipping instincts in the Negro, and the particular brand of Baptist Christianity which the Negro of the South has so largely adopted. It has even been compared to "Green Pastures" for its richness of spiritual content. Underneath this surface aspect, however, it really identifies, rather than distinguishes these two expressions of the Negro. It leaves one with the impression that the Baptist revival meeting differs very little from the pagan orgy in the forest in the honor of the moon, at least in emotional quality.

New Republic—*March/April 1933*[25]

Theatre Notes

by Stark Young

To my mind, Mr. Johnson, in this scene and sometimes in the wood scene, shows up the stuff laid on *The Emperor Jones* at the Metropolitan to a degree that is shocking, not only his music, but the singing as well, not to speak of the décor. . . . No other black play could compare in the full diapason of Negro quality, in the subtlety, and in the directing [with that demonstrated in the last act of *Run, Little Chillun*]. . . . There are moments when the music and the effect depart toward what might be called opera, and take on thus, at the same time, another beauty. Now and again come the hymns and spirituals, and now and again come moments where Mr. Johnson creates more entirely in his own right, and with fine success.

Journal of Negro Life—*April 1933*[26]

"[The New Day Pilgrims] elicit no recognition, they are merely baffling . . . it is to be regretted . . . that *Run, Little Chillun* was not as factual, as true to the lives of Negroes in the deep South as that part of it devoted to depicting the little church community of Baptists."

Saturday Review of Literature—*April 1933*[27]

The review deals primarily with the two choric scenes that were characterized as soundly operatic, using the standard operatic devices, not as mere conventions, but as the proper means for achieving the end in view. These scenes reveal what the writer of the "music-drama" must have intended: "A kind of performance in which the visual, and the auditory aspects of an event would be completely integrated, so that the tone of the voice and the flexions of the body would seem interchangeable."

Audiences, driven by some deep fear, seem to accept, most easily, such symbols of "contented indigence." Their endearing comic heroes are always "transparent, outspoken, ineffectual fellows, too scatterbrained to be dangerous," too engaged in foolishness to develop the hard skills of job-getting, or of making the best deal.

"In *Run, Little Chillun*, one sees a Negro genius [my emphasis] an attractive positive ability, . . . with a conviction, a liquidness, a sense of esthetic blossoming, and a gift for spontaneous organization which is capable, I believe, of actually setting the spectator a-quiver as he participates in the vocal and mimetic exhilaration taking place before him. No amusing picture of heaven here—nor 'backward superstition'—but an insight, a well-rounded biological pattern, a 'way of life.'"

Of these reviewers, only Burke considered *Run, Little Chillun* an unqualified success, indeed, a work of genius.

The *New York Times* critic also gave the work high praise as the abbreviated summary below confirms.

New York Times—*March 2, 1933*[28]

Hall Johnson Singers

Negro Spirituals

Run, Little Chillun boasts a large cast of some two hundred performers from Harlem. They have reached the Lyric Theatre after many months of hard work. Hopefully, they will have a long run. Hall Johnson was the playwright, composer, and arranger, and while the theme of the play deserves little discussion the performance of the spirituals is magnificent, sometimes, and very good all the time. The play is divided into four scenes, two of which are devoted to music and the other two, to the drama, pitting religious primitivism against conventional black Baptist faith. The orgiastic dance scene in the first act can hardly be surpassed. The same must be said for the revival scene. Johnson directs the choir and Merlin takes care of the other elements of production. The dialogue sometimes drags, but it is ably compensated for when the singing begins.

New York Herald Tribune—*March 2, 1933*[29]

Run, Little Chillun

Negro Drama by Hall Johnson Presented at Lyric Theatre

by Arthur Ruhl

Run, Little Chillun, directed by Hall Johnson, who is also the playwright and composer, opened at the Lyric Theatre last night. Despite an absence of dramatic unity and some bad dialogue, the singing was excellent, and at one spot in the final act, the audience actually stopped the show with their applause, demanding but not receiving an encore.

Set in the South, the plot is based on the conflict between the primitive New Day Pilgrims and the traditional Hope Baptist Church. The drama is further complicated by a tragic love affair between the parson's son and the beautiful Sulamai of the Pilgrims group. The worship of the New Day Pilgrims took place in the moonlight, in a forest grove, and was accompanied by "munbo jumbo," culminating in an orgiastic dance in which most of the principals removed their clothes.

Sulamai gets her man and takes the pastor's son to one of the nocturnal worship services. As the service becomes more and more pagan, Jim grabs Sulamai and drags her from the scene to a more staid Christian environment. The dance orgy seemed quite impressive, but was at times artificial.

The final act was little more than an authentic Negro Baptist revival in which the spectacular singing of the spirituals led the audience to stop the show with its applause. Jim is finally able to escape Sulamai's seduction and return to his church and to his wife, fully repentant. Fredi Washington as Sulamai and Ashton Burleigh as Jim were not totally convincing in their roles.

Thus, the New York run was short—only 128 performances. How then do we account for the unqualified success of the play on the West Coast? The Los Angeles run was 480 performances, four times the duration of the New York run. This was followed by a run in San Francisco and offers of a lengthy road tour, which was not permitted by Actors Equity (the union) because the production had been originally funded by the Federal Theater Project and was considered to be unfair competition to the regular companies. A number of these productions were *too successful* for both the government and the union and when private angels wished to buy them and tour them, the actors' union fought it. Indeed, the Los Angeles run of the show did not end for lack of public demand but because the federal government abruptly terminated the funding for the Federal Theater Project on June 30, resulting in a walkout of sixty members of the cast. The *Los Angeles Examiner* addressed the situation in an article dated June 15, 1939:

Los Angeles Examiner—*June 15, 1939*[30]

More Raids Planned on Federal Hit Shows

New "raids" upon Federal Theater Project (FTP) hit shows were planned yesterday by the private production syndicate, which Tuesday took over the FTP smash hit *Run, Little Chillun*. This was learned as five supervisors recently fired from the project were disclosed as the active organizers of the raiding group that boasts assurances of "unlimited capital from 10 Hollywood sponsors and one New York producer." Willis Lusher, discharged FTP technical director, told the *Examiner* in an exclusive interview yesterday that the raiding of *Run, Little Chillun*, in which sixty cast principals resigned from the FTP to continue under his banner, was his own idea. "I own the show now and am dealing for production rights to 'Volpone,'" he said.

The answer to this question of the difference between the critical and public reception of the play as originally produced in New York and that of the West Coast revival may be found in a confidential report on the FTP addressed to Mr. Rochester Gill and dated May 16, 1939. It is excerpted below:

> It is interesting to note that the interpretation which Clarence Muse has given to *Run, Little Chillun* is in direct contrast to the manner in which it was presented in the Lyric Theater, New York, where it ran for 128 performances. Players have been instructed to *play the piece for laughs*, and much of the action borders on the side of *burlesque*, with conscious intent to appeal to *an audience which has been accustomed to laugh at the Negro on the stage* [my emphasis]. But there are also moments when the audience laughs *with* the players, boldly pats its collective foot in unison with the contagious rhythm of the music, and shares the anguish of the aged leader of the flock whose son had strayed from The fold. . . . One finds . . . a cast that is outstanding for individual performances that made the play *Run, Little Chillun the smash hit of 1938-39, and the all-time national record holder* [my emphasis] for Federal Theater productions. More than 300,000 people have seen the show at the downtown Mayan Theater, Los Angeles.[31]

The report confirms the opinion expressed above and arrived at independently.

Reviews
There is no better way to evaluate Hall Johnson's historical position than to view him through the eyes of the competent music critics of the time. Frequently, research on significant black Americans reveals that they have little history, as their achievements have not been recorded. This is the case with many movies that the Hall Johnson Choir appeared in or contributed to the soundtrack of, without being credited. However, Johnson's work with the choir in concert and theater was so unique and so extraordinary that it was acknowledged as such by a multitude of critics. Because access to reviews of seventy-five years ago is so difficult and so limited and because one cannot fail to realize the magnitude of his accomplishments after reading the *complete* reviews of *Run, Little Chillun* and the West Coast concerts—which are nowhere collected save in Hall Johnson's memorabilia—the following reviews are included (in a digested and summarized version due to copyright restrictions) to give the reader a glimpse of the contemporary response to *Run, Little Chillun*. The complete reviews are preserved in the Hall Johnson Collection.

New York Evening Journal—*March 2, 1933*[32]

Spirituals in *Run, Little Chillun* Mainstay of Play at Lyric

The discovery and adoption of the primitive but fertile life of the American Negro as a subject for playwrights has interesting but differing results. The work of *genius* [my emphasis] Hall Johnson, famous as a composer and choral director, in this genre is, indeed, fortuitous. *Run, Little Chillun*, which opened last evening at the Lyric Theatre, ranks, unquestionably, with the best of the Negro Folk Dramas, *Green Pastures*, though with slightly less appeal. The spirituals, chants, and incantations are moving and superbly sung, the outstanding element of the show. They are so carefully woven into the dialogue that they become a part of the fabric of the whole. At times, the work becomes a virtual opera.

In his portrayal of a community, Johnson pits a pagan religious group against an orthodox Negro Baptist church. He pits the sensuous Sulamai against the meek Ella in a contest for the love of Jim, who breaks away from his church. Sulamai loses her life because of the wrath of the pagan, rather than the Christian, God, in a stroke of dramatic irony. The acting is above reproach.

Morris Piper *(Morris High School, Bronx, New York)*— *March 9, 1933*[33]

Run, Little Chillun

by Harry Morris

Mr. Hall Johnson, who recently brought his choir of spiritual singers to Morris for a very inspiring concert, has opened a play at the Lyric Theatre on Broadway, which demonstrates once more his inimitable *genius* [my emphasis]. Having already to his enviable credit, the composition and arrangement of all music in the highly successful *Green Pastures*, this new venture establishes him beyond doubt as our foremost composer of Negro spirituals

The simple but dramatic tale concerns the conflict between a migrant troupe of moon-worshippers, called the New Day Pilgrims, and the devoted congregation of the Hope Baptist Church situated in a little southern town. This conflict is intensified when Sulamai, an uncontrollable butterfly of the town, transiently steals the affections of the local pastor's son from his dutiful wife. And consequently, she inveigles him to such an extent, that he finally consents to attend one of the back-to-nature meetings of the N.D.P.'s. From the moment Sister Louella Strong emerged from her shadowed corner quite flat-footedly and announced in a husky articulation her intention of getting ready for "church" and Sister Mahalie Ockletree shook a vehement finger ambiguously about, saying "Somethin's jest gotta be did," I was completely enthralled.

But the tale is secondary. It is the music. *Run, Little Chillun* is opera! The second and fourth scenes, which deal with the New Day Pilgrims' meeting and the Baptist revival, respectively, are sung with such depth of power and beauty of expression that they are unforgettable. The native chant will echo again and again in your ears, and the wild passionate dance, which I have often tried to capture in words, will assume a sustained phantasmagoria before your eyes. As for the last scene of the revival, when Sulamai is dramatically struck by lightning, I am left without words to express the operatic crescendo of emotion that stormed my heart. Let it be said that this is opera entrusted to the Philistine appreciation of Broadway. *I do not think it would be blasphemy against Handel, if "Run, Little Chillun" should ultimately insinuate itself into the Metropolitan Opera House* [my emphasis].

New York American—*March 16, 1933*[34]

"Marilyn's Affairs" but Principally about Another Entertainment, *Run, Little Chillun!*

by Gilbert W. Gabriel

Having attended another show on the night of the opening of *Run, Little Chillun,* my words to be added to the chorus of praise for the show are long overdue. *"Two of the four scenes . . . are pretty nearly the most exciting pieces of stage ensemble I have ever met"* [my emphasis]. Forgive the artlessness of the other two acts and wait for the "orgy in the moonlight" and the revival scene. *"These are truly grand!"* [my emphasis]. Hall Johnson, the choral director memorable for the music of *Green Pastures,* has now provided us with the script, the music, and the singers. But the play is not just the work of one man, for it comes from the heritage of the race for the past two hundred years and therefore deserves triple honors and awards!

It is needless to promise magnificent singing for Johnson's singers would be hair-raising even to Moussorgsky's ghost, so rich, beautiful, and skillful it is. *"Go and hear them, and laugh at the maestros of the Metropolitan Opera when they deny the possibility of a Negro Grand Opera"* [my emphasis].

Pictorial Review: A Monthly Survey of Events in the Creative World—*July 1933*[35]
The Pace of the Arts

Run, Little Chillun, Run, fo' de Devil's Done Loose in de Lan'

This title song has become the emblem of *"the most tumultuous evenings in the theater"* [my emphasis]. Hall Johnson has written a folk drama so arresting that the audience is carried along on a wave of excitement until it vibrates with the actors at the climactic moments. The plot centers on the conflict between a cult of moon worshippers, and the Hope Baptist Church, where Jim, the pastor's son is enticed away from his wife and the church by the temptress, Sulamai.

Jim finally returns to his own church and prays for forgiveness and asks for the prayers of the congregation. Sulamai arrives to tempt him, yet again, and is struck with a bolt of lighting, proving the wrath of the Almighty God.

It is the powerful forest scene in the first act and the revival scene in the second that move the audience to show-stopping applause. The music drama is distinguished by its racial and spiritual exaltation and by its passionate expression. *Run, Little Chillun* is the first, and only, successful Negro music drama to have been written by a Negro, and it masterfully merges the spirituals with the dramatic action. Johnson feels that the performance of spirituals needs the dramatic interpretation to be complete.

Only a year ago, Hall Johnson Choir was enlarged to 175 voices for a performance of *Let Freedom Ring* at the Roxy Theater on Lincoln's birthday. The choir began the rehearsals of *Run, Little Chillun* in September of 1932, without backers or a promise of production. Frequently, the choir did not know where the next meal might come from. After five months, they found a producer, and their persistence has paid off in extravagant praise.

"The Greatest Negro Musical of All Time" was the heading of Charles Wakefield Cadman's telegram to Johnson after attending a performance of *Run, Little Chillun*. Cadman continued, "*In all my musical and theatrical life, I have never been so profoundly moved and thrilled* [my emphasis], and I want to tender to you and every member of your great organization my sincerest congratulations. The work is not only thoroughly American, it is epochal."

San Diego Union—1938[36]

Little Chillun Scores Hit on Savoy Stage

by Ruth Taunton

Last evening, Hall Johnson's *Run, Little Chillun* opened for a five-day run at the Savoy Theater. Should you fail to see it, you will miss the best theater production ever to play San Diego. Johnson wrote the play, wrote the music, and directs the large chorus for the performance. Thoroughly American, *Run, Little Chillun* is an accurate depiction of Negro life and psychology, with magnificent acting and singing by a cast of sixty.

Simplicity Keynote

Set in a small southern town, the pastor's son returns from college to be seduced away from his wife by Sulamai, who tries to get him to join a cult of moon worshippers, the New Day Pilgrims. The old pastor's dream of a pagan group, singing the chants and dancing the dances of Africa, becomes a reality that competes with his orthodox Hope Baptist Church and the revival meeting, with the religious ecstasy of the believer directly translated to the stage.

Pasadena Sun-News—1939[37]

Music Is Superb in Negro Show

The superb Negro acting company that made dramatic history with their Los Angeles Federal Theater production of this play now plans to take it on a national tour. The spiritual drama that played for 126 performances on Broadway and broke all Federal Theater records with full houses for a year in Los Angeles opened last evening at the Civic Auditorium in Pasadena. Hall Johnson is music director, and the cast, led by Jess Brook, features the original leads.

Vocal Orchestration
The music of the play can only be described as superb, with a breadth and completeness that challenges the orchestra, resonant and hair-raising in its passion and excitement, as it evokes the memories of a race through religion and faith. Equally vital is the acting, alternately, expressing reverence, joy, pathos, fear, and the triumph of salvation.

San Francisco Examiner—*July 23, 1938*[38]

Lovely Singing in *Run, Little Chillun* Drama

by Florence Lawrence

Run, Little Chillun, an all-Negro music drama, opened at the Mayan Theater last night and is characterized by great music and singing, and is thoroughly entertaining. Staged by the Federal Music and Theater Projects in a united attempt to put this Hall Johnson drama to music over to the best advantage, the cast includes many singers with lovely voices and some acting skills, too, which promises to register favorably for the players. The principal actors also reveal excellent voices and fine acting ability. Hall Johnson, of *Green Pastures*, and singer/actor Clarence Muse have combined their talents as playwright and arranger to bring this work to Los Angeles. (The reviewer is wrong here as Muse had no part in writing the book or arranging the music. He was the stage director.) The large cast of 150 is seen to best advantage in the camp meeting scene of the New Day Pilgrims, and in the revival scene of the second act. The conflict between the pagan and the Orthodox sects, and the struggle of the individual characters create substantial dramatic tension. One's enjoyment was enhanced by a multitude of beautiful voices among the soloists and in the chorus. The actors also were well trained and had a great deal of natural ability. Despite its length, *Run, Little Chillun* promises the audience both novelty and excitement. Stand-outs in the cast were Jess Lee Brooks, Ruby Elzy, Roy Glenn, Prince Modupe, and Florene O'Brien. The capacity crowd rewarded the performance with enthusiastic applause.

Variety—*July 23, 1938*[39]

Run, Little Chillun

Superbly written, scored, and acted, Hall Johnson's *Run, Little Chillun* opened last night at the Mayan Theater under the sponsorship of the Federal Theater Project. It is, by far, the most impressive of the productions offered by the federal government in the coast division. Its capacity audience was thrilled throughout the performance. Written by the Negro choral director Hall Johnson, both book and music, the music drama rivals *The Green Pastures* and, at times, surpasses it. Clarence Muse's direction of the large cast is above criticism. The acting of Florence O'Brien and Jess Lee Brooks is of star quality.

The Negro spirituals create an effective milieu for the drama, which is built around the seduction of a pastor's son. When the temptress is killed by a bolt of lightning, Jim returns to his wife and to his church. The exciting and exotic dancing of the forest scene creates a spectacular tableaux, balanced by the fervent sincerity of the spirituals in the revival scene.

San Francisco Examiner—*January 14, 1939*[40]

Run, Little Chillun Is a Musical Treat

by Ada Hanifin

Any operatic maestro would survey the final scene of the first act of *Run, Little Chillun* covetously. The show opened at the Alcazar Theater with an all-Negro cast of 150. During this forest scene, the stately Negroes intone chants from their African heritage as a part of the moon-worshipping ceremony in which nature is God. Written by the conductor, Hall Johnson, this music is more affecting in its sincerity than the consecration scene in Verdi's *Aida*! Joseph James, the High Priest, has the makings of a first class Ramfis.

Spiritual Meeting

In this music drama, the music reigns supreme. In the revival meeting in the final scene, the mass choir sings ten Negro spirituals, interspersed with scripture readings and testimony, drawing directly from the church service of the Negro Baptists. There are interjections from the congregation when a worshipper is overcome with the "spirit." It is this scene in which the title song, actually composed by Johnson, is sung, and not without an explosive response from the audience, who demanded that it be repeated. It must be said that the solo dancer of the forest scene, who served to ignite the orgiastic frenzy, would also eclipse any of those in the triumphal scene of *Aida*.

Much Spirit and Zest
The Federal Theater has black gold in *Run, Little Chillun*, for it is the program's first hit show. Any shortcoming in the acting is compensated for by the spirit and enthusiasm of the players. The pace of the actors' delivery was frequently too fast for the audience to catch all the words, especially with the part of Ella.

San Francisco Chronicle—*January 14*, 1939[41]

Run, Little Chillun Proves to Be Rousing Theater, Bounces Audience out of Seats

by John Hobart

After several postponements, *Run, Little Chillun* finally made it to San Francisco where it opened Thursday evening at the Alcazar Theater. A big show with many actors and singers, it did not disappoint as it is an extraordinary show that should liven up San Francisco's season. Sponsored by the Federal Theater Project, the music drama is filled with enervating rhythms, and what it lacks in polish, it makes up in enthusiasm and sincerity.

Cult Dances, Songs
Act I concludes with orgiastic dance tableaux, which is the culmination of an African nature-worship ritual of the New Day Pilgrims. The celebration includes "weird" dances and "weird songs," which extol the greatness of their faith. Despite the "hokum," the audience is jolted out of their seats, as it is exciting theater. The climactic scene, however, is the revival scene, which comes at the conclusion of act II. This scene, almost a literal translation of an authentic Baptist church revival, integrates the music and the acting with an electrifying effect. The near hypnotic effect of the preaching, praying, and chanting leads the congregation to spontaneous outbursts of spirituals that are fervent, joyous, and ecstatic. It is a transcendental scene that climaxes when Sulamai, the temptress, is struck down at the church door by a bolt of lightning.

Cast of Born Actors
The world knows that Negroes are natural actors. The direction of Gordon Lang and Jester Hairston has produced a cast that acts with naturalness and abandon. Although *Run, Little Chillun* may not be finely chiseled, it will do much to raise the pulse of the San Francisco season.

Synopsis

Setting	A town in the South
Period	Anytime
Characters	Thirteen males and sixteen females in the children's choir, Pilgrim's choir, Pilgrims, orchestra, dancers, townspeople, novitiates

Hall Johnson prepared the following synopsis for inclusion in the program for this production:

In a town in the deep south, an exciting soul-saving contest is going on between the members of Hope Baptist Church, led by Pastor Jones, and a mysterious sect, calling themselves the New Day Pilgrims. The latter worship in the woods, amid pagan rites and ceremonial orgies. For some time past the deacons of the Baptist congregation have viewed with alarm the falling off in attendance at their services, and a business committee has constituted itself to call on the Rev. Jones to talk things over. They think the Pilgrims are the cause of all the trouble. Tongues are wagging that Jim, the pastor's own son, who has an affair with Sulamai, although he is married to a good woman, is about to join the Pilgrims and will attend their next camp meeting with all its orgies. The pastor cannot bring himself to believe this awful news. Witnesses testify, however, that they heard Sulamai brag about it. Ella, Jim's wife, confronts Jim, who admits it isn't just Sulamai, as Ella conjectures, but Jim's own curiosity mixed with serious doubt about the church in which he has been brought up, that prompt him to a keen desire to go to the camp meeting, at least once. Ella and her prayerful entreaties do not bother Jim, but he hesitates when thinking of his father. However, Sulamai has no trouble in playing on Jim's jealousy of Brother Moses, the Pilgrim's preacher, to induce him finally to come with her.

Brother Moses is indeed a silver-tongued orator. Expounding the union of God, nature, and joy as ONE, he acts as an apostle for Elder Tongola, the Prophet of the New Day Pilgrims, who "knows all." The Elder never utters a word, but makes Brother Moses speak his thoughts. As the moon rises in the woods, the worshippers begin to sing and dance. Jim is among the Novitiates. Sulamai, carried away by the pulse-accelerating rhythm, throws off her garment and "self-expresses" in a frenzied dance, which makes Brother Moses mad with desire. Jim, seeing this, dives into the mass of dancers and loading Sulamai on his shoulders, carries her off.

Three nights later, Jim, who has seen enough of the New Day Pilgrims, promises Ella to accompany her to church. However, at the crossroads, Jim, under the pretext that he has to pick up something that he forgot, calls on Sulamai. He hands her a letter from the New Day Pilgrims, requesting both Jim and Sulamai not to attend their meetings at any future time. Jim taunts Sulamai with Brother Moses, but Sulamai protests that she loves only Jim. When Jim persists in his intention to go to church that night, Sulamai plays her trump card: She is going to have a baby, and if Jim leaves her, she is going to strut up and down the street parading Jim's baby under the stuck-up noses of the Hope Baptist women hypocrites. Jim proposes that they leave together by the two o'-clock train that night, and start all over again in another place where they are not known. Sulamai refuses. She wants to stay here. As he is about to leave, Jim sees Brother Moses, who has come to tell Sulamai that although he is supposed to have arrived at a point of evolution where he is immune to women, he cannot live without Sulamai. He is going to ask the Prophet Tongola for permission to leave the Pilgrims. There is a train at two o'clock . . ." Matrimonial Special?," sarcastically exclaims Sulamai. No! Always there seems to be a division of love, a divided allegiance, between her and God. A terrific storm is drawing near. Brother Moses promises to meet Sulamai at midnight in the Hope Baptist Church, but is aghast at her condition, that he must not ask Tongola nor anybody else's permission.

At the Hope Baptist Church, Rev. Jones is holding the fort for the Christian God in a quaint and semi-barbarous riot of singing, moaning, wailing and weeping. A woman evangelist has "packed them in," the Rev. Jones encourages the congregation to come forward and give testimony. Among those that do is Ella, who claims that her Jim, in answer to her prayer, is going to be restored to her and to the band of the faithful. Just at this moment, Jim enters the church. His father's sermon cites the Lord's forgiveness, but seeing Sulamai, he tells of Jehovah's wrath and vengeance. Sulamai escapes the hostile atmosphere and leaves the church. The thunderstorm comes nearer and is extraordinarily terrifying. Jim hurries out of the church, but returns soon and proclaims himself saved. Sulamai reenters, and as she stands isolated from the rest of the group, themselves around Jim and Ella, is struck dead by lightening. The face of Brother Moses is seen at the window. Tongola has had his revenge.

Hall Johnson was especially concerned that the audiences for *Run, Little Chillun* understand clearly the dichotomy between the religious philosophy of the Hope Baptist congregation and the New Day Pilgrims. To facilitate this, Johnson inserted the following statement in the program of the 1938 Los Angeles revival at the Mayan Theater:

Theology of the New Day Pilgrims

The Elder Tongola has spent a hundred and fifty years in all parts of our world teaching black people that they sorely need a new religion based upon and developed out of their own essential nature and not grafted on through contact with other peoples. He tells them that God is not a testy old superman living somewhere above the skies but that He is the All-Power, manifesting himself through nature. Man, the human being, is a part of that nature, he is supported by that power, and the realization of this truth must inevitably bring joy. Ineffable joy of life in nature, not tears of remorse and repentance, is the sign of the divine touch. Sin has no existence as fact but is only a sense of guilt inculcated by wrong education. The human body is not an object for shame or concealment but should be regarded in the same way as one thinks of the trunk and branches of a beautiful, fruitful tree. There is nothing obscene about a tree. All of which does not mean that man should content himself on the plane of the lower animals. On the contrary, the very presence of laudable ambitions and right desires is proof of the owner's capability to realize them, but he can only do this by working with, not against nature. The same law that produces great trees develops great men, and there is joy, always ever-increasing joy.

The Music of the Play

Act I

All songs in this act are original works by Hall Johnson.

"Processional"—"Credo"—"Moon Music"—"Tongola Dance Music"—"Sulamai's Song"

Act II

"Steal Away"—"Amazing Grace"—"Oh, Jesus, Come Dis-a-Way"—"Done Written Down My Name"—"I'll Never Turn Back No Mo'"—"Oh My Lovin' Brother"—"Do You Love My Lord?"—"Great Gittin' Up Mornin'"—"Nobody Knows de Trouble I See"—"Run, Little Chillun" (composed by Hall Johnson)—"Ser Glad"—"Return, Oh Holy Dove"—"O Lord, Have Mercy on Me"

It is a measure of Hall Johnson's greatness that he did not die a very bitter man. By all rights, *Run, Little Chillun* should have made him very wealthy. The record-breaking Los Angeles and San Francisco runs attracted the attention of Hollywood producer and director Frank Tuttle, who bought the option rights for producing the play with the original cast in 1939. According to Martha Ennis in her interview with Johnson, "They signed the contract last week, and from the looks of it, the screen credits will all be to Hall Johnson. He is to be story consultant, technical advisor, composer, scorer, dialogue director, and musical director. Tuttle calls the play an 'Ebony Nugget,' and expects no 'censorship troubles' over the fact that it is an all-Negro play."[42] Why this film did not happen is probably due less to kismet, than to the fact that the federal government and the actors' union united to try to block all commercial ventures of FTP shows, and were largely successful in doing this because, according to the union, it represented unfair competition for privately produced shows.

Again, in 1951, attempts were made to turn *Run, Little Chillun* into a movie. In a letter dated October 2, 1951, agent Carlo Lodato wrote to Johnson and indicated that if he wished him to present *Run, Little Chillun* to film companies, it would be necessary to provide him with a script of the music drama and a term option. He also asked to be put in touch with Johnson's agent so that they could discuss details in regard to motion picture rights. Lodato's letter is preserved in the Hall Johnson Collection.

As Johnson did not have a personal agent and was in the middle of the Berlin tour when Lodato made this request, there is no evidence that Johnson made an appropriate response. It is clear that nothing came of it, and for the second time, Johnson was denied the possibility of real wealth from his creative efforts.

Incredibly, and perhaps sadistically, eight years later, in 1959, there was a determined effort to make a film version of *Run, Little Chillun*, which, had it been successful, would have made Hall Johnson's final years economically secure. As the excerpted correspondence, which went on for more than eighteen months, will show, the venture was to fail again because of inexplicable barriers. Once again, Johnson was doomed to disappointment as the problems were never resolved and the project was dropped. Like Moses, thrice, he had seen the Promised Land, but he was not to enter it. A detailed discussion of the racial factors which prevented *Run, Little Chillun* from becoming a motion picture, and a summary of all the letters of Arthur Landau can be found in chapter 1, "A Historical Account."

Formal Structure

Any discussion of the formal structure properly should begin with a definition of the total work. Hall Johnson called *Run, Little Chillun* a Negro folk drama. However, this appellation totally ignores the music, which most critics consider more important than the script. The definition is further complicated by the use of two completely contrasting styles of musical composition appropriate to the dramatic characterization. In the first act, all of the music is original and classical as distinguished from the folk idiom. In the second act, the music is in the folk idiom, either spiritual or hymn. So the question remains, what is *Run, Little Chillun*? Is it drama? musical? folk? operatic?

The most discerning critics attribute to this work the characteristics of the operatic idiom. The opera with dialogue hearkens back to the singspiel of which the operas of Mozart provide numerous examples, including *The Magic*

Flute. Johnson's treatment, however, uses the chorus as a protagonist and incorporates features that are most frequently associated with Richard Wagner. The form most closely associated with the Wagner operas seems to also fit Johnson's treatment—"music drama."

The original music in act I, scene 2 is through-composed ("Processional," "Credo") with a distinctly modal flavor that represents the primitive heritage of the moon worshippers. The structures of the spirituals and hymns in act II include those most frequently found in folk music: the stanza form; verse and chorus (bipartite form), and call and response form. Act II also has one aria, "Sulamai's Song."

III. *Fi-yer*—A Negro Music Drama

The following information is taken directly from Johnson's script, which is available in the Hall Johnson Collection:

Act I—Three scenes
Act II—Three scenes
Act III—Three scenes
Act IV—Three scenes
This play was not produced in Hall Johnson's lifetime.

Author's Notes

Negroes are emotionally the most flexible people in the world, but a great many people do not know this. However, the easy transition from laughter to tears, from wild excitement to contemplative calm, is not the result of any mental instability or a too facile reaction to external stimuli. Rather its root is to be found in the Negro's natural love of histrionics and the luxurious *enjoyment* of giving in to his feelings. These same feelings are just as easily restrained or even cleverly disguised at will; for the Negro, very early in his history, was compelled by circumstances to master the fine art of dissembling.

Fi-yer deals with happenings affecting two generations of people on a southern plantation. Part 1, deals with the older people and has the flavor of serious drama, with music and ballet tending toward the operatic. Part 2, about the youngsters, is deliberately lighter, with comedy possibilities and modern singing and dancing. The music is an integral part of the action and the story moves right along through orchestral motifs as well as through the texts of the songs.

***

The action takes place on the Killingsworth Plantation in the South.
The time of the action in part I is about 1914.
The time of the action in part II is about 1932.

Cast: Uncle Hiram—Aunt Hester's Husband; Sam Simpkins—Elmira's latest husband; Mary—Daughter of Hiram and Hester; Bob Graham—Plantation Owner; Sister Elmira Waterberry—President, Pastor's Aid Society; Rev. William Brown—Pastor of the Church; Aunt Hester—A Faith Healer; Jabe Simms—A Farmer; Baby Tillie—Aunt Hester's Granddaughter; Little Tom Berkeley—A Neighbor's Son; Sister Prunella Jones, Idella Johnson, Euphrasia James, Sophony Jackson—Pastor's Aid Society; Aunt Patsy Pruitt, Sister Dogy Doolittle, Brother Ben Barnes, Brother Daniel Davis—Pillars of the Church; Satan—Ruler of the Infernal Regions; Assorted Fiends; Harlem Boys and Girls; The Three Little Habits, Ghosts, Haunts, Spooks, Imps, Werewolves, Vampires, Medicine Men, Witches, etc.

A Historical Perspective

The earliest mention of Johnson's folk operetta *Fi-yer* appears on the June 15, 1937, concert program of the Hall Johnson Choir at the Wilkshire-Ebell Theater in Los Angeles. The program "American Negro Folk Music and Choral Music by Negro Composers" consisted of three groups of traditional spirituals and folk songs and three groups of composed choral works by H. T. Burleigh, Will Marion Cook, Hall Johnson, and William Grant Still. The two Johnson compositions were the "Banjo Dance" (from the operetta *Fi-yer*) and the first performance of his "War March of Peace." However, *Fi-yer* appears to have been completed in California in 1939. It will be of interest to scholars to know that an earlier version of the play called *Goophered*, in two acts and three scenes is extant.

Sometime in the spring of that year, newspaper reporter Martha Ennis interviewed Johnson for an article about *Run, Little Chillun*, his folk drama that had been enjoying a successful run of almost a year at the Mayan Theater in Los Angeles. In the final paragraphs of her article, she mentions the composition of *Fi-yer*: "Hall Johnson hasn't found these activities sufficient to use up either his energy or his creative urges. In his spare time the first few months, he has written the score and script for a new drama, 'sort of an operetta,' which he calls *Fi-yer*. It is on its way back to Broadway and it may turn up in white lights there next winter. But at the root of all his work, all his varied forms of expression, is a passionate vision."[43]

About the same time, a Los Angeles paper published the first news about the creation of this new work:[44]

Hall Johnson Works on New Negro Folk Opera

Composer and choir director, Hall Johnson is writing a new folk opera called *Fi-yer*. The play is not yet complete, but Johnson and his choir are already busy rehearsing it. With Mr. Johnson, the music always comes first.

Run, Little Chillun, now playing for nearly a year in this area, is the first effort of Johnson's to utilize the music of his race as material for a stage. The plot of *Fi-yer* revolves around a Voodoo woman, and its music has hypnotic possibilities. By writing both the libretto and the music, Johnson has an advantage over most composers in music theater in keeping the work authentically American. Although his roots are in Harlem, his music is not Broadway, but hearkens back to his native Georgia. He integrates the drama, melody, and vocal effects to make a musical statement about his people.

The Music of the Play
Words and music composed by Hall Johnson.

Act I
"Cotton Song"—"Fi-yer"—"You Ain't Livin' Unless You're Lovin'"—"Death Is a Liar"—"In His Own Good Time, in His Own Good Way"

Act II
"Lullaby"—"Elegy" (a Negro sorrow song)

Act III
"Cotton Song" (Chorus)—"Good Times" (chorus in the style of a lively spiritual)—"John Henry Green Hits Broadway"—"The Cotton Strut" (song and dance)—"What You Goin' ter Do" (duet)—"Goopher Song" (Uncle Hiram and male chorus)—"Howdy-Do Miss Sylvie" (John Henry and male chorus)—"Pull Together Sisters"—"Hush-a-bye Tune" (Tillie)—"Pastor's Aid Song"—"No Crystal Stair"—"Banjo Dance"

Act IV
"Simmon Tree" (opening chorus)—"July Sun Chorus" (picnic scene)—"Cold Winter Blues"

Despite the spectacular success of *The Green Pastures*, and the notable success of *Run, Little Chillun*, Johnson was unable to find a producer for *Fi-yer*. The work lay fallow from 1940 until 1953 when the Robert Breen office expressed interest in the work. In a letter dated April 7, 1953, Johnson writes the following to Mr. Breen:

> While you were still in England, I received a telegram with your signature asking me to send the book and score of my musical play, *Fi-yer* to your New York address. I telephoned your office and talked to a lady who was representing you, Mrs. Watson, I believe. I explained to her that I had only one copy of the script and needed to have it by me as there had been some show of interest in

the neighborhood. I was sorry that I didn't have another copy available, especially as Mrs. Watson told me that you hadn't managed to look at it during the time it was in your office before.

Sometime later, it occurred to me that you might be interested in reading a synopsis of the play. So after much delay for the above-named reasons—I am sending one along. It is pretty full and will, I think, give you a very clear idea of what the story is about although unfortunately, it can offer no notion of the quality of the music, which is at least three-fourths of the play. Aside from that, I really believe the synopsis presents a better picture of the motivation and emotional progressions involved than can be had from reading the simple lines of the script. . . . In case your interest should reach the point of wanting to hear the music, it would be much better if I should come to New York and give you a little demonstration with a few actual voices. . . . There is action all the time, underscored by music. . . . The two longest scenes (the Picnic and the Vision) are almost entirely singing and dancing—with wonderful opportunities for effective choreography, and stage pictures. The Vision Scene in particular, will accommodate any number of details which, in any other setting, might shock the more puritanical members of the audience. As it all takes place in hell—where one would expect to find it—the good people can settle back and enjoy it without any strain on their self-righteousness. . . . I have been playing around in my mind with a special added attraction for Satan's floor show: a barber-shop quartet composed of Alexander the Great, Julius Caesar, Napoleon Bonaparte, and Adolf Hitler (top tenor). And Count Dracula in person, could present the six vampires who, of course, could not be expected to be too virginal in their approach.[45]

Despite Johnson's persuasive art, the Breen office did not choose to produce the show. This may have been because of the cataclysmic social changes that had taken place in America during the decade of the 1940s. The emphasis on equality and integration made the "all-black" show and the "all-black" choir a relic of an earlier period.

Formal Structure

Of the three musical plays that Hall Johnson wrote the music for, *Fi-yer* most closely meets the criteria for the standard opera as it includes arias, duets, ensembles, and choruses. It also boasts a set dance scene as do the grand operas with classical ballet scenes. In Johnson's script, he calls the work a "music drama," a carefully considered nomenclature describing a careful integration of dialogue and music. As this work is secular, the forms are very similar to those used in the traditional Broadway shows: stanza forms, bipartite forms, and song forms. The title song, "Fi-yer," follows a characteristic form of a spiritual, with a two-part chorus, repeated for each verse. As with the standard opera, *Fi-yer* has an orchestral accompaniment.

IV. *Son of Man*—A Negro Easter Cantata

There were two major New York performances of Hall Johnson's cantata, *Son of Man*—one in 1946 and one in 1948. They took place at New York's most prestigious venues, New York City Center, home of the New York City Opera, and Carnegie Hall, the home of the New York Philharmonic and a hostel for world-class performers. Not only were the choruses unique for their tremendous size, they were unique for their racial makeup. The 1946 chorus was an all-Negro chorus assembled by Johnson from the black churches and singers that had worked with Johnson in various performances since the creation of his professional choir in 1925. The second chorus was a barrier-breaking phenomenon in 1948, a fully integrated chorus with singers from the best black and white choirs in the city. It was a testimony to the high esteem in which Johnson was held because of his record of professional achievement as conductor, teacher, arranger, and composer. The two posters created by Johnson to promote these concerts are here replicated:

Premier—New York, New York
First Public Appearance of
The Festival Negro Chorus of New York City
Hall Johnson, Conductor

in a New Easter Cantata

SON OF MAN

a Musical Meditation in the Negro Idiom
with Text and Music Composed and Arranged by

HALL JOHNSON

The moving human story of the Christ told in
Soul-searching Old Spirituals, Dramatic Musical
Episodes, Spine-tingling New Songs
by a
Superb Chorus of 300—Fine New Solo Voices—Striking Instrumental Effects

Monday Evening, April 15, 1946 at 8:30 P.M.
NEW YORK CITY CENTER
131 West 55th Street

1948 Performance—New York, New York
THE INTERRACIAL FESTIVAL CHORUS
500 VOICES
HALL JOHNSON, CONDUCTOR

Juano Hernandez, Narrator
Carl R. Diton, Organist

presents the soul-stirring cantata

SON OF MAN

Good Friday Evening
March 26, 1948 at 11:30 P.M.

Carnegie Hall

57th Street and Seventh Avenue
New York City

Composer's Notes[46]

This is the story of the last days in the earthly life of Jesus, the man. It is told in music; sometimes in the simple but eloquent style of the older spirituals—sometimes in more highly developed original compositions. The dramatic incidents are clarified and connected by scriptural verses, read—not acted—by a dignified narrator against the musical background. The cantata is scored for Mixed A Cappella Chorus, Solo voices, and Narrator, with occasional accompaniment of Organ, Brass Choir, Harp, Tympani, and other percussion instruments.

Son of Man is presented neither as a brilliant concert occasion nor as a doctrinal religious service. The atmosphere during the performance should rather be one of serious meditation. The lines of the first solo voice, "Come on, brothers and sisters, let's talk a little while about Jesus," are addressed to everyone in the room with that intention. The singers will remain seated, except for solo passages, and the audience is requested not to applaud except (if desired) at the intermission and at the conclusion of the performance.

It seems particularly appropriate that the present performance of *Son of Man* should have as its sponsor the Interdenominational Ministers Alliance of Greater New York and Vicinity. After all, this wonderful old Negro music had its birth in the early Negro Church and served as spiritual food and drink for an oppressed people who had little else to go on except perfect faith and an abiding hope. What then could be more fitting than that an organization of churchmen should once again offer this grand old music, developed from the primitive sources into more modern forms, to bring a new message of faith and hope to a world so sadly in need of both? And what could possibly be a more perfect time than the Easter season for retelling once again the immortal story of Jesus, the Son of God, who sometimes loved to call Himself the *Son of Man?*

The Cantata, *Son of Man*, is the story of the last days on earth of Jesus—told in music—Negro music—sometimes in the simple but eloquent style of the older spirituals—sometimes in the more highly developed original compositions. The dramatic incidents are clarified by scriptural verses read—not acted—by a dignified narrator against the musical background. The story begins with the Last Supper, continues through the scene in the Mount of Olives, the agony in Gethsemane, the betrayal, arrest, trial, crucifixion and comes to a tremendous climax with the Resurrection.

Musical Requirements

An effective performance of *Son of Man* requires two choruses, soloists, an able reader for the narration, and an organist. Most of the music is sung unaccompanied but the organ is necessary for some of the solo passages and large climaxes. The instrumental effects may be greatly enhanced by occasional use of a few brass instruments, a harp and tympani, but these, while desirable, are not indispensable.

Two choruses—"Action" and "Grand"—The "Action" chorus is a very highly trained group which sings the more difficult dramatic music used to "advance" the story. . . . It should number about 50 to 75 singers, according to the size of the auditorium. The "Grand" chorus is composed of singers combined from church choirs, local choral organizations or any interested individuals with good voices and some experience. This larger group is used at frequent intervals to add weight and solemnity to the music. Their portions . . . are not technically difficult and may be easily learned in a few rehearsals. . . . The entire chorus being assembled only for the last rehearsals. . . . The "Grand" chorus should be as large as possible, so long as a reasonable balance is kept between the male and female voices. H.J.

In a pamphlet developed especially for groups that might wish to present this work, Johnson goes on to discuss such mechanics of production as expenses, publicity, credit to individual performing groups, and payment to members of the "Grand Chorus." A copy of the original program follows:

THE CANTATA

Son of Man
Introduction
   When I Was Sinkin' Down
   Come On, Brothers an' Sisters*[47]
   You Won't Find a Man Like Jesus

Man of Sorrows
  Man of Sorrows*
  I Feel Like My Time Ain't Long
  Judas Was a Weak Man
The Last Supper
  Den We'll Break Bread Together
  'Tis Midnight, and on Olive's Brow
Gethsemane
  I Got to Lie Down
  Po' Little Jesus, Cryin' in de Garden on His Knees*
  Dey Didn't Know He Was de Son of God*
  They Led My Lord Away
The Trial
  I've Been 'Buked
  Look What Dey Doin' to Jesus*
  Pilate! Pilate! Pilate!*
  Woe Is Me!* (Judas Repents)
Calvary
  The March up the Hill
  The Crucifixion (Male Voices Only)
  Terror! Darkness!*
  Lament of His Followers*
Victorious Vision
  Ride On, King Jesus
  He Is King of Kings

Intermission
Midnight before the First Easter
  Sabbath Has No End
His Friends Remember
  Were You There?
  Ain't Got Time to Die (Peter, the Rock)*
  Take My Mother Home (John and the Mother, Mary)
  I Will Arise and Go to Jesus (Mary Magdalene)
At the Tomb
  Mary Come a-Runnin' on a Sunday Mornin'
  Weepin' Mary (Women's Voices)
  Oh de Angel Rolled de Stone Away
  The Magdalen and the Master*
  Hallelujah, King Jesus! (The Angels)*
The Glad Tidings—Finale
  Christ Is Risen*
  Lord of Love*

Participating Choirs and Conductors

Interracial Fellowship Chorus	Harold Aks
Union Congregational Church	Ionia Bacchus
Grace Congregational Church	Helen Hagan
Mt. Morris Presbyterian Church	Arthur Phillips
St. Luke and St. Martin's Episcopal	William King
Metropolitan Community Methodist	Charles Alford
Riverside Guild Choir	Ralph Harrel
Mt. Olivet Baptist Church	Lorenzo Dyer
Sam Wooding Singers	Sam Wooding
New York Interracial Chorus	Clifford Kemp
Salem Methodist Episcopal Church	Rudolph Grant
Mother E. M. E. Zion	Leonard Matthews
Collegiate Chorale	Robert Shaw
Williams Institutional C. M. E.	Howard Johnson
Celestial Choir	Edith Brinnard
Mt. Calvary Methodist Church	Louvenia White
Abyssinian Baptist Church	Howard Dodson
Philharmonic Male Chorus	Elfrida Wright
St. Marks Methodist Church	Van Whitted
St. James Presbyterian Church	Melville Charlton
Hall Johnson Choir	Hall Johnson
Schubert Music Society	Edward Margetson
Church of the Master	Clarence Whiteman
St. Phillips Episcopal	Walter Witherspoon
Refuge Temple	David Mells
St. George's Episcopal Church	George Kemner

A Historical Perspective

The probable genesis of *Son of Man* has been discussed in an earlier chapter in relationship to Emil Ludwig's book of the same name. This theory would seem to gain added credibility when one considers that all of Hall Johnson's earlier major works were entertainments—musical plays, folk dramas, or shows. In Johnson's own words, the *Son of Man* was to be presented as a "meditation." This seems to be something of a caveat as the work is most certainly as "Christian" and as "religious" as the passions of J. S. Bach. While Coleridge Taylor Perkinson[48] compared the work to Handel's *Messiah*, a comparison to Bach's *St. Matthew's Passion* would be more accurate as the primary protagonist in *Son of Man* is the chorus, with the traditional spirituals functioning much as did the chorales in Bach's work. There are solo movements that indeed correlate to the arias in Bach, and the function of the recitatives is fulfilled by text delivered by the narrator. Given the fact that *Son of Man* was composed and assembled in such an incredibly short time (the choir was formed in January for an April performance), one might reasonably theorize that the use of a narrator to move the action was a compromise mandated by the need for expedition, as true recitatives would have all required original composition as they would have been through-composed. Ideally, such recitative would have been delivered by contrasting voices and would have required time for composition and teaching to selected soloists. *Son of Man* was also an expression of a functional need. Hall Johnson's vision of a "heavenly choir" was necessarily a heavenly host, that is, a massive choir (note three hundred voices for the first performance, and five hundred voices for the second). One is reminded of Berlioz's declaration that a thousand violins playing a C major scale would sound wonderful. Although Johnson had touring choirs as small as twenty voices, from his early appearance at the Roxy Theater with Waring conducting, Johnson's reputation allowed him to attract and command two hundred or more voices whenever needed throughout his active career. As early as 1930 and the Broadway run of *The Green Pastures*, Johnson had assembled a group of three hundred singers in New York, which he divided into the *Green Pastures* choir, a concert choir, and a reserve choir. Much of his ability to attract singers was based on his ability to envision significant projects for the singers and to successfully realize them, whether Broadway shows, concerts, movies, radio performances, and so on. As with Bach, most of his composition and arranging seemed to be totally functional as is obvious with *The Green Pastures*, *Spiritual Moods I and II*, *Jus' Keep On Singing*, and the many movie scores.

The following article adds significantly to one's perspective on *Son of Man*, and was published just prior to its New York debut. It is digested here in my own words.

New York Post—*April 12, 1946*[49]

300 to Sing Easter Cantata

by Henry Beckett

Monday evening's performance at New York City Center will feature two premiers, Hall Johnson's three hundred–voice Festival Negro Chorus of New York, and his new cantata, *Son of Man: A Musical Meditation in the Negro Idiom.*

Hall Johnson, whose name has been associated with top Negro choral groups for many years, will unveil two brand new products at the New York City Center on Monday evening. Item one is the Festival Negro Chorus of New York, a group of three hundred mixed voices organized and conducted by Johnson. Item two is a new Easter Cantata, *Son of Man*, composed and arranged by Johnson and subtitled *A Musical Meditation in the Negro Idiom*. The new chorus grew naturally out of Johnson's desire to find an artistic use for the many singers he could not use in his smaller core group. The structure of the Festival Chorus, organized in January, is to have a professional component of one hundred voices, and a nonprofessional component of two hundred singers. What Johnson found was that the quality of the singers in the larger group was so high that instead of devoting a full year of rehearsals to the preparation of the cantata, he was able to prepare it in a mere three months for its debut performance. He also considers the Festival Chorus as a means of providing education and employment to talented Negro singers in the cultural contributions of the race. His objective is expressed in the motto "Let our music work for us."

Son of Man represents a change from Johnson's usual absorption, almost exclusively, with the Negro spiritual, as it includes much original material and a variety of musical forms and styles. The spirituals that are included are less familiar ones. While much of the work is a cappella, organ, brass, harp, and percussion are used at climactic points.

The performance evoked a most moving poem from the poet Leo Liberttison, which he wrote as he listened. On the following day (April 16), he sent Johnson a letter expressing the following sentiments: The performance was *not* a concert, but a deeply moving experience. He commented that the chorus was both sensitive and eloquent and that Johnson's control of the three hundred voices defied analysis. He gave his reaction in the form of a sonnet, which cannot be reproduced here because of copyright restrictions. It has been preserved in the Hall Johnson Collection and is named, "How Many Are the Years (To Hall Johnson)." I believe that the "fair use" doctrine will allow me to quote several lines:

> How many are the years your towering form has seen
> Drift past, discarding their tear laden freight of pain?
> How many are the sighs your hands have drawn.[50]

The 1946 premiere with the Negro Festival Chorus appears to have been ignored by the New York critics. The 1948 performance by the Interracial Festival Chorus received extensive coverage. The digested reviews from the *Herald Tribune* and the *New York Post*, which follow, confirm the audience response and the generally favorable critical response. *Son of Man* remains unpublished although a complete score is extant. Unfortunately, the copyright complications that would arise in attempting publication are legion as the work includes many of Johnson's spirituals published by different companies, each owning the copyright to individual selections.

Reviews

New York Herald Tribune—March 28, 1948[51]

Son of Man Cantata Has Carnegie Hall Premiere

On Friday evening at 11:30, Hall Johnson led a large chorus comprised of members of twenty-six choral groups, in a performance of his cantata, Son of Man. The work is based on Christ's final days and is comprised mainly of traditional and composed spirituals. It is musically effective and expresses deep and genuine religious sentiment. The original spirituals were not as convincing as the traditional ones and lacked passion and intensity. The singing of the chorus and of the soloists was excellent, and the sustained applause of the audience confirmed the success of the work much as if it were the St. Matthew Passion of Bach.

New York Post—March 28, 1948[52]

Hall Johnson's Son of Man Is More Than Good

Hall Johnson's Easter Cantata, Son of Man, premiered at New York City Center in April 1946, received its second New York performance on Friday evening at Carnegie Hall. It was sung by a massed choir consisting of twenty-four choral groups, and totaling five hundred voices. There were few changes from the initial performance, and a large audience, representative of music professionals, music lovers, and other who wished to enter into the spirit of Easter received the performance enthusiastically. Described by Johnson as a musical meditation, the tone of the work is set by the opening number, "Come On Brothers and Sisters, Let's Talk about Jesus."

One listener was heard to say that the work moved him deeply, causing him to empathize with the suffering Jesus, and likening this suffering to that of an oppressed people. The cantata is carefully composed, moving from the simpler spirituals, to the intricate "Christ Is Risen." A sincere religiosity was communicated, and at times, the work of the ensemble was spine-chilling. Juano Hernandez was the narrator and Carl Diton, the organist. Conceptually, the cantata is arresting and most profound. More judicious selection of the small ensemble and more rehearsal time would add immeasurably to the total effect. The score might be revised so as to improve its unity and movement. While too much repetition made for moments of dullness, this was compensated for by the thrilling moments provided by movements like "Pilate! Pilate! Pilate!"

"Crucifixion," "Take My Mother Home," and "Christ Is Risen." These movements exhibit a "passion, intensity and grandeur" that should make the work "immemorable" [*sic*][timeless].

Formal Structure

Structurally, the design of *Son of Man* is analogous to that of the Baroque passion, as it is an extended form for soloists, chorus, and occasional orchestra, semi-dramatic in nature, with subject matter dealing with the Easter scriptures. As the Baroque cantata is much shorter in duration than the passion, it is interesting to ask why Johnson didn't call his work a "passion," given its length. As with the passion, *Son of Man* has an evangelist in the role of the narrator who tells the story and advances the action, a function traditionally carried by the recitatives. The other clear analogies are the solos to arias, the spirituals to the chorales, and the chorus to the Baroque chorus.

Within the larger framework the forms used in the spirituals are the traditional ones: stanza form, bipartite and ternary forms supplemented by auspicious use of dissonance, descriptive effects, and obbligatos. Some of the original music makes effective use of through-composed form as does "Pilate! Pilate! Pilate!" Other original pieces in the style of a spiritual like "Ain't Got Time to Die" assume traditional spiritual structures.

V. *Toward Freedom (Let Freedom Ring)*—A Short Cantata for Mixed Chorus, Solo Baritone, and Orchestra

Since 1927, the Hall Johnson Choir had been featured on the annual Lincoln's Memorial Show at New York's Roxy Theater. In February 1932, Johnson had been asked to design a stirring act for the show, which was called "Let Freedom Ring." For this performance, he assembled a group of two hundred black singers and created a major work for the event, which he named *Toward Freedom*. Because his notes have been preserved we are able to observe the careful planning and the organizational skill which he applied to every compositional task. First he carefully defines and limits his assignment:[53]

Toward Freedom

A Composition for Mixed Chorus, Solo Baritone, and Full Orchestra
(Should last about 25 minutes)
[Page 1]
   The text emphasizes the inherent freedom of mankind—from a universal point of view—rather than individual or nationalistic freedom; In other words, Freedom with each other instead of *from* each other.

The text, while wishing to get over the "feeling" of this important truth, avoids everything which sounds like argument, or philosophical discussion, or propaganda of any sort. There is rather a roughly poetic approach which makes full use of metaphor and symbolism. It must not be dull or "preachy."

Next, Johnson addresses questions of form, media, and textual development:

[Page 2]
Outline of thought, content, development of the concept. (What the text expresses in symbol and metaphor.)

Episodes or Sections
1. Short orchestral introduction
2. Choral—The people disturbed and anxious ask "What is this Freedom?" Some think one thing, some another.
3. Baritone Solo—Explains the essential nature of Freedom. Freedom not to be confused with the manifestations of Freedom.
   a. Not the waves of the ocean, but the wetness of all *water*.
   b. Not the circulation of the air whether mild breeze or rough hurricane, but the *oxygen*.
   c. Not the free motions of life, but *life* itself.
4. Chorus—People grasp the idea and discuss it in rapid, excited counterpoint. Ending in question—How is this freedom won?
   a. We have sought it always.
   b. Wherein have we failed? Fought for it? Died for it?
5. Baritone—Explains: Mankind has always measured *freedom* in terms of its manifestations—looking for it *without*, instead of *within* in the essential nature of man. Man, like the elements, is one in essence, no matter how widely separated in application.

From this brief sketch, Johnson developed the elaborate scene that appears below in its entirety, including stage directions, texts, and music:

Let Freedom Ring

The stage for this presentation—as has been explained—is arranged in three levels, resembling long narrow tiers, one above the other, so that the picture will give the effect of friezes. The lowest level is occupied by the singers, the second by the pantomimists, and the highest by the Roxyettes and the ballet, either together or alternately. (It is necessary that these three stages should be capable of being lighted together and absolutely separately—so that the action on one level can, if necessary, go on without the slightest change of scenery or costumes.) Only the singing never stops throughout.

The story and meaning of the action of this piece is narrated clearly in the texts of the songs. This could be further helped by titles on a screen if desired or found necessary. The emotion of the songs is translated into action on the levels above—more or less literally by the Negro pantomimists—more sublimated by the ballet on the top level.

The scenic details could be worked out either suggestively or quite realistically on the second level, with the actors either quite symbolic or in actual characters. The upper ballet is always conventional.

The Score Requires the Following Scenes

Scene I: Africa:

A Jungle—dark, indistinct figures; chanting against tom-toms; possibly a tribal dance interrupted by the attack of the slave-traders. Sudden confusion and black-out.

Transition:

The chants and cries settle down into a plaintive wailing-song which is to suggest the transportation of the slaves across the sea. Would suggest interpretive ballet here to illustrate leading away into slavery.

Song: "Strange Lands, Strange Things"

> Strange lands, strange things,
> New gods, new kings,
> Old homes done fade away,
> Dark night, darker day.

Scene II: Mississippi Slave Boat

Stirring heavy song in swinging minor. In the half-light, men, stripped to the waist are moving slowly—Women and children lie huddled in little heaps on the floor. Their swaying motions are quite diverse in direction but uniform in rhythm. There are other sounds—the regular swish of the propeller in the water—an occasional steamboat whistle. When called for by the words of the song—there could be rhythmic rattling of heavy chains with now and then a sudden crack of a whip.

Song: "Down de Mississippi Boun'"

> 1. Wris'-chains, ankle-chains,
> Down the Mississippi boun'
> Wris'-pains, ankle-pains,
> Down de Mississippi boun'
> River, what has darkies done to you?
> River, what you totin' darkies to?

Oh, wris'-chains, ankle-chains,
All down de Mississippi boun'
Oooh, Oooh—all down de Mississippi boun'.

2. Whip cracks, bleedin' backs,
   Down de Mississippi boun'
   Woun's burn, eye-balls turn,
   Down de Mississippi boun'
   River, you lef' Mammy on de sho'
   Won't you take me back to see her jes' once mo'?
   Oh, whip cracks, bleedin' backs,
   All down de Mississippi boun'
   Oooh, Oooh, all down de Mississippi boun'.

3. Hearts sore, weep no mo'
   Down de Mississippi boun'
   Heads bare, mumble prayer,
   Down de Mississippi boun'
   Lordy, Lordy, Help us thro de night.
   Won't you make dis driver take us to de light,
   Oh, hearts sore, weep no mo'
   All down de Mississippi boun'
   Oooh, Oooh, all down de Mississippi boun'.

This song starts somberly in male voices—rises to a wild pitch in the second verse, and settles down to a hush (almost) in the third.

Transition:

A strong *Prophetic Voice* rises from out of the choir while a figure typifying its meaning rises in the scene and carries out in pantomime what the Voice says. The choir responds in tone and the actors in motion. The Voice says, in effect,

Voice—Oh, Chillun, don't be so down-hearted; look up a little while. You still got one thing lef' and dey ain't nobody kin take it from you.

The above free passage leads into a vigorous, bright, syncopated spiritual which gathers force and swing as it goes and makes an ecstatic contrast to the dark boat-song. The verses are sung by the *Voice* and the chorus swings into the following refrain:

Song: "Keep On Singin'"
Refrain:

Keep on singin' and you can't die;
Keep on singin' and you can't be buried;

> Tell God to give you a song,
> An' jes' a keep on singin' it
> All day long.

The (Beat) scene closes on this religious dance (which could also be carried out by the formal ballet).

Scene III:

This scene should suggest expanse—a very large cotton field with a broad stretch of sky above. In the foreground (left) is the front of a cabin with a *stoop* and a *practical* door. The whole scene should be worked out more realistically than the others since it has to support a bright light to represent high moon.

Action:

At the close of the bright song of the last scene, the choir has started quickly into "Nobody Knows de Trouble I See, Lord," and is still singing when laborers are discovered working slowly in the field. It is near noon. Their downcast appearance and measured gestures fit the slow ebbing waves of the song. However, from time to time, one or two stop a second and scan the sky under their hands as if expecting something.

Suddenly the song is rudely interrupted by the Prophetic Voice. An actor runs on the scene with a whispered message which is passed all through the crowd (with differing receptions by different people)—some go on working, some stop and whisper together in knots. There is more looking up and a greater air of general expectancy. In the choir, the Voice is saying:

"Oh, chillun, don't you feel de time is coming? De tim's don been for tol' by de wise men and de elders for de las' hundred years." (The 12 o'clock whistle blows for dinner. Pickaninnies run on stage with dinner pails. The general excitement increases as the people quit work and prepare to eat.) The Voice goes on:

> Yes, Sir, I can feel it in de air an' all through each an' every bone—
> Good times is a comin' soon
> Trouble gwinter bus' lak a big balloon.

Choir picks up the refrain with these words and dashes into lively song. The people in the picture assume positions of ease and begin to work in the song. One or two begin to eat. An old man goes into the cabin and comes out immediately with a guitar and a banjo—two boys take these and begin to play in the song. The children form a ring and dance around or there could be clog specialties or anything like that for a lively minute.

Suddenly everything stops abruptly—music, dancing, everything. There is a second of tense silence. After a second of pause there comes a faint trumpet call from a distance *above*. Another second of hush then the Voice goes on:

"Yes, chillun, de Lord is rollin' up His sleeve. He is gittin' ready to stretch out His mighty arm for de salvation of His po' black people. He is makin' ready to speak and I know what he's fixing to say. Can't you hear His voice of thunder ridin' thro' de wide arches of Heaven an' echoin' in the bottomless dep's of de sea?"

Song: "Free at Las'"

Free at las' free at las'
Thank God A'mighty, I'm free at las'.

This song is done with a swing that will stimulate the liveliest motion and give great opportunity to both actors and ballet. While all this music is going on, the actors are showing more and more animation. Appropriate actions denoting astonishment and awe should accompany the first (faint) trumpet call and the *Voice* then follows. The atmosphere of mirth inspired by the "Good Times" song gradually gives way to a more solemn mood and through "Go Down Moses," the gestures and movements are most solemn and dignified.

Following the *series of three trumpet calls*, the action changes again After the first, at the words "Bow Low"—everybody assumes a position of reverence. Some incline their heads, some kneel. After the second, at the words "On yo' knees," those standing drop to their knees and those already kneeling fall face downward on the ground. After the third and longest call, at the words, "Arise and Shine," a messenger rushes madly on the scene in a frenzy of joyous excitement, proclaiming the [coming] of freedom.

The people rise hastily and crowd around him. When they realize what has happened, they are all affected differently. The younger people jump up and down, embracing each other; the older people wave their arms and clasp each other's hands; some laugh and weep on each other's shoulders; some of the children jump about, others cling to their parents in amazement. All this, during the singing of "Free at Last." The ballet on the top level should be dancing in the wildest joy. The song continues. After a few moments of rejoicing together, the people exit left, rather hastily, leaving cotton baskets, etc., in the field. The scene fades out but the ballet above continues to dance to the song.

At the end of the song ("Free at Las'"), the Voice and the choir resume:
Voice:

Well, chillun,
Dis is de beginnin' of a new day an' a better day,
But it's also gwinter be a mighty hard day,
You're gointer meet trials and tribulations dat you never met befor'
Now everyman is his own man
And everywoman is her own woman
An' yo' got to stan' up an' take yo' place
Like men and women.

Here the scene lights up again and the ex-slaves reappear from the left—marching diagonally up stage in a long line. They are carrying bags and bundles of all sorts and holding children by the hand. Their tempo is moderate but their heads are high with hope and they are smiling). The Voice continues without interruption by stage action:

> De worl' ain't gointer look the same to yo'
> An' yo' ain't gointer look de same to de worl'.
> But yo' get to go forward, yo' can't go backwards
> Yo' done been through too much to git weak-kneed now,
> An' de same faith an' de same songs dat brought you dis far,
> Will carry you on jes' as far as yo' got to go.
> (Sing) So, keep on singin! an' you can't die,
> Keep on singin' and you can't be buried.
> Praise God. He gives you a song
> So jes' keep on singin it' all day long.

By now, the line of ex-slaves has trailed off the scene. As the last chord of the above song die out—the orchestra bursts into "America." The full choir sings augmented by choirs in the upper boxes.

> Our fathers God to thee,
> Author of liberty
> To thee we sing.

Here, the full stage is lighted up disclosing for the first time the choir. The women make a long row behind the men. In the exact center of the row of men are six trumpet players who join in with brilliant fanfares. The big organ also joins at this point.

> Long may our land be bright
> With freedom's holy light,
> Protect us by thy might,
> Great God, our King,
> A-men—A-men.

Tremendous A-men (not Ah-men) finale with antiphonal replies from the different groups of singers. Three of the six trumpets could effectively be placed out of sight somewhere in the top of the back of the house.

In spite of the seriousness of this theme and apparent solemnity of its treatment, it will be found that the wide variety of moods, types, tunes, and rhythms will make dullness impossible. In fact, with proper direction, the audience should be made to experience every emotional reaction from very sad, to very gay. It has great possibilities for flexibility without danger of spoiling.

Two reviews of this performance, one by Edward Perry and one by Henry Beckett, appear in chapter 1. Both decry the absence of Hall Johnson from the podium and castigate Fred Waring for doing a less than competent job as conductor. The reception of *Toward Freedom* was positive although part of the work had to be cut because of time restrictions. While the *New York Post* critic called for a future complete performance of the work, there is no evidence that it was performed again in New York after the Roxy engagement. Apparently it was performed at the University of Southern California on July 20, 1942, as a letter from Max Krone in reference to the return of the orchestral parts has been preserved. Krone indicated, in a letter of January 30, 1952, that the parts had been located in the library, but the conductor's score was not there and had probably been taken by Johnson. It appears that Johnson rewrote the conductor's score as it only exists currently in a penciled sketch. This performance, apparently a West Coast premiere, was confirmed by a review in the *Pacific Coast Musician*, dated August 1, 1942: "Hall Johnson conducted his Negro Choir in the first performance of his *Toward Freedom*. The composition is built along lines of simplicity but is tremendously effective. Needless to say, his choir gave it a rousing interpretation."[54]

VI. *Spiritual Moods* for Male Quartet and Orchestra

On or about September 1, 1952, Hall Johnson received a commission from the Jubilee Singers through their agent Irwin Parnes.[55] The letter, dated August 30, said in part,

> The Jubilee Singers hereby commission you to compose and arrange a thirty minute composition based upon Negro spirituals. This piece is to be for full symphony orchestra and Male Quartet. The title will be *Spiritual Moods*, with the subtitle *Jubilee Songs*.
> The composition will be based upon and will include the following Negro songs:
> "Go Down Moses"—"Swing Low, Sweet Chariot"—"Joshua Fit de Battle"—"Were You There?"—"Witness"—"Every Time I Feel the Spirit."
> These songs are to be connected by original orchestral material.
> In deference to your recognized authority in this field of music, the Singers agree to make no changes whatsoever in your arrangement—either of the music or the text of these songs. It is particularly understood that the dialect forms in the text are not to be changed into correct English, as that would necessarily impair the rhythms of the songs.

It is understood that you release to the singers exclusive publication rights for this composition for a period of five years from date of this agreement. It is also understood that you grant to the singers exclusive performing rights to this composition for the same period of five years from date of this agreement.

You will receive standard record royalties as composer. You will receive for your services as composer-arranger the sum of $500. Two hundred and fifty dollars is being paid to you in advance and the remainder will be paid on or before February 19, 1953.

You agree to complete the full score and provide the necessary parts on or before October 12, 1952, and that the score and all parts will be sent to me in Paris by air mail parcel post in care of Marcel de Valmalete, 48 Rue La Boetie, Paris 5, France. I am hoping that the piano score will be in the hands of the *Jubilee Singers* long before October 12, so that they can give the work adequate rehearsals. Postage to send the score and parts will be paid by the singers.

If the above is in accordance with your understanding, would you please sign two copies and return them to me in the enclosed envelope. I know that you are making quite a concession to provide *Jubilee Songs* at the above fee and on behalf of the Jubilee Singers, I wish to offer you my sincere thanks.

Respectfully,

Irwin Parnes[56]

Incredibly, Hall Johnson accepted the commission for reasons that must have been primarily economic and agreed that for the munificent sum of $500 he would compose a thirty-minute work on six spirituals, write a score for full orchestra, and make a piano vocal part and all the instrumental parts, plus a conductor's score, between September 1 and October 9, a total time of roughly five weeks. Within a week of beginning the score (without returning the signed contract) Johnson received, from Parnes's Waldorf Astoria lodgings, a short letter dated September 7, 1952, in which he informed Johnson that the Jubilee Singers had been invited to perform with the National Symphony Orchestra of Luxembourg, on September 30. Parnes indicated that he would like to premiere the work on that date and wanted to know if it could be completed by that time. It would be necessary to have the vocal parts by September 11 and the orchestral parts would have to be in Paris by September 26.

Parnes's request, if granted, effectively reduced the time for the preparation of the vocal score to less than two weeks, and the time for the completion of the entire job to three weeks. Johnson wired the following reply:[57]

You should have completed score and parts in Paris by September 22, at latest, for adequate quartet rehearsals. This gives me only until September 17th to finish and mail. Possible only if I work night and day. Will do, if you wire additional $500 immediately, on receipt of this wire. Not a minute to lose. Otherwise, original dates and conditions must stand as per present contract. Music, contracts, and letter already in special delivery mail. Please reply immediately. H.J.

Parnes wired back his response at two o'clock in the morning on September 10.

Wish I could oblige you with the extra two fifty [?] but as you know there is a famine of money in this quarter. Will count on receiving score and parts as per original contract. However, if you could possibly complete work in time for Luxembourg Symphony performance, it would be wonderful publicity and good credit all the way round. Best regards.
　　Irwin

One would assume that the matter was now settled and that the Jubilee Singers would receive their commissioned masterpiece in Paris on September 22. Apparently, this was not the case. Not only did the group not receive *Spiritual Moods* on September 22, they did not receive it on October 22. On October 29, Johnson wrote the following letter to Irwin Parnes, manager of the group:

Suppose you received the orchestral sketch which I sent some time ago. Had hoped to hear from you about it but suppose you are in motion—which always delays things. Today, I sent you a cable suggesting you arrange some substitute material to use for your orchestral appearances until I can get the completed score and parts to you—or else, postpone your dates in some way. I have found it is simply *not humanly possible* [Johnson's emphasis] to prepare such a big job in the few weeks we had allotted for it—in all good faith. But good faith does not stimulate composition nor put a million notes on paper. You must remember that this was not just an arranging job (of already written music) but a composing job as well—and a fascinating one. I knew from the beginning that there was not sufficient time (especially since the men had to learn the score), but I let you persuade me against my better judgment and, now that I am in it, I want to finish it. Apart from the pressure of time, this is the most enjoyable job I have ever worked on—and I think it is my very best work to date. I have devoted every minute to it—since the beginning—working night and day—putting off my publishers and stealing time from my nightly rehearsals. The score itself is almost finished. The parts will take a couple of days to copy and only a few hours to duplicate. But then, there is the mailing time. I am still working night and day and will mail it at the first possible moment. That is all that can be done. I know you will be disappointed now but you will be glad later—because this composition will place your group in an entirely new field of performance. And it must be a perfect job throughout—including the singing. It all needs more time.

Please let me hear from you.

H.J.

Certainly, the Jubilee Singers, now in the sixth week of their concert tour, without their magnum opus, must have been more frantic than disappointed. However, Parnes, their manager, had anticipated the further delay and rescheduled their first orchestral engagement. His letter, written on October 25, four days before Johnson's, crossed Johnson's letter in the mail and said:

> Thank you very much for writing out and sending on the vocal score—you were quite right about the need for preliminary rehearsals for the singers. . . . We are looking forward to the performance of *Spiritual Moods* in Tunis.

For Johnson to accept the commission and promise delivery by a date he knew was impossible was unpardonable. However, it is understandable in view of his financial condition if one recalls that he had said to his manager the preceding December, "I don't know where my next dollar is coming from." He also had failed to land the Paris Festival job with his own choir, or the *Porgy and Bess* job in the spring and summer of that year. So the premiere of *Spiritual Moods* did not take place until the Jubilee Singers' engagement with the Grand Symphony Orchestra of Tunis on November 29, 1952.

Spiritual Moods created a sensation (my emphasis) at its world premiere under the direction of Louis Gava. The Jubilee Singers (Starling Hatchett and Robert Perrin Bradford, tenors; George Goodman, Baritone; and Daniel Andrews, bass) received eight curtain calls, and the work was hailed in the Tunisian press as "music of expressive power and enchantment, sung by great voices that form a veritable single instrument of precise intonation."[58] The group gave 110 concerts in Europe, North Africa, and the Near East before returning to the United States in February for a coast to coast tour, which they kicked off with a U.S. premiere with Thor Johnson and the Cincinnati Orchestra. Following their U.S. tour, the group toured South America for three months and sang the South American premiere in Buenos Aires.

Matthew Kennedy, in a letter to Johnson dated July 12, 1953, described the Buenos Aires reception:

> A few nights ago we had the pleasure once more of performing *Spiritual Moods*— this time with the Buenos Aires Symphony. The reception was fantastic! There

was such insistence by the public that it was necessary to repeat from the beginning to the conclusion of "Joshua." Everyone here says they never witnessed such an ovation. One gentleman says *the only similar demonstration that he can recall took place thirty or so years ago for Caruso!* [my emphasis]

Sincerely yours,

Matthew Kennedy

P.S.—July 16, 1953

This Cordoba performance evoked an even bigger demonstration!"[59] [my emphasis]

The Jubilee Singers' tour eclipsed all other groups in disseminating the "gospel" of the spiritual around the world in their concerts that presented both the unadorned a cappella form and the spiritual used as the material of an extended symphonic composition. The *Los Angeles Sentinel* addressed just this point in its edition of January 22, 1953, and has graciously consented to a full reprint of their article:

Los Angeles Sentinel—January 22, 1953[60]

Jubilee Singers End Tour Abroad

The Jubilee Singers will conclude a five month tour of Europe, North Africa, and the Middle East, February 8, with two farewell recitals in Paris, amid all the glory ever attributed any ensemble in the world today. The famed ensemble, which traces its origin to the original Fisk Jubilee Singers who toured Europe seven decades ago, is under the auspices of the United States State Department. They have already given 110 concerts on the current tour and have been hailed by audiences in 18 countries.

In Israel, where the singers toured on behalf of a quasi-governmental cultural organization, The Jerusalem Convention Center, their arrival set off a series of receptions, parties and celebrations culminating in their meeting the new-elected president, I. Ben-Zvi. In Vienna, a thousand cheering people poured from the concert hall, following the singers into the street, applauding as they drove off in their taxi-cabs. France-Soir, French newspaper, commented on the "indescribable enthusiasm of a fanatic, shouting audience," and the *Herald Tribune*'s Paris edition reviewer: "The Jubilee Singers packed the Salle Gaveau to standing room capacity with an enthusiastic, insatiable audience, which, at the concert's end clamored for more."

Typical of their European reviews was this comment by the music critic of the *Jerusalem Post*: "Who would deny that Negro spirituals rank second to none in folk music? The charm of these critics does not lie in the shouting of a congregation, but in their subtlety of effect conjures up sounds of Aeolian harps."

The Voice of America transmitted two special broadcasts of spirituals throughout Europe. The ensemble recorded recitals for the British Broadcasting Company in London, and radio stations in Paris, Zurich, Stockholm, Cologne, Munich, Luxembourg, Rome, Holland, Monte Carlo, and Madrid.

VII. *Spiritual Moods II* for Male Chorus and Orchestra

In late July 1955, Johnson received a second commission from the Jubilee Singers to write a second suite of spirituals for their 1955 tour. His response on July 19, to Mrs. Myers, the group's current director, follows:

Dear Mrs. Myers,

It certainly was good to see you again and to hear that your work has been meeting with such success. Of course, that was no surprise to me, knowing the intense devotion and spirit of dedication that has always animated your efforts. That is why it is always such a pleasure to work with you or for you, which brings me to the immediate subject of this letter:

I was thrilled to hear of the fine reception given the *Spiritual Moods* I wrote for you in 1952 and delighted to know that you want me to do another similar composition for your programs of the coming season. Nothing would give me greater pleasure and, if I undertake it, I will try to make it even better than the first one. You know my standards for the quality of my work and you also know that my interest in the success of your work is still the same. But the three years in between have brought changes in my situation which will make it absolutely impossible for me to prepare this composition July 19, 1955, for you except at a cost greatly exceeding the amount you paid me for the first work. And here are the reasons:

First, you must bear in mind that this is not a question of simply *arranging* a group of melodies (like a medley) for voices and orchestra; this is largely a matter of actual, original *composition* of a large, symphonic-type work which must have not only style and brilliance of execution, but, above all, unity of idea. It must be one organism, with beginning, development, growth and a logical brilliant climax. Otherwise, it would not be a single composition, but merely a string of tunes—loosely connected—such as any third-rate man could turn out in two weeks for a few hundred dollars. I would not sign my name to such a thing and, if I did, you wouldn't want it. It just wouldn't be good enough for *your* high standards—and you are acquainted with mine. And, don't forget, after the composition is all completed and scored for full orchestra and voices, I have to extract all the instrumental parts for each player's stand—besides making you a vocal score (with orchestra cues) for your preliminary singing rehearsal. All this *in three weeks!*

In an ordinary business commission, where my sympathies were not involved, I would ask for a job like this from $3,000 to $5,000 and—best of all—

three months time instead of three weeks. As it is, on account of my sincere friendship for you and my great admiration for your work, I am willing to do this—for you—for $2,000 and in the very uncomfortable space of three weeks—because I know that it is all the time you have. $1,000 of the amount is to be paid on the signing of the contract, and the remaining $1,000 on delivery of the completed job. By working at it night and day, I can get it ready in three weeks—but I won't be able to do anything else within that period. Which brings me to an explanation of why I have to demand so much more this time than I did before.

In 1952, when your representative approached me about doing a large orchestral composition for you, I was interested and anxious to help—just as I am now—only with this difference: at that time, three years ago, I had just arrived here, more or less, on a vacation. I had not begun to do any work here—so I had plenty of time—and you had plenty of time to wait. I was living at my sister's home, so I had no expenses. Even at that, I asked him for the very moderate amount of $1500. He quickly told me that you could not pay that much. Not being under any immediate pressure either for time or money, I lowered the price to $1,000. He then told me, very candidly, that $500 was all you could pay. I told him it was a ridiculous sum and *nowhere near* what the job was worth, but as I would enjoy doing it and had the time—and since I was so much in sympathy with your work, I would do it for that amount. It has been a long time since I had had time for a long composition like that, so I enjoyed every moment I worked on it—and when I heard how successful it was in your concerts, I felt repaid: by the pleasure of creating it and the knowledge of having helped you in your work:—*not by the $500.*

Now, three years later, everything is different. I remained here and started a very active studio. What with our regular choral rehearsals, a large class of individual pupils and trying to keep four publishers supplied with compositions and arrangements, I am busy as a bee from morning to night seven days a week. Some days I hardly get time to eat properly until late at night. So, if I do this composition with you, it will mean suspending all my regular work, which, unlike most schools, does not normally fall off during the summer. This will not only curtail my means of livelihood but will interrupt the plans of my students, some of whom have just come in to study beginning this summer. Still, because I know how badly you need this new piece and that you would not feel satisfied to have anyone else do it, I am willing to attempt it—if we can get started right away; the time is so short—even working on it every minute.

The price I am asking is still only half of what I would ask anybody else under my present working conditions. So you see, the truth of the matter is that I am not raising my figure to you this time. I simply did the first one for *my own pleasure* and took what you had to pay. But, as things are now, I can't afford such pleasures. I can't even take time out to read a book with a free mind. So, if you wish to do this, please try to understand that in 1952 I had much time and small expenses. Now I have more expenses and practically no time. If I am to do it, we must begin immediately. Every moment is precious.

Sincerely yours,

Hall Johnson[61]

Mrs. Myers agreed to Johnson's terms, and three days later, he confirmed the agreement with this letter:

July 22, 1955

Dear Mrs. Myers:

According to our several recent conversations, I understand that you wish me to compose and arrange a musical composition for the "Jubilee Singers," whose manager and director you are. This composition, provisionally entitled, *Spiritual Moods No. 2* is to be based on a series of Negro spirituals, bound together and developed by original material into a piece of twenty to twenty-five minutes duration and scored for male voices with a background and accompaniment of full symphony orchestra. I am to deliver to you the full orchestra score, parts for each player, and a working vocal score with orchestral cues on or before August 11th, 1955.

It is further understood that you are to have exclusive performing rights for this composition for a period of ten years, beginning with the date of delivery, and that I am to have printed credit as composer on every program where it is performed.

For this work, you are to pay me the sum of $2,000 as follows: $1,000 on the signing of this contract and the remaining $1,000 upon delivery of the above-named items. If these terms also constitute your understanding of the agreement, our two names and that of a witness on the lines below will give this letter the force of a legal contract between us.

Signed:

Hall Johnson[62]

The cover page of the completed work contained the following information:

Spiritual Moods No. 2
For Male Chorus and Orchestra
By Hall Johnson
Los Angeles, 1955

You May Bury Me In De Eas'
Trampin'
In Bright Mansions Above

I Want To Be Ready
City Called Heaven—
Ride On, King Jesus

While it is not known when Johnson completed *Spiritual Moods No. 2*, the fact that he signed a contract to deliver it in three weeks, when he knew that it could not possible be done in less that three months (based on the earlier composition), simply confirms that he was forced to make such promises out of desperate economic need.

Notes

1. Library of Congress, "The Booker T. Washington Era," part 1 of *African American Odyssey: An Exhibition at the Library of Congress*, ed. Debra Newman Ham, 10 (Washington, DC: The Library, 1998).

2. J. Brooks Atkinson, "New Negro Drama of Sublime Beauty," *New York Times*, February 27, 1930.

3. Arthur Ruhl, "Marc Connelly's *The Green Pastures* with All Negro Cast at the Mansfield," *New York Herald Tribune*, February 27, 1930.

4. John Anderson, "*The Green Pastures*," *New York Journal*, February 27, 1930.

5. George A. Leighton, "*Green Pastures*," *Cincinnati Enquirer*, February 7, 1932, 1 (Entertainment section).

6. George A. Leighton, "Green Pastures Holds Over at the Grand for Another Week," *Cincinnati Enquirer*, February 14, 1932.

7. Clifford Bloom, "A Lovable Lawd," *Des Moines Iowa Register*, April 2, 1932.

8. Isabel Morse Jones, "Green Pastures, Musical Masterpiece of Scoring," *Los Angeles Times*, June 26, 1932.

9. "*Green Pastures* Proves Delight," *Spokesman-Review*, July 10, 1932. Reprinted with permission of the *Spokesman-Review*. All rights reserved.

10. "*The Green Pastures* Returns," *Christian Science Monitor*, February 13, 1951. Reproduced with permission from the *Christian Science Monitor*, www.csmonitor.com. Copyright 1951 *Christian Science Monitor*. All rights reserved.

11. "*Green Pastures* Revived in Inspired Production," *Boston Traveler*, February 13, 1951. Reprinted with permission of the *Boston Traveler*. All rights reserved.

12. Elinor Hughes, "*The Green Pastures*," *Boston Herald*, February 13, 1951. Reprinted with the permission of the *Boston Herald*. All rights reserved.

13. Cyrus Durgin, "*The Green Pastures* Returns to the Colonial, Delightful as Ever," *Boston Daily Globe*, February 13, 1951.

14. Ward Morehouse, "*Green Pastures* Is Superbly Played in Revival," *New York Sun*, March 16, 1951.

15. Otis L. Guernsey Jr., "*The Green Pastures*," *New York Herald Tribune*, March 16, 1951.

16. John McClain, "Marshall Inspiring in Timeless Drama," *New York Journal American*, March 16, 1951.

17. Morehouse, *"Green Pastures* Is Superbly Played."

18. Asterisk (*) indicates an original composition by Hall Johnson.

19. Martha Ennis, "One Man Show" (unpublished article). Courtesy of the Hall Johnson Collection (Rowan University, Glassboro, NJ). All rights reserved.

20. Eileen Southern, *The Music of Black Americans* (New York: W.W. Norton, 1971), 432.

21. Hall Johnson, "The Theology of the New Day Pilgrims" (program notes for the 1938 production at the Mayan Theater in Los Angeles). Courtesy of the Hall Johnson Collection (Rowan University, Glassboro, NJ).

22. Burton Rascoe, "Reflections on *Run Little Chillun*'s Failure," *New York World-Telegram*, September 4, 1943.

23. Ingres Hill Simpson, "Hall Johnson, Preserver of the Negro Spiritual" (Master of Music thesis, University of Cincinnati College-Conservatory of Music, 1971), 22–26.

24. Richard Dana Skinner, "The Play," *Commonweal* (April 1933): 665. Copyright 1933 Commonweal Foundation, reprinted with permission. (For subscriptions: www.commonwealmagazine.org)

25. Stark Young, "Theatre Notes," *New Republic*, March 22, 1933, 60; April 12, 1933, 245.

26. Carl Cramer, *"Run, Little Chillun*: A Critical Review," *Journal of Negro Life* (April 1933): 113.

27. Kenneth Burke, "Pattern of Life," *Saturday Review of Literature* (April 1933): 13.

28. "Hall Johnson Singers," *New York Times*, March 2, 1933.

29. Arthur Ruhl, *"Run, Little Chillun,"* *New York Herald Tribune*, March 2, 1933.

30. "More Raids Planned on Federal Hit Shows," *Los Angeles Examiner*, June 15, 1939.

31. *W.P.A. Federal Theater Project Report* presented to program director Rochester Gil, May 16, 1939, on the scope and success of the program, confirming that Hall Johnson's play, *Run, Little Chillun*, was a smash hit and the all-time record holder of the Federal Theater shows. Courtesy of the Hall Johnson Collection (Rowan University, Glassboro, NJ). All rights reserved.

32. "Spirituals in *Run, Little Chillun* Mainstay of Play at Lyric," *New York Evening Journal*, March 2, 1933.

33. Harry Morris, *"Run, Little Chillun,"* *Morris Piper*, March 9, 1933. Review is quoted directly. Courtesy of the New York City Board of Education.

34. Gilbert W. Gabriel, "'Marilyn's Affairs' but Principally about Another Entertainment, *Run, Little Chillun!"* *New York American*, March 16, 1933.

35. *"Run, Little Chillun, Run, fo' de Devil's Done Loose in de Lan"* *Pictorial Review: A Monthly Survey of Events in the Creative World*, July 1933.

36. Ruth Taunton, "*Little Chillun* Scores Hit on Savoy Stage," *San Diego Union*, 1938.

37. "Music Is Superb in Negro Show," *Pasadena Sun-News*, 1939.

38. Florence Lawrence, "Lovely Singing in *Run, Little Chillun* Drama," *San Francisco Examiner*, July 23, 1938.

39. "*Run, Little Chillun*," *Variety*, July 23, 1938.

40. Ada Hanifin, "*Run, Little Chillun* Is a Musical Treat," *San Francisco Examiner*, January 14, 1939.

41. John Hobart, "*Run, Little Chillun* Proves to be Rousing Theater, Bounces Audience out of Seats," January 14, 1939.

42. Ennis, "One Man Show."

43. Ennis, "One Man Show."

44. Clipping from an unidentified newspaper found in Johnson's papers. Courtesy of the Hall Johnson Collection (Rowan University, Glassboro, NJ). All rights reserved.

45. Hall Johnson, letter to Robert Breen, April 7, 1953. Courtesy of the Hall Johnson Collection (Rowan University, Glassboro, NJ). All rights reserved.

46. Hall Johnson, notes prepared for the performance of *Son of Man* and for the use of conductors who might wish to perform it. Courtesy of the Hall Johnson Collection (Rowan University, Glassboro, NJ). All rights reserved.

47. Asterisk (*) indicates that words and music were composed by Hall Johnson. Remaining music arranged by Hall Johnson.

48. Perkinson is my contemporary and a distinguished twentieth-century Afro-American composer and descendant of Coleridge Taylor.

49. Henry Beckett, "300 to Sing Easter Cantata," *New York Post*, April 12, 1946.

50. Leo Liberttison, "How Many Are the Years" (unpublished poem written during the Carnegie Hall performance of *Son of Man*, April 15, 1948). Courtesy of the Hall Johnson Collection (Rowan University, Glassboro, NJ). All rights reserved.

51. "*Son of Man* Cantata Has Carnegie Hall Premiere," *New York Herald Tribune*, March 28, 1948.

52. "Hall Johnson's *Son of Man* Is More Than Good," *New York Post*, March 28, 1948.

53. This outline was scribbled on two loose pages found in Hall Johnson's papers and is found in the Hall Johnson collection under "Writings of Hall Johnson." Courtesy of the Hall Johnson Collection (Rowan University, Glassboro, NJ). All rights reserved.

54. "All-American Program at USC," *Pacific Coast Musician*, August 1, 1942, 7.

55. Irwin Parnes owned one of the leading concert agencies in America whose roster boasted such artists as Mischa Elman, Percy Grainger, John Brownlee, Claudio Arrau, Roland Hayes, Marjorie Lawrence, and others.

56. Letter from the Irwin Parnes Concert Agency commissioning Hall Johnson to compose a work for male quartet and orchestra, weaving the said spirituals into an

extended work called *Spiritual Moods*. Courtesy of the Hall Johnson Collection (Rowan University, Glassboro, NJ). All rights reserved.

57. All letters referenced are preserved in the Hall Johnson Collection (Rowan University, Glassboro, NJ). All rights reserved.

58. Matthew Kennedy, undated letter with program of the November 29, 1952, concert with the Grand Symphony Orchestra of Tunis. Courtesy of the Hall Johnson Collection (Rowan University, Glassboro, NJ). All rights reserved.

59. Matthew Kennedy, letters to Hall Johnson, July 12 and 16, 1953. Kennedy was the music director of the Jubilee Singers, and these letters detail the tumultuous reception accorded the singers and the music in Buenos Aires and Cordoba. Courtesy of the Hall Johnson Collection (Rowan University, Glassboro, NJ). All rights reserved.

60. "Jubilee Singers End Tour Abroad," *Los Angeles Sentinel*, January 22, 1953. Reprinted by permission of the *Los Angeles Sentinel*. All rights reserved.

61. Hall Johnson, letter to Mrs. Myers, July 19, 1955. Courtesy of the Hall Johnson Collection (Rowan University, Glassboro, NJ). All rights reserved.

62. Hall Johnson, letter to Mrs. Myers, July 22, 1955. Courtesy of the Hall Johnson Collection (Rowan University, Glassboro, NJ). All rights reserved.

CHAPTER FOUR

~

Literary Expression

Nothing so clearly reveals the personality, intellect, spirit, and dimensions of Hall Johnson, the man, as do his writings. It is these writings (along with those of the people with whom Johnson corresponded)—all preserved in the Hall Johnson Collection at Rowan University—that have provided much of the basic source material for this book. They fall into three categories: essays, letters, and poetry. Because of space constraints, only a representative but significant sample of writings in each category has been included.

As one might expect from the leading authority on the Negro spiritual and American folk songs, most of Johnson's essays dealt with these genres, though he did write essays dealing both with philosophy and government. Of the six essays included here, one was for a lecture-demonstration in which he discussed the spirituals and folk songs and used his choir to illustrate the lecture through the performance of representative music. Another is clearly written for one of a series of radio broadcasts with his choir on WMCA. Two others were written for broadcasts on the Voice of America, which featured his commentary and his choir's performance.

Regrettably, Johnson's most important essay, "Notes on the Negro Spiritual," had to be omitted because of its length. Interested readers may find it, as well as Johnson's classic and extended essay "Government," in the Hall Johnson Collection and in Eileen Southern's book *Readings in Black American Music*.[1]

Johnson's correspondence is divided into several categories: letters of recommendation; letters to management, foundations, producers, and publishers; and letters of self-promotion.

These letters have been preserved because in the age of longhand corre-spondence, Johnson took the trouble to have them typed with a carbon copy. These, and sometimes draft copies, were retained for his file. This, unfortu-nately, was not the case with his personal letters, and while we have his re-spondents' letters, only a few of Johnson's personal letters are preserved.

The quality and quantity of Johnson's poetry can only be described as ex-traordinary. He intentionally set out to write a volume of poetry, as is evi-denced by a frontispiece and a carefully constructed introduction to the vol-ume. The poems can be grouped into three categories: poems of love, poems of God, and poems of man. The most representative poems in each category have been included here. One familiar with the historical period cannot fail to compare Johnson's poetry with that of his dear friend Langston Hughes. As one who once read Hughes's work published regularly in the *New York Post* in a column captioned "Simple Sez," I would characterize Hughes's po-etry as "ethnic." Because of this, he was adopted and adored by the majority society. Johnson's poetry, on the other hand, would have to be characterized as "universal," for he eschewed dialect, and neither the style nor content of the poetry would reveal that the poet was a black man.

All of the essays, letters, and poems are published here for the first time. They represent only a portion of a much larger body of work preserved in he Hall Johnson Collection at Rowan University.

The Essays of Hall Johnson

Some Aspects of the Negro Folk Song[2]

With the introduction of Negroes as slaves into these United States, there be-gan to come into being a large body of songs which would never have existed but for the presence of these newcomers. Much time and ink have been used in discussions as to the actual source-origins of these songs. It would seem quite evident and natural, ignoring controversial details, that they should be the general product of the fusion between what the Negro brought here and what he found here. These reactions, set to music, became what are now known as the folk songs of the American Negro.

As these songs began to grow in number, they attracted the attention of mu-sicians the world over. At an earlier date than most people are aware, the bet-ter examples were collected, written down (very poorly, be it said), and issued in book form. Visiting Europeans went back home full of praise for the beauty of this strange new music and when, soon after the emancipation of the slaves, a group of Negro singers made a tour of Europe, the conquest of the old world was complete. In America, the interest in these songs has been of slow but steady growth. There are now very many collections with copious reading matter sincerely and expertly prepared. The phonograph companies, together with the radio, have been of invaluable service in familiarizing the public with this type of music which really has to be heard to be appreciated. In short, it is generally conceded by now that the folk songs of the American Negro represent the most important contribution that America has made to the musical world.

These songs have been studied and discussed from many points of view. There are the historical and geographical angles. When and where did these songs begin, how did the passage of time affect their form and content, and how many variants of the same song are to be found in different districts, even of the same state? Have they any sociological value in showing the relation of Negro life to its surroundings, what is the actual literary worth of the more or less poetic texts, what is the theology expounded in the words of the spirituals, and, finally, how does this music rate just as music, pure and simple? All these aspects of the subject have found interpreters in print and the interested reader will be especially intrigued (and amused) by several recent volumes which profess to prove that the Negro has added nothing new to American music-culture—no, nothing at all!

It is the intention of this article to try to shed a little light upon a few of the less obvious factors which have helped to make this music what it is, and to cause it to sound like it does. For, after all, music itself exists only in its performance. The notes on the paper are merely its symbols, a sort of record for preservation and consultation. Indeed, in the case of Negro music, this record can usually be only an imperfect approximation, for the peculiar quality of the Negro voice (together with its trick of kneading, as it were, the tones of the scale) produces effects which refuse to be apprehended by our present system of notation.

Let us begin by assuming that this music is both interesting and important in our cultural scheme (otherwise, there would not be so much discussion of it either way). That it is essentially good and worthwhile, may be argued from the infinitely small number of its detractors as compared with the multitudes of musically developed people who love it. The next thing to notice is the huge volume and great variety of this material. Hundreds and hundreds of songs in all kinds of moods and patterns—from the long drawn-out wail of the more somber spirituals to the brittle laconic phrases of the reels—with texts embracing every experience known to the singer—whether religious or profane. Such a vast output (and of such high quality) in a few hundred years would have to have almost ideal conditions for growth and development. This was true.

It is a matter of common knowledge that the greatest of our composers have been those who had terrific struggles of one sort or another, with life. Those who had no economic or spiritual problems have left music which pleases us but does not move us profoundly. It would seem that the very circumstances which go to improve quality tend to impede quantity. But to offset these difficulties, the trained composer has two things of inestimable value: a conscious scientific technique to extend his natural gifts and the opportunity to study, either for imitation or evasion, all the great music which preceded his own. If he is a poor man, his greatest problem is leisure time to think and write.

The ideal "set-up" for the creator of fresh music seems then to consist of (1) the desire to create, (2) thorough technical equipment, (3) knowledge of what has already been created, and (4) time to develop and record his creations. For the slave-composer of the Negro folk song, the first and last of these conditions were present to a greater degree than could be possible to any group not in physical bondage and the very lack of the other two was turned by them into an advantage which did more than anything else to help the quality of the music.

(1) Under slavery the urge to make songs was not merely a desire, it was a dire necessity. Deprived of the right of free individual functioning, both mental and physical, it was a matter of life and death for those vigorously live people to have some sort of emotional outlet, a safety valve which would keep them from going to pieces under pressure. Turning their experiences into songs, whether sad or gay, served this purpose as nothing else could have done. Singing these songs to each other helped lighten the burden and gave them a sort of unrestricted conversation in music which could never have been permitted in spoken words. (2) In the absence of scientific training, they turned to the greatest of all teachers, Mother Nature, and from her learned a technique which enabled them to express perfectly their deepest feelings. When they sang about rooks and mountains, the music became massive and firm; when they sang of the river, the measures flowed with breadth and majesty; when they looked at the stars, their voices soared toward that Promised Land which they knew must be above the stars because it was most certainly not beneath them. The technique thus evolved was simple and natural and, like everything simple and natural, very adequate. (3) Ignorant of the music of the past, they were not tempted to imitate it but struck out unhampered into new fields of harmony and counterpoint, Whatever hymn-tunes may have sifted down to them from the white churches underwent a startling transformation in this strange new alchemy and emerged revitalized with new beauties. Those who love to call attention to the fact that certain famous Negro spirituals are undoubtedly based upon certain Southern Methodist hymns, far from belittling the Negro's gift for originality, are only paying a compliment to his great natural musicianship and his superior natural taste. (4) Leisure to sing and to make songs presented no difficulty. Their daily toil engaged the muscles only and left the mind free to make what beauty it could out of a physically circumscribed existence. The masters, far from discouraging the slave-singers, noted that their work was always better when they sang and gave them every inducement to keep it up. Even today, in some sections of the South, the fore-

man or leader of a band of workers is paid a bigger salary if he can sing himself and keep his gang singing. So there was no lack of the practice which "makes perfect" and the results were recorded on that most durable of "lines and spaces," memory.

The vast number of these folk songs is easily accounted for when one considers that, over a long period of time, they were constantly being worked on by thousands of people who had every reason to keep working on them. The fact that all these people were undergoing practically the same experience gives the product of their efforts a great unity of thought and feeling, since the general inspiration was drawn from the same sources. The great variety in the style of the music comes from the ability of the old-time Negro to change his mood at the "drop of a hat." Being only a piece of well-kept property, he did not have to support himself; being all slaves together, there were no long-continued political or business feuds to perpetuate hatreds; no rivalries in love could be taken too seriously under a system where human beings were mated like cattle and whole families could be sold at a moment's notice. The mood of the slave-singer changed with the experience of the moment and, of course, the song changed with the mood. So these people were not always dissatisfied and gloomy as are the wage-slaves of today, nor were they the silly, childish creatures they often pretended (for their own reasons) to be. Having no responsibility in the material world beyond the will of their masters, they lived their own private lives in the realm of the imagination, where they could enjoy all the good things denied them on a lower plane. And right there lies the secret of the creation of the Negro folk song of slavery days. Imagination always has been and always will be the Mother of Everything New, just as Will is its Father. Nature does the rest.

This is not the place to go into a discussion of the various types and forms of Negro songs. There are many books which do this at great length and with numerous musical illustrations. But it may not be amiss to remark that this process of song-making is still going on in these post-Lincoln days. Slavery does not always rattle its chains and there will always be need of new emancipations. Naturally, the newer folk songs concern themselves with current experiences just as the old ones did. Spirituals are still being "made up" in the rural districts where the vested choir is still unknown. The old "reels" and "hoe-downs" have left their humble origins and made their influence felt in every ball-room in the world. Nowadays couples are no longer separated by the auction block but they still separate and, for this world-old occasion, the Negro song-maker has invented a very special and definite type of song—the "blues." The true "blues" are genuine Negro folk songs following a set structural pattern and not to be confused with emanations from Tin Pan Alley which call themselves by the same name. There is also the long, narrative folk ballad composed around some particularly dramatic happening such as "Casey Jones," "The Titanic Disaster," or "Scottsboro." But by far the most socially and musically important of this latter group are the "Songs of Protest" from the chain-gangs and the peonage districts. This is a growing group of tremendous significance because of their dramatic comment on present-day conditions. Fifty years from now they will furnish eloquent documents of these times.

Of the future of the Negro folk song, its possibilities for development into larger forms, who can tell? Many people seem to think that it has great possibilities and many composers in both Europe and America have tried to exploit them. Solo arrangements of spirituals appear with increasing frequency on the programs of nearly all the better recitalists and radio artists. Negro singing-groups specializing in their own folk music are still in demand for concert, radio, and motion pictures. There is no reason, after twenty or twenty-five years of this, to suppose that Negro music is just a fad in the concert hall or just "nice for a change." Anything rising from such deep sources must of necessity be too powerful to be lost or ignored and must contain somehow the seeds of immortality.

European and American composers have for a long time been asking occasional tentative ventures in this field. There have been fantasies and overtures on actual Negro themes as well as operas purporting to be in the Negro manner. These have all been good and interesting music worthy of performance. Several symphonies by Negro composers have gone a long way in the right direction and it is to be expected that the best exponents of this type of music should be those closest to it. What is really needed at this moment for composers who wish to write in this vein is a closer and more prolonged study of the *grammar* of the Negro idiom. For a Negro fantasy, it is not enough simply to refer occasionally to a well-known Negro theme while the development is along the lines of the regular old sixes and sevens. A libretto based on even the best Negro story but decked out with all the continental tricks of La Scala, even with a dash of jazz thrown in, still never make a genuinely convincing Negro opera. It requires more than that.

To keep the Negro flavor throughout an extended composition it is necessary, first of all, to understand the true Negro feeling toward music. To the primitive American Negro (and, after all, it was he, and not the present generation, who invented the flavor), music was not something objective which he touched or handled or which touched him. It was something which he himself *became*—body and soul. His musical utterance was patterned after his speech and he learned to make his melodic accents and inflections follow those of the spoken line. Hence, the feeling of naturalness and ease in a really good Negro folk song. How could those old singers have "let loose" and "enjoyed themselves" while singing if they had had to bother about a badly-set word or a false inflection in the tune?

A good-sized text-book could be written on the subject, "What makes Negro Music Sound Negroid?" So many people have the opinion that it is a question of special harmonies and rhythm. There are important factors, but not nearly so much as the unique counterpoint which results from a church full of people, each having his own conception of how the parts should go. And then it is well to know when the accent should slide into the middle of a note instead of plopping on its nose and when a tone should be diverted from its natural urge toward another tone in the scale or even raised or lowered a bit from its actual pitch. And, above all, how to make a melody note indicate naturally the underlying harmony when the other parts are not being sung—all this is essential if the composition is to sound racial throughout. It will be done some day and, when it is, everybody will recognize it and enjoy it just as we now enjoy the simple *Negro Folk Song.*

The following notes were obviously prepared for a radio show on Afro-American music as the choir had a regular Sunday afternoon series of half-hour concerts on New York's "Christian station," WMCA, in July of 1944. Regrettably, one page has been lost. The discussion, however, is both interesting and informative.

Some Distinctive Elements in African-American Music[3]

What are the characteristics of Afro-American music? Before answering this question, let us review the basic elements of music: rhythm (the regular succession of accents or impulses), melody (an agreeable succession of sounds so formed to give expression to an idea), and harmony (the quality of being pleasing to the ear said especially of the agreement of musical sounds). The distinctive elements in Afro-American music are found in the manner in which the Afro-American treated these basic characteristics in music. From rhythm, the transplanted African devised syncopation (a shifting of the regular metrical beat). For his melodies, he made use of the pentatonic scale (a scale of five notes which was used by the Chinese and other Asian countries).

Now, we turn to the texts of these songs, what can we say about them? The poetry of the songs is unique in that the songs were built around the words and without fail, the important words fell on the important part of the beat. The rhythm of the texts was attained by stressing some of the letters of the alphabet (the B's as in the song "'Bettah Day a Comin'") and by eliminating other letters such as the R's and G's at the end of a word. They became "dee" or "duh." (An example of this is found in the song, "You May Bury Me in de East," and in the song, "Go Tell It on duh Mountain." Some think there is beauty in the quaint pronunciation of the words, and at times, their still quaint and more charming mispronunciation. In the text of the sacred songs, the contents more usually composed from biblical events and adapted to the slave's life. In the body of the non-sacred or secular songs, the texts generally represent events in the daily life of the Negro.

Afro-American music is a combination of all of these factors: syncopation, the pentatonic scale, unison singing, and a combination of part singing, plus the poetry of the lyrics.

In addition to these more basic factors there is something else. I think the music of any nation grows out of the culture of that nation. As a consequence, this, too, gives it a kind of uniqueness. American society is largely thought to be a rather overt, enthusiastic, and bubbling kind of entity in which the people, along with their less positive aspects, are noted for being friendly, outgoing, and what you might call, somewhat daring. It is on such a foundation as this that I am going to try and demonstrate the thesis I have just presented through two major categories: the sacred songs and the secular songs of the Negro. In relation to these aspects of the American character, the Afro-American folk idiom has invaded the culture and enhanced the creativity, originality, and imagination of the American society.

The Sacred Songs
In the book entitled, *American Negro Songs*, John Work divided the spirituals into three groups. The first is the *call and response type*, as found in "Swing Low, Sweet Chariot." The melody of this song is based on the pentatonic scale. (Play record)—The second type is found in the *slow, sustained, long-phrase melody*, as represented in "Nobody Knows de Trouble." In this song, the pentatonic scale is also used and the melody could be played on the piano by using only the black notes. If we start with F# and build the pentatonic scale, we will note that the fourth and seventh tones of our modern diatonic scale have been omitted. (Play record—Marian Anderson, band 1)—The final type is represented by a segmented, syncopated, melody as in the song, "Joshua Fit de Battle." In this well-known song, the syncopation is a strong element plus the biblical story (Chapter IV, Book of Joshua). (Play record—Johnson recording) . . .

[Page four of the essay is missing.]

How have trained composers utilized these musical ideas? In an article in the *Century Magazine* (Feb. 1895), Anton Dvorak, the famed Bohemian composer, advocated the use of southern melodies as the foundation of a serious school of music to be developed in America. He said, "I was led to take this view partly by the fact that the so-called plantation songs are indeed the most striking and appealing melodies that have been found on this side of the water. There is nothing in the whole range of composition that cannot be supplied with themes from this source." In reference to H. T. Burleigh, he said, "Among my pupils, I have discovered a young colored man of talent upon whom I am building strong expectations." Shortly after making this statement, he wrote the "New World Symphony." Let us listen to major themes from this work. (Play "New World Symphony.")

Secular Songs

[One must examine] the work songs for a clear reflection of life during Reconstruction days. These songs were composed while the laborers were working. For certain types of work where rhythmic group action made the work easier, a special type of song became necessary. When the group was whipping steel, hammering, or drilling the work was coordinated by one of these songs sung by a leader. The rhythm was adapted to the type of work. (Play "Water Boy").

The Voice of Rhythm

To say anything really significant about the beginnings of the Hall Johnson Choir without mentioning my maternal grandmother would be like telling the story of Christopher Columbus with Queen Isabella left out. For like the historic jewels, which became more than just costly trifles for the decoration of royalty, the grand old Negro songs and stories of my grandmother, garnered during the last thirty years of slavery, were not only the delight of my youth but turned out to be the richest treasure of my later years. All day long, she would move about her work in house or garden with a long, level, rhythmic stride like an Indian on the trail, always humming softly to herself as if the sound came from the motion or the motion depended upon the sound. But at dusk, she would sit on the front steps, surrounded by us children, and sing song after song—song after song.

Our home was on the side of a steep hill and, from where we sat, we could see, not far away, half hidden by stately magnolias, the old house where she had spent her young days. Sometimes, when memory became too insistent, she would stop singing and tell us a story of the old place and time. Memories of her master, a kindly city doctor, long gone to his rest; of his three young daughters, her mistresses; of her own two sisters; of the day the Yankees came and of that great day when she had learned at noon that she was free and by sun-down had rented her own little house and moved into it with my mother; then a child of eight. Then, more songs. As I looked back upon those days it seems to me that, as I listened, it was not so much the tunes that moved me as the picturesque words uttered in her soft, high, quavering voice, like a beautiful oboe talking. Then she would suddenly discover that it was "getting" too chilly out in this "night-air" and, for one more day, the magic hour was ended.

And there were other times when, working all alone in the kitchen, the hum would change to full voice. "Blessed Be the Name of the Lord!" was one of her favorites. Higher and higher, warmer and warmer, "Blessed Be the Name of the Lord!" still walking and singing. The measured footfalls never break their rhythm as the song turns to ecstatic shouts of "Glory! Glory to His Name!" We children, playing on the back porch, draw away from the kitchen door but watch it expectantly between solemn glances at each other. We know from long observation that "Grandma" is "getting happy." In another instant she will come striding out onto the porch, arms in the air, tears streaming down her face, sobbing and shouting in her soft quavering voice, "Honor! Honor!" We know that, with the same rhythm, she will sit on the edge of the porch with her feet on the nearest of the high back-steps and rock slowly back and forth as the crisis dies. Then she will dry her eyes on her kitchen apron, smile blissfully to herself, then, rising, with a little after-prayer of perfect peace, she will stride on back into the kitchen and go on preparing the dinner. As soon as we hear her humming again, we children resume our noisy play. In those days I did not realize what it meant when Grandma sang at her work until she "got happy." But now I know that God—not the Lord of the Churches, but the very God of Hosts—occasionally visited my grandmother in our kitchen and that, for two or three minutes of mortal time, she would be the honored guest at his Welcome Table.

Although time and change have long since broken up our family group, the spell of the old songs and of my grandmother's singing remains fresh upon me. Seventeen years ago, when I first organized a group of singers to help preserve this music in is primitive form, I was in no doubt as to the origin of the inspiration. Years of training and professional experience had only served to increase my feeling of reverent wonderment at the effortless perfection of the best of these songs and, without realizing it, I had slipped into a life-work: (1) to collect and preserve these old songs in their early shape, (2) to identify and protect the present day derivates of Negro folk music, (3) to aid in the fullest possible development of this music for the future. To add strength to this effort, I have recently organized the Festival Negro Chorus of Los Angeles, a non-commercial group of amateur singers whose whole object is to make use of the traditional Negro music in every beneficial way. Although less than two years old, this organization has already demonstrated that this music is potent for many purposes besides mere entertainment. We have sung for many racial and patriotic occasions, presented new compositions by Negro composers, presented young Negro artists in concert, and provided six scholarships for talented youngsters. We are already formulating plans for the creation of a building devoted to our work and hope eventually to own a fleet of buses.

I have written at some length about my grandmother, not only because she personally was my deepest source of inspiration but because she represents, in retrospect, all that is best in the Negro spiritual and, without doubt, the Negro spiritual is the noblest and loftiest, both in conception and expression, of all folk music of any period and in any part of the world. The simple, rugged poetry of the texts, the unfailing rhythmical and melodic rightness of the tunes, the unerring precision of detail shown in the treatment of every single accent and inflection, not just a succession of differing verses crammed, no matter how uncomfortably, into the same time. These are the signs of a master craftsman and, here was a whole race of masters.

And why was it a whole race of masters and how did they develop their techniques? For this reason: In the ordinary free community there are usually only two or three individuals who have both talent and the urge to develop it. If they are lucky or extremely tenacious, they usually work up to some sort of opportunity to find time, teachers, right environment, and financial means to develop whatever native gifts they may have. Often they find they have nothing but the urge.

Now, imagine several million people, bursting with something to express, finding a way to express it, having plenty of time to study and practice and every external encouragement to do that and nothing else. These ideal conditions lasted for nearly three hundred years under one super-teacher, oppression. Who could help becoming a great artist and a great creator of art forms?

This was the exact situation of the Negro slaves in America. Human beings, living under an inhuman system. They certainly had plenty to sing about and they were denied every other means of expression except singing. This served not only as relaxation for the singers and as entertainment for the masters, but it was also a real safety valve, relieving an emotional tension which otherwise would have been unbearable. They had plenty of time for practice for they could sing, even while working, and because they worked better while [singing] the master not only permitted it but actively encouraged it. Sometimes a fetid swamp produces a rarely complicated and strangely beautiful flower.

Another important function of the slave music was to serve as an actual method of communication. Thoughts they dared not express in clear speech sounded harmless enough when couched in the quaint symbolism of the words of these apparently innocent and child-like songs. Because of this necessity, a peculiar musical form was developed; a song with long rambling verses, which go into the minutest detail of a given situation, followed by a short repetitious refrain, usually of four powerful lines, which clinches and reiterates the emotional drive of the song. Various other unique forms arose out of other moods, all having that peculiarly articulate quality which the function of actual communication required. This trick of substituting song for speech did not always require the use of a whole tune, sometimes only a single phrase sufficed. Indeed, it is not uncommon, even now, to hear a conversation where one of the speakers will suddenly complete his thought with a charmingly expressive fragment of a song which will give, better than in any other way, the exact nuance of his meaning. In this way, song has become, to the more primitive type of Negro, much more than merely singing, it is a sort of musical cloak which can conceal as well as embellish the thought.

The changes brought about by the emancipation of the slaves were soon reflected in the racial musical idiom. New labor conditions, life in cities, new forms of church, and various places and forms of amusement all had their effect. The old reels and coon-shouts became first ragtime, then jazz, and now swing music. This more profane rhythm crept into the city church and the dignified old spirituals gave birth to a lusty, zestful litter known (for want of a better name) as "gospel songs." With greater matrimonial freedom a new type of love song arose and flourished. When amatory relations became a matter of personal desire and not an incontestable device to increase the master's human stock—a disenchanted love-bird could freely go away, leaving the other one no better consolation than to sing the "blues," a distinctive type of folk song which resembles nothing but it self. The most drastic change, however, came when the ex-slave found himself working a farm on shares for very little money, or working on the chain-gang for worse than none at all. Then, the grand old work songs of the cotton field and the levee turned into bitter "songs of protest." Some of these are magnificent and may be favorably compared with the finest of the spirituals. It is of significant interest to observe that this development of the old traditional music is rapidly growing, both in quantity and in quality.

Naturally, the theater, mirror to whatever is going on, has made prodigious use of all this entertaining material. First, there were the old minstrel shows: white men writing imitation Negro songs to be sung by other white men in blackface. Since neither writers nor singers could do anything but seize and burlesque the mere externals of the Negro art, these confections can have no real value in our discussion, beyond noting the sincere flattery which is always implicit in imitation. A little later on, when Negroes learned to write for themselves and got a chance to do their own singing and dancing, they blessed the American theater with a flood of melody that is still remembered and cherished. The best songs of Will Marion Cook and J. Rosamond Johnson (two of the best known names of the period) still sound as fresh as the day they were written. A little later came the wave of Negro revues led by the sensational *Shuffle Along* and *Black-Birds*. It was then that the Negro chorus girls showed Broadway what dancing could be like. Although these outgrowths seem, at a casual glance, to have nothing to do with the old traditional music, a little closer scrutiny will reveal that they are only newer versions (to fit newer times) of the same old genius. There is the same rhythmic drive, whether in singing or dancing; the same concentrated emotion that enjoys itself first before going out to other people who then cannot fail to feel it. All this is a direct gift from those no-so-remote ancestors who literally had to sing and dance themselves out of themselves in order to keep on living. This and this alone is the unique and unconscious heritage of every great Negro artist. Individuals of other races may understand and share it, but only the Negro race has this form of "group-possession." It is the voice of the simplest and, at the same time, the most powerful engine that nature has devised—the voice of Rhythm—the voice of Rhythm beating against the bars. It is the effect of the shock which occurred when that which had always been free and untrammeled became suddenly and without warning, "unfree" and untrammeled. The shock has somewhat subsided but its repercussions linger on and are always ready to swing into eloquent and insistent vibration whenever the stimulus is present. It is the same thing which in the old days produced the Sorrow-Songs and the Songs of the Promised Land; the same thing which made my grandmother rent her house before sun-down on the day of liberation and, years later, made her "get happy" in the kitchen. It is the reason why, when Bill Robinson dances, every toe in the audience wants to wiggle. It is the living opposite of everything dead and perfunctory. It is the difference between vitality and mere vigor. It is power crying for release.

The production of the motion picture *Cabin in the Sky* offers an unrivaled opportunity to display this ancient chemistry in most of its modern manifestations. Here is no folk play, in the ordinary sense of the term. The action takes place in a town which affords all the seductive allurements of a great city and the characters are as sophisticated as their means will permit. There are still the saints and sinners, the church and the cabaret, apparently the same familiar furniture of most Negro plays. Kept in the old grooves, it could have been dull and dated; straining after extreme modernity, it might have come out merely vulgar. Neither happened. This always-good material has simply but wisely been poured through the magic filter of genuine creative Negro lyricism, keeping what was needed of the old and flavoring what was brought in of the new. The results is a charming blend of techniques, ranging from the quaint dignity of the oldest miracle plays down to the ultra-unhappiness of the present day revue, all held together by the common group-genius of the interpreters.

The story itself is one of primitive emotions. All real emotions are primitive. Here is the struggle to do right, besieged by every inducement to do wrong; here is a marital devotion bordering on mother-love, willing to go any lengths to protect the loved one; rarest and finest of all, here is shown the mellowing effect of a tolerance which can forgive endlessly just to preserve the right to go on endlessly forgiving.

The widely different roles are in excellent hands. Kenneth Spencer as the Lord's General and Rex Ingram as Lucifer, Jr., genially sardonic son of an illustrious father, continue into this year of grace 1942 the ancient Apocalyptic battle for the soul of man. Eddie "Rochester" Anderson as Little Joe Jackson, the man in question, gets a six month's stay against death and runs into more exciting problems in this marginal reprieve than in all the rest of his years put together. Bunyan's immortal Pilgrim was a snail compared with Little Joe's Progress and Dr. Faustus had no imagination at all on the subject of what to do with a few extra years. Lena Horne, as Georgia Brown, Little Joe's major problem, makes you wonder how that gentleman managed to live so long as it was a perfect bit of casting. Ethel Waters as Petunia Jackson, the patient, forgiving, but still very human wife, is the strong, though flexible hub around which all these brilliant spokes revolve. Only she could be equal to a job like this.

And then there are the group-scenes—and we have to talk about Negro music again. Both the cabaret and the church scenes are somewhat stylized but not to the point of artificiality; just enough to carry out the flavor of fantasy which pervades the whole play. But this is music in the raw. Once again the jet black muse speaks from across the waters, through all the years that preceded the first slave ship, and no tom-tom is needed to recognize her voice. It sobs in Duke Ellington's saxophones, shouts a triumphant shout from the brazen gullets of his trumpets and trombones, and fairly shrieks with savage glee when one of the possessed young dancers throws his girl clean over a table to inaugurate the bronze bacchanale. My grandmother never imagined anything like this.

She would be much more at home in the church scene. For in spite of its formalization, this episode projects a strong sense of realism during the few minutes required to fulfill its mission in the story which, of course, is an abortive attempt at the salvation of Little Joe. Two songs, a sermonette and one "testimony," are done with a genuine sincerity that really deserves to achieve better success with Joe. The "Little Black Sheep Comes Back Home" but, before he can be securely locked up in the fold, he slips out again—even while "The Old Ship of Zion" is "Landin' Many a Thousan'." Somehow he just can't seem to "Get on Board, Get on Board."

The "Cabin" is well tenanted when it comes to individual singers. The rafters of the little church ring under Kenneth Spencer's fine, resonant bass. A marvelous extension of her acting, and in the same seductive key, is the singing of Lena Horne. The "torch song" is not a pure, legitimate offspring of the old Negro music. Many forces have had a hand in its begetting and, generally, it is too much inclined to take after the "Curse of the Aching Heart" side of the family. But even the worst torch song is better when a Negro singer strikes the match. In the case of Lena Horne, the torch is not only a flame, it is a beacon. Even "Rochester," he of the gritty glottis, is bewitched to the point of singing back to her.

Of Ethel Waters, who has always been a great singer, it can only be said that, all these years, she seems to have been saving up for the "Cabin" for, in this picture version, she is at her amazing best. Probably due to her increasing powers as an emotional actress, her singing art has definitely deepened and broadened. Here is a woman who has learned by doing; for although she disclaims any formal knowledge of the science of music, she is undoubtedly the finest natural musician I have ever known. A player has some external help, in the way of an instrument, to suggest musical ideas. Ethel Waters has only her ear and her voice. She can make countless variations on a theme, never singing a song the same way twice, and her uncanny ability to improvise, paraphrase, and to otherwise elaborate on even an unfamiliar melody reminds one only of those fabulous Hungarian Gypsy violinists who have always been the wonder of the world of music. Her command of one-color would make Berlioz write a new book on orchestration. This voice, which seems to have no range limit in any direction, seems also to have no real need of words to convey a feeling.

With her tone alone, she can smile, weep, scold, pray—anything she wants to do. Everything about her art is so racial that sometimes—when it is the right song—I have the feeling that she is singing for the whole race; that all the Negro women who have ever lived, loved, suffered, and hoped are singing from her throat.

And so, to my mind, the "Cabin in the Sky" is the latest and most authentic demonstration of the use of the Negro idiom in singing, dancing, and acting as applied to the art of the motion picture. It has no bearing whatever on the subject of what Negroes themselves have been, are now, or will be in the future. It is simply a brave, new confirmation of the validity and durability of their creative impulse, an impulse which had its birth in the sheer necessity to create. The story itself could be about any racial group. Its sole claim to freshness and distinction is in its handling and performance. But that is enough—with people who talk when they sing and sing when they talk.

In 1950, Hall Johnson was approached by the Voice of America to prepare two programs on American folk song for international broadcast. In response to this request, Johnson prepared "Folk Songs of the United States of America," which he delivered in two parts and demonstrated through performances by the Hall Johnson Choir. These programs were so successful that they led the State Department to select the Hall Johnson Choir to represent the United States at the International Festival of the Arts in Berlin in 1951.

Folk Songs of the United States of America—Part I[4]

Music, as a means of expression, appears in the earliest stages of even the most primitive group-cultures, always employing as its first vehicle that oldest of musical instruments—the human voice. The poorer efforts are forgotten and the more satisfactory creations remembered and preserved, coming down to later generations under the general heading of "folk songs." These songs naturally exhibit quite definite points of resemblance or of difference, depending upon the degree of separation existing between the respective singers, whether this separation be geographical, social or simply mental—and a perfectly equipped laboratory for observing this principle in action is—the United States of America.

To begin with, the discovery of the continent of North America brought, among other things, the discovery of the American Indian—and a priceless opportunity to study a whole racial culture developed through centuries of complete isolation and hitherto untouched by any foreign influence. Here, indeed, was the ultimate in separation. The American Indian had learned his arts and sciences with only nature for schoolmaster and, significantly enough, music, both as art and science, was practiced with the greatest ardor. It was even believed to have magical properties as a therapeutic agent and, in severe cases, the Indian medicine-man usually supplemented his regular treatment with the performance of a song sent down by the Great Spirit for that special purpose—maybe for that particular patient. There was also, of course, music to go along with their games, battles, and important tribal ceremonies.

Totally unhampered by any suggestion from already existing models, this indigenous music poured itself into molds of untrammeled imagination and came out with characteristics peculiar only to itself. The rhythms were arbitrary and irregular, conforming to no apparent pattern, and the idea of harmony had evidently never even come up for consideration. Add to this a whole series of exotic tone-colors and unfamiliar vocal techniques, and we find something which must have sounded strange indeed in the ears of the new-comers. Let us listen to a "Ta-Wa War Song," with accompaniment of drum. The name of the singer is Swift Eagle. ("Ta-Wa War Song")[5]

That doesn't remind [you] very much of the singing in the seventeenth century England, does it? The first two important English settlements in this country, one in the North—the other in the South—were separated by a dozen years in time and several hundred miles of space but their basic problem was the same—how to survive and flourish in the new country. At first there was little time to think about music and, anyhow, even back home, their native national reserve had already formed a rather austere and practical approach to the art. The Northern group found little in their new surroundings to induce a more lyrical attitude toward life and, for long years, music with them was chiefly for religious worship, with the rigors of their daily existence finding apt reflection in the sparse harmonies of their hymns. ("Wondrous Love")

This song, "Wondrous Love," is an early New England expression of Christian faith—sounds comforting but not very warm. The settlers in the South, however, encountered two potent influences which gradually tended to loosed up the inherited stiffness of their music. Immediately, there was the bright, temperate climate, heightening the new-found sense of freedom and adventure; a little later came neighbors—and from a more romantic homeland, France. Soon, the songs of the South began to put on a more colorful dress, long before the music of the North had ventured out of the homespun of the meeting-house. Listen to "Lady Gay," an early example from the Appalachian Mountain regions. ("Lady Gay")

This song shows how singing may be affected by a change in the weather plus a different point of view. But by far the most powerful element in the music chemistry of the entire country came over with the very first ship-load of Negro slaves. Arriving in the early morning of American Colonization and trained only in the ancient but highly articulate cultures of Africa, they soon learned that the only thing they could continue to call their own in this strange new world was their songs and their singing. So they sang—and, miraculously, nobody stopped them—and so they kept on singing. This became the unique occupation of their creative minds when hands were busy and bodies were bent under the will of the master; the sole safety valve for pent-up emotions accumulated by their daily miseries and, somehow, the sure prophetic ministry foretelling better things to come.

As time dragged on and succeeding generations of slaves forgot the ancient rites and songs of the home-country, they began to adopt not only the religion of their masters but the church hymns that went with it. These were mostly pretty tame melodies but well harmonized and, with this new harmonic vocabulary added to their rich native gifts, the slave singers proceeded to create an eloquent literature of religious folk-music absolutely new in the world. These they called "spirituals" and we listen now to one of the oldest and best. In these few measures are tones of the firmest determination which soon mount in a soaring melody of aspiration to illuminate the simple, rugged words: "You may bury me in de East, You may bury me in de West, But I'll hear the trumpet sound in dat mornin'." ("You May Bury Me in de East"—Choir)

But the early spirituals were not all gloomy. These singers had songs to fit every mood. Among the many technical innovations brought over from Africa was a sort of musical form of "question and answer," bandied back and forth between a leader and the crowd. Often, in a religious ecstasy of joyous affirmation, the American slave singer would break forth—fairly erupt—in this style. "Have you got good religion? Certainly, Lord!" ("Cert'ny Lord"—Choir)

Meanwhile, the French influence was spreading, localizing itself in Charleston and, especially, in Louisiana, where the lilting rhythms and charming patois tinted the songs of the slaves as well as those of the "big-house." This one has been salvaged from the olden times and we hear it now in a concert version sung by the distinguished tenor, Roland Hayes. It is called "Mitche' Bainjo," in English, "Mr. Banjo." ("Mitche' Bainjo")

Soon, the acquisition of vast tracts of land in the far West offered a fresh and exciting invitation to hardy pioneer spirits in search of adventure and prosperity. First in covered wagons, then by stage coach, and finally by rail;—hordes of sturdy pilgrims confront[ed] new experiences, and, out of these experiences, made new songs. Songs of the great fighters: Davy Crockett, Santa Anna and Buffalo Bill; songs of the railroad: John Henry, the Negro giant who laid the tracks, Casey Jones, the heroic engineer, and Jesse James, the dreaded bandit who robbed the early passengers; Paul Bunyan and Johnny Appleseed, the supermen of construction and agriculture—all these and many more have found immortality in a tune. Time will permit us only one example. Here is a typical ditty built up around the daring exploits of the redoubtable Jesse James. ("Jesse James")

So much for the glamorous heroes of the early West. But the bone and sinew of the period and of the region was the picturesque though anonymous "cowboy"—for cattle was wealth and he tended the cattle. Whether driving his herd over the endless miles of a lonely trail or guarding them as they slept underneath the prairie moon, his was a lonesome job and, to keep himself company, he sang. Sometimes gay, sometimes plaintively wistful, his songs are usual about his work and breathe a sort of robust nostalgia which is greatly admired by thousands who have never even seen a cow. Listen to "O Bury Me Not on the Lone Prairie." ("Lone Prairie")

And another, in a different mood and strictly occupational. *Dogie* is the name given to the young calves which have no mother in the herd. Being orphans, they are the object of the cowboy's special care. ("Get Along, Little Dogie")

We said earlier in our talk that the early Negro slaves were *allowed* to sing. That is a slight understatement. Soon they were *encouraged* to sing, for their masters found that work went better and faster when it was done to the rhythm of their singing. Then, as their songs improved in variety and charm, they were *commanded* to sing—for guests at the "big-house." Naturally, in time the word got around—reports of this new musical phenomenon burgeoning in the South; Northern newspapers commented on it and, finally, the general public paid it the sincerest of all compliments—that of imitation. Theatrical companies were formed with white men made up as Negroes and performing exclusively Negro songs, dances, and comedy. These troupes were known under the general name of "Minstrels" and enjoyed the greatest popularity from 1843 until well into the present century. Composers of the day extended themselves in the efforts to write songs in this popular and lucrative style but most of them succeeded in capturing only surface values. One man alone of this group came near suggesting in his own work something of the genuine qualities of his Negro models—Stephen Collins Foster. His songs and ballads are still known and loved. Here is one of the most familiar—"Way Down Upon the Swanee River." ("Swanee River")

And again, from the pen of Stephen Foster, this one in a lighter vein, "Oh, Susanna!" ("Oh, Susanna!")

We have spent the last half-hour in a rather fleeting glimpse of some of the ingredients which have gone into the making of the Folk Songs of the United States of America up to the beginning of the present century. So rich are all these sources that several hours could be profitably spent with each separate one. Next week we shall consider their contribution to the contemporary musical scene with, perhaps, a bit of speculation as to their future in the cultural life of America.

Folk Songs of the United States of America—Part II[6]: Their Present and Their Future

In our talk last week we saw how various groups of people came from the old world to the new, bring[ing] with them the songs of their native lands. We noted also some of the characteristics of these songs, differing widely in the beginning but gradually blending into each other as the singers settled down amicably side by side in their adopted home. But behind this blending process several other factors were increasingly active, each one more powerful than the mere circumstance of physical nearness.

Agents for Unification

First and foremost, born with the federation of the original thirteen colonies, was the democratic tendency toward removing the barriers of class distinction; then, the steady and rapid improvement of travel facilities, reinforced by a thriving journalism soon made for a readier interchange of ideas of all sorts; later still, the thorough distribution and standardization of public schools, even in the rural districts, tended to form a national mold for public attitudes and opinions. The diverse racial strains gradually lost their sense of separateness and became Americans all.

But, of all the agencies for defining and refining popular trends in music, the latest and greatest is—the radio. With a maximum of variety and a minimum of effort, everybody can now become familiar with the music of everybody else, past or present, and under circumstances where the services of a music teacher might be absolutely unavailable and even a record collection impractical. For instance, if they both have good receiving sets, the Saturday matinee broadcast of the Metropolitan Opera Company sounds just as well to a gas-station attendant in the heart of the Mojave Desert as it does to a suburbanite in New York's Westchester County. Indeed, instead of amusing himself by making up his own folk songs while waiting for an occasional motorist, the music minded gas-dispenser can (and probably will) be switching his dial to an illustrated lecture on the fertility songs of some pastoral African tribe.

(A few bars of Western Music—Pause—African Song)

So completely now, thanks to radio, is the music of the whole world available to all the world.

American Folk Song—Present Time

At this point it may be of interest to see what has happened to some of the early American folk songs during these three hundred odd years of constant blending and progressive modernization. Here we find that, with groups as with individuals, increasing prosperity always brings more time and larger means for the expression of tastes, whether natural or acquired.

In the Cities

So, as the primeval wilderness gave way before the processes of civilization, the church-loving Northerners naturally turned toward oratorio and the symphony; soon Bach and Beethoven were heard in Bethlehem and Boston. In 1790 the romantic French brought the first grand opera to New Orleans in the far South and by the time the Irish and the Italians came over in great numbers to add their touch of tonal leaven, the musical outlook in America had become richly self-conscious. In the larger cities, at least, there was no further need for folk song.

In the South
The early British settlers in the South, however, ha[d] raised a more luxuriant, more richly varied crop of music and, when they began to spread westward from their Appalachian hills to the Ozarks, they left in their wake a wide belt of songs and dance-tunes still to be heard in the rural districts of the region. But, in the process of merging into the new nation, they did not lose this musical record of their early American experiences. Instead, for many generations they have maintained numerous singing-societies and periodic festivals (or meets) to enjoy and to keep alive the quaint, archaic-sounding hymns; the tender, wistful love songs; and the devilishly gay ballads and fiddle-tunes which they have created. Listen to this rendition of a love-sick mountain maid, "Black Is the Color of My True Love's Hair." ("Black Is the Color of My True Love's Hair")

And here's a fiddlin'-tune for dancing: "Turkey in the Straw" ("Turkey in the Straw")

The last two selections give a fair idea of the so-called Hill-Billy approach to melody making. Although no longer in a state of dynamic evolution, this music, treasured by creators and listeners alike, shows no signs of disappearing from the American scene.

In the Far West
One cannot speak with much certainty, however, of the future of the cow-boy songs of the far West. What with the prodigious growth in number and size of the great western cities, plus the thorough-going mechanization of the cattle industry, especially with regards to transportation, the mise-en-scene of the American cow-boy is not what it was a few score years ago. But his picturesque costume, together with the incredible physical dexterity demanded by his calling, makes him still the most glamorous idol of millions of youngsters the world over. Although he, himself may be less frequently in evidence, the tradition of his prowess is very much alive on movie and television screens, in the rodeo, and even in the ubiquitous comic-sheet. His songs, while no longer enjoying the immense vogue of a few years ago, are still regular radio fare. Here is one which brings, even to city dwellers, a peaceful breath from the wide-open spaces: "Home on the Range." ("Home on the Range")

French-American
The Creole songs, born of the admixture of French influence in the South, have never spread very far from their native Louisiana. Too exotic in essence to exert a really popular appeal on a national scale, they are absolutely ideal for adding to concert programs just that touch of fresh charm and variety which is

always welcome. Here is "Mitche Bainjo," in English, "Mister Banjo," sung by the distinguished tenor, Roland Hayes. ("Mitche Bainjo")

Neighboring Foreign Influences

Then, there are several groups of people who, while not natives of the continental United States, are still too near for us to have escaped their musical message. Within quite recent memory the Afro-Spanish rhythms of Brazil and Cuba [came] to pay us a visit and [were] met with such a warm welcome that they stayed on in our own dance music. A richer and darker French visitor from Haiti still leaves an occasional calling-card and, once in a while, a slow and slumbrous ditty fresh from Broadway will display unmistakable symptoms of the Hawaiian epidemic which ravaged our musical shores some thirty-five years ago. ("A Hawaiian Touch," if desired)

West Indian Invasion

But the most distinctly different contribution comes, oddly enough, from our nearest island neighbor—The British West Indies. It is called by the natives Calypso, and consists in a long rambling musical narrative on the subject of whatever might be the big news of the moment. It is of the very essence of folk song, being a spontaneous group-expression improvised right on the spot. Employing no bizarre unmusical devices, the special quality of the Calypso may be traced to its two most constant features: First, simple but fresh-sounding melodies intoned in a voice-quality and a linguistic dialect, both exclusively West Indian, coupled with an irresistible trick of mismatched accent, the musical stress falling upon the weak syllable of the word and vice versa. This combination of novel elements merits for Calypso a unique place among the folk songs of all singing peoples.

The most expert practitioners of this art are honored personages among the group and, for further prestige, have a custom of adopting professional names and titles of impressive sonority. Three of the best-known Calypso performers in New York City are called, respectively: "The Duke of Iron," "Macbeth," "The Crest," and "Willie the Lion." Let us listen to a Calypso song preserved and recorded by (Artist to be selected): (Calypso song)

That might be called the musical progeny of foot-loose African rhythms mated with self-contained British Psalmody. A tribal medicine-man at the harpsichord—or is it rather Mr. Handel bewitched by the trombone? Whatever it is, the dry, sly humor of the Calypso song caught the ear of our music vendors quite a few years ago, and started a vogue which is still prevalent in the amusement centers of the larger cities.

Negro Influence (Cause of It)

Now we have seen, even though very briefly, how all the ethnic groups arriving to make the new country have gradually pooled together, along with their other assets, their folk songs, for the enjoyment of the composite group which is the whole nation. Even the humble Negro slave made his unwitting contribution, and right here is a shining example of how the fact of separation was not physical but social and unbridgeable. Forced to live within the narrowest physical and mental limitations, the Negro slave soon set himself perfectly free in the only realm left open to his yearnings, the realm of music. And for the very reason that, even here, he had no guide except his own creative intuition, he discovered a dark and lonely path which belonged to no one but himself but was too rich in beauty to be ignored by those to whom every other path was open. ("I've Been 'Buked or Motherless Child")

Negro Influence (Spread of It)
Then, as the Negro continued to sing his plaintive songs which hid the tears so deep beneath the smiles, the whole world gradually began to listen. As early as 1874, highly cultivated audiences in Europe, Australia, New Zealand, and South Africa fell under the spell of this new music from the new century, brought to them by student singers from Fisk University, one of the earliest of the Negro schools. In the American Minstrel Shows, the white performers with blacked-up faces soon had to compete with dusky singers and dancers who had inherited the genuine article by right of succession. Along with a warmer type of melody came a simpler feeling for rhythm which came to be known as "rag-time." The music businesses made the most of it and, by the turn of the century, the singing and dancing, even the conversation, of the entire country had felt its effect. For with the greater melodic and rhythmic freedom, this music immediately communicated stronger suggestions of action and *release* and, through all the intervening years, under many forms and called by many names, it has steadily developed itself to meet and help relax the growing tensions of American life. In our age we know it best under the general name of "jazz." In its essential nature it is much more than the mere making of sound, it is a special *impulse* to expression. In its application it may be all things to all people, from an unmitigated nuisance to a venerated cult, but one thing is certain, in one form or another, it shows every sign of remaining with us indefinitely. (Jazz Music—To be selected)

The "Blues"
But the early Negro bard was not always feeling gay. Personal freedom has a way of bringing personal responsibilities and the problems of life, especially in the larger cities, could sometimes be clarified if not solved, by a little philosophizing in songs. The musical result is apt to be what its creator aptly calls a "Blues." Extremely simple in structure, the genuine blues gives the effect of a single musical wail uttered three times, usually with an instrumental accompaniment of some kind. The "low spirits" of the singer are reflected in monoto-

nous repetitions both of words and musical phrase. (Old-Time Blues—To be selected)

Modern, Artificial Blues

Of course, the strange appeal of this highly exotic song form was quickly imitated and exploited to the last degree by the tune-smiths. Commercial "blues" on every conceivable subject soon appeared. Some kept the traditional three-line form, some ignored it completely, but the vogue was definitely launched and continues till the present day, with all sorts of modifications and embellishments. Here is a recent sample, with a low-down jazz-band replacing the lone guitar accompaniment. If anything, the melancholy mood is brightened by the added tone-colors. In this ditty, a disillusioned lover complains, "I Can't Stand Your Treatment Any More." ("I Can't Stand Your Treatment Any More"—Performer to be selected)

Gospel Songs

About twenty years ago [1935], a new off-shoot of Negro Folk Song appeared and invaded the Negro church with overwhelming success. There adroit mixtures of idiom, half spiritual, half pure jazz, are known as Gospel Songs. In melody, harmony and rhythm, their music structure is much simpler than that of the old spiritual but, do not be deceived, this is only the frame-work. In actual performance, these Gospel Songs encourage improvisation to the extent that each different leader may let himself go in his own private version. Here is a typical example: (Gospel Song to be selected)

As a Business

Although confined to religious subject-matter and appealing to a limited public, the Gospel Song is a perfect illustration of the old folk-song impulse working under modern conditions. It is created within a separated group, mainly Negro Methodists and Baptists, with composers and singers moved only by spontaneous inspiration. The only difference is that this modern manifestation is consciously organized and highly commercialized. The outstanding exponents of the art are still honored as of old by the tribe and, in addition, the best of them enjoy the financial security of well-paid guest appearances and record royalties. They have a solid national organization with its own publishing companies for music and a monthly magazine; all together creating a business which runs annually well into seven figures. Once again, the tom-tom pays off.

Negro Spirituals on the Concert Stage

Throughout all these evolutionary ups and downs, however, the old traditional spiritual has consistently demonstrated its universal appeal. It is no longer the exclusive property of its originators but is found in the repertory of all American choral groups of whatever race, whether in concert, churches, or schools. Although originally and essentially for group singing, solo arrangements of Negro spirituals have long held a choice position on the recital programs of the best-known American singers. These solo adaptations usually necessitate the accompaniment of piano, which is not at all in the tradition but can be musically very satisfactory, given a fine melody and an arranger with taste and understanding. Let us listen to "Ride On, King Jesus," sung by the promising young Negro baritone, Robert McFerrin. ("Ride On, King Jesus")

Negro Influence on the Dance

And, of course, because genuine Negro music is preeminently based upon insistent rhythm, it was not long in renovating the dance-music of the world. The pompous strut of the Cake-Walk, the nervous twitch of the Charleston, the stealthy stride of Boogie-Woogie, are just a few of the endless succession of rhythmic tricks pulled out of the magic hat. And because human muscles gladly spring into voluntary action as a relaxation from involuntary labor, the American Negro has always spent much of his leisure inventing dance steps to go with his songs, translating his age-old, instinctive dancing urge into the moods and tenses of his present life. Note the difference between the old "buck-and-wing" steps of slavery days, and the quite recent "Lindy-Hop," performed by a couple and embracing a wide variety of physical posture and all available space. How indicative of the expansion of the dancer's thought-horizon during the intervening years. Also assuming the necessary technical skill, Negro instrumentalists bring something peculiarly their own to the playing of dance music not necessarily their own, as all lovers of dancing know and, especially during the period between the two world-wars, many of the most popular night spots of Europe and America were gladdened by ensembles of these rhythm-ridden troubadours. (Play popular European jazz favorite)

Influence on Popular Composers

Naturally, this powerful exotic and entirely new musical flavor brewed and distilled in a new country has not failed to exert its influence upon professional composers of music. The popular music of nineteenth century America immediately built up its milk-and-water ditties with injections of the new drug. After the emancipation, as young Negro men in the theatre learned to write their own music, the infiltration became even stronger. In fact, during the reign of rag-time, practically every tune-smith on Broadway was trying to write Negro songs with Negro words. The two most genuine talents to emerge from that period, Irving Berlin and, later, George Gershwin, freely admitted the anyhow rather obvious Negro influence in their output of the time. Still later, the gifted Gershwin developed it further in his opera, *Porgy and Bess*. Listen to a few measures from the scene where Bess unexpectedly meets the villainous Crown.

(Picnic Scene from *Porgy and Bess*)

Influence on Serious Composers

Gershwin was by no means the first serious American composer to attempt to use the Negro idiom. In fact, he was only the most recent of an earlier group whose announced rhapsodies or overtures on Negro themes were developed well enough along conventional academic lines but failed to catch the elusive but so necessary Negro spirit. Coming at a later period when the style was generally familiar, Gershwin was more successful than the earlier men. Several highly trained Negro composers have attempted symphonies, cantatas, and suites in their own racial idiom with a better chance of good results but, with the possible exception of William Grant Still, they have had little opportunity to be heard.

(Excerpt from Still's *Afro-American Symphony*)

Jazz

The Negro idiom as structure, [possesses] that combination of qualities and dissimilarities which would identify it, even on paper, among all other types of music. For the proper assimilation of all these constitutional earmarks in this composition, more time is required than any non-Negro composer has so far seen fit to invest. But as for the understanding of the Negro approach to *performance*, especially the manifestation known as jazz, that is another matter entirely. For the language of jazz speaks through music to universal human impulses for beneath and beyond all music or any other consciously practiced art, indeed, to the sources of being which cry out for expression of any sort. Jazz is not a manner, it is a *mood*, and being such, is immediately understood and answered by all who feel a sympathy for it. It is also easy of imitation by a clever musician who likes it well enough to practice its techniques. Contrary to popular opinion, it has no esoteric principles or secrets, which is the main reason for its wide-spread popularity. Born among an oppressed people, its voice is a rhythmical cry for release, from whatever may be binding and release in whatever direction. Posing a universal problem, this musical protest has found echoes among well-known composers of Central Europe and it is said that the most lucid analyses of its nuances are to be found in the writings of erudite musicologists, not of America, but of France. And all this is a part of the cargo brought to America with the very first shipload of slaves from Africa. (A few measures of drums)

Primitive Source Still Active in U.S.A.

In order to round out the picture it must be kept in mind that the making of folk song at the very source may still be observed among the Negroes in the remote rural districts and smaller towns of the deep South. Any event that impresses them deeply enough goes into a song. Many years ago the ballad of Casey Jones, the brave engineer, went into American musical history; later was the one recounting the sinking of the Titanic; more recently, and not so well publicized, a terse and gripping saga of the trial of the Scottsboro boys. Present day researchers assure us that, in spite of the space-annihilating devices of modern science, such isolated areas still exist where untaught but music-wise Negroes still "make up" their songs without effort and in total ignorance of the fact that for so many decades, a singing and dancing world has been so vastly enriched by the offerings of their dusky muse.

Plantation Cries

So we see that, of all the early groups who came singing to America, the Negro is the only one whose music continued to evolve until it was able to make a dynamic individual contribution to the culture of the entire world. The other groups, when their pioneer labors were over and they had settled down into the busy life of the new nation, left off entirely the making of new songs and contented themselves with preserving the old ones as keepsakes to be brought out and used on special nostalgic occasions. And this is as it should be, for the old folk song had done its work and served its purpose. It had kept the group together as long as it was a group apart, and with the forming of new national ties, it was simply no longer needed. The best folk songs of all nations, however, are practically indestructible and will always be in demand by international audiences everywhere. Such is the elemental vitality of a truly great folk song that no matter how arranged or rearranged, the intrinsic qualities can never be quite smothered or concealed. Too much of real living and thinking has gone into its creation and the subtle magic somehow always comes through.

Now, by way of conclusion, a few measures from the late George Gershwin who, in his brief career, came nearer than any other composer to creating a musical speech which might suggest and epitomize the manifold voice of American life and thought. This little chorus from the opera, *Porgy and Bess*, is entitled, "I'm on My Way" ("I'm On My Way"—Warfield, Price, Henderson)

Lecture-Demonstration on the Origins of the Negro Spiritual[7]

Sunday, March 21, 1954

Welcome! I'm glad to talk to an interested audience. We are always presenting the finished product, but today, we are able to analyze the works of music, to take them to pieces, instead of putting them together.

Singing is a combination of natural causes. Almost all animals have voices to express emotional reactions. Examples are the voice of the giraffe and the last "song" of the swan. The sounds they make vary; cats meow, dogs bark, hens cackle. The life of primitive man is characterized by war cries, incantations, and the medicinal songs of the American Indian. Individuals give off emotional sounds (laughter included) according to natural pitch. Great crowds rarely vocalize together spontaneously, except under mass emotional stress. Usually the shouters are leaders of some kind, or officials: any public speaker (orator) occupational—watchmen on the city wall—town criers—train callers—hog callers. Now the watchmen have become whistles and chimes from city hall clocks. The town-crier has become a city newspaper, a radio newsman. Train calling still persists; I suppose hog calling also persists.

Rarely is a great crowd permitted to yell at the same organized time, but the old Indian war cry has become the games and sports college yell. However, when the yelling is controlled by laws of music, ordered variations in pitch, duration, rhythms, changes in volume (dynamics), harmonic modulations, varying tone colors, this is music. Whether done by an individual or by a group, this is singing. Good singing is nothing more nor less than beautiful yelling. The simple definition of music (old catechism) is the art of making agreeable sounds. Now as to what is agreeable—opinions may differ—as in other matters. (Tell two stories: "Asiatic Little Boy")

Back to Singing—Folk Song
Coming from the human body, itself an instrument, it is the oldest form of musical expression. In reproducing and lengthening the most pleasant natural utterance, primitive man found relaxation. Imitation of the steadily recurring sounds of nature—the sea waves—footfalls in walking—brought a sense of rhythm. The adaptation of (beating) percussion instruments with the songs, gave pulse to the songs and brought excitement. Primitive man enjoyed singing and dancing—the relaxation and the release—the stimulation—the excitement. Like anything else pleasant, it first became contagious, then habit-forming—spread and grew into folk song.

Negro Singing—Why It Had to Be
Right here, let me ask, "how many composers (not great or even professional composers) have tried to write a song?" Anyhow, you have all analyzed compositions for your own student work and for your projects. Then, from your study of great individual composers, their needs for expression, their working methods, you can readily appreciate the mental and emotional toil which produced the Negro songs.

(1) Time: Because their conditions were originally peculiarly their own and remained so for a very long time, their peculiarities of expression crystallized and remained different, as they were not absorbed into the melting pot, as with other immigrants. Their songs had time to grow.

(2) Necessity: Because they [the Negroes] were not free (as they had been) they were not happy, and had to have an outlet. No free people would sing all the time—(as they did)—too many things to do. American Indians had tribal songs—but for occasions only—war, religious, medicinal. But the Indians had always been free and remained so—preferring extinction, to slavery.

The Negro slaves had to sing—to keep alive—it gave them not only relaxation, but a philosophy, and a hope.

(3) Practice: All music teachers know the value of practice—no progress without it. Well, these people practiced their singing constantly with every spare breath. With them, it became more than just a way of life— almost involuntary organic action. Also, they were encouraged by their masters—as they worked better. (Tell about the tobacco factories in North Carolina, the paid song leaders and the cotton picking phonographs [the phonographs to supply the missing singers—Charley McCarthy's Show])

So their music made them feel better themselves, work better, and give great pleasure to others. So with limitless time for practice and experimentation— with the encouragement of the controlling powers—and underneath all that compelling, that constant driving urge for release from an apparently incurable situation . . . no wonder they made good songs!

Folk Songs Transplanted

We have seen something of the emotional and economic causes of Negro Folk Song. Now let us look at some of the more technical peculiarities. What are the identifying characteristics? In what way does it differ from all the other folk music? Why has it left? Why does it still leave its mark on all the music and dancing of the world? For this statement is no exaggeration. To prove it, however, would require several full length concerts of all kinds of music composed in the past 150 years.

Now, the true Negro idiom is never so noticeable as when looking over the music of other people. They brought with them memories of the drums—the tom-tom, and the wild rhythms of tribal dance, and mixed it with what they found here (fascinating new melodies—) strange tunes—but all too pale, songs colored by Spanish, Portuguese, French, and English vowels. Above all, as they began to adopt Christianity, the Methodist and Baptist hymns, with their simple austere strength, made a strong appeal. Let's take a sample—and see what happened—still happens, for that matter. We all know the basic rhythms of music are 2 and 3—or combinations of duple and triple.

(1) Now the primitive African favors 2, and its combinations—the jump— the shout—the Charleston.

(2) His approach to ensemble singing (in the pre-missionary days) was contrapuntal rather than harmonic.

(3) He found the regular diatonic major and minor scales too limiting— tried in-between tones, but occasionally raised the 6th step in minor and lowered the seventh in major.

(4) Then as he began to love the harmonic combinations—tried to sing the whole triad in melodies, this brought strange and wonderful embellishments— still in gospel songs.

So let's take a simple hymn, one in 3/4—a rhythm new to him (PLAY). He would first of all find this too fast as well as too bare—to give vent to his feeling. Even today—with the average musically untrained Negro congregation—even with organ or piano accompaniment, it might come out something like this. (Sing "Amazing Grace")

Pseudo-Spirituals
We know what religion means. We also have a general idea of what a Negro is. Let's define folk song a bit.

Don't get the Stephen Foster songs, as fine as they are, [they are often] confused with the genuine Negro songs. Nor the early Minstrel Songs—written by white men for white performers blacked up with cork. Above all, don't mistake the Broadway product for the real thing just because it uses a lot of hallelujahs and amens.

Within the last few years, I have heard radio announcers identify the following songs as Negro Spirituals: "The Glory Road," "Sweet Little Jesus Boy," "Ol' Man River," "Shoutin' in the Amen Corner," "Sing You Sinners," and "Great Day." Not too long ago, a popular tenor (who ought to know better because he was born and reared in Georgia and sings Negro Folk Songs very well) remarked that "Water Boy" was his favorite spiritual, and then sang it. The second verse refers to the singer as a gambler whose pockets have been robbed of silver and gold by cards, hardly a religious theme. "Water Boy" is an authentic Negro Folk Song, but a chain-gain Work Song, not a Spiritual. The rarest candidate from Broadway however, seriously announced over the radio as a Negro Spiritual, was "I Can't Help Lovin' That Man of Mine," from *Show Boat*. So you see, there are all kinds of aspirants for the honor, and the conscientious listener will not be too hasty in either direction.

Variety Endless
Variety is endless in Spirituals, more than in action songs of work and play. A spiritual does not have to be extremely old to be authentic. Neither does it have to conform to any special musical mood, form or pattern, may be any tempo or rhythm, simple or complicated, and from dirge-like solemnity, to the exact opposite. Here is a very old and quite characteristic one: "You May Bury Me in de Eas'." It was a particular favorite of Dr. Henry Krehbiel, out of the few American musicologists who have paid serious attention to the Negro Folk Song. It is in the minor mode, but note the strange use of the raised 6th step. (singers stand for first line—"You May Bury Me in de Eas'"—unison, then harmony, hum and two verses.) Now a quite different one, with a leader, and congregational response, but not at all in the liturgical vein: ("Cert'ny Lord"—Singers sit.)

Now, we must remember something that is so often and so easily forgotten. We often confound the idea of civilization with that of mere complication, and it is quite human to suspect that whatever is different from our own must also be more than a bit inferior. For example, it may not occur to us that, if fresh food were free and always available, there would be little need of refrigerators. In other words, an original culture which satisfactorily meets the demands of its environment is all that is absolutely necessary. More than that is extra—and may be a nuisance, if not wanted.

The early slaves, brought by unfamiliar forces directly from Africa, found themselves suddenly in a completely new world, where the only familiar sights were the sun, moon and stars. Some had been kings, chieftains, and soldiers in their home country, men accustomed to authority over other men like themselves. Many perished en route, or soon after landing. In those who survived, authority had to become diplomacy, governed by expediency, but their moral courage, their curiosity and, above all, their imagination remained undulled.

Those who became house servants were often taken to church; the larger churches had slave galleries just for them. And sometimes, there were special religious services for slaves only. On these occasions, the minister's text was always, and invariably the fifth verse of the sixth chapter of St. Paul's letter to the Ephesians: "Servants, be obedient to them that are your masters according to the flesh, with fear and trembling, in singleness of your heart, as unto Christ." But although the slaves soon accepted Christianity and used it as the basis of all their songs, I have never heard of a single song which reflects the sentiments inculcated in this passage from St. Paul.

On the other hand, the stories of the old Bible heroes and prophets struck an answering note; the saints and sinners of the New Testament gripped their imagination with a force that still holds and as for Jesus, Himself, he became at once, not a Deity to be worshipped at a safe distance on Sundays, but a dear friend to take home and talk to. No literature of any other people has ever expressed, in song or story, the close personal relationship with the Son of God as is so constantly exposed in the songs of the American Negro in the days of his bondage. And how could it be otherwise. Jesus had made promises, and they took Him at his word. What else could they do? He was their only hope.

Those who heard the sermons and hymns in the master's church hurried back to the slave quarters to spread the good tidings to the field hands and other slaves who spread it still farther. Black evangelists carried the story from plantation to plantation. Secret prayer meetings were held at dead of night in out-of-the-way places. And the songs poured forth: songs of faith, hope, love and aspiration, prayer-songs, songs of exhortation to the strong, of encouragement to the weak, and warning to the luke-warm. Long narration songs about the exploits of the legendary old warriors of the Lord, but all revolving around, and coming back to *my* Jesus, as they called him—my Jesus.

What a closeness to the subject, what a musical technique, and what handling of the text and words. The English language to them was new. They were not hampered by any classical, literary traditions, so they handled it as they pleased, dropping a syllable here, adding a syllable there, changing the sound of a vowel to get more sonority into the singing. In short, they were unconscious masters of their craft, molding words and music together with one intention only—to release the fire that was burning in their hearts. This was all they had, and it had to be good. Listen to a few samples: (singers stand and move with songs).

The Letters of Hall Johnson[8]

Letters of Recommendation for Young Artists

From the earliest years of his professional career, Hall Johnson was actively involved in the encouragement, development, and support of young talent. Once he had become established in the field, one of the ways he could help was by lending his name in the form of a recommendation. In the precomputer age, only a few of these recommendations have been preserved, and only a few representative ones are included here as an example of his generosity and selflessness.

Wathea Sims Jones

To Whom It May Concern:

Mrs. Wathea Sims Jones was a regular attendant at my classes during the last four years of my work in Los Angeles. She also did a considerable amount of individual coaching with me personally besides some study in voice production with other teachers under my sponsorship. The entire record is as follows:

From November 1940 through April 1943—4 hours weekly, Choral classes in oratorio, opera, classic and folk music. In all—512 hours.

From October 1942 through April 1943—2 hours weekly—Individual coaching in solo repertory including interpretation of oratorio solos, Lieder, concert songs from the recognized literature and folk songs. In all—56 hours.

From January 1943 to April 1943—2 hours weekly—Voice building with Valdemar Banke—under my sponsorship. In all—24 hours.

I should like to add that, throughout my association with Mrs. Jones, I found her to be a conscientious and extremely talented student with well-balanced judgment and discriminating taste.

Hall Johnson

August 25, 1949

Georgia Laster

Michaels Memorial Award

Gentlemen:

It has come to my attention that one of my very favorite young singers, Miss Georgia Laster, of Los Angeles, is among your applicants for this year.

I am sending this line to say that I hope she may attract your most favorable consideration for, of all the young singers I know at present, this young woman has the most perfectly balanced assortment of qualifications to make a truly remarkable artist. Personal charm, sound musicianship, creative imagination and a beautiful voice are all hers. She is a good student and a hard worker.

Other people who have heard this young lady will give you the same report, for she always captivates her audiences. What I wish to emphasize here is this: After years of self-sacrificing hard work and now on the very brink of a brilliant career, this girl needs and deserves financial aid. At this critical period, it could spell the difference between great success and a great loss to American music. At present, we are not overburdened with really fine native singers, as you know. Please, do what you can for her.

Sincerely,
Hall Johnson
February 4, 1954

Shirley Carter (Verrett)
The Blanche Thebom Foundation

Dear Friends of Music:

Kindly permit me to say a word in reference to Miss Shirley Carter, the gifted young mezzo-soprano. My acquaintance with this young lady goes back six or more years to her native California—when she was very young and trying to "find herself" as a singer. I had the pleasure of helping her with her studies for a period of time and found her—quite aside from her remarkable vocal gifts—one of the most intelligent and dedicated students I have ever known. She literally wants to know everything about her art—and applies herself accordingly.

Immediately, upon her arrival in New York City, she began to experience the encouragement and success I had predicted for her. She is now well launched on a promising career. Her teachers are delighted with her bright and unspoiled personality as well as with her vocal abilities. Her audiences succumb at once to her fresh, wholesome appearance and, a few minutes later, to her beautiful singing. In a word, Miss Carter has all the potentialities for an extremely brilliant career. She needs further study with master teachers and for this, she needs financial assistance. Anyone helping this young lady may be sure of bounteous returns; even in the short time she has been before the public. Her success has already eliminated all element of speculation. When you get to know Miss Carter, I hope you will share my opinion.

Sincerely,
Hall Johnson
October 3, 1960

Eugene Thamon Simpson

To Whom It May Concern:

When Eugene Thamon came to study and work in New York in 1959, the musical community of the city soon recognized and welcomed a very valuable member to its ranks. This young man began immediately to attract signal attention by the variety and even development of his musical gifts, and is still making a generous contribution as pianist, organist, singer, teacher, and choral conductor.

Recently, Mr. Thamon has decided to concentrate his efforts toward the operatic and concert fields as a *singer*—and small wonder. His voice is a rich bass—resonant but flexible, even in quality and elastic in dynamic range. With his broad musicianship and general academic culture, he already commands a wide and varied repertoire which he delivers with taste and distinction. A pleasing presence and an amiable personality, coupled with the highest moral standards, lend significant support to his artistic qualifications.

I can wholeheartedly endorse Mr. Thamon for your commendation.

Hall Johnson

N.Y.C—6-15-'62

Letters to Management

From its Town Hall debut in 1928 until its return from the International Arts Festival in Berlin in 1951, the Hall Johnson Choir had a single capable manager—William C. Gassner. After Gassner's plans for the choir to participate in the Paris Festival of 1952 fell through, not without a substantial disagreement between Gassner and Johnson, there is no evidence of his functioning in this capacity. As a professional organization, the Hall Johnson Choir was finished. The correspondence included, from Johnson to Gassner, has been selected to best illuminate Johnson's personality.

December 1951

Dear Mr. Gassner:

In view of the fact that we have had so many misunderstandings recently, that our verbal agreements do not seem to register the same way in our respective memories, and that a continuation of this state of affairs is certain, sooner or later, to lead to serious embarrassment of some sort, I thought it advisable to clarify the situation a bit (from my point of view) on paper. Then, if any later confusion should arise, this letter will show to anyone concerned exactly what my attitude was on the date of its writing.

My most recent cause for dissatisfaction has to do with your recent visit to the State Department in Washington. When you first mentioned it—in a general way—I made no objection. It was over the telephone, you set no specific time for the trip, and I thought, naturally enough, that we would be talking again soon—which would give me time to think it over and discuss it with you later.

When I came to your house to talk it over, I found that you had not only written them and received a reply but had written again—this time with definite dates. This time, I voiced several objections:

1. I felt that the move was premature—that we would be in a stronger position if the first action came from them.

2. I said that I considered that the matter should be arranged through Mr. Breen, since he was responsible for our appearance in the recent festival and I knew he was working hard for a repetition for 1952—with us included. It seemed to me a bit like "going over his head."

3. Then I brought up my regular old argument—that the choir was not in adequate shape and there was no way of knowing when it would be. I hastened to add that I would not again go abroad, or anywhere else with a group which did not represent my very best effort. I repeated what I have said to you *so often*, that I cannot get results from a group of people who come together at the last minute simply because there is an engagement—and they want to work. I emphasized this point *particularly* this time because I know that, while you understand it at the moment, you do not remember it for very long. Like any other layman, you naturally think, when you see me standing before a group of singers, that they ought to sound wonderful.

This time, however, you seemed to agree with me and promised me that you would write and postpone your visit until our ways and means were clearer. I believe you did write—and receive a reply—leaving the whole visit to the indefinite future. At least, that was my understanding.

This all happened very recently. Imagine my surprise when you telephoned me last Monday announcing that you had *just returned* from Washington where you had a conference with six very important people of the State Department about the Hall Johnson Choir! When I asked you what was mentioned, you said (1) "that our budget was too tight" and (2) "that next time, we should visit more places." Then, when you saw that I was displeased because you had *broken your word* to me (by going in spite of our agreement at your house) you protested that what you had said "could not do any harm" and that you "hadn't talked any business." By that, I suppose you meant that you hadn't talked any "figures." (This is what a business man usually means by the word "business.") Of course, you emphasized that you told them what a "hit" we were in Germany, but that alone was not a justifiable reason for the conference. They had been hearing that over and over again—from Germany—and, more important still, from entirely disinterested people who would have no motive for plugging our success. You were trying to *sell* them something.

Thinking it over now, I see where harm has been done—and along the lines of the same three objections I made at first.

1. I think our business position has been weakened by our running to them first—and so soon.

2. I think Mr. Breen has every right to be surprised, hurt, and even angry. Since the whole thing was his original idea and he was still working on it, I think he should have at least been notified, if not consulted.

3. When you promise (or even intimate) that I can deliver an engagement of such pretensions, knowing as you do my serious problem with the choir personnel (so recently discussed), you are putting me in position which is quite false and dangerous now, at this moment, and still more so if I should be unable to deliver when the time arrivers. This embarrassment will only be aggravated if I ask them now to advance money to help me build a group from scratch—which was another one of your suggestions. A request of this sort would have been easier to make if the inquiry about the engagement had come from them.

So you see, Mr. Gassner, I am not very happy about your trip to Washington. Another situation which has disturbed me greatly is that three months after our return from Germany, I still have received no satisfactory financial accounting from you for the business end of the tour and—from all indications—there is no prospect of any. You don't even *mention* it any more. I readily concede that the extenuating circumstances you offer did certainly make the keeping of an accurate account more difficult but I fail to see why even these circumstances have made it *impossible*. Indeed, I feel that, *until* this matter is settled, you are not holding up your end of our contract and, unless this is done, there is absolutely no *legal* obligation to consider you further as our business representative.

These two matters (the Washington business and the lack of the German accounting) constitute my chief causes of dissatisfaction at this moment. There are quite a few others, but they need not be discussed at this writing. I find the whole present relationship between us very new and very disturbing—after the many years we have worked together in comparative harmony. I have given much thought to the entire situation and honestly cannot see where I have been at fault.

Please let me have your *written* thoughts concerning all this. I don't mind talking it over—but we have done that so often—and our memories do not seem to work the same way.

Thanks for forwarding Mrs. Gassner's nice card—and Happy New Year to you.
Hall Johnson

January 10, 1952

Dear Mr. Gassner:

Thanks for your letter dated January 3rd. It reached me Sunday, January 6th.

Am glad you agree with me about the advantage of writing for clearness. In the course of your letter you asked two questions which, I believe, sum up everything you want to know at this moment.

1. You write, "I am asking you whether you have had any communications or negotiations with him (Mr. Breen) about Europe or any other matter?"

The answer is "no." I have not had (and have not now) any business negotiations with Mr. B. (or any one else) about Europe or any other matter. As a matter of fact, I haven't the faintest idea where my next dollar is coming from. Which brings me to your second question:

2. You write, "Should I agree to pay you one hundred dollars, would you feel that I had made a perfectly satisfactory accounting of the entire trip?" . . . and later, "If you feel that the one hundred dollar settlement is entirely equitable, and satisfactory and will let me know, I will mail you a check immediately."

The answer is—I shall be more than happy to receive your check for $100 as soon as possible. I have a huge dental bill which I must try to reduce a bit—as I am still going to the dentist every other day. I cannot honestly say that I feel this arrangement would be "entirely equitable and satisfactory" but, at this moment, it would be so helpful that, in consideration thereof, I would promise to close up the discussion about the figures on the Berlin tour from now on.

Now, I feel that our recent exchange of letters has done much to clear up the situation—at both ends—and please be assured that my friendly personal attitude toward you will never be affected by any of our business discussions—past, present, or future.

Sincerely yours,

Hall Johnson

Letter to Foundations

January 9, 1946
The Rockefeller Foundation

Gentlemen:

In making application for financial aid for the Festival Negro Chorus of New York City, I wish to call special attention to one point: The Festival Chorus is not a theatrical or musical project solely for business or entertainment purposes. Its aims are first, last, and always, educational and cultural—in the broadest sense of those words. It seeks to unite and centralize in a group effort of immediate value all the rich native talent which usually has such great difficulty in reaching individual expression. The crying need for such an effort is most apparent to all those who, like myself, have had both the opportunity and the necessity to study the situation over a period of many years. The Self-Help plan for improving this situation is clearly outlined in the accompanying circular. The idea is simply to use what we have in order to get what we need.

The physical equipment for the project is being very generously supplied by the New York City Center of Music and Drama, who will also handle all the business of our Chorus. Numerically, the Festival Chorus is growing by leaps and bounds. Many already existing groups, church choirs, etc., will combine with us for our public performances and we hope to make an outdoor appearance next summer with at least five thousand singers. It would be difficult to overestimate the good influence of such a group in our community.

The only problem we have at present is the financial one of getting our Supporting Chorus firmly launched. This group is to be not only the "breadwinner" for the whole movement but the artistic core which will work daily to advance the cause of American music in general and of Negro music in particular. This will take a lot of time from a lot of people and it will be necessary to give them each a little money—not as actual salaries based on value of services but simply as a gesture and a "binder."

This Supporting Chorus should have a period of ten (10) weeks of intensive training leading up to their first public performance.

Yours sincerely,
Hall Johnson

Letters to Producers

In early 1943, Hall Johnson was approached by the George Jessel Office about a New York revival of *Run, Little Chillun*. The letter reveals the developing schism between Johnson's slow and deliberate approach to choral preparation and the exigencies of "modern" Broadway, which typically prepares a show in three weeks of intense rehearsal. Additionally, Johnson was concerned that his standard and reputation for choral excellence, well established with the original productions of *Green Pastures* and *Run, Little Chillun*, be maintained in any revival:

April 20, 1943

Dear Mr. Cooper,

Was glad to hear from you over the week-end through your communications with Clarence and Miss Shaw. Am glad the contract seems to be getting into a generally satisfactory state at last. . . . .

Right now I am worrying about another part of the matter. I have every confidence in your intentions to do the play as soon as possible and as well as possible. I have never had any doubts in this regard. However I really [do] believe that you are underestimating the gravity of the chorus situation. That is quite understandable since you did not see the early New York production and so cannot possibly realize the tough comparisons our chorus will have to go up against. That production was not much to look at but, oh—how those people did sing! To begin with, there were nearly two hundred of them and they had been singing that same music together all day every day for five months—while a producer was materializing. Really, it was the last word in choral perfection;—ask any of the old-timers who heard it.

I tremble when I think of the handicaps I am going to experience in approaching that standard of my own work. In the first place this crowd will be only half the size—(2) at present there is nothing like the wide range of selection for voices—everybody was idle in '32—now everybody is busy—or can be—(3) for the same reason, the rehearsal hours will be shorter. During the preliminary period (before the official rehearsals begin) I can only demand of the singers the time they have free and there will be many who will get free for the show who will have to keep working during this training period.

November 29, 1951

Dear Mr. Breen:

In thinking over our recent trip to Germany for the State Department, I had put down some notes about things I wished to remember. Knowing your absorbing interest in the whole project of the Berlin Festival, and being gratefully aware of your sincere appreciation of my own efforts through past years, I thought you might like to know some of my impressions and reactions. Since there always seems to be so little time for conversation, I decided to jot down some of these for you and you can glance at them during a chance leisure moment.

Along with these notes is a copy of an interview which I prepared for a Voice of America broadcast to Germany. I may have told you that it was through an invitation from the Voice of America that we were able in the past two years to send several programs over the air to Germany—with an English translation. While it contains my honest opinions and reactions, still the fact remains that it was prepared for German ears and is necessarily only partial—something like a "thank you note" to a charming week-end hostess. I have further impressions, even convictions, which must be for home consumption only. I am sending you some of these—for whatever interest they may have.

For one thing, when I say that the German audiences received us with warm or sincere "enthusiasm," it is a gross understatement. You yourself saw how they "carried on" in Berlin at the Titania-Palast, each of the three appearances successively more exciting than the preceding. Well, even our Saturday evening audience in Berlin was no preparation for the torrential demonstrations in some of the later and less cosmopolitan cities where the halls were filled to over-flowing with "home-folks." This I was not expecting. I was prepared to find that the Germans, on all musical levels, would like our songs and our singing. No nation has ever been more devoted to group singing of all kinds. When we did our first broadcast over the Voice of America two years ago, scores of air-mail letters came pouring in from all over Germany—saying the most wonderful things and full of questions betraying the liveliest interest. The program directors told me at the time, that no previous broadcast over their station had ever met with such a warm and immediate response. I attributed much of this to the novelty of the material and to their surprise and curiosity at hearing me conduct the program in intelligible German. Still, I felt sure that all who heard the broadcast, liked the songs and, when I knew that we were actually going to make the trip, I was most curious to see how they would be affected at closer range. Maybe the people who wrote the wonderful letters were all well-educated people with broad interests—maybe it would be different with the "general run."

As you know, Berlin, in mid-September was full of visitors from everywhere—even from the Festival —so, although I was told that the huge audiences at the Titania-Palast were 90% German, I had no way of knowing how "typical" they were. Then too, the Berlin concerts had box office and ticket problems which might easily have kept the poorer people away. In the ten cities we visited later, there was no doubt. Admission was free—tickets on request—first come, first served. And they came—in throngs—spilling out of the doors. A cross-section of all ages, sizes and types—from the bearded, bespectacled, learned-looking Docktoren and Professoren in the front rows, to tiny tots wedged together on the stair-steps and applauding as vociferously as their elders. Not since our earliest concerts in the States—twenty-odd years ago, when any kind of choral concert was a novelty, have we received applause of such sheer volume. The audiences don't whistle in Germany as they do here, so the aggregate noise hasn't that shrill quality which is so noticeable at such demonstrations in this country. They do more actual shouting—at the top of their voices—and when they get tired of this they go into something else which is a bit startling until you get tired of it: they add to the handclapping, a strong, steady stamping of feet. You will probably remember some of this from our Berlin audiences, but they were no match at all for Munich and Vienna and some of the university towns. There used to be an old expression for tremendous applause: "The house came down." I thought of this on several occasions when, at the end of the concert, nobody got up to go home—then, suddenly, that ominous-sounding rhythmic thunder would start. Of course, there was nothing to do but sing another song—if only to make sure the roof would stay up. As soon as they knew we were coming back on stage to sing again, this noise would—not fade out gradually—but break off very sharply into a death-like stillness, waiting for the announcement of the encore song. After this song, the whole business would start all over again. It was uncanny. I never did get quite accustomed to it, but it was fascinating and I was always sorry when the lights had to be turned out—which usually seemed the only way to bring matters to a close.

As I said before, I expected the Germans in general to like our music, being a choral-minded people, but I was certainly not prepared for *this degree* of overall approval and, more especially, for their absolutely uninhibited way of showing it. Ever since my earliest student days I have always respected and been quite familiar with the traditional and firmly established self-esteem of the

Germans in matters musical. In view of their enormous, century-long contribution to the development of the art, I have always considered it natural, well-earned, and justifiable—and certainly, it is present in even the most liberal and broadminded of their musicians. So, I had expected our offerings to be received with a certain amount of favor tinged with maybe a *wee* bit of condescension—with probably here or there an occasional "looking down of noses"—quite sweetly. You know what I mean. Well, nowhere was there even the faintest whiff of anything like that. If there was one thing that stood out above everything else with these audiences—from the youngest to the oldest—from the lowest to the highest—it was their absolute sincerity. I was not only surprised, but delighted. Here was an audience which could really be reached. However, and much more important, it was a crowd that wanted to be reached. Whatever barriers, emotional or otherwise, they may have erected—consciously or unconsciously—against mental intrusion, seemed to have been removed—consciously or unconsciously—and they found themselves exposed—mentally and morally naked—to this music which was, at one and the same time, simple enough to disarm their suspicions and great enough to demand their respect. As the tour progressed (and as my surprise grew a little calmer) I found myself trying to analyze the reasons for the extreme vulnerability (that is the word) of these people to our songs, and quite gradually, several facts began to emerge in my mind which seemed to offer a solution. Looking back over the whole experience after several weeks of being back home, I am sure that some of these factors make sense—and I should like to know if you agree with me, first as to their relevance, and then as to their importance.

1. It is a long time now since the Germans as a nation have been able to luxuriate in that mental condition of calm supremacy which, before the First World War, shaped and colored all their attitudes in matters of creative art. It may be that the succession of events in a rapidly changing world has somewhat shaken their native self-assurance in this field as in others. That is only to be expected. Anyhow, the adults with whom I talked (mostly musicians, actors, and teachers of one sort or another) impressed me as being a particularly open minded group with no hostile preconceptions to block the entry of new ideas. The youngsters were lively and sparkling with curiosity and conversation. Most of the teen-agers spoke excellent English.

2. The second thing I noticed was that, with all their readiness to talk, the older people *asked very few questions*. I had expected that they would want to know from us all about conditions in the United States, etc. But there was absolutely none of that. They wanted to talk about *themselves* and their own problems. Backstage, after the concerts and at the little receptions which usually followed; in the shops, restaurants and hotels—whenever I talked with them—I got the feeling that, more than anything else, these people wanted to be *heard and understood*. And finally, this thought came to me:

3. We represented to the "home" Germans, not only a new group of singers singing a more or less unfamiliar type of music but a completely new ethnic group and, in some ways, quite different from what they had expected to find. Naturally their preconceptions had been conditioned by their early education and I really think they were surprised and pleased to find us quite civilized! You must remember that, apart perhaps from occasional anonymous groups dressed in impersonal army or navy uniforms, most of them were seeing and talking with a sizeable company of Negroes for the very first time. While they knew that we represented America, still there was nothing in our presence to suggest the military might of America, the conqueror. To them, we were so many new *ears*, and if they could believe our songs, *sympathetic ears*. So, released by the songs and reassured by our personalities, they talked freely and sincerely. People are usually sincere when they are anxious to talk about themselves.

When our German audiences came backstage after our concerts, it was not just to ask for autographs and to say how much they enjoyed the music. They did this too—but that was not all. Their faces, even before they spoke, showed very plainly that they had received much more than merely aesthetic satisfaction. They told us of our clubs and schools, of what they were trying to accomplish in their work and invited us to visit them the next day. Many asked for copies of our songs—even for additional word sheets (which we had with both English and German texts). In Mannheim, there were several boys who were members of a choral group specializing in—of all things—Negro spirituals! Their chorus, I was told, had been organized in a nearby Quaker Center by the two young American Negro officers who at the moment were away on leave in the States. So I didn't get to meet the founders. However, judging by the enthusiasm of the boys who talked to me it must be a very worthwhile undertaking. Later on, I met two young women—one in Frankfurt and the other in Vienna—who had developed choral groups among the poorer children of these two cities. They asked me for copies of our songs. I gave them what I had along with me and promised to send more. These girls were so grateful.

Two other incidents, I can never forget. After one of our concerts, a young man—a handsome student type of about twenty-three—came up onto the platform and shook my hand. His face wore a strange bewildered expression and his voice as he spoke, was shaky with emotion. He said our songs had affected him as had nothing else in his whole experience. He could not explain his feelings in words—nor even to himself. He only knew that he had been greatly helped and would have to go home and think about it.

The other incident happened near the end of our tour when the evenings had become quite chilly out-of-doors. Always, in addition to coming backstage to greet us at the end of the concert, a great many of the audience had a way of gathering around our bus to wait for us to come out and to give us a parting wave or a final handshake as we left for good. On this particular evening, I noticed in the backstage crowd four quite elderly people, a man and three women, who seemed to have been particularly moved by the songs. I talked with them for only a few moments because at the end of this concert we had to stay on for a while to make some special recordings for later broadcasting purposes—so we hurried everybody else out of the hall as quickly as possible. Nearly an hour later, we came out into the cold night air to go home. Not another soul was in sight. Our bus was standing at some distance away—looking quite deserted. But, as we reached it and prepared to step inside, four tiny figures detached themselves from the shrubbery along the roadside and came up to say "Good night, and God bless you." It was our four little old friends who had been waiting nearly an hour in the cold to say, once more, how happy we had made them. Everybody else had probably reached home and comfort long before. This may not sound like much of a story to you but if you could have seen their faces, you would quickly understand why I shall always remember this occurrence.

And then, there were the times when we sang for informal groups like the workers—2,000 of them—at the big AEG Turbinenfabrik in Berlin. We entertained them during their entire lunch hour—in a huge workshop with a balcony running all around it. All these people in working clothes, mixed up on two levels, with all this weird fantastic-looking machinery—the whole thing suffused with a strange bluish light. It looked like a painting begun by Gustave Dore and finished by Salvatore Dali. You should have seen it. When we left them, many of the young men and women took to their bicycles and escorted our bus quite a distance down the road, cheering and smiling until they had to turn around and go back to work.

But most informal of all—and sometimes in the most out-of-the-way places—we would stop for refreshments and gradually a group of farm-hands or other laborers would congregate around our bus. As novel as this sight was to us, we must have presented an even stranger spectacle to them. We would all beam and smile at each other and then try out all our different brands of German. As soon as they discovered that we were a group of singers there was nothing for it but to sing a song. Who could resist such an audience—and with the blue skies and the green fields for a backdrop? It was delightful—apparently to all concerned.

These little incidents which I have recounted will always remain for me, I think, the highlights of our tour—simply because they arose out of actual close contact with the German people and did not have to happen in the "line of duty." Of course, I am pleased with the reviews written by the professional newspaper critics. These were not condescending nor over-generous; neither were they carpingly critical. Just thoughtful, sincere, intelligent, and quite unbiased analyses of our work. Some of the best were written by men who are evidently masters of their craft, and I am particularly proud of these. I am proud also of the letter of commendation and appreciation received from Mr. Mc-

Cloy, Mr. Lettenich, Mr. Espinosa, and our Mr. Schnitzer, who worked so hard to get us all over to the scene of the action.

And because you know that I am more interested in music as a social agent than as mere entertainment, you will understand what I mean when I say that I have several other letters which brought me even deeper satisfaction—and of a different kind. The first was from Professor Doktor Tiburtius, on behalf of the Berlin Senate. In the middle of a very grand letter, he says that the Berlin public was deeply conscious "not only of your splendid musical performances, but of the strong appeal for self-examination and human brotherhood which gives such a gripping character to your presentations."

Later, in Bremen, I received a letter on the official stationery of a local organization which began: "Die Deutsche Abraham Lincoln Gemeinde bids you welcome in Bremen and everywhere you appear in Germany. You may be assured that your coming is of great aid to our aim and work of making people understand that all of us are brothers . . . and whenever you sing, rest assured it will be as hearing and listening to old friends. Signed: George Henry Distler, President and Founder of the German Abraham Lincoln Community."

Then there were warmly sincere expressions from the American directors of the U.S. Centers in several cities. These are valuable because they come from our own fellow countrymen who have lived for a long time very close to the problem and so are *familiar* with it from all points of view. As a memento of two wonderful days spent in Bremen, the directors of the Office of the High Commissioner in that city prepared for me an extremely handsome souvenir book, complete with photographs, press notices, and a letter signed by their Chief of Public Affairs Division, Mr. Allen Y. King. His letter begins: "The appearance of your choir in Bremen was a complete success, musically, culturally, and socially, both for the Germans who heard the choir and met its members, and for us in the office of the Land Commissioner for Bremen. The Germans continue to state enthusiastically that the choir was one of the finest musical organizations ever to hit Bremen."

He continued this in the paragraph I liked: "You deepened the understanding and appreciation for the United States and its way of life, serving as the highest type of ambassadors of good will to the German people. Your visit will be long remembered and appreciated. The recurring question is, 'When will the Hall Johnson Choir return again?' We hope your time in Bremen may likewise have been pleasant and profitable to your group and that you will wish to come back."

I wanted to shorten this quotation but I couldn't. Mr. Paul D. Behtel, Director of the Amerika-Haus at Nuremberg writes, "This was *the* outstanding musical event of the year in this city and I should like to take this opportunity to thank you and the fine members of your choir again for the many friends you have made for America by this outstanding performance." With his letter he enclosed two photographs taken during our concert in Nuremberg; one of the group on stage in the middle of a song and the other of the audience immediately after the finish of a song. This second one, you *must* see. It gives you, at one glance, a clearer picture of the typical audience reaction than I could describe in pages of words.

Everywhere we went, the directors of the American Centers said, as if by pre-arranged agreement, one thing, which to me was interesting and important; that, apart from the enjoyment of our singing and the novelty of our songs, it was most helpful to them in their own work to have the Germans see a totally different aspect of American culture as exemplified by our appearance and behavior. I had not thought too much about that beforehand, but I suppose it had its value. In any case, the American directors seemed to think so—and they ought to know. Particularly enlightening along these lines were Miss Helen Imrie in Hamburg, Miss Naomi Huber in Mannheim, and Mr. Walter Donnelly, the American minister in Vienna. Mr. Donnelly not only invited us for a leisurely visit to the legation where he took photographs and discussed current events, but came out the same evening to our concert with Mrs. Donnelly and Congressman and Mrs. Lucas from Texas. This all-American quartet sat in the front row in the historic Brahmssaal and added mightily to the applause.

Of course, there were times when we performed for *unseen* audiences. In Berlin and Vienna, we made news-reels; in Hanover and several other towns, I gave personal interviews over the radio (real tests for my German). Practically every one of our concerts was also recorded. In Berlin and Nuremberg, two very special programs were designed, so I was told, particularly for broadcasts over the Russian Zone. So, you see, we missed *no* opportunity for usefulness during the short time of our tour.

Oh yes! I nearly forgot one performance which I enjoyed *so* much—and this time, the audience was *very* visible and neither Germans nor Russians, but our own G.I.s. After the first leg of our flight back home, we stopped for dinner (and other things) at a military base in Keflavik, Iceland. And here were all these soldiers—no telling how long some of them had been there—and literally *starved* for entertainment. After an excellent dinner, we sang for them until the pilot called us back on the plane to continue our journey—not too long a time for such a music-hungry audience, I'm afraid. They literally drank it up—and we hated to stop singing when we had to. If I had known the situation on arrival, we would certainly have sung first and eaten dinner in whatever time remained. If you had seen those boys, you would have realized it was *just that important.* There can be times when music is more necessary than food, and this was one of those times. The next morning, we were getting off the plane at Idlewild and it was hard to realize that we had dined just a few hours before in Iceland. The planes fly so fast. So does Father Time. New things come and go—and are no longer new. The tour is over, but I shall always be grateful for the experience—the most *active*, the most educational, and I like to believe, the most useful three weeks of my whole life.

Now, Mr. Breen, I have spent a lot of time (it seems difficult to condense it) telling you how the German people seemed to have been affected by our tour; now I want to tell you how it affected me—and this requires much fewer words. Music, as you know, is capable of, and in the course of the world's history, has been put to many uses. We of the Western hemisphere are quite familiar with it as entertainment and for ceremonial purposes, because it is in those capacities that we usually require its services. We also know a good bit about its chemical action on elementary human emotions—how it can be, at times, either a stimulant or a sedative, and at other times, a catalyst or a safety valve. What is not sufficiently well known—consciously and scientifically *realized*—is the *inherent* power of music to transmit actual and definite ideas. I don't mean the thoughts that may be expressed in the *words* of a song, I mean the tune itself—without words of any sort. If it is a great tune to begin with, then, projected in the right manner by the right performer toward the right ears, its magic never fails. This is the secret of the best of the old folk songs and Negroes learned it more thoroughly than anybody else, simply because they practiced it *constantly*—through many generations. Their tunes had to mean something then—and they still mean something today—because, basically, human nature does not change.

It was to preserve and demonstrate this peculiar quality of the old type of Negro song that we started our choir away back in 1925. It was never intended to be an outfit for entertainment purposes only. Its commercial success was then and still is due to the universal appeal of the tunes; the words only serve to make the inner meaning of the melodies a little more articulate—just as good choral arrangements render them more acceptable to the modern ear. And because, very *social* early in our activities, I discovered the tremendous potentialities of group singing as a unifying agent, selecting, of course, the best material for professional engagements.

As you know, we have often presented these very large "festival" groups in important performances—sometimes, interracial. Through the activities of these large choruses, we have raised funds for scholarships for talented youngsters who needed financial help, and twice a year for the past five years, have presented in a series of "New Artists Concerts" three or four finished performers who needed a boost towards a professional career. Knowing my convictions on the subject of "singing together"—especially for youngsters—many churches, schools, and settlement houses—including the Community Education Department of New York City—have cooperated in my efforts—giving me welcome access to all their classes, and using in their exercises little songs I have written for that special purpose. I have programs and circulars of all the things I mention.

The last paragraph was added not to impress you with what a big "humanitarian" I am, but merely to show you how long and how steadily I have been working along the lines of the socializing functions of music. I suppose my interest is partly humanitarian, and partly scientific. I have never analyzed my own feelings about it; I only know that it is my work. I simply *have* to try to do it—and it always gets results. However, with my longtime interest and endless experience in this special use of music, you can imagine how I was affected by what I saw in Germany. I have worked here in the New York area with natives and immigrants. For eight years, I worked in Los Angeles with its heavy influx of Orientals, Mexicans, and underprivileged Negroes from Louisiana and Texas—but nowhere have I noticed in any of these people what I felt about the Germans. And what I felt was not the *presence* of something new or strange, but the total *absence* of something very familiar. Those I met with seemed to have so much more, in mental equipment, than some people I know here, but there is one thing that even the most unfortunate person on our shores gives out, unconsciously even, with the first glance from his eye. It was that spark which I missed in even the most animated look from the German people I met in Germany. (Those I have met in this country have it—in abundance.) It is not a question of intelligence, self-consciousness, nor any of those things—nor the lack of them. It is something quite difficult to pin down with a word. But for want of better, I will say that what I missed was the "*sense of the individual.*" I have asked myself if my judgment was colored by what I know of their history and their form of government—and the answer is "no." I believe if I had been set down among them quite suddenly—as an absolute stranger from another planet—knowing nothing at all about them—I would still have had that same feeling of something missing. And such a necessary something. How can your choices and actions have any value unless they are determined by you yourself? In this country it may not always work out in practice, but at least, the concept is always present—and we work and wait. The Germans seem never to have had it and consequently don't miss it—but what a hole the lack of it leaves!

It is my firm belief, based on the way they responded to us, that our songs *disturbed* this condition and made some of them aware, if only vaguely, of this vacuum and of the need to fill it. Young and old, they all give the impression of children—waiting to be told. Intangible as this impression is, it is still very definite and I cannot be the only one to have sensed it. Of course, I had no personal contact with their "ruler types" nor with their "tough element." Those I observed were workers—from the *middle*, but are they not the important ones?

What I should like now—more than anything else in the world—is to go back again—and for a longer period of time, not only in order to visit a greater number of places, but to spend a little longer time in each place. We should leave in the late summer, in time to visit (and appear at, if possible) some of the European music festivals, and then—make an extended concert tour through Germany. On this tour, the dates for the formal concert appearances should be spaced far enough apart to allow time to visit local groups and organizations in each city. We had so many invitations of this sort before, but there was no time to accept. With this arrangement we could also make little impromptu stops along the way in places where a fulltime concert would not be expected, nor even necessary. This would be a wonderful thing to do, since it would reach people who would never find themselves anywhere near a concert hall.

Another new angle which could be worked in on a more leisurely trip and would certainly bring the most marvelous reactions: to sing not only for the Germans, but with them—our songs and some of their own—in German. These would be very easy to prepare in advance—and singing with them in their own language would be a magic key to open many doors. Now don't get the idea, from my enthusiasm on these subjects, that I wish to go over and *preach* something to the Germans. I am sure they would have all their defenses up immediately and, anyhow, preaching is not my work. The songs would do all that is necessary—without a spoken word of any sort. Music has that power—none the less effective for being "sugar-coated." And music, as *sheer propaganda* (in the finest sense of the word) has never been given a thorough trial by us. You mentioned this fact in your excellent article in the *New York Herald Tribune* of October 14th. The Assistant Secretary of State for Public Affairs, Mr. Edward W. Barrett, developed it still further in a recent address to an international conference at Town Hall, New York. Much of his speech was reported in the New York Times of November 15th. I wish all the executives in this department of our government could be made to realize what a powerful (and inexpensive) "weapon" they have been overlooking.

The unique feature of music as propaganda is its "insidious method of attack." First, you are attracted by its beauty, then, as the melody sticks in your memory, you begin to feel its meaning. You say to yourself, "Now I have that song," but it is really the song that has taken possession of you. By that time it is too late to do anything about it. It keeps hammering at you in your quieter moments, you can't forget it and—worst of all—you can't argue with it. It has slipped in under your guard and there it remains and gradually incorporates itself into your thought system—where slowly and subtly it begins to do things to you. All this time, you are quite unconscious of the whole process. You only know you like the song.

So often, during those three weeks of our German tour, some members of the audience would shake my hand and remark with fervor, "Musik ist die allerbeste Sprache" (Music is the universal language)—and it is true. Music is the best of all languages from two points of view: (1) It is the only form of articulate communication which is immediately understandable by everyone without need of translation. (2) It is not only universally understood but universally loved. Cases of allergy or immunity to music are rare indeed and many an ear which will turn deaf to the cleverest of speeches will gladly open to the simplest of songs. In any case, if the Germans say that "Musik ist die allerbeste

Sprache," we have nothing to lose by a small experiment in taking them at their word. What do you think?

Now, Mr. Breen, please pardon the length of my "reflections" on paper. I hope you can find time to read this far. Anyhow, I have had a good time getting it out of my system.

Thanks, and hope to see you soon.

Sincerely,

Hall Johnson

Letter Regarding Berlin Tour Incident

Johnson wrote two letters to Robert Breen on the same day. The first details Johnson's explanation for keeping one German audience waiting for almost an hour before the choir arrived. The letter was handwritten in tiny script and certain words are undecipherable, even under a magnifying glass. Based on the meaning suggested by the context, I have inserted these missing words in brackets.

First letter to Robert Breen:

February 10, 1952

Sorry for the annoyance of the past week or so. I asked for a few minutes conversation because [an explanation] of [the] details [is] not good on phone. If you [were not] unlisted [this] letter would [not] have [been] written [to] Mr. Bob Breen. [With the] customary agreeableness [your secretary] said you would call. [When you didn't,] I kept calling. If you had said finally "no," I would have written them [*Porgy and Bess* producers]. Doubly sorry when [I] found you were not only busy but ill.

Glad (in another way) because if Mr. Watson [was] not annoyed he would not have come out with [the] charge from Berlin [relative to the] final concert in Germany.

Of course, I recall that unfortunate incident. How could I have forgotten it? [Johnson's emphasis] I had arrived in time and was waiting [on pins and needles] every one of those forty (?) minutes for the [choir's] bus to arrive. I also realized the circumstance of situation which was due—not to carelessness or irresponsibility—but to circumstances which had unexpectedly and unavoidably taken place during the day. I explained those circumstances to you and Mr. Schnitzer, who were the only two authorities around at the time. Mr. Schnitzer said that it was not so bad because Mr. W. was late too and had just arrived at the concert. Later, I explained to you that we had got up early to entertain the employees at the AEG works at 12:00 noon at their distant factory—had then to come back to the Bahnhaus for (the necessary) brunch and then to go into a long—and even more necessary—rehearsal for the evening concert. Then they had to go to the various hotels and dress and get back to the concert.

It was really the rehearsal which took up the time. We were doing a completely new program (for the first time) and, without that rehearsal . . . our last concert in Berlin would have been a matter of "guess-work and heart-failure" (which the audience would instantly have recognized) instead of the brilliant success it was. When I explained this to you, you said you thought I had acted wisely under the circumstances. Being a performer yourself, you could easily imagine how I felt, that this show, being the last, must be the best.

Another thing which delayed the singers that evening—when the bus stopped to pick up Mrs. Powell (the "St. Louis Blues" ; "By Myself" girl), they found her quite ill and some little additional time more [was] used to get her into shape to go and perform; you can imagine how the program would have suffered without her presence. As it all turned out, once the concert started, the audience seemed to have forgotten all about the delay. They were as enthusiastic and as unwilling to go home at the close of the show as ever.

Since that time—nearly four months ago—nobody, not a single person, has made even the slightest reference to our lateness on that occasion and . . . I thought that the whole thing had been thoroughly explained and forgotten. Imagine my utter dismay when I learned from Mr. W. only yesterday (and this not officially, he explained, but merely in the course of a telephone conversation)—that this incident is not only remembered, but is being held as a black mark against the group and against me *personally*—although I, personally, was not late. Furthermore, (and this was a shock!) certain high organization officials who are interested in your future theatrical activities have advised that I may not be a dependable risk for employment—on account of the regrettable incident that Saturday evening in Berlin. Mr. W. says that I owe these officials an apology. This, I should like very much to offer, in writing, if somebody will kindly tell me who these officials are. Soon after the end of the tour, I received highly commendatory letters from Mr. Lettinich, Mr. Schutze, Mr. Espinosa, and Mr. McCloy, with nothing but praise and appreciation for our splendid cooperation throughout. Not too long ago, in reviewing certain little episodes concerning, I asked both you and Mr. Schutze if there was any complaint to be made about me, personally, and you both assured me there was *none*. Last month, I sent N.Y. greetings to a good many people in Germany—among others, Mr. McCloy. Only *last week* I received the most cordial response from him, saying, among other things, that people were still talking about our concerts in Berlin. (Mr. M. came to another town, in our third week, to hear us again.)

So, if I can find out who the displeased officials are, I shall be only too happy to write them the sincerest of apologies—explaining that I would have written sooner but just learned, only yesterday, about their displeasure. Also, if they distrust my dependability, they should know (though I shan't include it in my letter) that, in the theater, punctuality is an *individual*, not a *group* responsibility. Nobody has to be rounded up in buses and, if anybody should be so ignorant as to think he can arrive late, the stage manager will know how to take care of that.

So, please, Mr. Breen, kindly let me know the names of the persons to whom apologies and explanation are due. I cannot be happy, no matter what happens or doesn't happen, as long as I know this "black mark" is being held against me. I am sure that you and Mr. Schutze understood the Berlin situation at the time. Somebody evidently doesn't—until this day—since Mr. W. told me that you "came to my defense." I knew you would. Thank you. Now, please tell me, to whom did you have to defend me? I want, more than anything else, to clear this up. This is an *entirely new* experience for me and also, will you kindly show this letter to Mr. Donnelly?

Mr. W. said that word of my short-comings had reached him. This, of course, can only do me harm in his eyes, which I would regret exceedingly. He was not in Germany with us so he couldn't possibly know how our time was filled up in Berlin, or that we gave concerts in ten other cities in the following two weeks—with extra performances, broadcasts, radio interviews, and extra recording sessions for subsequent broadcasting if the occupation radio systems (still in use) are informed and even being granted two other countries. All this sandwiched in between the regular concerts and the daily transportation problems. He might get the idea that all I did in Germany was to flout authority and come late for concerts—and I wouldn't want that to happen. I want him to remember our very first conversation—over the telephone, before I had even seen him. I said to him, "all I want is a chance to do what I know is my best work—and I have *never* had it." There was a smile in his voice as he answered, "you are going to have it now." I have actually lived on that promise ever since—and I don't want anything to happen to change it. So, please show Mr. Donnelly this letter.

Also, please believe, my dear friend, that I feel certain you have always had confidence in me and my high artistic ideals. But for that, I am sure we wouldn't have been in Berlin to begin with. I treasure this regard and approval more than I can tell you and it was this very desire—not to let you down—plus the needs of the singers—which made that last (unfortunate) rehearsal in Berlin *so* necessary. Without it, you would not have liked the concert that followed—not at all, believe me.

It is this same sure knowledge of what I can do—(if I can get the chance to prove it)—this same drive toward perfection, that I want to put at your future disposal—if it can be arranged. I don't want your forthcoming presentation to be just two hours of more yelling and screaming and waving of hands—and *shadows*—(let's not forget the shadows!)—and *no words* in the story and no letters in the words. And you know *this can happen* with the best of intentions from all concerned. It is not enough just to tell the singers what to do—they all think they are doing the proper things all the time. That is because they listen only to their pretty voices—when they listen at all. They have to be shown and taught and drilled—and that takes time and the knowledge of a specialist. But it does produce ensemble—and that is the rare (almost unknown but easily recognizable) quality I want your performances to have. A comfortable opportunity to produce one truly marvelous group of singers, such as I know my people can make—is my whole and only desire and I am still hoping that you can help it along to our mutual benefit.

Hall Johnson

On the same day, Johnson addressed a second letter to Robert Breen:

Proposal for Preparation of Porgy and Bess *Choir*
February 10, 1952

Dear Mr. Breen:

Here is the plan I wished to suggest to you about assembling and preparing the singers. With it I am sending along another letter which I hope you will read first.

The thing I did not want to discuss over the telephone or in writing was actually figures. Figures can look so cold and hard (and so much bigger) on paper but can always be reasoned out and adjusted satisfactorily in a conversation. Well here goes. My plan is exactly the same as outlined in getting together the company for the *Green Pastures*, in which production the singers also had to do minor parts and understudy roles. I kept a large choral group in training for five months before the official rehearsals began. All this time we were looking for actors for the main roles—especially "De Lawd"—as well as the minor parts. Applicants who applied direct to the down-town office were sent immediately to our choral rehearsals uptown where the best ones remained in training until the final auditions which took place just before the official rehearsals began.

During this preliminary period, no promises were made to anybody about a job in the show and no special attention was paid to any music belonging in the show. The rehearsals differed in no way from our regular year—round rehearsals except that the attendance was more uniform and the interest more lively because the singers all knew the show was "coming up" sooner or later. This went on from the first part of August until January 18, '51 when the professional rehearsals started. By that time, the basic technique of the chorus was so firmly grounded that it was not at all upset when they started learning the stage action. Whatever happened to the show later, whatever weaknesses it may have had, everybody commanded the singing.

Now the choral and casting problems (aside for "De Lawd") of the *Green Pastures* were extremely simple compared with what yours will be with *Porgy and Bess*. Not only must you have ample understudies and "minor role" people—all of whom must be singers—but the music itself is much more difficult and will have to be much more thoroughly learned—because your chorus is something moving about the stage in separate groups, maybe, and not seated in a row watching a director—as in much of *Green Pastures*.

So you see if you want to be ready by September 1st, you have just about five months from now until the beginning of stage rehearsals. Exactly the same period of time the *Green Pastures* had—but with more exacting work to do and a more versatile group to assemble—*all singing actors*. That is why I have been so impatient to get started, all this work to be done—and time flying so rapidly. You see, these preliminary training periods do not require all day, every day (as the theater rehearsals will later on). They are held in our regular rehearsal room up town, at first only three evenings per week. The singers are not being paid anything during this period and are using only their spare time between their regular activities. Their interest is in the training—and the prospects. Meanwhile, a concert or two may come up to add further inducement along the way. I had hoped the Paris Peace Congress engagement would have fitted in that capacity. That would be a perfect "builder upper" for this preliminary period. Maybe it is still not too late, as the congress office has already printed handsome announcement brochures—bearing our picture along with others. This would be pure magic to help get some good new voices—especially men. (They all want to see Paris.) I would start the whole machinery with a couple of advertisements in the best Negro papers, simply inviting serious young singers to audition for the Hall Johnson Choir. There would be no mention of your name, or of *Porgy and Bess*, or the Festival. The mere fact of advertising (carefully worded) would stimulate enough curiosity to get the desired results without holding out any more specific bait.

Now that I have explained the machinery of this preliminary period, let's talk about the cost. For a similar preliminary period of five months—up to the actual rehearsals with the selected cast, the *Green Pastures* company paid me the sum of $2,500. (My agreement with them was for a flat fee—not a weekly salary. I prefer that arrangement for work of this type.) This was paid in several installments. I still have their check stubs with the amounts and the dates, which I can show if necessary. I will try to make the same arrangement with you for the term beginning from the present date until the day you start your professional all day rehearsals with your selected singing cast on the actual music of the play. You understand, of course, that Equity will not allow the people to study the actual score of the play (as such) unless they are being engaged and paid—and during the preliminary period they are neither . . . legally, they are simply in my rehearsal, learning choral techniques which will prepare them to study and perform any score, anywhere. If they went to the Westminster Choir School at Princeton, they would have to be paying for this same instruction themselves. But, there is no law to prevent you and your casting director from visiting these rehearsals as often as you like—with an eye to casting possibilities. By that time, we should know all about the musical activities of every one in the rehearsal as they all will be pretty well trained chorally before you even consider them as dramatic possibilities, or even as mere types.

For this sum, covering this period, I would . . . agree to work every evening to assemble and train a large group of singers, including any applicants you may wish to send through your regular casting office (they have all got to learn to sing together). In the daytime hours, I would be available for any special auditions or conferences when you wanted me and, in addition, I would pay all expenses connected with rounding up and holding together this group of singers, such as letters, telegrams, telephone calls, etc., and believe me, this last item can amount to plenty in five months. The only thing I might ask for would be a small donation to our Salvation Army Center rehearsal hall on account of the extra time we would be using it. I am sure you wouldn't object to that. As a matter of fact, I don't think you will really appreciate the value and economy of this whole preliminary idea until the day you start with your stage rehearsals and actually see how much work has already been done in the earlier period— and how far ahead you are with your show. Why not give it a trial, beginning now?

If you and Mr. Davis should decide to act on this suggestion—which you surely must admit is both practical and economical—the main thing that I would ask is that you begin right away. I should like to put the first ad in several papers for the end of this week. Then, by March 1st we should have a wonderful showing of people. Remember, your names or the name of the play will not be necessary for the ads and at no time in the whole preliminary period will you ever be involved in any obligation of any kind. As to payment, I should like $1,500 now to get started and the balance at some later mutually convenient date.

Yours sincerely,
Hall Johnson

Apparently, Robert Breen had already decided not to hire Hall Johnson for the preparation of the tour production of *Porgy and Bess* as he shot back an immediate response to Johnson's letter by telegram:

February 13, 1952

Hall Johnson
634 St. Nicholas Avenue

Regarding letter number one: Main point. Mr. Watson wishes to stress was that people concerned with *Porgy and Bess* Management had learned of Berlin incident and have qualms. Regarding letter number 2: We are not prepared to enter to your suggested arrangement at this time. Your citing of *Green Pastures* arrangement prompts us to inform you that this arrangement [was] not completely satisfactory to the producers of the *Green Pastures*. There were reservations about the wisdom of the arrangement, method of work, and results achieved. Therefore, as I told you in our last telephone conversation everything must remain in abeyance as pertains to possible arrangement with you until other production factors iron out. Spoke with Mr. Harrity today and he is most eager to finalize arrangements and attempt to go ahead on choir TV program.

Robert Breen[9]

Johnson made one more effort to secure the lucrative and badly needed job of providing and preparing the chorus for the fall production of *Porgy and Bess*. After an interval of six weeks, he wrote yet another letter to Breen. To understand the urgency of these negotiations for Johnson, one must recall his words in his January 10, 1952, letter to his manager, William C. Gassner: "*I haven't the faintest idea where my next dollar is coming from*" (my emphasis). This, only three months after a historic tour of Germany as a part of the first American festival group ever funded by the State Department. So desperate was Johnson's economic plight, that he willingly accepted from Gassner a payment of $100, in lieu of the full accounting for the Berlin tour which he was due. (See correspondence of January 10.)

March 20, 1952

Dear Mr. Breen:
   It has been just about six weeks since I had my last communication from you. I refer to your wire of February 13th saying that you were not prepared at that time to enter into the arrangement I had suggested for the preliminary training of the chorus for *Porgy and Bess*. I did not mind that at all. It was only a suggestion and, while I was sure that you agreed with it in principle, I could readily understand that there might be difficulties in the way of its immediate adoption.
   Then the wire said arrangements with me must remain at the standpoint of our last telephone conversation until other production factors were ironed out. I understood you were referring to our very last conversation—when you called to tell me that it had been decided in the meeting of directors that I was to have charge of the choral work in the production and assured me that this decision would stand. Since that conversation, I have telephoned your office several times but assumed that you were too busy to return my call.
   Naturally, as time continues to fly, I find myself rather anxiously awaiting a personal, official word from you. Meanwhile, I hope that everything is pointing in the direction of a fine and successful performance. As ever,
   Sincerely your friend,
   Hall Johnson

Unfortunately for Johnson, Breen's original decision remained unchanged, and the job of preparing the *Porgy and Bess* chorus went to some other conductor. Johnson might have spared himself some embarrassment and a needless waste of time had he only listened to the advice of his manager, William C. Gassner, who, in a short letter dated January 26, 1952—more than two weeks before his letters of February 10—advised him thus: "I forgot to mention that Mr. Breen and Blevin Davis are the principals in the *Porgy and Bess* negotiations, *they seem to leave you definitely out* [my emphasis], but I am sure it is a price question and no reflection on you."

In my opinion, Gassner's last phrase relative to the price question was added to soften the blow of Johnson's loss of yet another project. Johnson's unwillingness to accept his manager's judgment and his attempt to push the deal through personally is one indication that his concept of the concert and theatrical business was relatively unchanged since 1930 and that he was no longer competitive with younger conductors and newer groups.

The six-month period between the Hall Johnson Choir's final concert in Vienna and Johnson's final rejection as conductor of the *Porgy and Bess* represented the unquestioned demarcation between the life and death of the Hall Johnson Choir, and between Hall Johnson, the choral titan, and Hall Johnson, the choral "has-been." Three crushing events occurred within the period. The Hall Johnson Choir was invited as a featured group to the Paris Festival, which featured some of the world's greatest ensembles, but the choir had neither the money nor the singers to return to Europe in eight months. The best offer Johnson got was round trip transportation for the choir in exchange for three additional concerts in Paris. Only one month before his telegram of February 13, Breen sent Johnson the following cable from Paris:

January 14, 1952

Johnson Choir offered two way oceanic transportation in exchange for three concerts Paris Festival in May. Johnson might accept if you could guarantee tour elsewhere. Cable immediately as Johnson must give decision today. Regards.
    BoBreen[10]

Of course, Johnson was forced to reject the offer, for in addition to transportation, three weeks in Paris would require money for room, board, and ground transportation for the singers, which he did not have. Additionally, he no longer had a resident group, a fact which he acknowledged in a letter to Gassner the previous December.

The second disappointment during this period was the rejection of the choir for the production of Virgil Thompson's *Four Saints in Three Acts*. Thompson liked the voices of the singers but frankly told Johnson that his play required young performers and that Johnson's singers were too old.

Johnson's third disappointment, his rejection for the *Porgy and Bess* choir, was the last straw. One familiar with the choral music business in 1952 cannot read Johnson's letter, with his proposal for working with the singers for five months before the beginning of the professional rehearsals, without realizing that he was hopelessly out of touch with the times. In 1962, I participated in a Grammy-winning recording of *Porgy and Bess* highlights with William Warfield and Leontyne Price. The choral director was Leonard De Paur, and the orchestra director was Skitch Henderson. The recording took perhaps three recording sessions, with a single hour rehearsal for the chorus before each session. The modern professional chorus consists not only of professional voices, but of singers who are professional musicians and are prepared to give a stylistic reading of most standard repertoire with little or no rehearsal. The AGMA (American Guild of Musical Artists) and AFTRA (American Federation of Television and Radio Artists) singers of the fifties and sixties—as well as of today—typically would have done many concert performances of *Porgy and Bess* and would be unwilling to donate five months of their time to do what they could do in three weeks or less. I had the good fortune to work with three of the black choral giants of Johnson's period— Johnson himself, William Dawson, and Edward Boatner—and to know Eva Jessye. Of the four, only William Dawson kept pace with the professional growth in the field. Johnson, Jessye, and Boatner all continued to rehearse as if they were working with musically illiterate singers, and by doing so, drove all the trained singers away. Dawson, who remained active in the American Choral Director's Association until his death, came to New York to record broadcast music for SESAC (Society of European Stage Authors and Composers, in which I sang) and demonstrated the most modern and expeditious contemporary rehearsal techniques.

Letter to Disney Studios Regarding Preparation of the
Sprites for the Mickey Mouse Show
  January 20, 1956

  Dear Mr. Adelquist,
    You will probably recall that I wrote you not long ago saying that all the H.J. Sprite had received all their Mouseketreasures except *one* little boy who was out of town with his family at the time. Well, he finally got back and was im-

mediately given his full list of things. His name is Stanley Bragg. Am enclosing (on two sheets) a statement, signed by each of the original Sprites in the presence of their families, to the effect that they have received everything sent them by your studio. They are all very happy about the whole thing. So am I and so, I hope, are you.

This whole situation started with Mr. Damiani's first telephone call asking me to train a group of children for the TV Series. When I told him there were no children in our Music Workshop, he suggested that I assemble such a group and train them. He volunteered the promise that your studio would gladly pay any expenses incurred. He repeated this promise at each of the two auditions, with you and others present. So I took him at his word. I saw no necessity (at that time) of confirming this promise with you, especially when he told me to send in a letter itemizing these expenses.

Just before the photography, *I found that the studio had no intention of paying me anything for the training of the kids* [my emphasis] and Mr. Damiani had gone. I had put in hours and hours for two months, besides disarranging my regular teaching schedule to clear the after-school hours for them. So when I told the parents (of) this situation, they all agreed to pay a small percentage of the children's checks to the Workshop for training and placement. They knew that other schools charge tuition fees and agent's fees, but we had never asked the kids' parents for a penny. So far, so good; but when the checks arrived, the Sprites dropped out immediately, with their entire check, and have never come back.

This happened in the middle of June. The Sprites appeared on the screen on October 14th, four months later. The rehearsals had been going on steadily all this time, with newer and better Sprites replacing those who had disappeared. A few days later [after the T.V. showing] the Treasures arrived. Mrs. Jones [Wathea] didn't give any of the kids all the things at once, and for this reason, based on her long experience with small children, they had been making three rehearsals a week for four months—with no engagements—and no immediate prospects of any. She thought it would sustain more interest in the group to give to give them some things at the time, and the rest from time to time. She discussed this plan with all those present and they all liked the idea and looked forward to later presents. They knew she was keeping the other things for them. So she gave them all the more important things including the membership scrolls. Things were taken to the homes of the Sprites who had apparently dropped out after the photography. Of the two fathers of these kids, one said nothing. The other kept promising to bring his boy back, so we kept expecting him. They, of course, are the two who telephoned the complaint to you, and of course, the only two who had broken their promise about paying the small commission to the Workshop.

So, when we got your letter about complete distribution to those children who had participated, we immediately gave everything to the entire six. We had to replace some few little things that had been given to other children who were not of the original number, but who had been in faithful attendance ever since last summer. If you have ever worked closely with children, you will know that, in a group, you cannot give two or three something and not the others, without destroying the group. We had put in too much time with them to have that happen. It was no trouble to find duplicates for the few things that had been used in this way.

I understand your insistence that what you gave should go to the kids who were there. I hope, however, you will also see my end of it, that the group is more important than any individual or individuals, especially those who will not keep their word.

Both groups [Sprites and Sprouts] have improved vastly in the time since you saw them. Many people told me they saw your rebroadcast of the Sprites last week. They have had six months of training since that film was made. I wish you could have seen them entertaining the large audience last Saturday evening (see enclosure). They scored a tremendous success, with four nationalities represented in the group, and songs of all four. They make a wonderful picture and sound very, very well.

I hope that this matter is now cleared up satisfactorily and beg to remain
Yours sincerely,
Hall Johnson

The preceding letter demonstrates more clearly than any other the almost childlike naïveté of Hall Johnson in business and financial affairs. That a conductor of his years, who had made over thirty Hollywood films, would undertake the preparation of an on-camera group for Disney's Mickey Mouse TV series without a written contract clearly guaranteeing a fair and competitive wage for the director *beforehand* is simply inconceivable. In fact, Johnson's final major film was Walt Disney's *Song of the South*. Even in 1939, when *Run, Little Chillun* was breaking all attendance records in Los Angeles for Federal Theater Project shows, the entertainment unions were strong and did not discriminate in their representation of black performers, so Johnson knew quite well what his union scale minimum compensation should have been. With a distinguished record with Disney through his contribution to *Dumbo* and a distinguished body of work in the industry (which had prompted Disney Studios to *call him* for this job), Johnson could have expected to be paid above scale for his work with the Sprites.

When I interviewed one of the former Hall Johnson singers who knew, loved, and respected him much, his one reservation about Johnson's greatness was that additudinally, Johnson seemed "too old-fashioned." At the time of the interview, this seemed inexplicable in view of all Johnson had accomplished in spite of racism and segregation. However, after viewing his entire life with considerably more perspective, it does seem accurate to call his attitude in dealing with the white economic superstructure "antebellum." During slavery, the "proper attitude" was to give your best to the "master" and joyfully accept whatever crumbs he tossed you, even if it was nothing. While Johnson was confident of his abilities, over and over again he sold his genius to the white man for a pittance. Not unlike the American public, which seems largely content for the top 1 percent of the population to possess (a reported) 85 percent of the wealth, as long as the remaining 15 percent "trickles down" to them, Johnson seemed relatively happy to be famous, to perform and compose, despite the fact that he received little of the wealth generated by his talent. He never demanded from whites anything near what he was worth to them: not from the producers of *The Green Pastures*, who paid Connelly and Bradford more than a $290,000 over the same period that they paid Johnson less than $3,000; not from Warner Brothers, whose movie of *The Green Pastures* sold 6,000 tickets per hour at the Radio City opening; not from Gassner, who failed to give a financial accounting for the Berlin Tour; not from Rockmore and company, producers of *Run, Little Chillun*, who refused to clear production rights so that a movie could be made; and not from Disney for the development and the training of the Sprites. His whole life might have been much different economically had he only employed a capable and trusted personal representative to handle these matters for him.

The problem Johnson had with Disney regarding his distribution of gifts to performers who did not actually appear on the series (in order to keep them in the group) points to another characteristic weakness Johnson revealed in all of his negotiations after Berlin: his focus on personal goals (the reestablishment and perpetuation of a viable singing group) over the objectives of the studio/producer with whom he was working.

For example, in Johnson's negotiations with Robert Breen relative to the preparation of a choir for *Porgy and Bess*, it was evident from his correspondence of February 10, 1952, that despite the highly successful Berlin tour that he had completed the previous October, he no longer had *any* professional choir and that his plan for auditions, without mentioning *Porgy and Bess*, and his plan for five months of rehearsal prior to selecting a final cast were designed primarily to build another professional choir rather than to effectively and expeditiously prepare professional quality singers for the production. By this time, both Jester Hairston and Leonard De Paur, former students of Johnson, were exemplars of the change that had taken place in the industry. Every major "vocal contractor," the designation used by the unions (AGMA and AFTRA), maintained a list of vocally and musically trained singers who could instantly be fitted to the job at hand and perform it with dispatch resulting in important economic savings.

Similarly, in a city the size of Los Angeles, it would have been relatively easy to identify three dozen black kids with good voices, good looks, and good musical skills by canvassing the churches. By so doing, months of rehearsal and the corollary expense would have been avoided. The fact that Hall Johnson turned the Sprite project into six months of workshop rehearsals, three days a week, indicates that he was a man looking for a choir. Meeting a studio need was not his primary objective. Had this not been the case, he would not have given gifts from the studio—designed as a part of the compensation for the singers who appeared on the TV series—to nonperformers, admittedly, just to keep them in the group. It is unfortunate that his hard-earned reputation was tarnished by such a trivial error of judgment, making it impossible for him to demand the compensation that he had earned, but did not get. Sadly, his whole identity was tied to having a group, and this workshop flyer of 1956 speaks volumes about "how low hath the mighty fallen."

The Hall Johnson Music Workshop
wishes you a Happy New Year and asks you to
Come and *Join* in some *Music-Making*
Saturday Evening, January 14, 1956 at 8 o'clock
***
Not a Concert!! No Tickets! No Food!
just
Informal Entertainment! Good Fellowship!
and *Music!* and *Music!* and *Music!*
Choral Music of All Kinds
Fine Solo Voices of Ambitious Students
Selections by Well-Known Guests
Songs with Audience Participation
Special Attraction!
The Hall Johnson Sprites and Sprouts
The "Sprites" are aged 4 to 8; the "Sprouts" up to 14
***
Please come and bring your friends. Admission Free!
But please bring a small contribution toward the Building Fund
of the *Greater Ebenezer Missionary Baptist Church*
whose rooms we use. Now, let's see you on January 14th
and
Happy New Year!

Letter to Walt Disney Studios about Copyright Infringement

Dear Mr. S.

Thanks for your telephone call on Monday, April 3rd. I received the contract on Friday, April 7th. In the same mail was a second letter from Mr. Olin of the Walt Disney Company which I am including along with the earlier ones you requested. You also said not to hesitate to ask questions,—so here goes:

1. Have you a copy of the W.D. record album in question—DS—1205? Is a 12" or a 10"? Hairston says there is a difference. Ask him to get it to you, if he has not already done so. Your contract form refers to "the record entitled *Song of the South.*" The cardboard jacket of the 12" carries in huge (title) letters "All the Songs from Walt Disney's Uncle Remus"—and only the small letters at the bottom (under the big picture of Uncle Remus) "Music from the Original Sound Track *Song of the South.*" The album is known in the New York stores as "Uncle Remus," from the big outside letters. This may not be important (certainly not in our contract) but I want us both to be clear together about the same things; we are so many miles apart—if some detail should have to be discussed quickly. My name (H.J. Choir) appears 4 times, but *only* on the *disc.*

2. It is my understanding, both over the telephone, and according to the contract, that you will advance the money for any legal costs that may arise, at the time they arise, and deduct such amounts from my share, after the settlement is made. In other words, I am not to have any financial obligations whatever, during the discussion period. Is that correct?

3. Aside from the "realm of intangibles," just what are my damages? What do they owe me for? I had never even heard, or heard of, the times I was credited with performing. So there is no question of unlawful use of a recording I had already made. For the same reason, it could not be a case of plagiarism or infringement of copyright. I have no prior claim of ownership of either the singing or the songs. This seems more like the willful misrepresentation of a commercial product—signing my name to a job I couldn't have possibly done because (1) I was not even present and (2) because the quality of the work is too far below my well-known standards.

4. No matter what their reason or explanation might be, it is quite obvious that this accrued to their advantage and to my disadvantage.

5. This case really seems to fall more under labor laws than any other. In those days, if I had recorded the songs for the picture, I would have received one check to cover my total services. The singers would have been paid by the studio at a daily rate agreed upon. If I had recorded the songs for the Uncle Remus disc, the singers would have been paid by the studio at a time rate, but I would have received no check (unless by special added agreement). I would have been given a small percentage of the sales profits as royalties at stated intervals—as long as the record sold. For me, the picture recording and the record company recording have always been two different kinds of deal and

have always been handled as I explained, I have never known or heard of a case where a recording contract for a picture automatically carried with it record album distribution rights. Of course in the '30s and '40s, the record business was not what it has since become. Their record album was not released until 1959. It is quite possible that I still may have a claim on the Walt Disney Company for the *Dumbo* album.

Of course, my biggest hurt and most serious claim for damages has nothing to do with how much or how little the choir job would have been worth—if we had done it. My damage is in the realm of absolute "intangibles"; but nevertheless, very real: the blow to my professional pride, and to a reputation built up over a long lifetime of meticulous adherence to only the highest standards. For example: There is a beautiful melody in the W. D. album called "All I Want"—listed "Traditional." I never heard it before—but it is just the kind of Negro folk song we specialize in. As recorded, the arrangement is not at all in the racial style (how could they be expected to know?) but, worse than that, the diction is atrocious—simply for lack of consonants. Pure phonetics and clear articulation have always been our "pride and joy," and no singer who has ever been in three of my rehearsals could possibly turn out such sloppy words. Imagine how I feel to have the name of our choir signed to such singing. True, in "show business," good diction is desirable, but not too important. The opening chorus, "Song of the South," by the Studio Choir is a case in point. This would be quite effective—if you could only understand the words without straining the ears! At that, it is as good as the average movie chorus—but for me, the "average" is not good enough!

Someone may say that this record is especially designed for *children*, that children won't notice such things, and so I should not take this matter too seriously. This is not true. Mothers and fathers will enjoy this whole Disney Series and notice all the credits, and the children will not always be children. In fact, as long as one single "Uncle Remus" recording is still available anywhere, it constitutes an effective and absolute refutation of everything I have always preached (racially and musically) in every class, lecture, rehearsal, or performance. And this harm works everywhere—especially in places where our choir has not and will not be heard—and for all time, past, present, and future. It is really a body-blow to the structure of a life-time (See enclosed biographical notes). No amount of money can undo this harm—but the perpetuators should be penalized.

I can't expect you or anyone else to realize the depth of my feeling about this; only another creative artist, or perhaps a particularly dedicated teacher, might understand. I am mentioning this now—in advance—so that you will not expect me to be satisfied with the kind of adjustment that might adequately satisfy a claim of simple plagiarism or infringement of copyright—neither of which could do my reputation any harm. On the contrary, both are forms of flattery.

Sorry this letter had to stretch out to such proportions, but I do want you to know the ins and outs. You are well situated out there to know how the movie and record contracts may or may not overlap. I don't think I have any more questions so—Thanks a lot—and Good Luck!

Hall Johnson

The facts surrounding the performance of the Hall Johnson Choir in the filming of *Song of the South* become even more confusing with the receipt of the Disney Studio's response to Hall Johnson on March 3, 1961. The Disney Studio flatly contradicts Johnson's assertion that he and his choir did not do the movie.

Dear Mr. Johnson:

Please accept our apology for the long delay in answering your letter of December 4, 1960, inquiring about the identity of the Hall Johnson Choir named on our record "Original Sound Track from *Song of the South*." Part of the delay was caused by the necessity of going into old records, and we hope you will understand.

The answers to the specific questions contained in your letter are:

1. The musical director of the Disney picture was Charles Wolcott, and the vocal director was Ken Darby.

2. There were approximately 40 singers in the group.

3. The film itself was filmed for the largest part at the Goldwyn Studios. It is believed that the Hall Johnson Choir was working there at the time (in 1945 or 1946) and that the casting of the group for the Disney film was done by the Goldwyn Casting Department.

4. Yes, the group known as the Hall Johnson Choir recorded the original sound track for "Song of the South."

5. Yes, the group did call themselves "The Hall Johnson Choir."

6. The picture did not contain screen credits for the choir.

7. The group has not been used as background music in any other Disney theatrical but a portion of the choir was used on a *Mickey Mouse Club* television show, in about 1956. On the latter occasion the man known to the Disney people in 1945–46 as Hall Johnson remembered very well the same Disney people who worked on the film in 1945–46.

8. Nothing on the Disney film production schedule at the present time indicates the likelihood of a future engagement for the group.

9. *Song of the South* was released in 1946.

10. Our record, No. DQ 1205, was released in September, 1959.

We hope that this information will help to clarify the situation.

Very truly yours,

Walt Disney Music Company

After a careful examination of all available evidence, the most rational conclusion is the studio contracted a counterfeit Hall Johnson Choir to do the film, apparently without knowing it. It is possible and even probable that the singers were actually members or former members of the Hall Johnson Choir, or former members of the large Federal Theater Project Choir that performed in the record-breaking Los Angeles production of *Run, Little Chillun*. By 1945, Los Angeles was teeming with Hall Johnson singers. The *Green Pastures* choir, fifty strong, had traveled to Hollywood in December 1935 to make the film and remained to do many others. They had been joined by others to cast *Run, Little Chillun* in 1938 and 1939, as well as a production of *Mikado*, which Jester Hairston conducted. In addition, Johnson had formed the large Festival Choir of Los Angeles. It is not far fetched to assume that when he returned to New York for the revival of *Run, Little Chillun* in 1943, one of his ambitious assistants contracted a group of local Hall Johnson singers to do this film. The matter could have easily been settled if the studio had only produced the names of the singers it paid for the job. Lacking that, I believe that despite the fact that Hall Johnson himself was in New York, members of the Hall Johnson Choir did the movie.

It is not clear whether Johnson collected any damages from Disney as his choir had a long history of having several units operating simultaneously under different conductors. The receipt of the Disney letter was also only three months before Johnson suffered a stroke.

The following letter, though unfinished, accurately depicts Hall Johnson's attitude about infringement and bastardization of his work. In 1964, the great contralto Marian Anderson commissioned and recorded for RCA Victor an album of spirituals arranged by Hall Johnson that was called *Jus' Keep On Singing*. Included in the album was Johnson's arrangement of "I Been in de Storm So Long." John Motley was piano accompanist for the album. Two years later, in 1966, a brilliant young mezzo-soprano, Shirley Verrett, recorded the same song in her first album (I was one of the singers in the backup group), *Singin' in the Storm*, and included Johnson's arrangement (the title song) orchestrated by Leonard De Paur, who also conducted the recording sessions. Apparently, sometime after the release of the recording, Johnson, an inveterate record collector, walked into a record store, saw Verrett (a former pupil of his) on the cover, and purchased the album. The ensuing letter was written when Johnson discovered the inclusion of De Paur's (also a former student) orchestration of his arrangement, with the following description: "*I Been in de Storm So Long*—This beautiful expression of the many tired souls who have, in the words of another spiritual, '*been buked and scorned'* is heard in an orchestration by one of the great arrangers of Afro-American music, Hall Johnson."

Unfinished Letter to R.C.A. Victor Records Regarding Copyright
Infringement and Bastardization of His Arrangement
   The Musical and Legal Departments
   R.C.A. Victor Record Company

Dear Sirs:
   I enjoyed pleasant early experiences with Victor in the 1930s when you recorded the Hall Johnson Choir with all available technical equipment at that time. In recent years, I have not been so fortunate. My name has been used several times without permission, on my music, deformed by others, or (on music) which I did not write at all. My reputation will be damaged by these things as long as the current record exists. I need information so let's clear up terms and laws in general. I shall begin with the present situation (*Singin' in the Storm*).
   June 6th—I bought the album on account of the picture. Later, I was surprised by the key of this little song, as yet unpublished. I telephoned the producer—He called his secretary, who told me:
   1. She had phoned me, my secretary answered as I was asleep, but she knew the situation, and it is OK to go ahead. *My secretary knows nothing of this conversation.* The producer said he was sorry and would call me soon.
   2. I called him. He asked me which I preferred, straight payment or royalty. I said that I was willing to discuss either. He had to go out of town and would call me on his return.
   3. Weeks passed, I finally called and was shocked when he said "the company owns the rights to the song—from an earlier album." I denied that: The rights claims were relinquished for the previous album only.
   4. Wednesday, October 26th—Producer phoned with a *completely new story*. No mention of rights whatever. Instead, a grand mistake. He had meant to put Leonard De Paur's arrangement in the album, and accidentally, put mine instead. I was mystified. Was there a different arrangement? "Yes, of course. Leonard De Paur's had orchestration." That does not make the arrangement different. It only colors it! "Oh yes," said he. He has also changed the harmonies and the key is different. Then he offered me $100 to settle and forget the whole thing. I declined and requested a meeting. He agreed.
   Thursday, October 27—Producer phoned and shocked me by admitting the two arrangements *are exactly the same.* Would I please take $100. No! I insisted on meeting Monday as agreed.
   Overnight, he had become convinced that placing a few wind instruments onto my piano arrangement could not be considered an orchestration. *All it did*

was to spoil the clearness of my work! The *eight* different tone colors, tracing exactly my contrapuntal lines, threw the whole thing out of shape and balance, just as if streaky red, green and black stripes were clumsily smeared onto a new white house. The effect is not decorative, but deforming—and the original white house has disappeared. A *real* orchestration would have replaced my arrangement, not have *leaned crazily against it.* Yet, *this unmusical abortion* has been sent out into the whole world—under my name.

A genuine folk song has no individual authorship. The words and melodies are created by an anonymous group. The harmonies are generally sparse and rudimentary. Only the American Negro exhibits a marked predilection for rich harmonies and brilliant counterpoint. The folk melodies are (legally) in "public domain," but any development, such as variations, or improvisation, should be considered the property of the arranger. *Mr. De Paur may use about one-third of my melody.*

Johnson's letter stops here without a formal close. Though it is undated, it had to have been written after 1966. At seventy-nine years old, Johnson experienced declining health in 1967 and 1968. It is not certain that his letter to Victor was ever mailed or that his very legitimate claim was ever settled. Unfortunately, multiple infringements of his works continue today, and some of his publishers seem impervious to such theft, even when alerted to it. There is no way of telling whether or not this indifference is reserved for black composers.

Letters to Publishers

The following letter to Herbert Marks, owner of Marks Music Publishers, demonstrates Hall Johnson's frustration with the publisher after signing a contract to publish ten arrangements. (Despite continuous editorial hassling, Marks had published nothing of Johnson's in four years.) Johnson's many word emphases make the letter read much like a script with a perfection of construction and language that is uniquely his.

June 11, 1956

Mr. Herbert E. Marks
E.B. Marks Corp.

Dear Mr. Marks:
    Thanks for your letter of May 21st. I hope your trip to Mexico and California was both pleasant and profitable. Did you come to Los Angeles? If so, I am sorry we didn't get together for a little talk. I had written you last on March 28th and, without a line of response from you (or from your secretary, saying

that you were out of town), I was naturally at a loss how to interpret your silence of so many weeks. In the meantime, the situation was growing clearer in my own mind.

When your reply finally arrived, a couple of weeks ago, it completely ignored the main point of my last letter—the suggestion that we call our agreement off altogether. I now wish to change my suggestion to a *formal request*. I think I have both legal and moral grounds for my position.

In July of 1952, I entered into a contract with your firm for the publication of ten choral arrangements—to be delivered by me and issued by you in installments. I sent you the first installment. *In a few days, it will be July 1956,— four years later*—and still I have not seen a single proof-sheet. Instead, on *three* occasions, you or your representatives have made post-contractual demands and requests which, if acceded to, would not only vitally change the basic structure of my work but would do violence to my sincerest artistic principles in general. The first two instances occurred soon after the signing of the contract and had to do with (1) your editor's blue-penciled objections to my style of composition and (2) the insistence upon "optional" piano accompaniments. The third occasion was the very recent objection to the dialect of the texts. Since then, even though I immediately revised the first four songs to meet the first two demands, the intervening *years* have passed in silence,—with no action nor any sign of further interest from you—until your letter of February 24th, 1956—about the dialect. Needless to say, if any *one* of these stipulations had been mentioned with the contract in 1952—I would not have signed.

I have neither the desire nor the time to rehash the discussion about any of these three complaints brought up by you *after* the signing of the agreement. I have already given you—in detail—both the technical and artistic reasons for my stand. When you signed with me, I assumed that you knew the particular characteristics of my work. The entire musical world had long since accepted it and three reputable New York publishers had been distributing it for thirty-odd years. Anyhow, I submitted to the head of that department quite a few samples of my arrangements—from which he selected ten. Four of these have been with you now for a *very* long time, but I suppose you had not looked at them personally until quite *recently*. It could have not taken four years for you to notice that the texts were in dialect.

Now, I have already overcome my scruples enough to comply with the first *two* requests but, when you suggest that I modify and modernize the dialect, it was completely *out of my power* to agree. It was, to me, simply unthinkable—as if you had asked me to retouch the Mona Lisa with Max Factor cosmetics or to put a "Maidenform" bra on the Egyptian Sphinx! Even if I could have seriously considered such a thing, it would have been *technically* impossible. Other words just wouldn't fit. I had not the slightest wish to change your opinions—or those of your friends. I have nothing whatever to do with that, although I might add—quite incidentally—that my contract is with *you—not with your friends*.

And, of course, any and all opinions affecting this contract should have been brought forward *before* it was signed—*not four years later*. Still, it is these opinions which have occupied most of the space in the two letters you finally wrote.

Another thing—I realize that your business is many times bigger—in volume—than mine and that my contribution to your catalogue is not a matter of crucial importance but, even so, I must say, quite frankly, that I have never had business with *any* company that showed such a leisurely and casual approach to the important factor of *time*. For example, you keep ten of my best songs tied up—lying idle—for four years and then (February 24th this year) you write that the *proofs* of the first four songs are at that moment on your desk—ready to be put through,—and awaiting only *my* decision on a matter which *you* consider of the gravest importance. Would I kindly give this matter my most *careful* consideration and reply at my *earliest* convenience? It sounded urgent, I considered carefully, as requested, and replied as soon as I could— under the sudden new and rather upsetting circumstances. Naturally, I expected a fairly prompt reply—since it was *you* who demanded haste. *Three months* (thirteen weeks) later—on may 24th, to be exact—I received *three short paragraphs* from you—with *most* of the space (and all the major emphasis) devoted *once more* to the personal opinions of a mysterious and anonymous group of "certain individuals" whose opinions are wholly irrelevant to *my* business, although you show *very plainly* that they are a dominant factor in yours. *Not a word* about the (to me) *vitally important* suggestion I had made—after giving the matter the "carefully considered opinion" *you* requested. That was only indirectly alluded to in a portion of the last sentence of your letter: (I quote) "Accordingly, we shall (not should) forget about everything but getting out the very finest arrangements worthy of your name." Just like that!

Earlier, in the beginning of your letter, you say: (quote) "Your arrangements of the spirituals have gone to the engraver with the words *untouched.*" Who would have touched them—and didn't the proofs on your desk last February also come from the engravers? Most proofs do. Why make a second set before showing me the first?

Furthermore, I think I should be *asked* to "forget about everything"—not just have it announced to me that we *shall* forget it. That is not so easy—for me— after all the rigmarole we have been through for the past four years—with no results. I can forget it only if you consent to my suggestion to terminate our present old—but—still—virgin contract. In my last letter, I also offered a substitute agreement: to sen[d] you some modern material which might find greater favor with you, your editors and even with the Olympian hierarchy of "certain individuals." This suggestion apparently did not interest you, since it went unnoticed in your belated reply.

Honestly, Mr. Marks, I see no other solution. The blue pencil of your editor and the insistence upon "optional" piano accompaniments are proof positive that your staff will not enjoy preparing arrangements "worthy of my name."

You, yourself, do not like them—otherwise you would not be suggesting vital changes. Also, your own God-like indifference to the calendar leaves me agape and, back of all of this, looms the shadowy but oh-so-potent hierarchy of "certain individuals"—like a federation of ghosts on a medieval parapet. Really, it is too much for me. I can see not one single hope for harmonious relations ahead—and I cannot work under any other kind.

So I now change my recent *suggestion* to an entreaty: *please let me out of our agreement.* This is the last *long* letter I shall write you (I promise) and your reply can be as short as you care to make it. But *please, let it be soon*—(it can even be a telegram—collect) and *please* let it read something like this: "We hereby agree to annul the existing contract between us and to return all your manuscript music arrangements on receipt of the sum paid you as advance royalty on same."

This would be *such* a great relief to

Yours sincerely,

Hall Johnson

P.S. Quite aside from all this—my very kindest regards to you and to Dr. Greissle.

H. J.

Johnson's letter generated an equally heated response from Marks, a portion of which will be included to provide the necessary context:

June 21, 1956

Your letter of June 11 is so unbusinesslike [sic], sarcastically insulting and generally unfair that I was tempted not to answer it at all. Since, however, you are presumptious [sic] enough to say that you have both legal and moral grounds for requesting the return of your arrangements and the cancellation of the contract, let me state a few facts:

1. You signed a contract with us on June 26, 1952, calling for you to arrange ten Negro spirituals for mixed chorus. You received an advance of $300 upon the signing of the agreement. It was stated that we agreed to copyright and publish these arrangements before the end of the year 1953, providing the manuscripts were received by us before the end of the year 1952. . . . Your dispute with our editors regarding certain phases of the arrangements delayed the works received by us for a long time. Not being a musician, I do not feel competent to go into the questions involved here, but I should like to state that it was our intention and hope to publish the Hall Johnson arrangements as soon as possible for several reasons. We announced them in our catalog quite some time ago. We had invested $300 and considerable other money, time and labor trying to prepare them for publication. Finally, we did wish to have your name among many other distinguished ones in the list of works published by us.

E.B. Marks, President

Johnson's final letter was considerably more conciliatory in view of the fact that Marks had agreed to publish the arrangements in hand and to release Johnson from further obligation:

August 15, 1956

Dear Mr. Marks:

Thanks for your interesting letter of June 21st, which only an extra pressure of work has prevented me answering sooner. I quite agree with you that it is time to drop all discussion and confine all necessary correspondence to purely business matters. From the beginning, we have been approaching our subject from two entirely different points of view: mine, altogether musical; yours, altogether social. The only possible way to end it is to drop it. So—ok.

Now, about the business: I am quite satisfied with your decision to publish the four songs you now have—and let it go at that. I know you will do a good job on them and I will do everything in my power to increase their circulation.

However, it is incorrect to say that I sent you only four arrangements. I sent *seven. Three were returned to me* (March 12th, 1953) for optional piano parts, with a statement that the others would be "put into production in a matter of days." (I am re-reading that letter at this moment.) Returned were "Mos' Done Travelin,' " "When I'm Gone," and "By an' By." Are you sure your dates aren't a little mixed. If, as your last letter states, you didn't receive the last two manuscripts until May 1953, how could you possibly return three out of seven on March 12th, 1953—two months before you received any at all?

Two other little points about the business:

1. Until your last letter, releasing me from further obligation for the other six songs, I quite naturally considered all ten "tied up" with you. The ten titles were listed in the contract and I could not legally make any other use of them. That is why I referred to these songs as "lying idle" for the past four years.

2. In the very last line of your letter, you wonder if I really think I have lived up to my contract. I am very sure I have. All the long delay, and all the unpleasant argument were caused by stipulations and requests made by you and your music department *after the contract.* These were not promised by me over my signature, so I had every legal right to demur, argue the points—and even refuse to comply. I would most certainly have done all three if these requests had been made before the contract. The worst you can say of me is that I am "a bad fellow," but no court in the land would say that I deliberately broke my contract.

Hall Johnson

The following letter to Mr. Von der Goltz involves a dispute between Johnson and his second assistant conductor, Leonard De Paur. In a television production of *The Green Pastures*, conducted by De Paur, Mr. De Paur apparently claimed credit for the final two choruses: "Hallelujah, King Jesus!" and "Hail de King of Babylon!" both of which had been composed by Johnson.

June 14, 1958

Mr. Von der Goltz
Vice President
Carl Fischer Music Co.

Thanks for your letter of May 26th concerning the pros and cons of my claim to sole authorship of the two original songs in *The Green Pastures*. I read with great interest the two other letters which you enclosed—one from your attorneys, Gilbert and Gilbert, and the other from Mr. Rockmore, attorney for Mr. Leonard De Paur. Mr. De Paur, of course, was the musical director of the television performance of *The Green Pastures* recently produced by the National Broadcasting Company, which performance gave rise to the present discussion as to authorship of the two songs in question: "Hallelujah, King Jesus!" and "Hail, de King of Babylon!"

Quite some time ago I signed, in your office, a very brief and condensed, but absolutely true, statement of the facts in the case. The statement was sent to your attorneys—who secured a similar statement from Mr. De Paur by way of his attorney, Mr. Rockmore. Since Mr. De Paur's statements conflict in several instances with mine, your attorneys very kindly sent it on to me for my comments. I wish to thank them for this consideration—and here are my comments:

First, I must congratulate Mr. De Paur on his wisdom in dropping all further claims to any participation in the composition, "Hallelujah, King Jesus!" which was used in the recent television show substantially as I wrote it twenty-eight years ago. He now apparently confines his remarks to the second song, "Hail, de King of Babylon!" and, in this regard, makes one statement that is absolutely true: He did prepare for the telecast an altogether different setting for this song "which in no way infringes on Hall Johnson's original composition or any rights with respect thereto" (Mr. Rockmore's words—quoted from his letter).

Unfortunately, Mr. De Paur has been grossly misinformed on three very important points with regard to "Hail, de King of Babylon!": [De Paur asserts,] (1) "the words were written by Marc Connelly," (2) "it was a contrived (?) tune in the original production which was suggested to Hall Johnson by Marc Connelly." All tunes are contrived. The one in question was contrived by Hall Johnson and not suggested by anyone. [He asserts additionally,] (3) "the lyrics were part of Connelly's original script." These three statements (quoted from Mr. Rockmore's letter) are absolutely false and, coming from Mr. De Paur, have no other value than hearsay, and for one simple (and very natural) reason which should impress any lawyer: the contract with Mr. Connelly for the production of *The Green Pastures* was signed by the producer, the Laurence Rivers Company, early in January of 1930. The play opened several weeks later—on February 26th, 1930. At that time, De Paur was a youngster of 14 or 15, living in New Jersey, and going to school in Pennsylvania. I did not even meet him for the first time until a year or so later. At that time, he had no professional musical or theatrical experience of any kind and was never at any time connected with the production of *The Green Pastures*, which incidentally, remained unchanged from its first performance on Broadway in 1930 to its last. There was never any question of revisions or changes in drama or in music.

So you see Mr. Von der Goltz, I should not be expected to argue these questions with De Paur, who cannot possibly know what he is talking about—since he was not even in New York at the time. However, if the person who originated these false statements cares to confront me with them, I shall be very glad to submit contrary evidence that will more than satisfy any court.

Sorry I could not keep my comments down to the single "line" you requested, but brevity is not always conducive to clearness—and this situation requires clearness—once and for all time. Don't you agree? (This all happened, or didn't happen, twenty-eight years ago!)

Sincerely,

Hall Johnson

P.S. Kindly relay this to Messrs. Gilbert at the proper time.

In a recent discussion with the new publications manager of one of Hall Johnson's several publishers, I found it necessary to explain the difference between the easy solo arrangements found in their published collection of *The Green Pastures Spirituals* and the concert versions of the same spirituals that Johnson composed at a later date. The following letter of Hall Johnson, discovered subsequently, addresses this same issue with the publications manager of G. Schirmer Music in reference to "Po' Moner Got a Home at Las'."

September 14, 1961

Dear Mr. Heinsheimer:

Thank you for your recent letter. I am sorry I couldn't reach you before I left New York for an indefinite stay in California.

I am glad to have your opinion about the three songs. Naturally, at first glance, you might think that the arrangement of "Po' Moner Got a Home at Las'" is the same as in the book of "Thirty Spirituals." But if you will notice, that version is greatly simplified for the purposes of the book, and not at all suitable for concert performances. This arrangement now on your desk is being used in manuscript for concerts with great success.

Will you kindly compare the two versions again before making a final decision?
Very sincerely yours,
Hall Johnson

Of course Johnson was right and his tempered response, so different from his earlier intemperate correspondence to E. B. Marks (which appears above), was successful in getting the concert arrangement published.

Letter of Self-Promotion

Los Angeles Times Press Release

The Festival Negro Chorus of Los Angeles, Hall Johnson, conductor, will be guest artists in a concert of unusual interest Sunday evening, July 20th at Bovard Auditorium on the campus of the University of Southern California. The Negro Chorus will unite with the chorus and symphony orchestra of the university to present compositions by William Grant Still and Hall Johnson.

Mr. Still's cantata, *And They Lynched Him on a Tree*, is a dramatic musical study of the emotions attending a lynching. Its performance requires a white chorus, a Negro chorus, solo contralto (the mother of the murdered boy), a narrator, and full symphony orchestra. It has been called "The most powerful utterance since *Uncle Tom's Cabin*."

Hall Johnson will conduct his own composition, a stirring march for chorus and symphony orchestra, entitled *Toward Freedom*. In this music, the Negro, out of his long experience of slavery and partial emancipation, looks forward to a New Freedom, not for himself only, but for everybody in the world; a freedom, not only from oppression, but from the causes of oppression; a spiritual freedom from hatred, greed and hypocrisy, liberating the oppressor as well as the oppressed.

This concert is one in the regular series of the University Summer School. Bovard Auditorium is located at 36th Street and University Avenue. The concert will begin promptly at 8:15 p.m. and is absolutely free to the public.

The Poetry of Hall Johnson

Notes on the Hall Johnson Poetry

It is clear that Hall Johnson attached great value to his poetic efforts as they were more carefully preserved than any of his other works. The job of curating his memorabilia would have been immensely simplified had he given equal care and treatment to his music scores.

All of the poems were typewritten but only the carbon copies are extant. The fading and smudging of some pages dating back to 1908 required a magnifying glass to decipher them. Many of the poems originally bore no titles. At some later date, Johnson appended the titles in pencil. I have added titles where none were found and have indicated these additions with as asterisk (*). Some poems were dated, some were not. Those with dates will show them as originally written.

There is no attempt to organize the poems chronologically or by quality. They are, however, organized as to theme as they seem to deal with three great forces: love, God, and self. Just as Robert Schumann had his "song" year, Johnson seemed to write most of his poems in 1934. The reasons for this are unclear.

His poetry is frequently autobiographical as it refers to situations and stimuli in his life. You will note the poems on Marian Anderson, Will Marion Cook, and on drunkenness. In these poems, the inner workings of Hall Johnson are revealed far more completely than in any other area of his creative genius.

As was his custom, Johnson wrote some accompanying notes on these poems and organized them into categories that are roughly reflected in the organization I have used here. Unfortunately, the introductory notes and the page outlining the categories were not found in the same file as the poetry and had obviously (by the age of the paper) been sketched some time before many of the poems were written. All the poems were typed. All introductory notes were handwritten and are provided for the additional insight they bring into the creation of the poetry.

The Chemistry of Life in Action[11]

Love—is—altogether selfish, is manifest always as an appetite, the desire to be one with its object. The appetite changes, as the quality of love changes. The quality of love changes, as the sense of being changes. When the sense of being was altogether physical—as it became more mental—as it becomes spiritual—But love always remains selfish—.

Jealousy is the belief in other *selves* who can take away the object of our love. When love grows to include all, there can be no jealousy because the sense of individual being includes all life—hence, there is *nobody* to take away *anything*, because the magic sense of the words tell it there are no longer a sense of *bodies* or *things*—All is the self—which remains selfish, identifying itself with *all life* and *all real love.*

[These words] lay no claim to being poetry. They are simple verses, full of faults—only too apparent,—under but each expressing a thought or—a situation of the author. The stress of the times is bringing people back to simple emotions which antedate all words and will outlast all specific occasions. To the unlettered, everyday person who understands love—these lines are offered—.

Love is constant and changeless in quality—only its object varies. (What about love of possessions,—and possession love? of people?) In the final analysis, each man loves only himself. This takes the direction of—possessions and power, the flesh, works as such, works for humanity, humanity, love itself. At what point does love cease to identify itself with its object and realize that it is its own object? Unworthy objects pall and bring suffering—as love grows—self, it welcomes sacrifice (enlarging the self) until love is its own object and its own reward.

For the frontispiece of his poetry collection, Johnson designed a rather elaborate graphic that will be presented here in a standard poetry format:

Some Old Fashioned Lines for My Lovers
by
Hall Johnson
This book is not for the literary artist,
The cynic.
This book is for the simple—
Because more love makes more simplicity.
About love . . . and Love.
Living is simply one extended course in loving—
Grades—Classes—Teacher—(Experience)
Career (Love life) of race—
Compared to that of individual.
Of frustration, Disillusion, and Parting.
Largely Physical!

Poems of Love

Obsession
At night I cannot sleep but lie with fix'ed gazing
And scan the dim-arched ceiling that o'erhangs my bed,
Where my inflamed fancy limns with loving fingers
The fine and noble contours of your shapely head,
And when at length of gazing thus I feel a-wearied
And turn me on the other side to ease the strain,
My eyes encounter my long mirror's inky blackness
And there your flaming Southern eyes meet mine again.
Upon the city-streets I stalk 'mid busiest traffic,
Like some gaunt moon-mad Manfred on the Alpine heights,
Peering above the thronged heads of Mammon's children
To where your smile blends with and dims the city-lights.
In short, where'er I go, whate'er I would be doing,
Your form and face obtrude themselves without consent;

So have you witched me with your cool yet dev'lish beauty
And, all unwitting, robbed my life of all content.
What have I done to draw on me this dire obsession
Or have my fathers sinned that I must stricken be?
If prayer nor work can exorcise this apparition,
What hope is there in Earth or Heaven or Hell for me?
Why were you made so beautiful beyond description
And then placed just outside the reach of my desire,
Forbidden by the Word of God and laws of Nature
To even know the passion that your eyes inspire?
These eyes with which each fresh encounter's but a dagger
To deepen this Prometheus-wound within my flesh;—
While knowing that you're not for me and never will be
But turns the cruel knife and starts the blood afresh.
Oh, could I tell you but just once how dear I hold you,
Just one time lay my hand upon your black-silk hair,
Press just one kiss upon those eyes with fringed eyelids,
Or on that velvet neck,—there, just behind the ear.
Just once to feel your panting breath 'neath my embraces,
Those luscious lips, that quiv'ring form at my control,
To hear just once your heavenly voice with my name burdened;—
Ah! T'were too cheaply bought with my immortal soul. (1908 or 1909)

Memory

I heard a memory:—
All suddenly it came within a music so revealing
That my flesh leapt to the sound,
Earth and Heaven spun around
As the madness of it set my senses reeling.
I saw a memory:—
(All silently it rose from out a book I was a-reading)
Pale and tenuous as a wraith,
Yet as heavy as a sigh
That comes welling up through faith
When the tears long since are dry,
And the sadness of it left my heart a-bleeding.
I love a memory:—
Ah, love, is there no magic balm
Can ease this bitter ailing?
For 'tis all that's left of you
Lying out there in the cold.
So my weary thoughts renew

All the things we said of old,
Lest my soul grow sick and die. (1909 or 1910)

Excuse Me, Please

Never to have known you?
That would be too distressing.
Never to have loved you?
'Twere to have missed a blessing.
Never to have lived with you?
The rest of life were vain.
Never to have left you?
But I had to live again!

Friend

Friend, what are you, friend or lover?
Both of these—and something over?
Times I think you are my mother,
Or, at least, my double-brother:—
Being not me and yet of me,
All inside me, still around me,
Sharing every thought I think of,
Thinking ev'ry thought before me;
You the thought and you the thinker,
You the wine and you the drinker;
String and bow to all my music,
Music for my ev'ry meaning.
Friend, what are you, friend or lover?
Both of these,—and something over!

Border

Where were you going last night when I met you
In that pale land,—so far and yet so near,
Where light is music and where speech becomes no sound?
What did you say to me when I looked at you,
Trailing your filmy drap'ries in the winds of time
Which seem to blow but are not ever blowing,
In that still place where nothing moves but Mind?
Did you lean to me? Was it you who kissed me
And drew my soul to vortices unknown before?
Say, was it you, or was it God who kissed me?
Nay, do not answer me,—I'll ask no more.

Fusion

Ah, which is you and which is me,
Lost in this two-fold unity?
Is that your foot?
Is that my hand?
Could anyone tell, on demand,
The meaning of this solemn, sweet
And sacrificial mystery?
One thing alone I know,—
That you and I have reached
The promised land! (3-11-1934)

Knitter of Dreams

I dreamed you in a dream and knit you strong,
So we could be the two lips of one song
To sing upon the house-tops every day
And up-beat, down-beat this old world away.
But then, one day, you stayed away so long
And, when you came you had forgot the song—
I threw away my needles, for it seemed
I must have dropped a stitch
And you had come un-dressed. (3-1934)

Testament

Darling, if you should go before I go,
Tell them that I am coming,—
Tell them that never,—since the earth was young,—
Has any mortal loved another mortal
As I love you.—
Tell them that I would go to hell and serve out all my time
If that would make you more secure in Paradise;
Tell them that there are no flames in Hell
Could be as hot as my desire for you;
Nor any harp in heaven (halt) sweet enough
To sound the songs my heart would sing to you.
Tell them I only lived because you needed me
And then tell God I love him next to you—
And He will let me in.

Your Feet

Your feet are flanged panels running up and down my walls
Making that little more-than-silent sound
That strikes not on the ear but on the mind.

They leave no imprint on the faintest ground,—
They are so light and soft. In fact,
I never knew that you had feet; I thought
You were a creature all apart,—all wings,—
Until one day you lit, and doffed your wings
And waded through my heart.
Your feet are leaves that push apart the other leaves
Along my jungle path and tangle with
Those other huge and matted feet of jaguars
And swift pumas twisting through my mental grass.
The filth, the offal of the jungle mire,
Begrimes their feet and bunches all their toes.
But your ten toes are ever sweet and clean and stay apart
And talk to me—like tea caressing little silver tongues
In dead of night,—while they are wading
Through my heart.

Unrequited Love*12

The grape uncrushed can never give its sweetness out,
And so my heart, with all its store of love and pain,
Is mute, till mangled by your calm and cruel laughter
Which tells me that the love I gave was giv'n in vain.
Then bleeds my heart in music, as the grape bleeds wine;
The world drinks up my music and accords me fame.
But my sad heart,—for just one hour of perfect loving
With you, my love, would gladly give the world's acclaim.

Like a Light

My love goes on before you—like a light,
Parting the shadows which beset your path,
Lest you should lose your way amid the fog of things
Which seem to be, but are not really there.
You are too young to know that things are only things
And that the only real thing is my love for you:—
This love which goes before you like a light.
My love erects a platform,—as of steel—
Where you can sing and dance and take your stand
And beat your breast and trumpet to the winds
That whip about the shoulders of the coming man,
"Blow on, you winds of discord, winds of hate,
You cannot blow me down,—for I am strong—
Strong in the strength of my beloved one
Where love erects a platform as of steel!"

My love goes on before you like a light
Which God has lit and shelters with his hand.
You do not have to know your way; just keep
Your hand in mine and he will understand.
And if, upon your journey through the dark,
The sickly fumes of sense and self should rise,
Becloud your vision and bestray your feet
And falsify the witness of your eyes;
If you should lose my hand and stumble to the ground,
Be not afraid, but lie still where you are;
Remember me—and know that I am there.
Then breathe my name quite softly in the night.
My love will hear and find you, raise you up,
Set you upon your feet, regain your hand,
Steady your faltering footsteps, kiss your eyes,
And then go on . . . and on . . . and on before you—
Like a light.

Be Thou My Wine

Be thou my wine and pour thyself in me
Till I can stand no more of ecstasy.
Run through my every vein and fill me up,
Exquisite pain, the everlasting fee
That I must always pay and pay
For having worshipped thee.
Be thou my wine; withheld not from my lips
The precious spout where through my eager sips
Draw that dear essence which is soul of thee,—
The Holy Flame that sets my Spirit free.
Be thou my wine, release me, drive me wild
And be the sweet virgin father-mother
Of my unborn child. (3-14-1934)

Love Song

Who are my lovers? All who love.
Wherever they may be;
No matter whom or what they love
Or where or when or how they love
They all belong to me, my love,
They all belong to me.
You do not love the thing you love,
No matter how it seem,
All you can ever love is Love,

You cannot love a thing but Love,
The rest is just a dream my love,
The rest is just a dream.

Now, It Is Too Late*

The night is dark, the bed is warm,—
You ring my telephone;
You swear that I belong to you
And that you are my own.
You tell me all the pretty truths
I told you years ago
When paradise was yours to give
And all you said was, "No."
But now, I'm slightly old and tired;
My bed is used for sleep;
And you are middle-aged and fat,—
(Your beauty didn't keep.)
The ivory towers you tried to build
Have crumbled at the gate.
You need now what I offered then,
But now,—it is too late.
The lovely things you didn't do
Would have brought good,—not harm,—
When you were young and beautiful
And I was young and warm.

Worlds

The sweetest gift that I could ever give you
Would be if I could make you know what I know
When you are lying mute and yielding thus beside me,
Oh, my heart's friend!
If you knew this,
You could not get up presently and go out from me,
Leaving me lying, wordless, here in this bright Heaven
Which you alone, with your love, have created,—
World without end!

Summons

Beauty is dark. The daylight has no sound
That can approach the myriad voices of the night.
These age-old passions that bestir men's souls
Get up and walk each time the sun goes down—
And Pity fails to function in the dark.

So come, you heroines of ancient times.
Hey, Helen, Guinevere, and all the rest!—
Come, live your lives again.
Th' immortal tragedies that make you great
Are still worth living.
Paris still has his apples, Jove his crown,—
And love is love, the while the world goes 'round.

Soldier-Son

So you must go into the war and fight,
My boy who was my Baby,—who still is.
How will you do this thing you have not learned,
Who never raised a hand except to aid?
What do you know of strife?
Your picture in your uniform I place
Beside your little kiddie-picture on the stand.
You have not changed.
The eyes that look out at me are the same
Have held me all these years and drunk my love,—
Then gave it back to me,—and out to all.
Those eyes could never hate.
But now it's go you must across the seas
To kill your brother whom you've never seen;
And he has left his love and lies in wait
To try to kill you first.
But you and I know better, don't we boy?
We know man cannot take what man can't give,
That, spite of all stupidity and greed,
Life still must live.
Love sends us down strange, unaccustomed roads,
Whips us into the wisdom that we need.
When old truths die to make way for the New,
Something must bleed.
Now, so long, boy. And if this end the term
We had to spend together,—let's be gay!
We've had a lot of fun and learned a lot
In this old school.
And if it should be you who don't return,—
Well,—maybe it's because you need the rest,—
A sort of spring-vacation,—you know,—week-end home,—
Close to your other Father;—He knows best;—
So,—so long, boy.

Revery

If you could hear the things they say about me,
To see how I have altered since you've gone,
See how the world is wont to do without me
While I sit here bewidowed and alone.
I do not think that you would turn and leave me
If I am wrong and all the world is right—
I think you'd come and put your arms around me,—
I think you'd come and sleep with me tonight. (3-14-1934)

Renunciation

No, love, let's give it up,—
It cannot be.
You know that I love you
And you love me;
But all this dense hull of humanity
And all these mountains of modernity
Are much too much for us;—
We are not free,—
Not free to be what we were meant to be.
So let us stumble on a while, apace,
Content if we can look God in the face.
Let us get lost in Him, and on His breast
Of Love, our love will find its own
Sweet point of rest.

Offering

I come to you every day and every night,
Bringing you something in my eager outstretched hands—
Do not look at me, but look at what I have in my hands.
I bring you Beauty—and Beauty is the Body of God! (3-11-1934)

Lover

I don't love you as a lover,
But I love you like a father.
I can't love you as a sweetheart,
But I love you like a mother.
Who has ever had two fathers
Or but one and only mother?
I'm your father, I'm your mother,—
This and more, my heart's beloved.
I don't care if others love you,—

You may have a million lovers;
I want all the world to love you;—
But like me there'll be no other.
So, when they all love and leave you,
I'll be there to love and lull you;
On my breast and in my bosom
You will find your Only Lover.

My Brightest Sun
Is it my fault that both my hands have eyes
And that your beauty has no secret place
Which I may not spy out and, finding, drink my fill
Till I am drunk and drowsy with your touch
And melt in you?
No, Love, I am my world—and if you want to be its sun,
Who's going to stop you? God will not,—nor I.
He said, "Let there be light!"—and there was light.
So shine right on, my brightest, loveliest sun;
Shine through my night!

Kisses in Bed
Kisses in bed,
Kisses in bed,
Body to body,
Head to head;
The whole world drowned
In a sea of red
Passion to passion—
Kisses in bed.
Kisses in bed,
Kisses in bed,
What do we care
If we'll soon be dead?
Tonight we live—
We have Meat and Bread;
Turn to me, darling—
Kisses in bed!

Butcher-Boy
I had to get me down the town
Upon an errand grave,
But I can never be on time
Tho' 'twere my life to save.

And as I hied me down the stairs
As late as late could be,
There stood a little butcher-boy
A-smiling up to me.
His eyes outshone the morning-star
His lips,—a double thrill,
His throat invited kiss on kiss;
With love my heart stood still.
Said I, "God bless you butcher-boy
Whose glances shame the dawn;
You think you are a butcher-boy,
I know you are a faun."
But I swear I did not tarry,
Nor, in good faith, did I race,
Though I tumbled down the subway steps
At quite a lively pace.
My train was due at twelve past nine,
It now was nine-thirteen
And as I dropped my token in,
I saw a flash of green.
The tail-lights whizzed around the curve,
My haste was all in vain;—
I cried, "God damn you, butcher-boy,
You've made me miss my train." (3-18-1934)

Love Is . . .*

Love is a smile between two sighs
A sob between two kisses,—
And one must give what the other takes,
Supply what the other misses.
It is not love if it doesn't hurt,
The pain but makes it stronger,
So do what you must and will, my love,
I'll only love you longer . . .

One

I am so rich in love,
So weighted down with all the values God can hold,
I must have circulation for my wealth
And all the world must come and use my magic gold.

My warehouse sits atop a hill;
Come up, you needy, take your fill.

I always give, I never lend,—
So there's no interest to spend,
No broken promises to salve,
The more you take, the more I have,
I never bargain, nor refuse,
I always gain,—I never lose.

No stocks and bonds, no bulls nor bears,
No ticker-tape for frenzied stares,
No market-price to rise and fall,
If you want some, you must take all.
My Father keeps the books and He
Takes ev'ry order straight from me.
My cargoes dock the instant place,
For I can troll both time and space.
I am so rich in love,
Endowed so full with all that power can ever be,
Almighty God Himself, if He should wish to make another sea,
Could not pronounce that first all-devastating, all-creative word
Till He had come by me. (1943)

In Love

Once, when I was dreaming,
I dreamt that love was a room:
My room,—well-windowed with my heart's desires
And splendid with my dreams,—
But carpeted with all the little tattered rugs
Of prejudice, and sufferings, and lies
I'd sewn with selfish seams.
Then you passed through my street,
I watched you through the windows of my heart's desires
And asked you in—to be in love with me.
You came.
My love-room came to life and rang with song.
But you had brought your own frayed rugs along
And soon we found our patterns did not blend.
The love-song lisped,—then faltered to its end.
You went away.
Then, later in my dreaming,
I dreamt love was a searching ray.
Warm, but invisible, it leapt from heart to heart—
Each questing for that other ray, its counterpart,
To make each other whole.

You were my answering ray—I knew it well.
Again you came,—again the song did swell.
We burned our little rugs and cleared the air;
Our rays became as one and love again was fair.
But, when you stood before my windows open wide,
Your dreams could not take wing and soar outside,
For my dream-windows only served to view
My heart's desires—and yours could not get through.
And since my dearest windows, let you in no light,
What was quite wrong for you, for me was right.
You went away again.
And now I know what lovers all must learn:
When two rays truly join,—both room and rugs must burn.
Then love can build anew, with windows high and wide
To let two dreams go winging, singing,
Side by side.

Never Fear My Love*

Say, never fear my love.
A love like mine could never wish to shape you
To its mold.
It only would spread silken carpets all along the path
That leads to where your eyes have glimpsed the gleam.
And if that path—at some time,—even in a dream—
So much as brushes mine,—my love is met
And all the little paper currencies will change
To minted gold.

Parting*

They say you're dead,
They say they saw you die;
But I, who saw it too,—I say
It is a lie.
I saw them pack your body in a box
And clamp the lid,—
And all the beauty I had loved so long
Was safely hid.
But where's the box or lid,—however strong,
Can muffle the sweet echoes of our song,
That song supernal which is you and I?
If life lives, then that song can never die.
My love is not dismayed
Because you're hid from view.

What they hid was not then
And never had been you.
And so my eyes are dry,—alone here
In our nest,
Because I know that parting is not separation,
But a test. (First stanza—1933; Remainder—3-29-37).[13]

Moon Messenger

Lovely moon, so calmly sailing
Through the cloudy evening skies
In your gentle light unfailing
See how deep my sadness lies.
I can follow, sadly gazing
With my eyes your way pursue
But, in spite of all my craving,
May not go along with you.
In the wooded valley yonder,
Mid the shade-trees; leafy hands,
Where the mountain streamlets wander
Where a little cottage stands.
Go so softly to the window
Peep so gently through the shades.
There you'll see my sweet Elise
Fairest queen of all the maids.
Lovely moon, true friend of lovers,
Slip into her little room,
Bear this message that discovers
All my bliss or all my doom.
Tell her gently how I love her
She's the only world I know:
Laughing only when she's happy,
Weeping when her tears do flow.
Life without her loses measure
Days and nights are all the same
Work or play brings me no pleasure
Hurry back, Moon, let your moonbeams
Smile her message from above.
Say she bids me back to living
Tell me she returns my love!

*I Take You with Me**

I take you with me everywhere I go—
When things go right and bright we wave hosanna palms—

When things go bad and I am beaten to the ground!
I see you lying there where they have cast you down.
You—all I've got—I lift and hold up in my dusty arms
And weep my black tears into every bleeding wound.

Deception

Tell me, why are you then so beautiful and good?
Tell me, why do your deep eyes bathe me through
With all the tender warm, impenetrable sweetness
That every poet hinted at in all the song and story of the world?
Tell me why, when your loving arms go searching 'round me,
Instantly I know, as by one flash of more than sense,
All that gray bards have chanted since the world began
Or fair young shepherds piped upon their pipes-o-Pan,
Before all music found its core in you.
Then tell me if you can, what is this cruel law
That dents the perfect circle, crooks the perfect line,
Beguiles a knave in Heaven, a fool in Paradise,
And mirrors in false Time a false Infinity?
Why am I forced to live on your ungrudging All,
Knowing it is my own because you are my own,
And still not even wish to give you back in kind
What you are giving me?

Beauty-Pain

My heart is broken with the beauty of this world.
Oh, why does beauty have to hurt you so?
It is because it is passing,—always passing,
And that the self-same beauty never comes again
To search your soul?
Or is it, rather, that it does not, cannot pass
But, shining ever through the mind's sun-glass,
Produces a too-sharply-concentrated point of light
That burns a hole in your heart?
Or, maybe, 'tis because that fine, corroding line
'Twixt what this beauty is and what it ought to be
Becomes a sharp edge, like a jagged piece of tin,
And tears an ugly wound that never, never heals.
My heart is broken with the beauty of this world.

New Year's Resolution—1941

Love is a smile between two sighs,
A sob between two kisses,

And one must give what the other takes,
Supply what the other misses.
It is not love if it does not hurt,
The pain but makes it stronger.
So do what you must and will, my love,
I'll only love you longer. (1-1-40)

Sybil Sex
Listen, lovers, do not fret;
You can't understand it yet.
Learn the rules and play the game
But don't mistake the smoke for flame.
All this heat, this inner fire,
Only hints the real desire
And what seems the entering wedge
Is but gleaming outer edge.
Now we only see the fringes
Of that curtained door whose hinges
Turn but never open quite
Till our eyes can stand the light.
For you know—and know it well
(How you know you cannot tell)
That there's mote to love's embrace
Than frantic panting face to face.
Did you think this priceless treasure
Given just to bring us pleasure?
Life is _one_ and means to prove it;
Nature makes us learn and love it.
Every ecstasy's begun
From this longing to be one.
Each climactic groan and cry
Hears its echo in the sky.
Even knaves denying Heaven
In this moment feel them shriven,
Feel their baser senses freeing
Foretastes of completed Being.
In the Oneness, he-and-she
Means much more than you and me:
you-and-me's a false sensation,
He-and-she begets creation.
Male-and-female, he-and-she,
Piles the mountain, digs the sea,
Channels out the river-bed,

Pins the clouds high overhead,
Wakes the sun to make the morn,
Boosts the bud and points the thorn, .
Urges on orgasmic noon
Cushions soft the sunset's swoon,
Mutes the light with darkness deep,
Counts our breathing while we sleep.
All these things could never be
Were it not for he-and-she;
All this God could never do
If this *one* were only two.
Out of balance, he-and-she
Bursts the mountain, boils the sea,
Topples down the tallest trees
With a gale that was a breeze,
Hangs the black clouds with a shout,
Twists and tears the towns about.
Shakes the earth from core to crust:—
Live who can and die who must!
Back in balance, all is well;
Heaven once more transfigures hell.
Sun and tide come racing in
To absolve the land of sin.

Hymn to Sex

Thou two-in-one,
Doer of all that's done,
Maker of all that's made,—
The long right arm of That which never needed making,—
Thou never hast been two,—but only two-edged one.
Without thee, nothing moves—or even wills to move
From sun to sun—without thee, there could be no sun.
No up and down, no back and forth nor in and out;
No contact, shock, reaction, play or interplay;
No valve or plug or socket,—friction, cussion, blow;—
No breeze could turn to gale,—no rain to ice and snow;
The bravest of communications could not come or go;
Without thee, nothing is,—to be or know.
For thou alone, eternal two-in-one,
Art root and branch and principle of all that can be known or done.
The planets flirt with all their satellites, choosing none,
But keep their long, adoring gaze fixed on the sun.
The radiant sun smiles down upon the quiet sea

And, that day, ev'ry sailor knows that love is free.
The moon-maid makes a beckoning motion with her hand
And slavering tides come wallowing in to lick the land,
While farmers scan the wise old skies for signs of birth,
Then thrust the shy seed deep into the waiting earth.
Thou art the hammered nail, the buttoned button-hole,
The stalwart axis of each eager-trembling pale,
The thinkered thought that ripens into thing or deed,
The singered song with fright of love and joy and need.
Thou art all tensions, relaxations, push and pull;
All joinings, fusions, cleavings—to or from,—
The giver-taker, rhythm-ruler, weight-adjuster thou.
O tireless piston-rod, O universal suction-pipe,
All tractions, all repulsions, love and hate are thine,
Thou mortise in the tenon of the mind.
All these are but the two posts of the invisible gate
That lies between what claims to be created and the uncreate.
And thou, the keeper of the gate, the still calm doer of the done,
Thou know'st no seed can blossom, not a rill not river run
Until the Word is spoken and the gate-posts merge in one.
For all his puzzling mystery of two-of-you-and-me, of he-and-she,
Is locked between the twining twin gate-posts of know-and-be
And only Love-with-Understanding ever learns the secret of that lock
And only understanding love can ever see and take and turn
the invisible key.
Thou art the 'hesion that holds all of life in one,
Yet breaks it forth in myriad-imaged aspects of itself.
But only little man, by too much staring always out and down
And never in and up,—where lies the Source of All that Is,—
Mistakes the tool-chest for the ark,—the jewel for the crown,—
And only spells the letters of that magic Word whose sound,
Could he but hear it, would set free his soul
And spring his feet from out the clinging sod.
Save man alone, all others know thy works, revere thy chastening rod
And praise thy name, Eternal Sex, the strong thumb and fore-finger
Of the Living God!

Oneness

All the world's in Love,
There is no other place or way for it to be;
And, though we worldlings may not even guess it,
What are we but poor, faulty images of love,—

Love in motion,—desiring this or that,—
But always desiring?
What we desire is not important;
How we desire it always solves itself;
That we *desire* it is the only Fact—
And this fact takes on various forms and faces,
Veering with the weather-vane of our desires
As it is blown by storms or zephyrs
Of each present need.
And then, one day, the weary storms are spent;
The vane no longer quivers to the slightest breeze;
Motion has stopped.—Now Action comes to light
And, in that Light, both Fact and Object disappear
And only Urge remains, desiring only Urge;—
The One Love—Loving Love.
Now Urge, the Lover,—the beloved Urge,
Absorbing all desires into the One,
Comes boldly to the window-sills of Sense,
Where Fact and Object long had blocked the light,
And throws the shutters wide.
The One looks out. Number and Separation flee
Where nothing is to count,—nor any space between.
Where something is as nothing, how divide?
When only One exists, how multiply or add?
A thousand rows of trailing zeros cannot big
The initial Prime.
Since life is One,—containing all that truly is,
Then Unity *is now*,—there's nothing to unite.
Man feels this when th' extremity is dire,—
When Nature shakes the earth and rains down fire,
Man *knows* himself for *One*.
But "brotherhood," that fine sonorous word
So often spoken, so impossible to feel,
Is but the statement of expediency and guile,
Serving to salve the guilty conscience for a while
But soon forgotten when the need is past—
For this poor word is meaningless. It cannot last.
Born of Plurality and Separation, the twin lies
That would replace the Oneness with a "life" that dies,
This specious mathematics every law defies:
Pray, how can *one* be "brothers?"
This urge-to-oneness always has been there,

Still as the stillest depths of ocean are,
Unmindful of the glittering wish-waves in the sun,
Knowing that every wish,—if found or if foiled,
Must some day reach its term and,
Splattering into disillusioned spray,
Vanish into itself.
The urge-to-oneness waits—and is not moved;
Waits till the mist of motion clears away
And every dream of sense and little selves
Recedes before the vision of the wakened I.
Now points the vane to inward, to the all-embracing self,
And lo! The urge-to-oneness stands revealed
In all its might, erasing time and space.
Motion give way to Action,—fact to Truth,
To Perfect Power that, motionless, moves all.
For *Oneness* is the Action of the Truth of Life
And *All* there Is to Love.

Poems of God

Black Easter

Allegro Giocoso
Swing, censers! Anthems, ring!
Peal your bells, ye sons of God.
Wash your faces clean today,
Christ is risen from the clod!
Lento Dolorosa
Swing, nigger! Lynchers, sing!
Toll your bells, ye sons of men.
Wash your faces clean today,
Ye have killed your Christ again! (4-13-1934)

To a Crucifix

Jesus, you little long-eyed Jewish boy,
Did you have first to suffer, then enjoy
Your Godhead, with the light of all the pain
That had shone on Your soul grown bright again?
Ah, tell me, Nazarene of mystery,
Are there no roses on the road to Calvary?
What did you mean when, spite of piercing nails,
You gazed into the light that never fails
And cried, "Father, forgive them,—for I do"?
When you said, "It is finished," were you through?

Prayer

God, let me tell them what I know—
So they won't have to suffer so.
Who stalk around and grin with grief
While joy shouts out from every leaf—
Someone must tell them,—why not I?
God, give my soul its speech,
Or let me die. (3-11-1934)

And Acquainted with Grief

Man of sorrows, Man of sorrows,
Prophets say that was your name;
Son of God and Prince of David,—
Man of sorrows just the same.
Man of sorrows, Man of sorrows,
If that truly was your name,
Then you feel our ev'ry burden,
Then you know our ev'ry shame.
Did you often have to struggle
With this human flesh down here?
Did you weaken,—just as we do,—
When the devil came too near?
Man of sorrows, Man of sorrows,
By that token You are mine.
I could never weep and love you
Had you been ten-tenths divine.

Me Crucifixus

Hail, Brother Jesus, hammered to Your tree,
I feel for you,—but mine is killing me
By millimeters, while flying inches mark
Your passing grief;
And then, to boot, You lucky One,
You have Your thief,—
Your lover, John,—Your mother,
And those other two whose name is Mary, they
Will weep for You.
The nails that pierce Your lily-hands
Are new and strong
And make neat holes which saints will love to kiss
For long and long;
And soon your mortal enemies will re-appear

Revile Your Name,
Then break your legs for pity
And for very shame.
And then they'll take you down from there and give Your clay
To those who loved You so they could not run away.
Don't fear,—they will not dump Your body in the sod—
Tomorrow they will need you for their Risen God!
So, Brother Jesus, try to stand Your tree
A little while;—there is no hope for me.
The nails that clamp my members to this bark so rough
Are rusty with coagulations of the stuff,
Of my heart's-blood which trickles through the years
And falls upon the hungry earth in silent ruby-tears.
Earth licks her chops and stretches forth her craw
And, rolling, bleary eyes await the day
When putrefying flesh perforce must have its way
And I must drop like garbage in th' eternal maw.
As I hang here, there is no kindly neighboring cross
With lover-thief for rendez-vous beyond the tomb;
The fair St. Johns I might have known have long been lost,—
Since Mother Nature birthed me from an alien womb.
There is no one to come and take me down from here
Reach me the reed with bitter hyssop on the end;
No enemy, with cruel-kind, delivering spear,
To run me through and toss my carcass to a friend.
So, Brother Jesus, try to stand your tree
A little while;—there is no hope for me. (11-1934)

The Secret Door*

There is a door set deep within your house
Which may not open to let enter light nor air
Nor any human guest, however proud or fair.
For you yourself will never know 'tis there—
This secret door—
Until one day life crashes 'round your head;
You rest against this door—with senses dead,
It swings ajar—and lo! The banquet spread,
The Bridegroom—waiting—and the marriage-bed!
There is a Wisdom which may never come
Till all the wise men of this world have dubbed you "Fool,"
Till ev'ry bell and book and ev'ry chart and rule
And all the appurtenances of church and school
Have left you flat.

Gone are the safe familiar roads so lately trod,
Gone ev'ry earthy anchor, ev'ry staff and rod;—
Then speaks the Bridegroom, beckoning with a nod,
"Come, enter here. 'Tis time for you to learn
The nameless Name that changes man to *God*." (11-1937)

An Artist's Prayer*

Creator God,
Thou God of love Whose other name is Beauty,
Reach out and touch us—we are not so far from Thee,
Stare at us through all line and form and color
Till we catch Thine eye.
Shout in our ears through many—throated music
Till we hear Thy Voice.
Then—hold us close, Oh, God of Beauty,—close and still.
Soak all our inmost being with the very feel of Thee,
Till we have learned to name Thee by that Other Name
Which moves the mount and bids the dead, "ARISE!"
Come work with Me; I am not in the skies! (1943)

Changelessness

Because a flower withers or a robin falls,
That does not mean that Spring has come and gone
And will not come again.
The wind blows out my candle and the room is plunged in dark
And all the dear, familiar things are hid from sight.
The candle weeps a waxen tear, but I,—I know
There still is light.
All changing things but speak of That which cannot change,—
Triumphant love that locks the door on death and strife,
I am the ever-birthing Spring,—the inextinguishable Light.
I am Eternal Life! (5-24-1956)

Poems of Man[14]

Marian Anderson Singing "Die Allmacht"

Voice of a million years,
You banish all the sins and all the fears
I feared a hundred years ago,
Before I learned that sin and fear and God
Cannot exist together.
Then sing to me, oh Voice of Heaven,
And make me know that Love alone is valid,—
Hope and Love.

Then, if I had to die, Death would be sweet
With your sweet music sounding in my ears;
Only I know—(and, hearing you, I more than know)
I cannot die, and no one, ever since the birth of time,
Has ever died.
Then sing to me, oh Voice of Heaven.
You sing Eternal Life and make a fool of death;
Sing on—and make me live,
Breath of my breath!
Pure and putrid, pale and pious
Dance of "life out on the bias."
Though we know it isn't true,
Faute de mieux, we make it do.
So we dance the dance of sense.
Come on,—really, it's immense! (5-14-1952)

Will Marion Cook—In Memoriam
You took us many miles o'er land and sea
To show the people what a thing you'd found,—
A mine of God-sent music, welling up from caves
Whose unexpected riches waited on your hand,—
The master-hand to turn them into sound.
You stood before us, humble and yet proud,
And, at your call, all things took on new birth,
Old voices sang in new; the past awoke
In present splendor, as we climbed with you
To glorify the lowly of this earth.
And when we sang to suit you! Oh sometimes
The fires of heaven would light up in your frown
And, in one look of satisfaction and of love,
Proclaim your birthright, guarantee your throne,—
A king who knew his subjects and his crown.
And, sometimes, there were flames but not of heaven;
Your tortured soul would rise and lash and beat
Against the bars that held you from the full,
Keen realization of your dreams awhile
But could not sink you down in stark defeat.
Ah, master, we are blest that you were here
With us awhile, with thunder in your face.
You taught us how to sing,—and to be proud of singing,—
The theme you sang and never tired of singing;—
The rich, dark beauty of your rich, dark, singing race. (9-1944)

A King You Are

Do you feel hurt because your face is more than tan?
Do you feel less secure than any other man?
Hold up your head and walk;—What if you tread
Black Harlem's teeming sun-scorched bricks or thread
The burning tracts of dark Sahara's nights and days?
What difference makes it to your sovereign will and ways?
You're not a clown.
A king you are;—but there've been kings before,—
And rotten kingdoms fell when you were just a spore.
So, build your throne on Manhood, make of love your crown,
And all the kingdoms in this little world can never shake
Your kingdom down. (1-22-1943)

Where I Live

Where I live, there is no people,
Not a church and not a steeple;
No machines to stir up strife,—
Not a husband, not a wife;
No fine talk of foes nor brothers,
(Since there is no "We" or "Others")
No such thing as form nor face,
Creed nor color, group nor race.
Where I live, there are no masses,
No conceited, braying asses
Coveting the slaver's gains,
Forging "Freedom" with new chains.
Here, there's neither king nor despot,
Banquet-hall nor even mess-pot;
Not a sword and not a gun;
All Majority is One.
Where I live, there is a stillness
That knows naught of pain nor illness;
No diseases,—slow nor quick,—
(Since there's nothing to be sick).
No cold, fear of want, or needing
Anything; no laws for heeding.
Nothing happens or "takes place,"
Here there's neither Time nor Space,
Nor even Death, Plurality's oldest son.
Where I live, there is only Life,—
The One!!

Dreams

Dreams, dreams, wonderful dreams!
Dreams of our night-times and dreams of our days!
Dreams of strange magic, or God-born or Devil-born;
How deep your workings,—how subtle your ways!
Oh, how you torture us, oh, how you bite us!
Then, how you lull us and soothe us again.
Dreams, you make fools of us, knaves of us, gods of us,—
Then let us down again into mere men.
Dreams, dreams, intangible dreams,
All that is good or bad comes straight from you,
Ah, how we live for you, bleed for you, die for you,
Knowing the while you can never come true.
Still do we cling to you, loving you, hating you,
Rending the air with our "Wherefore" and "When"?
Come then, make gods of us, knaves of us, fools of us,—
Only don't leave us to be just mere men! (1909)

Self-Esteem*

Let me be simple, God,
And let me speak my mind.
Did you ever make anybody
Any better than I am?
And, if you did, how can you ever tell me
Unless we get away back in that little room
Where matter ends;—where the last pot boils over
On the latest stove—and there is nothing left
On any plate—and then,—
No plate?

Return from Singing in Germany
(after a concert tour of the Hall Johnson Choir in 1951)

What is this warm, sweet radiance
That follows 'cross the sea?
Oh, that is warm, sweet eye-light
A-comin home with me.
For I was late among them
And they looked into me
And found the answer waiting
That they had longed to see.
There is little need for word-sounds
To turn water into wine
When the love spills over the eye-sills

Till the very air's a-shine.
So now there's nothing else to do
Nor any place to go,
For light has spoken into light
And now—we know we know. (10-11-51)

***

So what then is the portrait of Hall Johnson, the man, that is revealed by his writings? We see a man of tremendous intellectual ability with an enviable command of the language as an instrument of expression in poetry, prose, and drama. His essays illustrate a high order of thought over a wide range of subjects—music, musicology, criticism, philosophy, and government. We see a man with the highest ethical principles, who devoted his life to the collection, preservation, dissemination, and popularization of the Negro spiritual, America's most unique contribution to the world's culture. We see a man who thought not as a miniaturist, but as a giant, with unbounded altruism, who had as a primary object uniting the nation through music. In pursuit of this objective, he detailed his grand concept in the organizational schema for the Alliance for the Development of African American Music and Sing Out America: A Nationwide Choral Plan to Help Children through Music. This conceptual grandeur and great organizational skill was apparent early and was observable throughout his career—when he organized and trained two hundred singers for the Roxy Theater in 1932; a large cast with double choirs for the 1933 production of *Run, Little Chillun*; a choir of three hundred voices for the New York City Center premiere of *Son of Man*; five hundred voices for the Carnegie Hall performance of the same cantata; and nine hundred singers for a performance at the Polo Grounds in New York.

Because they differ so widely in purpose, Johnson's letters reveal so much more of him. The letters of recommendation for young artists reveal a spirit of kindness and generosity, for he wrote many. The letters to management (Mr. Gassner) show a certain financial naïveté, some paranoid distrust, and the ability to become really angry if he thought that he had been cheated or that the management was willing to destroy his reputation by arranging performance commitments for which he did not have a choir that met his standards. The series of letters to publisher E. B. Marks are, for me, the most brilliant. Written when Johnson had been treated with condescension and was angry and aggrieved, they display a spirit of independence and one of complete equality with, if not superiority to, the white publisher whom he was addressing. They reveal Johnson's capacity for expressing politely the most biting sarcasm in a well-constructed, documented, and detailed explication of his viewpoint. Similarly, with the same authority, clarity, and controlled sarcasm, he eviscerated Von der Goltz of Carl Fischer Music and a representative of RCA Victor for copyright infringement. Finally, the letters to Bob Breen show a completely different side of Johnson, as he was clearly in the wrong when his choir arrived forty minutes after curtain time for its final performance in Germany. Here, we see in Johnson a spirit of true contrition, combined with attempts at flattery and other blandishment that he hoped would encourage Breen to assist him in landing a contract to direct a forthcoming production of *Porgy and Bess*. In truth, at this point in 1952, he was in dire economic straits and was forced to "bow low" in a failed effort to get the next job.

Johnson went on to create many more superb arrangements and compositions for solo voice and for chorus between 1952 and 1970. Painter, violinist, violist, choral conductor, composer, arranger, linguist, teacher, coach, and mentor to many, he has left an indelible mark on choral and vocal music in America and the world. His concert arrangements of spirituals are sung by world-class artists all over the world. His choral arrangements are staples of concert choirs in high schools and colleges and his best seller "Ain't Got Time to Die" currently has nine "covers" by other arrangers in publication. I shall never forget when, following a general audience with Pope John Paul II, the Rowan University Chamber Choir sang the High Mass in St. Peter's Basilica on Good Friday in 1995. At the close of the mass, no one moved in the congregation and the Celebrant asked the choir to sing three additional selections. The final selection was Hall Johnson's setting of "City Called Heaven." Immediately after the final chord had died, a congregant rushed to the choir loft and asked if he could please have a copy of the final number. I reached into my folder and gave him my copy. In every major city where the Rowan University Choir performed—London, Paris, Rome, Vienna, Salburg, Madrid, St. Petersburg, and Moscow—we included music of Hall Johnson, which was received with great enthusiasm. His influence on legions of conductors and singers has created a living memorial as they will continue to impart his knowledge of and love for the Negro spiritual for generations to come.

Johnson's professional life began with a series of honors: the Simon Haessler Prize for the best composition for chorus and orchestra upon his graduation from the University of Pennsylvania in 1910; director and arranger for the Pulitzer Prize–winning Broadway show *The Green Pastures* in 1930; the Harmon Award in 1931; and an honorary doctorate from the Philadelphia Musical Academy in 1934. His professional life ended just as it had begun, with another shower of awards. In 1962, the *Saturday Review of Literature* featured a Ruth Bernhard photograph of "The Hands of Hall Johnson" on its cover following its exhibition in New York's Museum of Modern Art. The same year, the City of New York honored him with the Distinguished Service Award. The Association for the Study of Negro Life and History bestowed on him the Heritage Award, and on his birthday, March 12, 1970 (only eighteen days before his death), he received New York's highest honor—the George Frederic Handel Medallion for his contributions to intellectual and cultural life.

What price glory? This "black genius," so called since the 1928 Town Hall debut of his Hall Johnson Negro Choir, was almost totally destitute in his last years. So proud was he that many close to him had no idea of his grave need (nor did I). Never working for a school or a church, he sacrificed economic security to realize his dream. The great tragedy is that though Hollywood approached him three times about making a movie of his music drama *Run, Little Chillun*, it never happened. He never had the big pay day. He saw the Promised Land, but was destined never to walk in it.

Notes

1. Eileen Southern, ed., *Readings in Black American Music* (New York: W.W. Norton, 1972). I anticipate the publication of the omitted essays and poetry separately, at a later date.

2. Hall Johnson, "Some Aspects of the Negro Folk Song." Courtesy of the Hall Johnson Collection (Rowan University, Glassboro, NJ). All rights reserved.

3. Hall Johnson, "Some Distinctive Elements in African-American Music." Courtesy of the Hall Johnson Collection (Rowan University, Glassboro, NJ). All rights reserved.

4. Hall Johnson, "Folk Songs of the United States of America—Part I." Courtesy of the Hall Johnson Collection (Rowan University, Glassboro, NJ). All rights reserved.

5. A song title in parentheses indicates that the named song was sung at this point in the radio program.

6. Hall Johnson, "Folk Songs of the United States of America—Part II." Courtesy of the Hall Johnson Collection (Rowan University, Glassboro, NJ). All rights reserved.

7. Hall Johnson, "Lecture-Demonstration on the Origins of the Negro Spiritual," March 21, 1954. Courtesy of the Hall Johnson Collection (Rowan University, Glassboro, NJ). All rights reserved.

8. Courtesy of the Hall Johnson Collection (Rowan University, Glassboro, NJ). All rights reserved.

9. Robert Breen, letter to Hall Johnson, February 13, 1952. Courtesy of the U.S. State Department.

10. Robert Breen, letter to Hall Johnson, January 14, 1952. Courtesy of the U.S. State Department.

11 . Hall Johnson, "The Chemistry of Life in Action." Courtesy of the Hall Johnson Collection (Rowan University, Glassboro, NJ). All rights reserved.

12. An asterisk (*) denotes that the poem was untitled and that I supplied the title here.

13. These dates have great significance as Hall Johnson's wife of twenty-four years died in December 1935, between the composition of verse 1 and verse 2.

14. Only seven of the eighteen poems in this section have been included because of limitations of space.

CHAPTER FIVE

~

Personal Recollections

The following accounts are presented as written by each individual, with two exceptions—the accounts by Elijah Hodges and George Royston, who were interviewed by telephone. The recorded interviews were then transcribed and submitted to the subjects for their verification before being added to the manuscript.

To ensure that key aspects of their relationship with Johnson were addressed, the contributors were provided with a list of questions to help focus their responses.

John Morrison

I was introduced to Hall Johnson in 1958, soon after I came to New York from Athens, Georgia. When I told Mr. Johnson that I was a native of Athens, he stared at me and finally spoke at length of points of interest there, some of which I had forgotten. I auditioned for him and made quite a fine impression which was later tarnished by my insufficient devotion to study.

I remember Mr. Johnson as a man who spoke with tongues other than English, with or without words, thought positively, charmed the ladies, and was a master musician with an ear that surpassed the pitch pipe. Bored, after spending more than an hour on one measure at one of his rehearsals, I initiated a discreet conversation with Joshua Cato (one of the original Hall Johnson singers and a basso profundo extraordinaire). A look from Mr. Johnson, somewhat pleasant but definitely electric, squelched the levity in an instant and without a word. I never made that mistake again.

After his stroke in the early 1960s, I once heard someone greet him, "We are happy to see you up and out again, Brother Hall," to which he responded, "I have forgotten that, you forget it too . . . I feel fine."

One Sunday afternoon, Mr. Johnson invited me to join him and two young ladies at a performance in The Village Gate. This was for me a great lesson in the nature of charm and sex appeal. Despite my youth, the ladies focused almost entirely on Mr. Johnson who kept them enthralled with stories of his experiences in Hollywood, on Broadway, and with many world-class artists.

One anecdote indicates his fluency in German. At the opera one evening, a friendly German couple spoke to him at length in English and later engaged in a conversation about him, in German. After listening to them amusedly and noting their inquisitiveness, he turned to them and said, with a straight face, "Why don't you ask me?" That evening was the beginning of a warm relationship which endured and later included a visit to their home in Germany.

It was a joy and a learning experience to know Hall Johnson, who was both a common man and a genius.

John Morrison
Tenor soloist emeritus, Riverside Church, New York City
March 12, 2001

Helen Duesberg

At the time of Hall Johnson's return from California (circa 1963), his mind was very much occupied with the "Freedom March" to Washington. He envisioned a grand mass expression in song from the thousands of "Freedom Marchers" with *Let Freedom Ring*, which he had used in the 1930s when he introduced the Hall Johnson Choir on Broadway. This time, it was to be accomplished with the cooperation of church choirs from all over the country. He composed special songs for this occasion (which I helped him copy) and had them Xeroxed by the thousands. This undertaking would necessarily require some organizational work to train the choir directors and would need support from the leadership of the March. When the Reverend Martin Luther King Jr. came to Friendship Baptist Church in Harlem (where I was organist), it was such a crowded affair that many had to be seated outside on the street where they could hear the service through loudspeakers. The whole street was closed to traffic. After the service, Hall Johnson personally met with Dr. King, Coretta King, and Reverend Kilgore in the small church office and presented his proposal. While Mrs. King showed interest, the idea did not catch fire with the ministers and thus did not materialize.

One of Hall Johnson's great regrets was the fact that recording technology was still in its infancy during the heyday of his choir. He had hopes of finding funds to prepare a choir and produce a definitive recording of Negro Spirituals in an authentic, unadulterated form before the passage of time could erase the memory of the performance practice. This recording would be preserved in the collections of the Library of Congress to inform succeeding generations of performers and scholars. The Community Church of New York, in an effort to acquire the needed support, initiated a drive whereby members of the congregation could, with a donation of $5,000, purchase a gold medallion, inscribed with the name of an artist of great merit, to be permanently displayed on selected church pews. A music reviewer from the *New York Post* chose two names for inclusion: Arturo Toscanini and Hall Johnson, who, in his opinion were the greatest conductors of their time. Among the notable individuals who became aware of this project was Robert Kennedy, who sent to Hall Johnson a very warm congratulatory letter acknowledging Hall's importance in introducing the Spiritual to the general public, thus enriching the history of American Music. After meeting Hall Johnson personally, he promised full support for the recording idea. His tragic assassination in Los Angeles put an end to this endeavor.

How can we define Hall Johnson's greatness as a conductor? The *Saturday Review* once featured a portrait of Hall Johnson's hands on its cover. His innate musical sensitivity and charismatic personality were legendary. Yet, all of this does not explain the magic with which he was able, with a few rehearsals, to transform almost any average choir into a beautiful, vibrant instrument (as from a factory violin to a Stradivarius). I was able to witness it on occasions when he was invited as guest conductor. As a rule, the choirs were well prepared and knew their notes, were ready and eager to start singing. Yet, there was not much of that during the rehearsal time with Hall. He would talk, talk, and talk, with the most imaginative ideas and comparisons. He would control the impatient choir like a restless horse. After this tedious process, the choir would grasp the rhythms and content of the music, and internalize them almost unconsciously, and the result would be sheer magic.

The same metamorphosis could be detected when he worked individually with professional singers, some of them illustrious performing stars. He was a perfectionist, very patient and kind, yet, a stickler for detail, very giving, and very generous with his time. A congenial host, he was frequently surrounded by a large circle of admirers, former choir members, disciples, and friends. A born leader, he was very cosmopolitan, magnanimous, and generous to a fault. When I met Hall Johnson, he lived in a cramped apartment, bulging with books, music, and photographs, many bearing images and autographs of famous personages he had encountered and befriended. An amateur photographer himself, he provided the most sophisticated captions for his pictures. He also had a remarkable gift for art. I remember a striking still life of yellow roses in a vase with blue hues in the background. He was multi-talented in many ways, fluent in German and French, and extraordinarily expressive in his writings, which were both philosophical and poetic.

The years I was privileged to spend with Hall Johnson as his friend and companion felt like years in a fairyland. He remained eternally young, ever a wellspring of imagination and innovative ideas.

Helen Duesberg
Organist emeritus, Friendship Baptist Church, New York City
April 10, 2001

Arthur Bryant

I had lived a rather eventful 30 years which included study at Drake University as a pianist, military service in Africa during the great war, and graduate study at Paris Conservatory, before I finally settled in New York during the mid-fifties. I was enrolled at Columbia University when one of my associates took me to a Hall Johnson Workshop (rehearsal). Hall Johnson was such a brilliant man that I was immediately drawn into his artistic circle. As Mr. Johnson did not own a car and I did, I was happy to offer my services to transport him whenever he needed help. As I only lived a few blocks from him, I also made arrangements to study Music Theory with him. For several years, our relationship existed on three levels: I sang in his Workshop Group, I studied Music Theory privately with him, and I was a personal friend who chauffeured him to concerts at Lincoln Center and at other venues and was exposed to his expert and incisive music criticism.

In the early 1960s, Hall Johnson had a stroke and returned to California to recuperate. As this effectively brought an end to his Choral Workshop, I decided to continue this work and started the Arthur Bryant Choir. The choir's greatest achievements were performances which featured Hall Johnson's music at the New York World's Fair in 1964 and 1965. The group gradually disintegrated by 1970.

How would I evaluate Hall Johnson in comparison with other conductors [I] have worked with? He was superb! He was fanatical about details. I liked that. I learned so much. I sat in on many of his coaching sessions with singers, and he was meticulous. He was a great musician. He was stern. You couldn't get by with anything. He was different and I knew he was correct. I was inspired and overwhelmed by his artistry which surpassed anything I had ever witnessed in conducting.

His artistic settings of the Negro Spiritual and his original works in this style are models for all who would work with this unique musical material and confirm its limitless scope and potential.

Arthur Bryant
Educator and choral conductor, New York City
June 2, 2001

Louvenia Pointer

It was perhaps providential that in 1939 I organized a group of Black singers to audition for the National Youth Administration Radio Workshop Choir which was to perform a series of radio concerts to advance both young singers and culture in New York. On the strength of our audition, my group was accepted and I was named as the director to plan and perform the series which ran concurrently with performances by Jazz Orchestra, Symphonic Orchestra, and dramatic productions. My work with this group, which rehearsed in the Ed Sullivan Building, brought me in contact with Robert Shaw (who rehearsed on a lower floor), Leopold Stokowski, Harry Burleigh, Dean Dixon, and many other well-known personalities, some of whom appeared as guests on my show or did their own broadcasts from the building.

However, it was my work with the Calvary Methodist Church Choir which brought me in contact with Hall Johnson who lived only a few blocks from the church. To my surprise and delight, I looked up from the score we were rehearsing one evening to find Hall Johnson observing. His generous expression of admiration for what I was doing with the choir soon led to a friendship. Subsequently, I attended many of his rehearsals at the Red Shield Club on 124th St. Many times, after the rehearsals, we sat and talked about everything musical.

In 1947, I met and married William Pointer, a member of the De Paur Infantry Chorus, then under the management of Sol Hurok. As I soon became pregnant, I was never able to tour with Hall Johnson and had to turn down his offer to go to Berlin for the International Music Festival. I was, however, able to sing in the revival of *The Green Pastures*, on Broadway, and received one of the greatest thrills of my life when Hall Johnson appointed me Assistant Conductor to do the choral work with the show for its Broadway run. Unfortunately, the run was curtailed and the show closed because of protests and demonstrations by the NAACP [National Association for the Advancement of Colored People] and other groups who felt that the show denigrated Blacks.

Hall Johnson's friendship and example had a salutary effect on my work as a conductor. To receive encouragement and compliments on my work from such a great man was inspiring. The very idea that he would leave his show in my hands gave me a sense of self-worth which no one else could have. On one occasion, he wrote me a letter of appreciation for the way that I had performed some of his works. Hopefully, I shall be able to locate it so that it can be included in this volume. How do I compare Hall Johnson with other conductors of this music? First, there is Hall. Then, much later . . . the others. Hall Johnson was the apex. He was the kind of director I adore. He paid attention to details of every sort. He let nothing go by. He took his time and worked diligently to get exactly what he wanted. Whether you thought so or not, he knew how important it was to the interpretation he was seeking.

He had a wonderful sense of humor. As great as he was, he had the human touch. He always knew how to relate. Shortly before he died, he came to dinner at my home. After dinner, he graciously allowed my children to perform for him. I wanted them to have the experience of knowing this great man.

If there is one thing that distinguishes his arrangements from others, it is his uncanny preservation of the original feeling and line, no matter how intricate the accompaniment. His arrangements are always authentic, never contrived. Many younger arrangers employ beautiful harmonies and exciting rhythms, but lose the feeling of the requisite authenticity. Hall's works, when properly performed, emphasize exactly what must be emphasized.

Louvenia Pointer
Concert mezzo soprano and choral conductor, New York City
July 20, 2001

John Motley

I believe it was in 1949 that I met Hall Johnson. This meeting was precipitated by the need to have him do a special arrangement for Marian Anderson to perform at a United Nations affair, and by my interest in his Easter Cantata, *Son of Man* (which had been performed at Carnegie Hall with a choir of 500 voices in 1948). I can recall visiting with him at the Red Shield Club only to learn that the music had been stored in the basement, and that the custodian had thrown it out. Hall and I had to painstakingly reassemble the cantata from various individual sections. In the years between 1950 and 1970, jointly, we conducted about 50 performances of this work in New York churches, the last, at Salem Methodist Church a week before Hall's untimely death.

My interest in Hall Johnson began when I first saw Leonard De Paur conduct. I was told that De Paur, founder of the famed De Paur Infantry Chorus, had been trained by Hall Johnson. I made a beeline for Hall Johnson and that is how we started. I asked him to make an arrangement of "He's Got the Whole World in His Hands" for Marian Anderson who was singing with my chorus at Philharmonic Hall on a program for Mrs. Roosevelt, Adlai Stevenson, Madame Pandit, and Sidney Poitier. This association led to even greater things. When RCA Victor asked Hall Johnson to write some arrangements for Miss Anderson to record, he told them that I should accompany her. As we had already worked together, she was delighted to comply. Not only did I accompany her on the album, *Jus' Keep On Singin'*, but, I toured Europe as her accompanist and coach.

Hall and I were inseparable. I would leave church on Sunday and go and sit with him until 6:00 a.m. the next day. Then we would go to breakfast before I left for work at the Board of Education. I spent all of my free time with him. I once asked him why he didn't do a lot of coaching. His response was, "I can't give 'way what I know 'les more sell it." He did however coach Shirley Verrett,

Robert McFerrin, and a number of other singers who became famous. He was expert both in German and French. We went to a concert of yours [Eugene Thamon Simpson's] one night at St. Martin's Church. I asked him where he wanted to sit; he replied, "I just want to get in off the street." He used my choir (the All-City Chorus) for "Son of Man." He would come to all of my concerts with the All-City Chorus at Carnegie Hall and Philharmonic Hall, and I would always acknowledge him. He was my inspiration. He was my everything.

Hall was a genius within himself. He was an original. His unique harmonizations are so right. Dawson [William] did a lot of contrapuntal writing in his arrangements but Hall's work is so authentic. He never beat a chorus to death. He conducted just the music.

I used to watch him [rehearse] at the Red Shield Club, all night long. His dynamic effects were extraordinary because he took the time to teach them. When they were preparing for their European Tour, there was no music, for everything was learned by rote. The full attention of the singer was always on him. Hall "talked" a man into bankruptcy in California as the recording time required to achieve the desired result was more than the man could pay for. It was said that during the German tour, he "cussed" the Germans out and told them that "nobody rushes me." Harry Belafonte brought Hall to New York to write arrangements for him, and made the fatal mistake of whistling at him in rehearsal and immediately lost his conductor, as Hall walked out. One night, at Convent Avenue Baptist Church, Hall was to conduct a massed choir in some of his works. The warm-up rehearsal spilled over into concert time and yet Hall would not bring the choir to the stage. Finally, in anger, he shouted, "Every Goddamn time I cut off, some son-of-a-bitch is still singing. They waited on me in Hollywood, they waited on me on Broadway, and they're gonna wait on me tonight!" Another time, we were rehearsing *Son of Man* at a church on 28th Street (Hall would always sit in the rear of the church and sleep while I was rehearsing), the tenors were singing "Pilate! Pilate! Pilate!" but were in the wrong place. On the word "Devil," Hall woke up and said, "Mr. Motley, the tenors got the Devil in the wrong place." In performance, Hall would only conduct one chorus, "Pilate! Pilate! Pilate!" I conducted everything else.

Hall Johnson knew that he had to bring our music to the world. He use to recall how his grandmother would sit on the porch and sing these melodies. In *Son of Man*, there is an aria, "Woe Is Me." It is as dramatic as "It Is Enough," from Mendelssohn's *Elijah*. I never heard a piece which describes so vividly what Judas did to Jesus. It is as great as any dramatic aria written.

You ask, "What was it about Hall Johnson that inspired me?" The genius of the man, as with Wilhousky, as with Hugh Ross, as with John Finley Williamson, drew me to Hall Johnson as it did to them. When Arthur Judson was managing the Hall Johnson Choir, Francis Poulenc threw a party which Hall and I attended. Josef Hoffman, the great concert pianist, also on the Judson Roster, played the "Star-Spangled Banner." On the word "see," to the usual sub-mediant harmonization, he added a striking major sixth which inspired Hall to write an arrangement of the National Anthem that is the greatest I've ever heard. Hall did everything for me. I depended on him for guidance.

I didn't know Hall Johnson's wife, but I did know his mistress (Madeline Preston). I know the girl that he went with for a long time when she was over at Columbia. He sent her to school. He was taking care of her. I don't know whether or not she is still around but she would have a lot to tell you. I will say that Helen Duesberg was something special. She saved his life.

Hall's contribution to the classical settings of the spirituals was unique. He created this genre. He started it all.

John Motley
Pianist and conductor emeritus, New York All-City Chorus, New York City
July 28, 2001

Thomas Carey

My evolution from a City College business major to an operatic baritone, performing leading roles in London and Germany, makes an interesting story, which I tell in my soon-to-be-published autobiography. My recollections of Hall Johnson have to be put in a context of my experiences with Eva Jessye and Edward Boatner, both of whom played important roles in my life.

In the 1950s, the dominant Afro-American personalities in the area of black choral music were Ms. Jessye (original choral director for *Porgy and Bess*), Edward Boatner, and Hall Johnson. I was fortunate to sing in Ms. Jessye's choral group from a very young age. She served as music director, mentor, and consultant, favorably influencing many aspects of my musical life. After I began to study voice, Boatner was an important influence as a language coach.

It was through Ms. Jessye that I met Hall Johnson. Although I never sang with him, I can recall being somewhat awestruck for he was so revered by the professional singers I knew and associated with, a group which included Elinor Harper, William McDaniels, and Eugene Brice, all of whom sang with me in the Metropolitan Opera (extra) Chorus. During this period, I studied and performed many of Hall Johnson's Spirituals. It is probably more to him than to any other that I owe my great appreciation for this music, which has resulted in an annual Spirituals Concert here at the University of Oklahoma for over a decade.

Hall Johnson's importance as a creative arranger and composer of spirituals is impossible to overestimate. His settings have remained an essential part of my concert repertoire throughout my career.

Thomas Carey
Concert baritone and Regents' Professor, University of Oklahoma
October 15, 2001

William Warfield

My pilgrimage to New York City was a circuitous one. My father, a minister from Arkansas, moved to Missouri, and then to Rochester, New York, where I ultimately attended the Eastman School of Music. I always aspired to be a concert singer in the tradition of Roland Hayes and Marian Anderson. It was natural that my studies should culminate in a debut recital at Town Hall in 1950, which fortunately met with great critical acclaim. I included some Hall Johnson Spirituals on this concert and was delighted to be approached by Hall Johnson after the recital and to learn that he "liked the way I sang his spirituals." From that first meeting, we remained friends until his death in 1970.

Over the years, he brought to me several of his arrangements, including a hand-written transposition of "Ain't Got Time to Die," which I still have in my library. Another piece which he brought to me which remains unpublished was "Oh Heaven Is One Beautiful Place I Know." When Dr. Johnson died, the archives did not have a copy of this work so I loaned them mine. I later loaned my copy to the late Wendell Whalum (then director of the Morehouse College Choir) who made a choral arrangement which I believe is published.

If I had to compare Hall Johnson with other conductors of the Harlem Renaissance, I would have to say that he was a giant. Not only was his conducting outstanding and his arrangements unique, but he inspired many younger people like Eva Jessye, Jester Hairston, Leonard De Paur, and John Motley, to great choral success.

One of the characteristics of Hall Johnson which contributed to his great achievement was his superior knowledge of folk dialect and his insistence of the proper use of it in the performance of his arrangements. I remember discussing the fine points of dialect with him over the phone for about two hours. Sylvia Lee has developed a complete list of his rules of dialect which would be useful to include in your book. Hall was also a stickler about having his arrangements performed exactly as he wrote them. One of his big beefs was that singers performed his spirituals too fast. Syncopations should not be rushed ("keep so busy praising my Jesus"). He would always tell you exactly what he thought.

Hall's contribution to the development and propagation of the spiritual is inestimable. He reached the masses by performing this music on Broadway and on the silver screen. Before Harry T. Burleigh, the spiritual existed primarily as a choral form. His arrangements brought the spiritual to the concert stage as a refined but simple solo form. On the other hand, Hall Johnson's arrangements will endure as they represent the epitome of this genre and elevate the material to the level of art songs.

William Warfield
International concert and operatic baritone
Professor, University of Illinois at Urbana-Champaign
October 17, 2001

Elijah Hodges

I auditioned for Hall Johnson in late 1935 as he was assembling his singers for the filming of *The Green Pastures*, which was to take place the following year. As Hall had several New England engagements to fill, he sent half of the group on to California and kept half in New York for the concert engagements. I remained in New York and finally traveled to Los Angeles in March 1936, as a lad of 17. We arrived at Warner Brothers and spent three to four months filming the choral portions of the movie.

At the conclusion of *The Green Pastures*, Hall had to return to New York to do a radio show. A small group of singers were chosen to do that appearance and to return to New York by car. When Hall's regular driver could not make the trip, I was chosen to replace him and thus became very close to him. While in New York, Hall suffered a bout of depression that lasted several months. We finally were able to get him back to California. I ended up living in the same house with Hall for three or four years. Miss Mays [Willie] did our cooking. I ended up doing much of the driving for him (as Hall did not drive). Hall and I were seen together so much that the choir members dubbed me "Junior" as I was like his son.

We returned to New York to do *Run, Little Chillun*, which closed after one night. The show had been a great success in California with companies in both Los Angeles and Oakland. Jester Hairston conducted the Oakland cast. The problem with the New York production was the unavailability of quality singers as most had been hired for Billy Rose's production of *Carmen Jones*.

Hall spoke German and French fluently. We would often go to concerts together and he would practice his languages on German or French natives in attendance at the concert. Frequently he would visit them later and speak only their language.

He always made sure that the Hall Johnson Choir got proper billing. There wasn't much being done by choirs in the movies after the Hall Johnson Choir. In the old days, Warner Brothers paid the rail fare for the whole 50-voice choir to travel to California, and we spent three to four months on the set on weekly salary. After that, they hired a bunch of contract singers from this area and called Hairston to direct them. He should have gotten credit for directing them, but I don't remember him having a set choir as such.

We did one recording for RCA which I have on tape from Jester Hairston. Most of the other conductors I sang with, particularly Jester Hairston and Leonard De Paur, studied with Hall Johnson. Perhaps Leonard was a little better although he would spend just as much time on one page. After *The Green Pastures*, we all stayed in California. We rented Masonic Hall and rehearsed every day from eight in the morning until twelve at night.

What made his work so outstanding? Well, he was six foot four inches tall and always wore a big black hat. He was a stickler for clean attacks and releases. No wrong note escaped him. While he would not embarrass a singer, you had to rehearse and rehearse until you got it right.

Hall was wonderfully helpful to me as a singer. During the period that we lived in the same house, he would play for me and go over my music almost every night. On many occasions, he would be called to the phone for a prolonged conversation, and I would sneak out, as I would have a date.

Hall was sought after by a number of women but was not the marrying kind. He had a very close relationship with a young woman whom I used to call my sister [Madeline Preston] but I am not aware that they ever married. As far as I know, she always maintained her own apartment in New York, which she shared at one time with Katherine Dunham.

Hall is guaranteed a place in history by the work of the Hall Johnson Choir alone. My life has been enriched by my participation in the choir.

Elijah Hodges
Professional chorister and studio singer, Los Angeles
November 8, 2001

Madeline Preston

Predestination must have played a role in leading me to Hall Johnson. As a resident of Westchester County, I rarely saw any of the Afro-American newspapers. I still don't recall how I happened to get a copy of the *New York Amsterdam News*, but there it was, an audition call for singers to perform in Hall Johnson's Easter Cantata, *Son of Man*, at midnight on Good Friday, 1948. So, fresh out of high school, I headed for the Red Shield Club on 124th St. in Harlem for the auditions. As I had been studying voice, I was prepared and sang the famous Bach-Gounod *Ave Maria*. Hall Johnson accompanied me on the piano. When I finished, he turned to me and said, "Very pretty voice, when you come back, bring the rest of it." (My voice was sweet, but light.) So, I made my debut with a choir of 500 voices at Carnegie Hall and then went on to become a member of the regular choir with the high obbligatos as my specialty. Later, I was cast as an angel in the New York revival of *The Green Pastures* with Ossie Davis and William Marshall, and in 1951, toured with the Hall Johnson Choir to Berlin, Germany, to sing in the International Music Festival.

Hall Johnson is still in my everyday thoughts. As I write, I am looking at the famous photograph of his hands by Ruth Bernhard that appeared on the cover of the *Saturday Review of Literature*; I know that I loved him the first time I saw him. He was an imposing figure, exuding kindness and gentleness. When I joined the Hall Johnson Choir in 1948, I was the youngest member. Before long, I was living with him in his apartment at 634 St. Nicholas Avenue. Because of the difference in age (which did not bother me) he would sometimes, with a chuckle, introduce me as his granddaughter. After the Berlin Tour, Hall returned to Pasadena, California, and lived with his sisters, Alice Foster and Susan Jordan. He took me with him and I remained until he introduced me to Katherine Dunham following a performance at the Greek Theater, which I thought was the most spectacular and exciting show that I had ever seen. I returned alone for two more shows and auditioned for Miss Dunham, beginning a relationship which has endured to the present. Hall and I lived together for about five years and although he called me his wife in private, we were never legally married. We remained close friends until his death.

I think of Hall Johnson less as a conductor and more as an orchestrator. He wrote the songs. He arranged the songs and he brought out the sound qualities of the various voices. That is why he called me a "piccolo" soprano. When he worked with a choir, he was thinking of the voices as instruments. He would mix baritones and sopranos, double the solo line, and do other distinctive textural things. I think of him as a fantastic composer who wrote *Chopin in Harlem*, and works for cello. People forget about this aspect of Hall Johnson who also was a vocal coach for many famous singers.

The man was a genius. He could watch television and write a musical composition simultaneously. I observed him making an orchestration for Marian Anderson while he was listening to the *Brahms Fourth Symphony*. I could never understand how that was possible.

When Hall Johnson was rehearsing, he was such a perfectionist. He would go over and over a point of diction until it satisfied him regardless of how impatient the choir became. When you heard that line in performance, it would be absolutely clear. His experience with the Belafonte Singers was short-lived because of this. It took so much time to get the perfection that he demanded, that he and Belafonte were forced to part ways. A series of younger conductors, De Paur, Howard Roberts, and Robert De Cormier, who were more willing to accept the compromises of modern studio recording, supplanted him.

I look forward to your book on Hall Johnson as the first which will accurately reveal the magnificence and magnitude of Hall Johnson's genius.

Madeline Preston
Professional chorister and member of the Katherine Dunham Dance Company, New York City
November 30, 2001

S. Carroll Buchanan

My first encounter with Hall Johnson (a.k.a. Brother Hall) was in 1948. I began NYU as a freshman in 1947 and had a miserable year academically. Consequently, at the end of the school year I dropped out. It was devastating to me. At that time, I was living in South Jamaica and met George Royston who sang the lead solo in "Ain't Got Time to Die" with the Hall Johnson Choir. After commiserating with George regarding my experience at NYU, he suggested that I meet with the great man. At the time, he was holding forth at a brownstone next door to the Salvation Army Red Shield Club on 124th Street in Harlem. I recall vividly the meeting. When I arrived at the building I met a very nice young lady named Madeline Preston who escorted me inside. I felt rather nervous at first, but within 10 minutes, I was at ease.

We discussed my plight and he asked me, "Buchanan, what do you want to do?" I replied, "I would like to study with you." To my utter surprise, he responded, "When do you want to start?" I said, "As soon as possible." With that, we began a relationship that lasted better than two years. Since I was very weak in music theory, it was this aspect of my musical training that we concentrated on. After my fourth or fifth visit, he asked whether I would like to join the choir. I began attending the Red Shield Club choir rehearsals forthwith.

Incidentally, the "Great One" took me on as a student free of charge. Because I began to miss lessons, he decided that I needed to be encouraged to make a commitment so he charged me $10.00 a month. What a paltry sum for one who could command much more.

I remember the names of some of the choir members: George Royston, Roger Alford, Parker Watson, Brother Cato, Bill Veasey, Sylvester Timmons, George Hill, Sister Mays, Enola Phillips, Occie Scurvin, Madeline Preston, Bertha Powell, and Moses LaMarr, all outstanding singers. I remember so well how Hall would occasionally have music he had written down on small pieces of paper that he kept in his jacket or shirt pocket. I also remember attending rehearsals of a small male ensemble that included Bill Veasey, Joe Allbright, Luther Johnson, and famed baritone Robert McFerrin.

At times, just prior to my lessons, I would meet Brother Hall and Madeline Preston in the dining area of the Red Shield Club. It was there that I learned a great deal about this amazing man. I learned that he was a linguist, and that he had attended the University of Pennsylvania and the Institute of Musical Art in New York City. He was from Athens, Georgia, and sang in his father's church choir [and] was not initially a choral man but a violist who, along with Marion Cumbo, played with the James Reese Orchestra and the Negro String Quartet. He told me about the beginning of the Hall Johnson Choir as a small group of singers that he started in the mid-twenties. I believe he said it had about 7 or 8 members. He also mentioned a concert that he gave at New York's Town Hall in the late twenties. I do not remember whether this was his first concert with the Hall Johnson Choir.

Once, when I mentioned to him that I was from Baltimore, he told me that he had appeared with Eubie Blake in the Broadway musical *Shuffle Along*. He was also acquainted with Meredith Birch, head of the African American Baltimore Boys Choir. I was always delighted when we had these conversations.

Brother Hall was the most deliberate eater I have ever known. It took him forever to eat a plate of food. I noticed, too, that two fingers on his right hand were discolored because he smoked incessantly and would have ashes dangling from the end of his cigarettes.

Through Hall Johnson, I met such giants as Leonard De Paur and Jester Hairston. During a Roland Hayes recital at Town Hall, I had the privilege of being introduced by Hall to Edward Boatner and William Dawson.

Due to my work schedule and family responsibilities, I was unable to remain with the choir very long. My tenure as one of his students ended in 1950 when *The Green Pastures* was revived on Broadway. Asked what I wanted to do, I indicated that I wanted to go to Juilliard. He said, "I think you're ready."

In 1963 I gave a performance with my choir, the Carr-Hill Singers, at the Convent Baptist Church in Manhattan. Brother Hall was there. The group sang several of his spiritual arrangements. After the concert we spoke briefly and his comments were complimentary. George Wilson from WLIB Radio recorded our performance. Little did I know that this recording, including the Hall Johnson spiritual arrangements, would be played on the radio for over a week during the mourning period following the assassination of President Kennedy.

From Hall Johnson, I received a wonderful education and will always remember his kindness, sensitivity, and brilliance. I know that he has helped many people and I feel honored to be among them. Through his blessings, I did go to Juilliard and returned to NYU where I was graduated with a B.S. degree in 1955. I ultimately earned an M.A. from Columbia University in 1962 and a Ph.D. from NYU in 1987. In 1963, in collaboration with George Hill, a former member of the Hall Johnson Choir, I organized the Carr-Hill Singers, a choir which lasted 40 years. Throughout all of this my experiences with Hall Johnson were a constant source of inspiration.

The last time I saw Hall Johnson alive was in the 1960s when George Hill and I picked him up at his St. Nicholas Avenue apartment and took him to a barbecue at George's home in St. Albans. I learned of his passing when I was in Africa with the Peace Corps. In 1948, he gave me a photograph that adorns a wall in my home. I will ever be grateful.

S. Carroll Buchanan
Educator and choral conductor, Sarasota, Florida
April 5, 2002

George Royston

The son of a prominent Baptist minister, I was born in Kansas City, Kansas, in 1916. My father took a church in Leavenworth, Kansas, in 1932 and I went to school at the Kansas Vocational School in nearby Topeka. Upon graduation, I entered Western University in Quindaro, but was forced to drop out of college when my father died in 1935. As fate would have it, the Utica Jubilee Singers were auditioning to fill a baritone vacancy that spring. I sang for them when they visited Western, and they hired me. My professional career began with them that fall.

I sang with the Utica Jubilee Singers for about five years until the group finally broke up in New York. This was fortuitous for me as I had married while singing with them and settled in Jamaica, New York. When the war broke out in 1941, I was not drafted because I had a child to support. Shortly after the onset of the war, my wife and I visited a bereaved friend in Harlem. Here we met a woman who was a member of the Hall Johnson Choir. Ms. Mack said that she had a rehearsal with the choir that evening and invited me to attend and meet Hall Johnson. As I was aware of his choral eminence and of the motion picture work of the choir, I was only too happy to accept her invitation.

I met Dr. Johnson at the rehearsal which was held at the YWCA on 138th Street in Harlem. He asked me to stay after rehearsal and to sing something for him. After he heard me, he worked with me on a selection and then told me that he would like me to sing the solo part in their next concert in Philadelphia. To this day, the "River Chant" is indelibly stamped in my mind. Needless to say, I started coming to the rehearsals and I say this, "Hall Johnson was the father of my career." When Frank Sinatra was told that Bing Crosby had died, this is what he said. I've thought about it a lot since. If Bing Crosby was the father of his career, Hall Johnson was the father of mine.

I stayed with the choir and occasionally we would find a gig somewhere and get paid $10.00 or so, but being in his choir got me into Broadway shows. The first was *Blue Holiday*, with Ethel Waters, Eartha Kitt, and the Katherine Dunham Dance Troupe at the Belasco Theater. It opened on Monday to great reviews and closed on Saturday. My second show was the revival of *The Green Pastures* with Robert McFerrin and William Marshall. There was no orchestra in this show, only the Hall Johnson Choir. Hall Johnson arranged all of the spirituals and added some original music. We played Boston, Philadelphia, and New York for a total of ten weeks.

The only vocal training I got was from a woman named Lola Hayes, who was a member of the Hall Johnson Choir and whom I met in the short-lived production of *Blue Holiday*. Although my voice was beautiful, my range was short, and Lola helped me to extend the range and to do the required professional singing without strain. This may well have been the start of the teaching career that made her one of New York's best known voice teachers.

A large part of Hall's rehearsals was teaching. Over half of each rehearsal was talking. I learned a lot from listening to him talk. Some of the things he preached about, he didn't do himself, or he would have stayed away from the bottle. But he couldn't. I know that we have composers, poets, and other famous men who imbibe too much. He taught me how to be a professional. "If you are going to be in show business you have to *be in show business*. You can't have one foot in and one foot out. You are either in it or out of it." He kind of indoctrinated me into that way of thinking.

I remained in the choir until 1952. A year earlier, I was a soloist on the international tour to Berlin and Vienna at which we represented the United States at the International Music Festival. In 1952, I joined the cast of Virgil Thompson's *Four Saints in Three Acts* with Leontyne Price and Inez Matthews. Originally, the Hall Johnson Choir was scheduled to do this work but Thompson felt that the members were too old as the casting called for young faces. We played two weeks on Broadway and two weeks in Paris. From Paris, we flew directly to Dallas, with a brief stopover in New York, for the opening of *Porgy and Bess* at the Texas State Fair. The show toured from 1952 to 1956. After the show closed, I decided to retire from the business, buy a home in Hollis, Long Island, and educate my two boys.

I rate Hall Johnson over all the conductors I worked with, although I worked primarily with him and Eva Jessye. What made Hall so successful was his ability to arrange things so that they were "listenable." I sometimes felt that some of his works (like the *St. Louis Blues*) were too intricate. His knowledge of music and his skill as an arranger made him what he was. He delighted in giving a well earned compliment and did not care for perfect pitch singers who always suffered if the pitch of the choir varied. His work with the spirituals was as important as any arranger in history. I only wish that people were aware of the many other works he composed. Perhaps this book will rectify the situation.

George Royston
Professional chorister, Virginia Beach, Virginia
August 10, 2002

Shirley Verrett

I think the year that I met Dr. Hall Johnson was 1952. It was late in the year, perhaps a year and a half before I left California to go to New York City. At the time, I was married to James Carter, my first husband. It was he, in fact, who wished me to meet Dr. Johnson to work on my interpretation of the Negro Spirituals with him. An appointment was made with Dr. Johnson, but before I met him, I attended a concert of his with his famous choir. I always liked choir concerts, but this concert was special for me, not only because the choir sang beautifully, but also because I was going to sing for this great man!

The designated day arrived and I sang for Dr. Johnson. I forget the place (it was not his home), but it was a rehearsal hall somewhere in Los Angeles. I sang about three spirituals for him. He was very complimentary and then surprised me by saying that I did not need to learn to sing spirituals, because, with a tweak here and there, my spirituals were just fine. What he wished me to begin thinking about immediately was German Lieder. I was astonished, but thrilled, to say the least. That is how the great musician and master of choral singing began to teach me German.

Yes, Dr. Johnson spoke German and French! My first Lieder composer was Brahms. One of the first songs he had me learn was "Von Ewiger Liebe." We worked together for some time, and then I was off to New York to appear on the Arthur Godfrey Show and in the Marian Anderson Competition. He also gave me a "saying" that I have used as a mantra to this day, *Hurry Slowly!*

Some time after I came to New York and entered the Juilliard School, Dr. Johnson moved back to his New York apartment. I think it was located on St. Nicholas Avenue. I went to work with him on this and that piece for a few times, and sometimes, I went just to hear his words of wisdom, and then, the *career* began to "take wings" just as he had predicted in Los Angeles. He had told me that I would not be returning to Los Angeles to live, once I began my vocal life in New York. He was absolutely correct! I lived in New York from September 1955 until my move to Ann Arbor, Michigan, in 1996, where I am now a Distinguished University Professor of Voice.

I am deeply touched when I recall what Dr. Johnson thought of me, and did for me.

Shirley Verrett
International opera and concert artist
Distinguished Professor, University of Michigan
December 1, 2002

John Patton Jr.

It was William Grant Still who suggested that I meet Hall Johnson. I had been invited to supper with Mr. Still and sang for him. I did not know that Mr. Johnson was living in Los Angeles and was very excited to learn this. I made contact, and we met on the campus of the University of Southern California.

I was twenty-one years old at the time and had a very limited repertoire ("Trees," "Thank God for a Garden," "Invictus," etc.). Mr. Johnson asked to hear me sing. I thought I was singing fairly well, when all of a sudden, he said, "Stop! Do you know any spirituals or songs by Black composers?" Well, I knew only a few of them: "Plenty Good Room" and "Nobody Knows de Trouble I See." He said, "You have an uncommonly beautiful voice, you should know more about your music." Mr. Johnson wrote out a reading list and said, "When you finish, give me a call, but do not call unless it is finished!" I do not remember all of them now; however, three remain deep in my memory:

1. "The Negro and His Music"   Alain Locke
2. "Negro Musicians"   Maude Cuney Hare
3. "The Mis-Education of the Negro"   Carter G. Woodson

That meeting gave me the motivation to study, to do research, and perform Black Music of Black composers. The meeting was also the beginning of a friendship that lasted until his death.

Hall Johnson became my mentor and my friend, and I am indebted to him. He was like a father and I am sure there are many who could say the same. He was an avid reader, and spoke several languages fluently. We used to exchange books. He would test you, and I became more critical in my thinking and more literate. I was fortunate to participate in the Hall Johnson Workshop in Los Angeles, and also, when I came to New York, to study at Juilliard.

I held part-time jobs at Handy Bros. Music, Galaxy Music, Columbia University Chapel, and Barnard College. The cost of living and housing was so expensive, but I still wanted to make my debut in New York City. Brother Hall came through and did not allow me to give up, and he encouraged me. Therefore, when my debut at Carnegie Hall occurred, Hall Johnson was there along with Nora Holt [music critic for the *Amsterdam News*], W.C. Handy Jr., and Langston Hughes. I was overwhelmed with joy and confidence.

Hall Johnson was a true "Renaissance man," and I was privileged to have known him. When he died, I was in Italy, but I arrived in time to attend his memorial at New York's St. George's Church. However, the original plan was to meet him and pick up my Ezra Pound books, and to have him autograph my record *Black Art Songs and Spirituals*, which opens with his "Fi-yer." I was saddened when I learned that his death was caused by fire.

When I arrived at his memorial, I saw and met the Brothers and Sisters (as Mr. Johnson called us) who had sung and known him. He had a vision of a "City Called Heaven" and he was sure "He Had a Home in Glory." I want to let the reader know a few of the people who came to pay their final respects: Leonard De Paur, William Warfield, Robert McFerrin, Inez Matthews, Katherine Dunham, John Motley, and many more.

I cannot fully describe the impact and beauty of the singing of his arrangement of "I Will Arise," sung by former members and friends from many places (no rehearsals), with John Motley conducting. What a sound! When we reached the cemetery, we locked arms, holding hands as the last words were spoken. As we turned to leave, Katherine Dunham said softly, "So long Brother Hall. Goodbye." I believe he was one of God's servants on loan to us, and God received him and said, "Well done, Brother Hall."

John Patton Jr.
Concert tenor and actor, Berkeley, California
March 26, 2003

~

Appendix A: Discography

Solo Recordings of Hall Johnson's Music on CD and LP

Albert, Donnie Ray	*Donnie Ray Albert In Recital* "Ain't Got Time to Die"	CNB-1402
Alexander, Roberta	*Songs My Mother Taught Me* "Give Me Jesus" "His Name So Sweet"	KTC-1208
Anderson, Marian	*Marian Anderson Spirituals* "Hold On"	LSC-2592
	Marian Anderson Spirituals "Roll Jerd'n, Roll" "Crucifixion" "Honor, Honor"	LM-2032
	Jus' Keep On Singin' "Oh, Heaven Is One Beautiful Place" "Lord, How Come Me Here" "Prayer Is de Key" "He'll Bring It to Pass" "You Go!" "Jus' Keep On Singin'" "Ain't Got Time to Die"	LM-2796

	"I Been in de Storm So Long" "I've Been 'Buked" "Le's Have a Union" "Oh, Glory!" "Ride On, King Jesus"	
Arroyo, Martina	*Spirituals* "City Called Heaven" "Witness" "Honor, Honor"	Centaur B0000057TC
Battle, Kathleen	*Great American Spirituals, Vol. 9* "Ain't Got Time to Die" "Ride On, King Jesus"	CDM-07777
	Kathleen Battle in Concert "Honor, Honor" "His Name So Sweet" "Witness"	DGG-445524-2
	Pleasure of Their Company "Ain't Got Time to Die" "Ride On, King Jesus"	B000002RNM
	Spirituals in Concert "My God Is So High"	DGG-429790-2
Blackmon, Henry	*Henry Blackmon Geistlijke Liederen en Negro Spiritual* "This Is de Healin' Water" "Cert'ny Lord" "Po' Moner Got a Home at Las'" "I Got to Lie Down"	SGLP-6047
Brice, Carol	*A Carol Brice Recital* "My Good Lord Done Been Here" "Witness"	ML-2108
Brown, William	*Fi-yer!* "Fi-yer!"	Troy-329

Conrad, Barbara	*Spirituals* "Wade in the Water" "Ride On, King Jesus" "Take My Mother Home" "Po' Moner Got a Home at Last"	LC-5537
Davis, Osceola	*Negro Spirituals* "Give Me Jesus" "City Called Heaven" "Ain't Got Time to Die" "His Name So Sweet" "Ride On, King Jesus"	ODE 715-2

Dever, Barbara	*The Best of the Hall Johnson
	    Centennial Festival: Art
	    Songs* (Hall Johnson
	    Collection)
	"Song of the Mother"
	"Foundling"
	"Mother to Son"
	"Crossing the Bar"
	"Dear, Could You Know"
	"Love Is a Plague"
	"I'm Callin', Yes, I'm Callin'"
	"Ain't Got Time to Die"
	    (original spiritual)	

Duncan, Todd	*Todd Duncan Sings Spirituals* "Witness" "Roll Jerd'n, Roll"	LP-50113

Fernandez,
    Wilhelmenia
	*Wilhelmenia Fernandez Sings
	    Favorite Spirituals*
	"Witness"
	"Honor, Honor"
	"Ride On, King Jesus"
		KEM-DISC 1010

Foreman, Blanche	*The Best of the Hall Johnson
	    Centennial Festival:
	    Spirituals* (Hall Johnson
	    Centennial Festival)	

"Wade in de Water"
"O Fix Me"
"My Good Lord Done Been
    Here"
"My God Is So High"
"I Been in de Storm So
    Long"
"Roll Jerd'n, Roll"
"I'm Gonna Tell God All of
    My Troubles"
"Oh, Glory"
"I Got to Lie Down"

Graves, Denyce	*Angels Watching over Me*	NPR-0006
	"Le's Have a Union"	
	"City Called Heaven"	
	"Witness"	
Holmes, Eugene	*Holmes Sings Spirituals*	AV-115
	"Witness"	
	"Let Us Break Bread Together"	
	"Swing Low, Sweet Chariot"	
	"Ain't Got Time to Die"	
	"Ride On, King Jesus"	
	"His Name So Sweet"	

Hopkins, Gregory	*The Best of the Hall Johnson
	    Centennial Festival:
	    Spirituals* (Hall Johnson
	    Collection)	

	"Ride On, Jesus"	
	"Le's Have a Union"	
	"Oh Freedom"	
	"Nobody Knows de Trouble I've Seen"	
	"Take My Mother Home"	
	"Witness"	
McFerrin, Robert	*Classic Negro Spirituals*	WLP-466
	"Every Time I Feel the Spirit"	

"Fix Me, Jesus"
"His Name So Sweet"
"I'm Gonter Tell God All
    o' My Troubles"
"Swing Low, Sweet Chariot"
"A City Called Heaven"
"Ain't Got Time to Die"
"I Got to Lie Down"
"Oh, Glory"
"Witness"
"Ride On, King Jesus"

Miles, John	*The Classic Spirituals*	Epiphany

"City Called Heaven"
"Ride On, King Jesus"
"I'm Gonter Tell God All
    o' My Troubles"
"Hold On"
"Give Me Jesus"
"Ain't Got Time to Die"

Mims, A. Grace Lee	*Spirituals*	HGM-8101

"Lord I Don't Feel Noways
    Tired"
"His Name So Sweet"
"I Cannot Stay Here by
    Myself"
"Take My Mother Home"
"Ride On, King Jesus"

Morrison, John   *The Best of the Hall Johnson
    Centennial Festival: Art
    Songs* (Hall Johnson
    Collection)
"Birthday Song"
"David"
"Life"
"Stillness"
"Swing Dat Hammer"
"The Courtship"
"He'll Bring It to Pass"
"Fi-yer!"

	Morrison Sings 16 Favorites "Keep-a-Inchin' Along"	
Norman, Jessye	*Spirituals in Concert* "Ride On, King Jesus"	DGG-426790-2
Price, Leontyne	*The Essential Leontyne Price* "His Name So Sweet" "Honor, Honor" "Ride On, King Jesus"	BMG-LC-0316
Quivar, Florence	*Great American Spirituals* "Honor, Honor" "I've Been 'Buked" "His Name So Sweet"	CDM-07777
	Ride On, King Jesus "Ride On, King Jesus" "Give Me Jesus" "Honor, Honor" "I've Been 'Buked" "I'm Gonter Tell God All o' My Troubles" "Witness" "Hold On" "His Name So Sweet"	Angel B000A9QLAO

Simpson, Eugene
   Thamon
	*Hear Me, Ye Winds and
	   Waves*
	"Wade in the Water"
	"Oh, Glory"
	"Witness"
	"Honor, Honor"
		Black Heritage
		Publications

	Thanks Be to Thee "I'm Gonter Tell God All o' My Troubles" "Fix Me, Jesus" "Le's Have a Union"	Black Heritage Publications
	Honor and Arms "Roll Jerd'n, Roll" "City Called Heaven"	Black Heritage Publications

"I Got to Lie Down"
"Honor, Honor"

Verrett, Shirley	*Singin' in the Storm*	LSC-2892
	"I Been in de Storm So Long"	
	Shirley Verrett Carnegie Hall Recital	LSC-2835
	"Honor, Honor"	
	"Oh, Glory"	
	"Witness"	
Weathers, Felicia	*Arias and Spirituals*	LC-5440
	"Ain't Got Time to Die"	
	"City Called Heaven"	
	"Jesus, Lay Your Head in de Winder"	
	"My Good Lord Done Been Here"	
Wilson, Robin	*Best of the Hall Johnson Centennial Festival: Spirituals* (Hall Johnson Collection)	
	"Honor, Honor"	
	"Steal Away"	
	"His Name So Sweet"	
	"Jesus Lay Your Head in de Winder"	
	"City Called Heaven"	
	"Way Up in Heaven"	
	"Give Me Jesus"	
	"Ride On, King Jesus"	

Choral Music of Hall Johnson on CD

The Best of the Hall Johnson Centennial Festival—Hall Johnson Collection

Choral Spirituals and Work Songs

Howard University Choir—Dr. J. Weldon Norris, Conductor
"Way Over in Beulah Land"
"Scandalize My Name"

"River Chant"
"Keep a-Inchin' Along"
"I Got a Mule"
"Ride On Jesus"
"I Couldn't Hear Nobody Pray"
"I'll Never Turn Bak No Mo'"
"Honor, Honor"
"Elijah Rock"

Music from the Cinema

Winston Salem University Choir—Dr. James Kinchen, Conductor
"Swing Low, Sweet Chariot"
"Swanee River"
"Mule Song"
"Walk Together Chillun"
"Cert'ny Lord"
"Rise an' Shine"
"Dere's No Hidin' Place"
"Go Down Moses"
"Lord, I Don't Feel Noways Tired"
"St. Louis Blues"

Choral Music from the Music Dramas

**Glassboro State College Chamber Choir—
Dr. Eugene Thamon Simpson, Conductor**
Run, Little Chillun (Tongola scene)
"Processional"
"Credo"
"Run, Little Chillun"
Fi-yer!
"Banjo Dance"
"Elegy"
"Good Times/Miss Sylvie"
Son of Man (Concluding scenes—Part I)
"I've Been 'Buked"
"Pilate! Pilate! Pilate!"
"Lament of Judas"
"Ride On, King Jesus"

An American Heritage of Spirituals (BWE-0097)

Mormon Tabernacle Choir—Albert MacNeil, Guest Conductor
 "Ride On, King Jesus"

African American Spirituals: The Concert Tradition
(Smithsonian-Folkways)

Florida A & M University Choir—Dr. Augustus Pearson, Conductor
 "I've Been 'Buked"

Howard University Chamber Choir—Dr. J. Weldon Norris, Conductor
 "Ain't Got Time to Die"

The Hall Johnson Song Book (Black Heritage Publications)

Virginia State College Choir—Dr. Eugene Thamon Simpson, Conductor
 "Cert'ny Lord"
 "I've Been 'Buked"
 "Lord, I Don't Feel Noways Tired"
 "When I Was Sinkin' Down"
 "His Name So Sweet"
 "Fix Me Jesus"
 "Honor, Honor"
 "Run, Little Chillun"
 "I'll Never Turn Back"
 "I Couldn't Hear Nobody Pray"
 "Elijah Rock"
 "City Called Heaven"
 "Ain't Got Time to Die"

Live from the Mormon Tabernacle, Rowan University Chamber Choir
(Video; Black Heritage Publications)

Rowan University Chamber Choir—Dr. Eugene Thamon Simpson/
Dr. Jester Hairston, Conductors
 "Run, Little Chillun"
 "City Called Heaven"
 "I'll Never Turn Back"
 "Ain't Got Time to Die"

Hush! Somebody's Calling My Name (BDC01)

Brazeal Dennard Chorale—Brazeal Dennard, Conductor
  "Ain't Got Time to Die"

Remembering, Discovering, Preserving (BDC4444)

Brazeal Dennard Chorale—Brazeal Dennard, Conductor
  "I'll Never Turn Back"

~

Selected Bibliography

"All American Program at U.S." *Pacific Coast Musician* (August 1, 1942): 7.

Bernard, Emily. *Remember Me to Harlem: The Letters of Langston Hughes and Carl Van Vechten, 1925–1964.* New York: Yale University Press, 2001.

Burke, Kenneth. "Pattern of Life." *Saturday Review of Literature* (April 1933): 13.

Cramer, Carl. "*Run, Little Chillun*: A Critical Review." *Journal of Negro Life* (April 1933): 113.

Ennis, Martha, "One Man Show." Unpublished article. Courtesy of the Hall Johnson Collection (Rowan University, Glassboro, NJ). All rights reserved.

Haley, James T. *Afro-American Encyclopedia.* Nashville, TN: Haley & Florida, 1895.

Kobald, Karl. *Franz Schubert and His Times.* New York: Alfred A. Knopf, 1928.

Leff, Leonard J. "*Gone with the Wind* and Hollywood's Racial Politics." *Atlantic Monthly* (December 1999).

Library of Congress. "The Booker T. Washington Era." Part 1 of *African American Odyssey: An Exhibition at the Library of Congress.* Edited by Debra Newman Ham. Washington, DC: The Library, 1998.

"*Run, Little Chillun.*" *Pictorial Review* (July 1933).

Simpson, Ingres Hill. "Hall Johnson, Preserver of the Negro Spiritual." Master of Music thesis, University of Cincannati College-Conservatory of Music, 1971.

Skinner, Richard Dana. "The Play." *Commonweal* (April 1933): 665.

Southern, Eileen. *The Music of Black Americans.* New York: W.W. Norton, 1971.

———, ed. *Readings in Black American Music.* New York: W.W. Norton, 1972.

Talbert, Horace. *The Sons of Allen.* Xenia, OH: Aldine Press, 1906.

Wright, Richard R. *Centennial Encyclopedia of the African Methodist Episcopal Church.* Philadelphia: Book Concern of the A.M.E. Church, 1916.

Young, Stark. "Theatre Notes." *New Republic* (March 22 and April 12, 1933): 245.

Index

Johnson, Hall: account of illness
(alcoholism), 15, 61, 64, 69, 72, 75,
128; approach to composition, 83;
art accompaniments, 92; Bible of,
59; breadth of concept, 89; choral
directors and concert artists who
studied with, 92; George Van Hoy
Collins, 71, 93; complete works,
140–59; composer and arranger, 7,
49, 164, 179, 334; developed the
spiritual, 92; Distinguished Service
Award, 96, 325; essays of, 22, 102,
224; folk music as a basis for original
creation, 228, 232; Manet Fowler,
62, 63; frugal existence, 57; George
Frederic Handel Award, 97; a great
chorus, 16, 83; Harlem Jubilee
Singers, 5, 6; Harmon Award, 11,
95, 164, 324; Heritage Award, 96,
325; Holstein Award, 94, 95;
honorary doctorate, 94, 324; honors
and awards, 94, 183; idealistic and
ambitious objectives, 90; immoral
lifestyle, 62; independence of spirit,
56; influence on choral and vocal
music, 91; interpersonal demands,
69; Jan Hall Jones, 75; Wathea Sims
Jones, 49, 74, 105, 253; musical and
theatrical personages (white)—
(Maxwell Anderson, Henry Beckett,
Ruth Bernhard, Millard Bloomer,
Robert Breen, Charles Cadman
Wakefield, Samuel Chotzinoff, Marc
Connelly, Walter Damrosch, Meyer
Davis, Lorna Cook De Varon,
Denishawn, Walter Donnelly,
Donald D. Engle, Guy Fowler,
William C. Gassner, Oscar
Hammerstein II, Willem van
Hoogstraten, George Jessel, Hans
Kindler, Max T. Krone, Fiorello La
Guardia, Jack Lavin, John Lindsay,
John J. McCloy, Howard McKinney,

Lauritz Melchoir, Newbold Morris,
Horatio Parker, Irwin Parnes, Russell
Potter, Robert Rockmore, Eleanor
Roosevelt, Robert Schnitzer, David
O. Selznick, Alexander Smallens,
Carlton Sprague Smith, H.
Augustine Smith, Benjamin
Steinberg, Leopold Stokowski, Virgil
Thompson, Channing Tobias,
Wanda Toscanini, Robert Wagner,
Fred Waring, John Finley
Williamson, Jasha Zayde), 81–83; A
Nationwide Chorale Plan, 323;
organizational and promotional skill,
83; perfectionism, 56; personal
recollections about, xiv, 327, 329,
331, 333, 335, 337, 339, 341, 343;
personal relationship with Polly
Celeste Copening, 3, 72; personal
relationship with Ronald ("Ronnie")
Dixon, 70, 79; personal relationship
with Helen Duesberg (see Duesberg,
Helen); personal relationship with
Jester Hairston (see Hairston,
Jester); personal relationship with
Madeline Preston, xv, 69, 77, 334,
337–39; personal relationship with
Aurelia Walkes, 78; personal
relationship with David Wells, 76;
personality of, xi, 40, 57, 83, 223,
254, 255, 329; poetry of (see poetry
of Hall Johnson); professional
friends and associates (black)—
(Adele Addison, Betty Allen,
Marian Anderson, Harry Belafonte,
Eubie Blake, Jules Bledsoe, Edward
Boatner, Lawrence Brown, Ralph J.
Bunche, Harry T. Burleigh, Dorothy
Candee, John Carter, Cecil Cohen,
Barbara Conrad, Will Marion Cook,
Marion Cumbo, Ossie Davis,
Sammy Davis, William Dawson,
Leonard De Paur, Nathaniel F. Dett,

~

About the Author

Eugene Thamon Simpson has made a career as a professional singer, pianist, choral conductor, arranger, and educator. He made his New York piano debut at Fischer Hall in 1956 and his vocal debut with the Boston Symphony at Tanglewood. His choral arrangements are published exclusively by Bourne Music. He has held professorships at Virginia State, Bowie State, and Rowan Universities. His choirs have appeared at Carnegie Hall, Lincoln Center, Kennedy Center, and the Mormon Tabernacle, as well as in London, Paris, Rome, Vienna, Moscow, and Madrid. He is the founding curator of the Hall Johnson Collection at Rowan University in Glassboro, New Jersey.

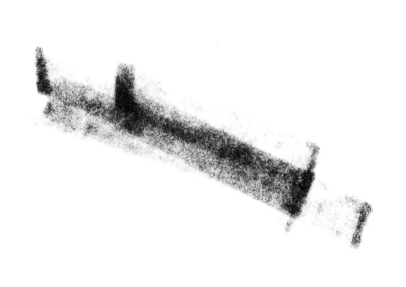